MAYORS IN THE MIDDLE

COLUMBIA STUDIES IN MIDDLE EAST POLITICS

COLUMBIA STUDIES IN MIDDLE EAST POLITICS

Marc Lynch, Series Editor

Columbia Studies in Middle East Politics presents academically rigorous, well-written, relevant, and accessible books on the rapidly transforming politics of the Middle East for an interested academic and policy audience.

Mayors in the Middle

INDIRECT RULE AND LOCAL GOVERNMENT
IN OCCUPIED PALESTINE

Diana B. Greenwald

Columbia University Press
New York

Columbia University Press
Publishers Since 1893
New York   Chichester, West Sussex
cup.columbia.edu

Library of Congress Cataloging-in-Publication Data
Names: Greenwald, Diana B., author.
Title: Mayors in the middle : indirect rule and local government in
occupied Palestine / Diana B. Greenwald.
Description: New York : Columbia University Press, 2024. |
Series: Columbia studies in Middle East politics |
Includes bibliographical references and index.
Identifiers: LCCN 2023053872 | ISBN 9780231213141 (hardback) |
ISBN 9780231213158 (trade paperback) | ISBN 9780231559744 (ebook)
Subjects: LCSH: Local government—West Bank. | Arab-Israeli conflict—1993- |
West Bank—Politics and government.
Classification: LCC JS7502.3.A3 G74 2024 | DDC 320.95694—dc23/eng/20240129
LC record available at https://lccn.loc.gov/2023053872

Cover design: Elliott S. Cairns
Cover image: AP Photo / Nasser Ishtayeh

CONTENTS

Chapter Five
Palestinian Local Government Under Israeli Indirect Rule:
Qualitative Findings   147

Chapter Six
Histories and Futures of Indirect Rule: Situating the
Palestinian Case in Comparative Context   183

TABLES, FIGURES, AND MAPS

TABLES

FIGURES

MAPS

A NOTE ON TRANSLITERATION

Throughout this book, I use a modified version of the *International Journal of Middle East Studies* guidelines for Arabic-to-English transliterations. In transliterations throughout the main text, I omit diacritics such as the macron (i.e. ā, ī, ū) used to indicate long vowels, or the dot (i.e. ḍ, ḥ, ṭ) used to distinguish certain Arabic letters. This is done for ease of presentation to the reader. In the bibliography, I maintain diacritics for all sources originally written in Arabic. In certain cases, I retain common transliterations of Palestinian places and names if they have been widely spelled a certain way in the English language (e.g., "Al-Bireh" instead of "al-Bireh", or "Beit Jala" instead of "Bayt Jala") or if I can verify that an individual spells their name a certain way in the English language that does not match the formal transliteration rules (e.g., "Shaka'a" instead of "al-Shaka'a", or "Audeh" instead of " 'Awda"). Individual terms that appear in standard English language dictionaries (e.g., intifada) are not italicized.

PREFACE AND ACKNOWLEDGMENTS

I set foot in Palestine for the first time on May 31, 2011. Earlier that spring, revolution and upheaval had swept through Tunisia, Egypt, Libya, Syria, Yemen, and Bahrain. From the privileged safety of my Ann Arbor apartment, I, like many others around the world, watched history unfold in the region. I had been awarded a language and area studies fellowship, but now it appeared that most of the region would be off limits. I watched Syria's descent into war with particular despair. I had been profoundly shaped by a summer spent in the country in 2006 and my subsequent time working for a Syrian-run human rights organization. With neither the means nor a principled justification for traveling to Syria amidst its horrific unraveling, I began developing a backup plan. Fortunately, in parallel, I had submitted an application to pursue a faculty-mentored research project in Palestine. At the time, and in language that now strikes me as technocratic and sterile, I proposed studying the political factors that shaped the size and nature of public sector employment in the Palestinian Authority.

Perhaps the language I used was a relic of my time spent in Washington, DC, before attending graduate school, or perhaps it was an indication that I was wary of writing about Palestine altogether. Former professors, mentors, and other researchers had warned me it was a "minefield," that trying to write one's first book on Israel and Palestine would kill one's career. On the other hand, my advisor, Mark Tessler, had written one of the preeminent political histories of the Israeli-Palestinian conflict in the English language. He was encouraging. So, once the University of Michigan approved my travel, I prepared for a summer of research and continued language study at Birzeit University's Palestine and Arabic studies program.

After my first trip to Palestine, there was no looking back. Still, as I write these words in the fall of 2023, I cannot help but feel that twelve years is barely enough time to call oneself an expert in anything. Just over one week before the wholesale destruction of the Gaza Strip began in October of this year, I delivered a presentation at the University of Michigan in which I aimed to consider potential sources of either stasis or disruptive change in the future political order of the occupied West Bank. The talk referenced Antonio Gramsci's idea of a "morbid" interregnum—an oft-cited quote that appears in the concluding paragraphs of this book—between two political equilibria or stages of history. Perhaps I could claim that subsequent events—the massacre in southern Israel, followed by the ongoing, almost incomprehensible, obliteration of the Gaza Strip, its infrastructure, its homes, its natural resources, its heritage, and, most of all, its people—validated some prior theory I held about the inherent instability of Israel's regime in the occupied Palestinian territories. I do not know if they have. Certainly many of us have made such arguments. But, when bearing witness, remotely, through a phone or computer screen, to the shattering of a people, words fail, past predictions wither away, and all one is left with is the morbidness and the enormity of loss.

As alluded to in the introduction to this volume, I have intentionally deconstructed and reconstructed this manuscript many times. Any remaining oversights, errors, or omissions are my own. Nonetheless, this book exists because I have benefited from the support of many brilliant and generous people along the way.

First and foremost, more than fifty Palestinians from small and large towns across the West Bank sat down with me for formal interviews. Many others, some of whose names I never knew, assisted in providing various forms of logistical support—arranging schedules, transmitting paperwork, chauffeuring, and fueling conversations with coffee and tea—during my multiple visits to Palestine between 2011 and 2019. Still others took the time to share their lives with me in more informal ways—on the phone, over a meal or coffee or nargileh, on a road trip, at their universities, in long taxi rides between cities, at art exhibits, in their villages, with their children, at their weddings, and in their homes. I, quite literally, could not have written this book without them. The Palestinian people are why I chose to write this book, hence I dedicate it to them.

Mark Tessler, more than any other, is responsible for my obsession with Israel and Palestine. Mark is brilliant and humble. From Mark I have gained a deep appreciation for both the privilege and responsibility we bear as foreign scholars trying to get things right. My other committee members at the University of Michigan, William Roberts Clark, Mark Dincecco, Brian Min, Anne Pitcher each challenged me in unique and invaluable ways, contributing to my development as a social scientist. Nathan Brown also generously connected me to some of his contacts in Palestine prior to my first trips to the region.

From 2017 to 2018, I wrestled with this manuscript during a postdoctoral fellowship at the Middle East Initiative (MEI) at the Harvard Kennedy School. Tarek Masoud, the faculty director of MEI, is one of the least boring people I know. I am very lucky to have him as a mentor, intellectual foil, and friend. No one challenges me more. At Harvard, I was also deeply fortunate to meet Hilary Rantisi, who codirected MEI. Conversations with Hilary were eye-opening, pushing me to ground my abstract social science language in the lived experiences of Palestinians. Readers will see just a small slice of Hilary's beautiful and rich family history referenced in the introduction to this book. My fellow fellows, Matthew Buehler, Jonas Bergen Draege, Allison Hartnett, Elizabeth Nugent and Hind Ahmed Zaki, defined my community while at the Kennedy School. I was, and continue to be, sustained by their wisdom and friendship.

The Department of Political Science and the Colin Powell School for Civic and Global Leadership at the City College of New York have been my academic home since 2018. I completed the bulk of this manuscript while here, and I am immensely thankful to have done so among such fascinating, amicable and funny colleagues. I am especially grateful to Nicholas Rush Smith for many thought-provoking and rich discussions over the years on, among other topics, apartheid, the making and unmaking of states, and how we know what we know. I have learned a great deal about the colonization and decolonization of India from a set of references supplied by Raphaëlle Khan. Colleagues including Bruce Cronin, Rajan Menon, and

Dirk Moses have generously provided feedback on my work. My department chair, Dan DiSalvo, and my dean, Andy Rich, have provided unfailing support and guidance. Whether over Zoom, in the hallway, over drinks, at an academic talk, or in a raucous faculty meeting, my colleagues have each, in their own way, brought energy and light to this process. I am also indebted to our professional staff and to the awe-inspiring students of the City College of New York. My students make me a better thinker.

I could not have completed this book without the help of a team of part-time research assistants, both in Palestine and in the United States. The brilliant H. J. researched the results of the 2004–5 local elections and helped arrange and provide interpreting for several interviews in 2014. Also in 2014, I met Ali Musa, who supplied excellent research, interpreting, and logistical assistance during my field visits in 2014 and 2019. Further, my research has profited greatly from discussions with Ali over the years about the nuances of Palestinian politics. His role in the 2019 interviews was particularly instrumental. Zane Jarrar generously coordinated with the United Nations Office for the Coordination of Humanitarian Affairs (OCHA) to obtain geocoded data on the location of Palestinian police stations and helpfully validated election results from the Palestinian Central Elections Commission. L. J. is a truly first-class Arabic-English interpreter; they also provided expert written translations of interview transcripts. Rabab Alhadae, Husam Kaid, Atsuko Sakurai, and Reda Souaidi worked with me during their time as CUNY undergraduate students. Reda and Husam did admirable data entry work, drawing on a labyrinthine set of budget files in Arabic; Rabab conducted valuable archival analysis of Palestinian news sources around the 2004–5 local elections; and Atsuko deployed her programming and geographic information system (GIS) skills to help complete an array of data analysis tasks, including measuring distances along Palestinian-accessible roads in the West Bank and validating municipal-level measures of the West Bank's security zones and built-up areas.

I am thankful to the Palestine Economic Policy Research Institute for providing me with office space and allowing me to participate in seminars with their brilliant researchers in 2014. Samir Abdullah was particularly generous and welcoming. I am grateful to B'Tselem for sharing some of its geocoded data, and for the extremely important work it does in the occupied territories. My thanks go, as well, to the Palestinian Ministry of Local Government in Ramallah for sharing the municipal budget files, and to Jamal Numan and the team that launched the Ministry's GIS portal. I also wish to thank Khalil Shikaki and Walid Ladadweh at the Palestinian Center for Policy and Survey Research. Although this book does not rely on survey data for its primary analysis, I have frequently drawn on the center's abundant archive of polls to understand the nuances of Palestinian public opinion.

Over the course of writing this book, I received funding from the United States Institute of Peace, the Rackham Graduate School and International Institute at the University of Michigan, the Project on Middle East Political Science (POMEPS), and the Research Foundation at the City University of New York. I could not have completed this book without their support.

This work was vastly improved from the tremendous feedback provided by attendees of the 2015, 2018, and 2022 American Political Science Association (APSA) annual meetings; the 2015 Political Economy Workshop at the University of Michigan; the 2017 Governance and Local Development Institute Annual Conference at the University of Gothenburg; the 2017 State Capacity in Comparative Perspective Conference at Harvard University; the 2019 Comparative Politics Workshops at both the CUNY Graduate Center and at Yale University; and a 2023 presentation at the CUNY James Gallery cosponsored by the Middle East and Middle Eastern American Center. I received in-depth feedback on this project at two book workshops. At the 2018 POMEPS Junior Scholars book workshop, Ian Lustick and Pete Moore read a full draft of a much earlier version of this manuscript. Their feedback, and the input from other colleagues at the workshop, was critical in forcing me to address tough questions about what kind of contribution I wanted this project to make. For the 2022 Minority-Serving Institutions virtual book workshop convened by APSA, John Jay College of Criminal Justice, and Howard University, Ana Arjona, Nadya Hajj, and Paul Staniland read a revised version of the manuscript. Their incisive critiques and suggestions helped push me over the finish line.

In addition, I am indebted to the following individuals, who have read and commented on portions of this manuscript: Fiona Adamson, Laurie Brand, Jason Brownlee, Matthew Buehler, Dan Corstange, Jonas Bergen Draege, Allison Hartnett, Amaney Jamal, Robert Kubinec, Marc Lynch, Tarek Masoud, Elizabeth Nugent, Sarah Parkinson, Wendy Pearlman, Dean Schafer, Jillian Schwedler, Nicholas Rush Smith, and Hind Ahmed Zaki. Further, Alexei Abrahams and Dana El Kurd have made studying Palestine as a junior social scientist a much less lonely experience than it could have been.

I am grateful to Marc Lynch for not only supporting this project as editor of the Studies in Middle East Politics series but also for his tireless work in cultivating an ecosystem to support junior Middle East–focused political scientists. POMEPS, which Marc founded, has introduced me to countless fellow scholars, enabled me to sustain necessary relationships and friendships within the Middle East politics community, and allowed my work to reach new audiences. Furthermore, many thanks are due to my editor at Columbia University Press, Caelyn Cobb, for her patience and support, and to the rest of the editorial, marketing, design, and production staff for their professionalism and clear communication throughout this process. Two reviewers solicited by the press engaged very closely with my work, contributing immeasurably to improving the framing and clarity of my findings. Hossam Abouzahr provided essential and timely assistance with Arabic transliterations.

My parents, Roy and Gail Greenwald, and my sister, Katy Greenwald, have always been my role models. I could not have gone "to the end of school" without having been inspired by their examples. Matilda Groff has grown up in parallel with this book, and I am so delighted that we share approximately 25 percent of our genes. Thank you, Brandon Groff, for all the music recommendations and ridiculous Reese's products. I have been nurtured and sustained by the McWilliams, McLaughlins, Zimmerings, Schiffs, Jains, Cyndi Morrison, and Maisie O'Brien. My late dog, Io, was a source of endless joy, comfort, amusement, and wonder. I cannot overstate how important friendship has been during these long years of learning and writing. My friends are my chosen family—some have been in my life since high school, and others I met within the last few years. My friends amaze, inspire, comfort, and entertain me. They give me life. Finally, I feel so lucky to be alive on the planet at the same time as David McWilliam. Dave, thank you, more than anyone, for your patience, your inspiring creativity, your (literal) warmth, and your love. I think I have finally figured this thing out. I think we are finally figuring this thing out. I love you more every day.

ABBREVIATIONS AND ACRONYMS

AISPC	All India States Peoples' Conference
ANC	African National Congress
CIVAD	Israeli Civil Administration
DFLP	The Democratic Front for the Liberation of Palestine (*Al-Jabha al-Dimuqratiyya li-Tahrir Filastin*)
Fatah	The Palestinian National Liberation Movement (*Harakat al-Tahrir al-Watani al-Filastini*)
Hamas	*Harakat al-Muqawama al-Islamiyya* (The Islamic Resistance Movement)
IDF	Israel Defense Forces
IMF	International Monetary Fund
INC	Indian National Congress
JDECO	Jerusalem District Electricity Company
MK	uMkhonto we Sizwe
MOLG	Palestinian Ministry of Local Government
PA	Palestinian Authority
PFLP	The Popular Front for the Liberation of Palestine (*Al-Jabha al-Sha'biyya li-Tahrir Filastin*)
PLC	Palestinian Legislative Council
PLO	Palestinian Liberation Organization
UNRWA	United Nations Relief and Works Agency

MAYORS IN THE MIDDLE

A FRAMEWORK FOR NATIONAL STRUGGLE

On June 2, 1980, a bomb exploded in the car of Bassam Shaka'a, the mayor of Nablus. Nablus is one of the largest cities in the West Bank, a part of historic Palestine that, by then, Israel had militarily occupied for thirteen years.[1] At the time, the territory was home to more than seven hundred thousand Palestinians and at least seventeen thousand Israeli Jewish settlers. The latter number had been growing rapidly since the inauguration of a hawkish, right-wing Israeli government three years earlier.[2] The attack against Shaka'a was carried out by members of the Jewish Underground, a hardline offshoot of the fundamentalist settler movement Gush Emunim ("Bloc of the Faithful"). Gush Emunim embraced the use of violence to promote mass settlement and Jewish sovereignty over what it deemed "the whole land of Israel," including the West Bank.[3] As a result of the attack, Shaka'a had both of his legs amputated from the knees down. He was targeted that day along with two others: Karim Khalaf, then mayor of Ramallah, and Ibrahim Tawil of the neighboring city of Al-Bireh. All three survived, but Khalaf was also permanently maimed.

Shaka'a, born to a prominent family in Nablus, had previously been a member of the Arab nationalist Ba'ath party. He spent time in Egypt and Syria, returning to Nablus in his thirties as a political independent.[4] Five years after Shaka'a's return, Nablus, like the rest of the West Bank, fell under

Israeli military rule. The 1967 war (the "Six-Day War" or *al-Naksa*, "the setback") displaced hundreds of thousands of Palestinians. Many had been rendered refugees following the mass flight and expulsions of the 1948–49 war (Israel's War of Independence, or *al-Nakba*, "the catastrophe"), and thus found themselves uprooted for a second time roughly twenty years later. In the wake of Israel's capture of the West Bank, Jewish Israelis began settling the land almost immediately, first in the form of military outposts facing toward Jordan, where Palestinian commando bases were stationed, and subsequently as full-fledged residential communities. Settlements were built either on land expropriated from private Palestinian owners or on formerly Ottoman-designated *miri* lands, most of which Palestinians had lived on, cultivated, and used for generations.[5]

During the first decade of occupation, in what some would describe as a "perplexing" move,[6] Israel allowed Palestinian municipal elections in the West Bank. The year was 1976, and, while a previous set of elections for local councils had taken place four years earlier, Israel had recently—and perhaps shortsightedly—expanded the franchise to include women and propertyless men.[7] By this time, the Palestinian Liberation Organization (PLO) had been internationally recognized as the sole legitimate representative of the Palestinian people, and it was politically ascendant. In towns and cities across the West Bank, local politicians like Shaka'a swept into office. These leaders openly opposed Israeli military rule and sought Palestinian national self-determination rather than, for example, a reattachment of the West Bank to the neighboring state of Jordan.[8] Unlike the mostly pro-Jordanian mayors and municipal council members who had come into office in 1972, the politicians elected in 1976 were, on the whole, younger, less conservative, and better educated; they represented an overt challenge to Israel's claims over the land.[9] While they did not always identify with specific political factions, they were, in general, ideologically supportive of the PLO. Thus, the 1976 local elections resulted in unapologetic Palestinian nationalists gaining formal governing power within historic Palestine for one of the first times in history.[10]

When my research assistant and I reached Shaka'a's house in Nablus in December 2014, we were almost an hour late. One of Shaka'a's friends and former colleagues greeted us on our arrival. He cautioned us that Shaka'a, then eighty-four years old, would need to speak slowly with frequent pauses.

However, his friend assured us, Shaka'a's memory was strong, and he was ready to answer our questions.[11] As our conversation began, Shaka'a told us that he had initially planned to boycott the 1976 elections. Much of Nablus had been without services since the previous council had resigned. When asked what convinced him to run, Shaka'a responded pragmatically: "Nablus was in need of electricity; it was in need of water; it was in need of many services."[12] He described how the municipality was in debt for two electricity generators that the previous council had purchased in an effort to avoid connecting the city to the Israeli grid. In the meantime, Nablus's residents were struggling to pay their bills, creating a budgetary crisis. In fact, electricity had long been a political issue in Nablus.[13] As mayor, Shaka'a would fend off Israeli pressure to connect the city to Israel's grid. He would also face regular interference from Israel in his efforts to extend lines to neighboring villages; in a 1982 letter he penned to his colleague in the city of Tulkarem, he recounted how occupation authorities arrested Nablus's municipal engineers and workers on site.[14] In the letter, he described these actions as part of Israel's broader strategic approach in the West Bank, writing, "all this coincides with the policy to annex the land with the intention to empty it of its population . . . to confront them [other regional and international actors] with a *fait accompli*." The nuts and bolts of municipal governance were running up against Israel's program of gradual, settlement-based annexation.

Despite having been elected to office, Shaka'a realized that his position—heading a major Palestinian municipal council under Israeli occupation—was potentially sensitive. Shaka'a recalled how, at the time, he had felt compelled to communicate to both Israeli military authorities and to the people of Nablus that "we," the newly elected council, "are not part of the occupation." He was tested on this stance even before taking office. In May 1976, Lina al-Nabulsi, a seventeen-year-old girl, was walking home from school when an Israeli soldier shot and killed her.[15] As the city mourned, the Israeli military governor of the West Bank placed a call to Shaka'a. Although Shaka'a had not officially begun his term as mayor, the Israeli official ordered him to task municipal staff with scrubbing political graffiti from the walls and removing posters that Palestinians had hung around the city in the wake of al-Nabulsi's murder. Shaka'a refused. He recalled telling the Israeli official, "This is why the last municipal council resigned. We will not do the same things. We are here to represent the people, not oppress them."

Speaking with Shaka'a, I began to understand that this earlier generation of mayors—their experiences, and the relationships they had with their occupiers—would shape the ensuing trajectory of Israeli rule in the West Bank. Mayors like Shaka'a became prominent oppositional actors rather than cooperative intermediaries within Israel's political regime. Instead of depositing the municipal budget in an Israeli bank, Nablus's municipal council members stored it in cash dispersed across their own homes. In 1979, after Israel alleged that Shaka'a made remarks supporting violent Palestinian resistance, he was arrested and threatened with deportation to Jordan.[16] The effort was unsuccessful—Shaka'a appealed the decision to Israel's High Court of Justice, and mayors across the occupied territories resigned in protest, convincing the Israeli military to drop the expulsion order.[17] Shaka'a was released from prison and defiantly returned to Nablus amid popular celebrations. The Israeli Arab journalist Rafik Halabi summarized the moment: "Now that the military government had reversed itself, the mayor of Nablus was more than a local figure, more than a national one: he had become an emblem, a power to be reckoned with in the West Bank."[18]

Ultimately, the capture of municipal institutions by Palestinian opponents of the occupation was short-lived. Shaka'a, along with other popularly elected Palestinian nationalists, was removed from office and replaced with an Israeli-appointed mayor in 1982. In addition, Israel banned the National Guidance Committee, an important organization of Palestinian business leaders, union representatives, religious leaders, and nationalist mayors, which included Shaka'a and Khalaf among its members.[19] Lessons had been learned. In 1986, Meron Benvenisti, a keen Israeli observer and former deputy mayor of Jerusalem, wrote, "Israeli authorities still view independent, elected municipalities as a security and political risk. When residents of the town of Dura . . . petitioned the High Court of Justice and demanded municipal elections, the High Court rejected their petition. The court accepted the authorities' position that municipal elections in the West Bank were a framework for national struggle and an instrument for the PLO to undertake subversive activities. Thus, the Palestinian community remains disenfranchised, even at the local level, and devoid of any autonomous authority."[20]

I found myself in Nablus again in July 2019, wondering if Palestinian municipalities could ever provide a "framework for national struggle" again. Bassam Shakaʿa had passed away just days prior. Posters featuring his portrait blanketed the city, while an enormous banner in his honor was draped from the multistory municipality building. His funeral procession drew thousands. In an environment of enduring Palestinian political polarization, it was notable that Shakaʿa was eulogized by leaders from Palestine's two most powerful and disparate political factions: Fatah (*Harakat al-Tahrir al-Watani al-Filastini*, or the Palestinian National Liberation Movement) and Hamas (*Harakat al-Muqawama al-Islamiyya*, or the Islamic Resistance Movement).[21]

The level of solidarity expressed after Shakaʿa's death surprised me at first. However, it soon reminded me of an earlier conversation with Hilary Rantisi, a Palestinian-American colleague and friend, about her late father, Audeh. Audeh Rantisi was elected deputy mayor of the city of Ramallah in 1976—the same elections that brought Shakaʿa to office. After the car bomb attack against Karim Khalaf, Rantisi—a reverend and a refugee from Lydda, a city from which the Israeli military had forcibly expelled tens of thousands of Palestinians in 1948—assumed the position of mayor of Ramallah.[22] Israel placed Rantisi under house arrest and targeted him with movement restrictions several times, but his defiance revealed itself in his sense of humor and sharp moral provocations, both of which often confused and disarmed Israeli soldiers. At the time, Hilary mentioned how all political factions and prominent families from Ramallah were represented at Audeh's funeral, paralleling what I would later see with Shakaʿa. As we spoke in her office on that fall day in 2017, Hilary reflected on how a number of her Palestinian friends and acquaintances had recently expressed nostalgia for the municipalities of the late 1970s and early 1980s, when Shakaʿa, Khalaf, Tawil, and figures such as her father had been in office. "Now," she remarked, "many mayors are just perceived as technocrats."

Indeed, the environment changed dramatically over the ensuing decades. Israeli military rule and state-backed settlement of the West Bank continued unabated. However, unlike Shakaʿa and his contemporaries, the mayors, municipal council members, and local staff whose activities form the empirical basis for this book worked under a new intermediary—the Fatah-controlled Palestinian Authority (PA), a vast organization created in the mid-1990s to take over select governing responsibilities in Palestinian communities in the occupied territories. The way Hilary described these newer generations of mayors stayed with me. Back in Nablus, I wondered if her impression that they were "just technocrats" was true. Had Israel and the PA successfully muted resistance from the corridors of Palestinian local government? Had the office of mayor been transformed from a platform for nationalist mobilization into a depoliticized provider of services, or simply another cog in a patronage-driven bureaucracy? Might the municipalities ever be transformed once again?

UPGRADING THE INDIRECT RULE REGIME
UNDER ISRAEL'S OCCUPATION

Since Israel gained control of the West Bank in 1967, it has, like the other empires and states that preceded it, experimented with various forms of rule. From the earliest days of the occupation, Israel attempted to delegate certain functions of government to Palestinians whom it hoped would serve as reliable agents or, at the very least, help sustain Israel's regime.[23] However, several years after the defiant mayors elected in 1976 were deposed, the outbreak of the first intifada—a mass uprising in the occupied territories—offered proof that Israel's cooptation efforts had not quelled Palestinian resistance and thus had not stabilized Israeli military rule. The intifada represented a culmination of Palestinian nationalist mobilization against the occupation; Palestinians coordinated on an unprecedented scale in a largely nonviolent resistance campaign that included the imposition of roadblocks, boycotts, strikes, and mass protests.[24] Israel responded to the uprising with force; an estimated 1,356 Palestinians and 253 Israelis were killed by the end of 1994.[25]

On the heels of this unprecedented display of Palestinian resistance, Israel's strategy to rule the West Bank underwent a dramatic transformation. The Oslo Accords—a set of agreements between Israel and the PLO signed in the 1993–1995 period—created a new, expansive, Palestinian governing structure with political authority centralized under the dominant party, Fatah, and its leader, the longtime chairman of the PLO, Yasser Arafat. In 1994, the PA was officially inaugurated and assumed responsibility for certain aspects of governance in Palestinian communities in the West Bank and Gaza Strip. In particular, much of the day-to-day policing of Palestinian communities was delegated to the new Palestinian security apparatus—a set of institutions that formed a vital and oversized part of the PA and were predominantly populated by Fatah loyalists. Following

Israeli military withdrawals from the Gaza Strip and the West Bank city of Jericho, Arafat, after nearly a full lifetime in exile, arrived triumphantly in Gaza, where he would soon be elected the first president of the new PA.

Instead of attempting to restrain municipal leaders, Israel's preferred intermediary would become the executive branch of the PA, including its policing and security organs, under the one-party control of Fatah. In cultivating such a relationship, Israel was pursuing a strategy of *indirect rule*, an approach used by dominant powers—empires, colonial states, postcolonial states, or specific governments within them—that do not want to or cannot, except at great cost, govern some subset of the population that they control. Under such arrangements, rule is carried out in part through collaboration with intermediaries from the "native," indigenous, or preexisting population.[26] Israeli continued its military rule over the West Bank and Gaza, in conjunction with the state-supported project to settle the territories—and the West Bank, in particular—with Jewish Israeli citizens. However, Israel entrusted the PA to take on the role of managing daily civil governance tasks within major Palestinian cities and towns, while the land surrounding these population centers was increasingly fragmented and hemmed in by Jewish Israeli settlements, Israeli firing zones, Israeli-designated state lands, and Israeli infrastructure built to serve the settlers and the military occupation.

The thousands of cheering Palestinians who greeted Arafat on his arrival in Gaza masked the stark divisions that the Oslo Accords had introduced into the Palestinian public. Numerous Palestinians did not cheer on the Oslo Accords or the creation of the new Palestinian governing authority. After all, the PA's authority was heavily circumscribed, both geographically and functionally. It was to have an elected president and legislature, but it did not control any geographic borders, thus it had no externally facing defensive capacity, nor was its central government empowered to collect many of its own taxes. It could not adopt its own national currency unless "mutually agreed" on with Israel, nor could it pursue urban planning or rural development throughout most of the West Bank without Israeli approval.[27] In the over 60 percent of the West Bank known as "Area C," Palestinian development—not to mention the presence of Palestinian police forces—was all but totally forbidden.[28] Finally, although the PA was established as a transitory arrangement, there was no guarantee that Palestinians would obtain statehood at the conclusion of the five-year "interim" period.

Influential political factions from both within and outside the PLO rejected the deal; critiques arose from politicians, academics, and militants alike, many of whom had decried arrangements for Palestinian "autonomy" without sovereignty since its reference in the 1978 Camp David agreement between Egypt and Israel. The famed Palestinian scholar and writer Edward Said called the Declaration of Principles "an instrument of Palestinian surrender, a Palestinian Versailles."[29] Ten ideologically disparate Palestinian opposition groups—including PLO members, such as the Popular Front for the Liberation of Palestine (*Al-Jabha al-Sha'biyya li-Tahrir Filastin*, PFLP) and the Democratic Front for the Liberation of Palestine (*Al-Jabha al-Dimuqratiyya li-Tahrir Filastin*, DFLP), and non-PLO groups such as Hamas and Palestinian Islamic Jihad—formed a nominal alliance based on their shared opposition to the Oslo Accords and their commitment to the continuation of armed resistance.[30] Fatah, for its part, was riven by internal divisions but soon came to be associated with *al-sulta* ("the authority") rather than *al-muqawama* ("the resistance").

HOW INDIRECT RULE SHAPES LOCAL GOVERNMENT

The creation of the PA introduced a new regime—or a new system of formal rules and informal expectations that determine the distribution of power within the political system.[31] It was one which, for some Palestinians at the time, hinted at an eventual path to Palestinian self-rule but which, for others, foreshadowed a reconfigured and more stable form of Israeli domination. Existing Palestinian municipalities in the West Bank and Gaza were subsumed under the new PA structure, while many new ones were also created. The central focus of this book is to develop an understanding of how Palestinians have engaged in everyday, local governance under this regime. This casts a spotlight on municipal-level actors, in particular—mayors, town and city councils, and their staff—while also illuminating how the local is connected to the national. From the historical and empirical record of the specific case of the West Bank, I develop a theory of how indigenous actors will pursue the core functions of states and governments—namely, coercion, extraction, and distribution—in such settings and some of the challenges they will face in doing so. In brief, I find that systems of indirect rule, when part of a regime of domination, produce different incentives and challenges for the governance projects of indigenous actors. Those perceived as regime intermediaries are likely to enjoy resource advantages yet suffer reputational deficits, while those perceived as regime opponents will likely benefit from reputational advantages while facing resource deficits. These conditions, in turn, shape the nature and type of governance strategies they pursue. In moving from the case of the Israeli-occupied West Bank toward more general propositions, I contend that my findings are most likely to be reproduced in contexts where indirect rule is part of a regime that promotes the domination of one ethnic, religious, racial, or other identity-based group over another while, nonetheless, facing considerable, sustained resistance.

First, I examine the precursors to, and origins of, this regime in the West Bank. I argue that the particular form of indirect rule that emerged from the Oslo Accords differed from earlier variants pursued by Ottoman, British, and Jordanian powers in Palestine and how it also diverged markedly from the strategy pursued by Israel itself before the 1990s. These regimes also depended on the delegation, or outsourcing, of local governance to indigenous Palestinian intermediaries. Tasks entrusted to the local level included the extraction of both taxes and labor and the provision of certain distributive goods. These earlier powers experienced both success and failure in their efforts to coopt local elites. However, I document how Israel differed from earlier empires and states in its approach to the West Bank due to its unique goal of exclusive annexation—namely, its intent to assert indefinite control over the territory of the West Bank, control that was to be strengthened through state-sponsored settlement to "right-people"[32] the land while politically excluding its existing population. Thus, I find that Israel's iterated attempts at ruling the West Bank via Palestinian intermediaries were distinctive in that they were driven by this logic.

Israel's approach to the occupied West Bank had two effects. First, it shaped the trajectory of institutional design such that the internal policing of the Palestinian population would become a predominant function of the Fatah-led PA, in turn facilitating Jewish settlement and territorial expansion. This contrasted with earlier imperial and state rulers in modern Palestine, where coercive capacity mainly rested with the center. Under these earlier empires and states, there was occasional but, overall, little formal reliance on Palestinian intermediaries for securing order through coercion and violence. Second, Israel's goal of exclusive annexation—and thus its need for a political regime that secured the domination of one racialized, ethnoreligious group over another—meant that Palestinian intermediaries would incur substantial reputational risks from collaboration.[33] These two conditions would influence the governance strategies of Palestinian mayors and the municipal councils they headed.

The empirical analysis in the second half of the book focuses on a time of heightened vulnerability for Israel's rule in the West Bank. To summarize these conditions in more general terms, this period combined a renewal of collaboration between the dominant state (Israel) and its preferred intermediary (the Fatah-affiliated leadership of the PA) while the intermediary faced mounting challenges to its legitimacy. The fissures in the indirect-rule regime had burst open with the outbreak of the second intifada—a much more deadly Palestinian uprising, which lasted from 2000 until 2005—leading to the temporary collapse of Israel-PA collaboration.[34] It was during this time when—for the first time since the 1976 polls that had brought an earlier generation of regime opponents to power—competitive elections were held for municipal office. Both Fatah and its main opponents—Hamas, PFLP, and independents and smaller parties—participated. As a result of these elections, challengers to the Israeli-PA regime would obtain formal governing power in Palestine for the first time. Following Hamas's landmark victory in general elections held in January 2006, Israel and international donors recommitted to strengthening collaboration with the Palestinian security apparatus, all branches of which ultimately answered to Arafat's successor, Mahmoud Abbas. Thus, the newly elected municipal councils in towns and cities across the West Bank found themselves governing in an environment of extreme political polarization.

How did Palestinian mayors and their municipalities approach governance in such a setting? Drawing on geocoded, local-level data on the political, economic, and security environment in the West Bank, an original and detailed data set of 107 municipal budgets from 2006 to 2012, and over fifty interviews conducted in small and large towns across the West Bank from 2014 to 2019, I analyze the activities of local governments, comparing those controlled by mayors affiliated with the regime intermediary, Fatah, with those led by its opponents. I find that nuanced relationships can develop between indigenous politicians at the local level. Indeed, in general terms, some will align with intermediaries who cooperate with the dominant state, while others will represent opponents who resist the state's project of domination. However, even in environments of sharp political polarization, blurry boundaries can characterize individual relationships between intermediaries and opponents on the ground, many of whom live in the same neighborhoods, share familial and professional networks, and are sometimes even friends. At the local level, ideological differences may even fade into the background at times.

Nonetheless, my analysis shows that local politicians representing Fatah versus those representing its opponents pursued distinct approaches toward local governance. I find evidence that municipalities led by Fatah underperformed their opponents in mobilizing revenue from their constituents while also forbearing from using the party's control over PA police forces to do so. Meanwhile, Fatah-affiliated towns took advantage of malleable budget constraints to spend relatively more on broadly desired, collective goods, such as electricity and water, than their opposition-led counterparts. On the other hand, I find qualitative evidence that opposition-led towns, in general, mobilized voluntary contributions from constituents and drew on other creative measures to reduce spending. Hamas-led towns, in particular, were more likely to increase their revenues over time and exercise fiscal discipline.

From these findings, I build the general argument that indirect rule induces intermediaries, such as Fatah, to perform politically risky governance tasks among their own communities. In particular, the dominant state usually depends disproportionately on the intermediary for one of the following two core capacities: the use of noneconomic, coercive force to police the indirectly ruled population, or the extraction of material resources or revenue from the population.[35] This introduces reputational costs for individual politicians and local-level actors who are associated with the intermediary and, thus, cooperation with the regime. In settings where the intermediary's legitimacy with the indigenous population is already weak, I argue that intermediary-affiliated actors will be more likely to reduce, or forbear from, the politically risky task (i.e., coercion or extraction) that is less central to their relationship with the dominant state. Further, intermediary-affiliated actors are more likely than their opponents to use distributive goods to enhance their local reputations.

I also develop an argument about how indigenous opponents of the regime, such as Hamas and others, will approach local governance. In general, these regime challengers may have fewer opportunities or fewer incentives to participate in governance via formal institutions. A subset of regime opponents may either capture formal political office or pursue "rebel governance" projects in the midst of armed conflict. In either case, they will find themselves in a different position than intermediaries. Relative to regime intermediaries, opponents of the regime face little to no pressure to fulfill the demands of the dominant state. Furthermore, opponents will often possess a legitimacy advantage over the intermediary. However, I argue, due to their ideological position, they are likely to face resource challenges when trying to develop the capacity to govern. They may face direct repression, sanctions, or other punitive measures carried out by the dominant state, the intermediary, or like-minded allies. Thus, my findings suggest that indigenous opponents of the regime will structure their governance programs around overcoming these resource constraints. This may mean increasing their capacity to raise revenue from their constituents or finding cost-efficient ways of achieving their productive and distributive goals.

CONTRIBUTION

Scholarship on Palestine, with rare and important exceptions, has not been fully integrated into mainstream political science. Those exceptions have enhanced our understanding of the role of civic associations in regime survival;[36] how movement structure,[37] inclusion in state institutions,[38] and mobility restrictions[39] shape resistance strategies and participation; how both time and movement interact to project power and structure Palestinian life in urban areas[40]; and how Palestine can assist us in theorizing about individualized (noncollective) types of regime opposition.[41] Dana El Kurd, in particular, has analyzed how the Palestinian Authority has reduced Palestinian political mobilization in the Oslo era, which she argues is explained by its reliance on international support.[42] El Kurd's emphasis on the polarizing effects of the post-Oslo regime in the occupied territories finds echoes in some of the local-level political dynamics explored in this manuscript.

Further, a body of important work by political scientists has explored local-level organization and mobilization among Palestinian refugees in the diaspora, examining diverse outcomes including the formation of diasporic social and political institutions across countries[43], militant group socialization and recruitment,[44] the enforcement of property rights in Lebanon's refugee camps,[45] and the use of information and communication technology to cultivate community protection.[46] Of particular theoretical relevance to the present work, Nora Stel applies the concept of the "mediated state" to theorize the relationship between the Lebanese state and the PLO during and after Lebanon's Civil War.[47] However, none of this work has adopted an explicit focus on day-to-day formal local governance in Palestinian communities under Israeli occupation. Through both its empirical and theoretical contributions, this manuscript contends that formal local politics provides an important window into the effects of indirect rule and its potential long-term consequences.

While there is a vast social science literature on the legacies of colonial institutions for politics, violence, and development, the example of Israel's attempted, gradual annexation of the West Bank provides a striking example of such colonial institutions in action. In the subsequent section, I elaborate on how Israel's indirect rule regime is in the service of a project that we can describe, without loss of precision, as settler colonization. Thus, looking closely at the local political institutions, figures, and experiences that characterize Israel's military occupation of the West Bank can inform the work of future social scientists and historians concerned with such legacies, taking care to note the ways in which contemporary colonization looks different from European colonialism in centuries past.

The Israeli-PA regime in the West Bank differs in important ways from some historical examples of indirect rule; for example, more authority is outsourced in urban rather than rural areas, and the intermediary party, Fatah, is itself a former rebel organization.[48] However, it also possesses some similarities to earlier cases—in particular, its emphasis is not just on the delegation of governing responsibilities to local leaders but also the exclusion and what Mahmood Mamdani calls the "containerizing" of indigenous populations.[49] In this sense, its *raison d'être* is to sustain domination based on racial, ethnic, or religious identity, something that unites it with earlier forms of colonial rule. In the present work, I trace the origin of Israel's particular form of indirect rule as it iterated from, or perfected, forms of institutional delegation associated with earlier state projects in the West Bank so that they served Israel's territorial and ideological goals.

The Oslo Accords promised to be if not a pathway to Palestinian self-rule, then at least a devolution of power to semiautonomous Palestinian political institutions. However, this book joins a body of critical writing on the agreements that characterizes them as a feature, not a bug, of Israel's settler colonial project in the West Bank.[50] The work of municipalities in

Palestine—repairing sidewalks and roads, collecting fees for services, providing electricity, hosting cultural events, maintaining public markets, upgrading infrastructure, maintaining a small staff—has evolved marginally over the ages. But, this book argues, the political context for this work has changed and, as a result, has shaped the nature of Palestinian governance and resistance at the local level. The creation of the PA introduced a well-funded and armed Palestinian political organization. With its thirty thousand policemen as of 1995, which would eventually grow to over eighty-three thousand by 2017,[51] the PA "transformed [the West Bank and Gaza] into zones where the ratio of police to civilians was among the highest in the world."[52] In parts of the West Bank and, originally, Gaza, this sprawling organization was intended to mediate between, on one hand, Israel's military occupation and settlement project and, on the other, the Palestinian people.

While much has been written about Palestinian politics in the wake of the Oslo Accords, to my knowledge, no book has been written on Palestinian local government under the Oslo regime.[53] I believe the stories of local government under Israeli occupation, in its contemporary form, are important to tell. I was attracted to the topic for two main reasons. First, because, despite centuries of foreign rule and occupation, Palestinians have been practicing a form of self-government at the local level since long before the Palestinian Authority, even before the modernizing influences of the Ottoman Empire arrived in the region. We would not consider all of these historical experiences to be comparable to formal institutionalized municipal government in its contemporary form, and the scope of the present work is mainly limited to the latter. However, local government has been, and perhaps will continue to be, a through line in the temporal trajectory of Palestinian political life under conditions of statelessness and foreign rule. It has also been a nexus of political agency and, at times, resistance against domination. Existing research on the legacies of colonial institutions suggests that these local relationships, routines, and institutional investments made under regimes of indirect rule can shape politics well into the future, long after ostensible national liberation is achieved.

A second reason to study local politics in and across the West Bank was because of a need I felt, as a foreign researcher first arriving in Palestine in 2011, to get out of the gravitational pull of Ramallah, the administrative capital of the PA, to understand how Palestinian-run institutions were functioning across the breadth of the territory of the West Bank. While the entire territory has fallen under military occupation since 1967, the geographic map of that occupation (a version of which is provided in map 4.1 in chapter 4) suggested to me that occupation might look and feel tangibly different from one locality to the next. Further, because the civil, legal, and institutional distinctions between Israeli settler populations and Palestinians play out at a hyper-local level, local politics in the West Bank is, in a sense, national politics.[54]

The research reflected in this book focuses exclusively on the West Bank—a portion of historic Palestine that is only slightly larger than the U.S. state of Delaware but in which over three times as many people reside. While broad narratives in international media tend to flatten the occupation and the lives of Palestinians living under it, my multiple trips to the territory revealed a land and a people teeming with diversity. A municipal engineer I interviewed in a town outside the city of Hebron told me "Studying local governance is good. You will have a lot of information to put in your book." They were right, and I hope the following pages do not leave them disappointed.

SITUATING THE STUDY OF PALESTINE

While, paradoxically, Israel/Palestine often seems to defy comparisons with other cases, as a scholar situating the case, one has no shortage of conceptual frameworks to choose from. On the whole, my research suggests that the local political outcomes I observe in the West Bank under the Israeli-PA regime are most transportable to settings in which a state or its political leadership are pursuing a project of domination such as military occupation, colonization, imperial conquest, or annexation of territory. In general, the West Bank is most immediately comparable to other cases that are generally unpopular with the indigenous population—in other words, they face sustained forms of opposition and resistance. However, Israeli rule over the occupied Palestinian Territories, and the conflict over the land in general, can be viewed through myriad conceptual frameworks. The most prominent are nationalist conflict, settler colonialism, and apartheid. By emphasizing the scope conditions of indirect rule, I do not eschew these other frameworks and ways of understanding the context. I next explicate the relationship between these frameworks and the one I have chosen. Each comes with trade-offs, both conceptual and, at times, normative.

Indeed, the conflict between Zionists and Palestinian nationalists that began to emerge in the early twentieth century and continues to this day is an example of a nationalist conflict between what we can characterize as two broad sides, each of which has its own vision for how the territory of historic Palestine should be ruled. There is a common critique that the term "conflict" is not appropriate for describing what has been occurring in Palestine/Israel since the early twentieth century because it implies some kind of symmetry in capabilities or righteousness across the two sides. This view becomes obsolete if we adopt an encompassing definition of the term, which merely depends on there being a conflict of interest between at least two political actors or organizations. Of course, in this case, one is represented by a state with a well-funded military whose sovereignty is broadly recognized by the international community, and the other is a stateless people facing subordination and discrimination by said state. Also on this side are the nonstate organizations that claim to represent them.

The asymmetry in capacity is obvious in myriad other ways, but it does not undermine use of the label "conflict" to describe, on an extremely basic level, the setting. However, situating my analysis within the universe of cases of nationalist conflicts would be simultaneously too broad and too narrow. It would be too broad because it would not allow me to precisely define the institutional setting within which local intermediaries and opponents operate within the West Bank. It would be substantively too narrow because, while my framework does assume a conflict between the dominant power and its indigenous adversaries, it is not always accurate to describe such conflicts as "nationalist." While most may meet this criterion, we can look at the example of Apartheid South Africa as one in which indigenous challengers—such as, but not limited to, the African National Congress (ANC)—framed their demands as seeking not national self-determination but, rather, equality and freedom within the existing state.

The historical approach to the land both within the Green Line (the name given to the 1949 armistice lines that define the de facto borders of "Israel proper") and in the territories occupied since 1967—adopted first by prestate Zionist settler organizations and subsequently by the state of Israel—is frequently described as settler colonialism. The concept is used so frequently in social scientific fields outside political science that it would be nearly impossible to cite all examples here. Within American political science, though, the concept is less frequently foregrounded. An important recent exception is by Lachlan McNamee, who defines it succinctly as "a process of state building involving the displacement of indigenous people by settlers."[55]

I find settler colonialism to be an appropriate label to describe Israel's approach to the West Bank, the focus of this volume, since 1967. Since that time, the Israeli state's overt sponsorship or, at least, tacit support for Jewish settlement in the West Bank is indisputable. Some readers will bristle at such an approach being labeled "colonial." The motivations of Israel may indeed differ dramatically from those of the colonial powers of the past, and certainly the symbolic and religious connection of Jews to the land is an undeniably important feature. Further, beginning in the 1930s, Zionism itself became associated with Jewish safety and survival under the threat of genocide, an association which still shapes individual attachments to the ideology. However, none of these factors changed the empirical features of the project nor its implications for Palestinians, in particular. A non-normative definition of colonialism would perhaps emphasize the establishment of political, economic, and social institutions in a populated territory by an external power. Normative implications follow when such institutions are paired with a project to extract value from the indigenous population, the claimed territory, or both, and justified with notions of cultural, ethnic, racial, or religious supremacy. The state-sponsored settlement of the West Bank since 1967—and, more generally, the approach to the Palestinian population leading up to, during, and following the 1947–49 war—has been oriented around the belief that Jewish access to the land and Jewish belonging in the state come before, and instead of, Palestinian access and belonging. I will touch briefly on the issue of labeling this ideology (and, in particular, whether it needs to include the concept of "race") later.

What distinguishes settler colonialism from other varieties of colonial rule? As Mamdani succinctly notes, "immigrants join existing polities, whereas settlers create new ones."[56] Further, as described by Patrick Wolfe, paraphrased by Lorenzo Veracini, "settler colonialism *is not* a relationship primarily characterised by the *indispensability* of colonised people. On the contrary, Wolfe emphasizes the *dispensability* of the indigenous person in a settler colonial context."[57] For Wolfe, "the primary object of settler-colonization is the land itself rather than the surplus value to be derived from mixing native labour with it."[58] Wolfe has thus argued that settler colonialism, although distinct from genocide, shares a logic of "elimination."[59] Noura Erakat argues, for example, that this eliminatory intent has been inherent in Israel's international legal strategy to sustain its occupation.[60]

In my explication of Israel's motives in the occupied West Bank, in particular in chapter 3, we indeed find strong evidence in Israel's intent to annex land exclusive of the population living on it, and we also see throughout the analysis of Israel's occupation of the West Bank that Israeli settlers carry their sovereignty with them, as Veracini aptly describes. However, while successive Israeli governments have certainly treated the Palestinian population in the occupied territories as dispensable, my narrative emphasizes instead the way in which Israeli politicians navigated the impossibility of elimination—an impossibility that arose from both the enduring nature of Palestinian resistance and, further, I would argue, ideological and normative constraints that prevented Israel from executing a campaign of violent ethnic cleansing of Palestinians at the scale required to be "eliminatory." For these reasons, the settler colonial nature of Israel's project and, more proximately, the governing institutions that grew out of that project define the scope of my analysis in the ensuing pages. I refer to some of these latter institutions as constituting an indirect rule regime. It is worth noting that the impulse to *contain* Palestinians—what Hilla Dayan calls a "regime of separation"[61]—is what generated the need for institutions such as the PA, through which Israel could rule indirectly. It is a matter of debate whether separation and containment were always intended to lead to elimination.

Finally, with the international community moved to address the violence and oppression being committed against Black South Africans in the 1960s and 1970s, crimes of apartheid were defined in international law via the 1973 International Convention on the Suppression and Punishment of the Crime of Apartheid, passed by the United Nations General Assembly. The concept was then incorporated into the 1998 Rome Statute of the International Criminal Court. The Rome Statute defines crimes of apartheid as acts "committed in the context of an institutionalized regime of systematic oppression and domination by one racial group over any other racial group or groups and committed with the intention of maintaining that regime."[62] The term has been used to describe the system in place in Israel, the West Bank, and Gaza by Palestinian, Israeli, and international human rights organizations, the latter most recently including Human Rights Watch and Amnesty International.[63] While the term gains traction in the international community at large, there is a somewhat distinct question of whether the concept of race is both appropriate and required to understand the institutionalized forms of violence, segregation, dispossession, and discrimination that Palestinians face. Erakat et al. have argued that racism is constitutive to Zionism and its settler-colonial character.[64] Race, while it makes claims to be derived from innate biological traits, is constructed by societal actors and institutions as something that is politically relevant (or not).

For the purposes of my analysis, what is critical is the belief that Jewish Israelis and Palestinians are two distinct peoples, and, most importantly for the purposes of understanding institutional development in the occupied Palestinian Territories, this supposedly fixed membership in one community or the other should determine one's political belonging and/or exclusion. So, the position that will guide this text moving forward is that race may indeed be an appropriate lens through which to view the institutional setting in the West Bank. While perhaps appropriate, it is not required for assessing the theory and findings that I present. I do not think much is lost by using the labels "ethnic," "religious," or "ethnoreligious" to distinguish the Jewish and Palestinian populations. Nonetheless, it should be clear that I consider apartheid to be an appropriate label for conceptualizing the institutional feature of Israel's indirect rule regime, as chapter 6 explicitly compares my findings from the occupied West Bank with local governance under South Africa's apartheid regime.

I am not the first to use the framework of indirect rule to understand Israel's occupation and rule in the West Bank, but I hope to build on existing scholarship by theorizing its functional form more explicitly and generating findings about its localized effects. Neve Gordon refers to the Oslo process as Israel "outsourcing" responsibilities for the occupation to the newly created PA: "Theoretically, outsourcing should be considered a technique employed by power to conceal its own mechanisms. It is not motivated by power's decision to retreat, but, on the contrary, by its unwavering effort to endure and remain in control."[65] In social science on the Palestinian case that either explicitly or implicitly adopts a rational actor approach to theory development, existing analyses have explored the implications of thinking of the Palestinian Authority as either an agent of Israel or an agent of its international donors, the United States being prime among them.[66] Furthermore, Youssef Mnaili characterizes the Israeli state's relationship to the settler movement in the West Bank as one of indirect governance.[67] In this case, settlers and settler institutions serve as agents, or intermediaries, of the Israeli state. Finally, although Somdeep Sen's ethnographic analysis of Hamas's rule in Gaza certainly does not depict the militant resistance group as an intermediary within the Israeli regime, he nonetheless documents how the movement is somewhat awkwardly positioned between anticolonial resistance and the "postcolonial" trappings of governance.[68] The local politicians who are the subject of the present work also end up enmeshed in some of these complexities—whether they represent Hamas, other opposition groups, or even, occasionally, Fatah, the ruling party.[69] It is my contention that such complexities have not, until now, been given sufficient attention.

NOTES ON METHODOLOGY AND SUBJECTIVITY

Social science is often concerned with causal processes—relationships of cause and effect that, under certain scope conditions, may be reproduced elsewhere. Despite this emphasis within my field, many scholars would not dare to offer generalizable insights from analysis of a single case such as Palestine. I do, indeed, write this book in the spirit of the scientific enterprise. That entails an inherently cyclical process of deriving propositions about social and political processes from empirical observations and further testing and refining those propositions with additional observations. This process must include places for both inductive and deductive reasoning, and it must be precise and careful about attempts to generalize. I discuss the former issue—inductive and deductive approaches—more later, but first I describe my thoughts on generalization.

The intent to seek generalizability or reproduction of one's theory elsewhere may sound unappealing to some readers. Along with such readers, I believe in the inherent value of describing one case, or one instance of a phenomenon, extremely well. Further, cumulative knowledge production may occur by summing these individual descriptive studies, but how are we to engage in this kind of aggregation? A familiar problem for comparative politics researchers is that no two cases are identical. Comparing across localities, regions, or countries necessarily entails not only traversing geography but also introducing differences in historical experiences; social, economic, and political circumstances; cultural traditions; and many more contextual features that shape human behavior. Even comparing the same geographic region over time brings on board myriad differences—those derived from merely changing the historical context—that may shape the empirical relationships one observes and thus the conclusions one draws.

In this book, what I aim to do is use variation within the case of the West Bank—both across localities and, to a certain extent, over time—to derive conjectures about causes and effects. The main empirical analysis is contained in chapters 4 and 5, and it draws on both quantitative and qualitative sources gathered through field-based research. However, these chapters are sandwiched between alternative exercises in "zooming out." First, chapters 2 and 3 retain a geographic focus on the West Bank, but they provide the historical context for understanding the origins of the explanatory variables in the subsequent analysis. Then, chapter 6 asks whether the causal propositions derived from the preceding chapters might apply in other regimes of indirect rule, starting with British colonial India and apartheid South Africa. Thus, while a primary purpose of this book is to describe Palestinian local politics in a particular part of historic Palestine during a particular period, a secondary purpose of this volume is to develop a theory about the effects of indirect rule on local politics and local governance. In the review of existing scholarship in chapter 1, I demonstrate that we do not yet have enough theoretical propositions about these effects.

As a final note on generalizations, I will say that the modest amount of space the non-Palestinian comparison cases take up in this book is not commensurate with the amount of time I have spent in either some form of obsession or anxious discomfort in trying to situate the Palestinian case comparatively. This is, of course, related to the preceding discussion of which framework or scope conditions one adopts to understand the phenomena of interest. Furthermore, related to the next subject I will discuss—the role of my subjective identity and perceptions in the research process—it took me a long time to settle on the framework of indirect rule as the most relevant and appropriate for my purposes.

My approach in this manuscript is neither fully deductive—in the sense of a unidirectional progression from theories to hypotheses to testing—nor fully inductive. I thus embrace an approach in keeping with what Sean Yom has labeled "inductive iteration," whereby the researcher moves back and forth between data and theory in a transparent, iterative way.[70] In this spirit, I use the first person quite a bit throughout the text to signal to readers when, for example, my own theories about causal relationships were adapted in light of new data. As described by Yom, I find that there are strong incentives for comparative politics researchers to hide behind the cloak of "deductive proceduralism" when my research process—which aims to deeply understand the Palestinian case, first and foremost—did not proceed in such a unidirectional manner.

My methodology also needs to recognize the nature of the Palestinian case. It is not an environment I would claim is data-poor, but it is one in which local government under the existing regime has not been systematically analyzed by social scientists. It is also a context in which it is not clear how well existing theory should or should not map. As I elaborate in the next chapter, literature to date in social science has largely focused on governance by states on one hand or rebel organizations on the other. The interplay between them has been an important area of emerging focus, but when developing intuitions about how the setting I characterize as indirect rule will shape local governance, I find it is most constructive to begin with fairly naive priors.

Implicitly, I also draw on a Bayesian approach as described by Tasha Fairfield and Andrew Charman, who, citing Cox and James, define "probability as extended logic," in the sense that the researcher asks, "Given this set of empirical observations, how likely (or unlikely) is it that my theory is true?"[71] This contrasts with conventional econometric-style statistical analysis, which asks, "Given my theory (or, more accurately, given the null hypothesis), how likely (or unlikely) would these empirical observations be?" This is a radical difference in how we think of probability and chance, and it is one that I find, quite simply, more intuitive. However, I do, in fact, conduct tests of statistical significance in the quantitative analysis in chapter 4, suggesting a frequentist rather than Bayesian approach. I pursue these tests, as I think the reader will discover, as a process of building a base of empirical observations from which I can assess the relative likelihood (or unlikelihood) of a given theory as true. Thus, as with the balance between inductive and deductive, there is a balance between Bayesian and frequentist approaches here.

The main critique of inductive iteration or a Bayesian-informed approach is that it is more susceptible to confirmation bias due to motivated reasoning by the researcher. I take the possibility of researcher-induced bias seriously in my work, because in our position as observers, visitors, and data collectors, we also develop normative opinions informed by our experiences. In other words, researchers are humans. However, I aim to protect against introducing this kind of bias by, when appropriate, transparently specifying rival theories, hypotheses, or hunches about which I believe equally compelling logic could be presented. I began my research process by learning about my case (Palestine) but without strong, fully deduced theoretical priors about how governance outcomes would vary *locally* within that case. Thus, in the spirit of Bayesian inference, I aim in this book—and in chapters 4 and 5 in particular—to distinguish logically prior information from data incorporated as new evidence.

Finally, a note on how my subjective position as the author of this work may have shaped the final product that you are now reading. I approached this research with both personal and institutional privileges as a white American scholar who was able to conduct her first research trips to Palestine carrying the affiliation of a reputable American research university. As I transitioned from my first postdoctoral appointment to my tenure-track faculty position, I adapted to a smaller research budget within a public university system that—despite its essential value as an engine of upward mobility for tens of thousands of students each year—some may consider less "prestigious" than the institutions from which I received my PhD and subsequent one-year fellowship.

Throughout this time, my ability to study Palestinian politics in Palestine is a privilege that is denied to the majority of Palestinians every year. Palestinians from the occupied West Bank and Gaza are denied access to Israeli citizenship. They possess PA-issued identity documents, which generally bar them from entering Israel without exceptional reasons to do so (i.e., on a case-by-case basis to visit the holy sites, travel as part of a vetted delegation, or access health care or visit family). Palestinians who were ever residents of the occupied territories, even if they currently live in the diaspora, are usually subjected to similar restrictions. Palestinians with foreign citizenship and without PA identity documents are often heavily scrutinized, harassed, or barred entry based on their national origin. While I have been subjected to unpleasant searches of both my belongings and my person while traveling to and from Palestine, it must still be acknowledged that I have been permitted to come and go from the country. Furthermore, I am generally permitted to cross back and forth between the West Bank and Israel proper—across both sides of the Green Line—while Palestinians who live within Israel, the occupied territories, or the diaspora usually face extreme hurdles to do so, if they are ever successful.

While in Palestine and Israel, I also present as white, female, and, to some, Jewish (my father is Jewish, leaving me with the "half-Jewish" label that is either well-understood, perplexing, or meaningless, depending on one's own connection to Judaism). I am able to read standard Arabic. I speak the Levantine dialect of Arabic with an intermediate level of proficiency, and thus I conducted all interviews with the presence of a native Palestinian Arabic speaker who could provide oral interpreting. I do not speak Hebrew but can read it at a very basic level.

My personal and professional background undoubtedly shaped the research process in, first, the evolution of the research question I sought to answer. My own perspective on how to understand political life in Palestine has shifted over the course of my studies. While in graduate school and beginning this project, I often described my interest as "Palestinian state-building." It was not that I believed the Palestinian Authority would necessarily become a Palestinian state, but I did assume that was what it was trying to do. It took years, including many field visits, to understand that "state-building" may not capture either the purpose of these institutions or the empirical conditions they were producing. I am a child of the 1990s, and I both went to college in Washington, DC, and became somewhat immersed in the Beltway bubble in the four years following graduation before transitioning to academia. Thus, I believe my perspective on Palestinian governance—or my imagination—was shaped and constrained by these experiences. My first trip to the West Bank in the summer of 2011 was transformative, as is the case with many foreigners who see the occupation up close for the first time.

Although I did not possess any preexisting attachments to the state of Israel, I believe my position as someone with Jewish ancestry did influence my attraction to Palestine and Israel as a geographic locus for my work. I was personally affected by a number of conversations with my paternal grandfather, who was an endlessly curious, loving, and multitalented man, a World War II U.S. Navy veteran, a reform Jew, and a person who, I am fairly confident, would have identified as a Zionist, although I rarely heard the term growing up. After I took my first trips to Israel and Palestine while in graduate school, I remember sharing some reflections with him. He would have been ninety at the time. In several conversations over the ensuing years until he passed away, I remember being moved by his sense of both the ideal of what Israel could be and what, in his view, it was tragically becoming. I believe there is a Jewish National Fund tree planted somewhere in Israel/Palestine in my family's name, on land that no doubt used to be Palestinian land, whether its confiscation was achieved through the market or sheer force. I grapple with this just as I consider what it means to be a descendant of settlers in North America. The latter is something that my paternal grandmother seems to have processed into a productive force, fueling decades of volunteer work at the Haffenreffer Museum of Anthropology in Providence, Rhode Island, where she developed an impressive amount of knowledge about the culture and traditions of the Wampanoag, Narragansett, and other indigenous Americans. I miss both of them and wish they could read this book.

It is possible that any of the traits just mentioned shaped how my informants perceived me and, thus, their responses to my queries. For this reason, I do my best to include long, word-for-word excerpts from my interviews in chapter 5 so the reader can have a sense of the full conversation and make these judgments themselves.

Finally, I have endeavored to consider, throughout the process of writing this book, the sensitivity of its subject matter and, more precisely, my argument about a seeming "principal-agent" relationship between Israel and the PA executive branch and use of the verb "collaboration" to describe Palestinian actors within this ecosystem. The reader should rest assured that words such as "collaborator," "agent," and "intermediary" were never used in my interviews with interlocutors in Palestine, as such labels can carry existential security risks.[72] In my writing, I also seek to avoid the term "collaborator" to describe anyone except those who might, in a setting of confidentiality, describe their own actions as such. In essence, this detaches such a label from, for example, the many thousands of Palestinians who work in the PA's bureaucracies. Direct collaboration is something that, with both theoretical and empirical justification, I believe we can consider as limited to those within an upper echelon of the intermediary institutions, such as the PA, that I describe. I do theorize that entire organizations (such as Fatah) within certain institutional settings (such as the Palestinian Authority) can develop a reputation as regime intermediaries—something I develop throughout the volume. I also try as much as possible to avoid layering normative judgment on to my description of how various Palestinian actors have behaved, or might behave, in the threat environments they have faced under foreign rule, past and present.

ROADMAP OF THE BOOK

Chapter 1 outlines the main theoretical argument of the manuscript. This theory emerges inductively from my analysis of the Palestinian case over the following chapters. Where indirect rule is carried out in support of what I refer to as a regime of domination, complex relationships develop between indigenous actors perceived as regime intermediaries and those who position themselves as regime opponents. However, ultimately, I argue that these two types of actors will approach local governance differently. Local actors affiliated with the intermediary will suffer weak or weakening legitimacy with the indigenous population. As a result, I predict that they will reduce their involvement in—or forbear from—those politically risky functions of governance (i.e., fiscal extraction or coercion) that are relatively less central to the dominant state-intermediary relationship. At the same time, I suggest that local intermediary affiliates will be less resource-constrained relative to local regime opponents, allowing them to invest relatively more in politically rewarding activities, such as distribution of goods and services. By contrast, local opponents of the indirect rule regime will possess a relative legitimacy advantage but face relatively greater resource constraints. Therefore, I suggest that, absent external support, such actors may exert relatively greater fiscal effort while also benefiting from voluntary (non-coerced) resource contributions from constituents. However, they may be required to restrain their distributive activities.

Many West Bank municipalities have been in existence for much longer than the PA itself, meaning that local governance provides an important window into the historical legacies of governance during conditions of statelessness. Chapter 2 draws on a variety of sources to outline the history of local governance in the West Bank under the late Ottoman period (1830–1919), the British Mandate period (1920–48), and the Jordanian monarchy (1948–67). I show that rule through intermediaries was not uncommon, but because of their varied goals in the territory, the approaches pursued by these earlier states would differ markedly from what Israel was to pursue in the West Bank.

Chapter 2 concludes on June 10, 1967, when Israel's victory in the preceding war against Arab forces left it in control of three times the amount of territory it had held just a week prior, including the West Bank. Israel made immediate efforts to incorporate East Jerusalem into the Israeli state, while the rest of the West Bank and its nearly six hundred thousand Palestinian inhabitants were placed under indefinite military occupation. Given Israel's objectives, and taking into account the existing legacies of local institutions in this part of historic Palestine, how was Israel to rule?

Chapter 3 traces the origins of Israel's indirect rule regime in the West Bank—as embodied in the creation of the PA between 1993 and 1995—and grounds its explanation in Israel's goals for the territory. Israeli state-building and occupation was unique in Palestine's contemporary history by being neither inclusive of the Palestinian population nor overtly temporary. While the ideological and strategic underpinnings of the successive Israeli governments between 1967 and 1993 varied, the minimal and maximal bounds for discourse, and for policy, ultimately constrained the type of self-rule that the PA would be able to practice. In particular, as the dominant power, Israel emphasized the delegation of internal policing to the new Palestinian Authority rather than, for example, fiscal extraction. This, as I illustrate later, contributes both to Fatah's reputational deficit with the Palestinian public and to the options available to Fatah-affiliated mayors and municipalities.

Chapters 4 and 5 provide an in-depth examination of how the indirect rule regime shapes governance at the local level, first by analyzing an original data set on local policing, taxing, and spending and, subsequently, drawing on qualitative observations from more than fifty field-based interviews and additional qualitative sources. Chapter 4 finds that the duration of time a municipality spent under Fatah rule is associated with lower levels of local revenue mobilization. Opposition-led municipalities, however, demonstrate strong revenue collection, specifically in areas where the policing capacity of their Fatah rivals is highest. Finally, Fatah-led towns seem to possess implicit resource advantages, engaging, for example, in more debt-financed (i.e., "soft budget") distributive spending.

Qualitative evidence marshalled in chapter 5 supports the proposition that Fatah-led municipal councils were more likely to forbear from revenue mobilization. Interviews with former and current mayors, municipal council members, and staff from across the political spectrum also suggest that Fatah's opponents at the local level faced both financial challenges and overt repression. They describe creative, and sometimes confrontational, strategies to boost revenues or reduce the costs of their operations. Chapter 5 also adds texture to the complex political positions of both local-level

Fatah affiliates and their opponents, demonstrating how personal and professional relationships experience the strain of indirect rule while continuing to carry on the essential work of local government.

Chapter 6 applies the findings from the preceding chapters to two comparison cases—the indirectly ruled parts of India under the British Empire and the Bantustans, or so-called homelands, of apartheid South Africa. This preliminary review finds that the South African case bears more similarities with the contemporary West Bank than colonial India, although it leaves open numerous questions about how to conceptualize political legitimacy, intermediaries, and opponents in each case. The chapter identifies several areas for additional research on direct versus indirect rule, urban versus rural dynamics, the experiences of everyday citizens, and other themes. I conclude with some reflections on how political dynamics in Palestine have evolved since the period analyzed in the preceding chapters and how a possible return to unmediated military rule in the West Bank might shape both governance and resistance in Palestine.

Chapter One

A THEORY OF LOCAL POLITICS UNDER INDIRECT RULE

"The main objective of keeping natives under their own law
is to ensure control of them."

THEOPHILUS SHEPSTONE, BRITISH COLONIAL OFFICIAL IN SOUTH AFRICA,
QUOTED IN MAHMOUD MAMDANI, *NEITHER SETTLER NOR NATIVE:
THE MAKING AND UNMAKING OF PERMANENT MINORITIES*

Existing literature in comparative politics has shed light on how both states and non-state rebel movements can develop the core capacities to govern. However, under colonial rule, military occupation, and other regimes of domination, political actors can emerge that do not wholly represent either the state or its challengers. Some territories—such as the indirectly ruled parts of British colonial India; the Bantustans, or "homelands," in South Africa and Namibia under apartheid; and today's occupied West Bank—have been subjected to a particular form of state control. In such settings, the dominant state or regime—such as the British imperial state, the apartheid government, or Israel—exercises disproportionate control over the territory and the lives of its established population.[1] These cases are known for the enduring forms of resistance that they provoked, such as India's pro-independence movements, the activists and organizations that fought apartheid, and the various wings of the Palestinian national liberation struggle. However, under these systems of domination, certain functions of local governance were also shared with, or foisted on, actors who mediated between the dominant state or regime and the local population. For example, in portions of colonized India, especially after 1858, rulers of the so-called princely states, landlords (*zamindars*), and estate-holders (*jagidars*) played this intermediary role. In apartheid South Africa, the chiefs and others who were appointed and coopted into running the bantustans ful-filled such a purpose.

Other examples abound of indigenous actors being mobilized to aid the efforts of dominant states and colonial powers. These include the Ottoman Empire's use of tax farmers in its peripheral territories and Great Britain's reliance on chiefs in Sierra Leone to arbitrate disputes and tax the popu-lation.[2] Much of Europe—including England, France, the Low Countries, and Prussia—were dominated by indirect rule arrangements until roughly the eighteenth century.[3] In the occupied West Bank, as subsequent chapters show, Israel initially attempted to cultivate local leaders to serve as inter-mediaries in Palestinian cities, towns, and villages but later settled on the Palestinian Authority executive branch, under the control of Fatah—until then, a party nominally committed to Palestinian national liberation—as its preferred go-between.

As I will elaborate, such arrangements are best understood as regimes of indirect rule, systems that, while sometimes defined as a more general form of delegated governance, subsume "local institutions—not simply individuals—into an overall structure of colonial domination."[4] As the epi-graph to this chapter exemplifies, imperial and colonial states have histori-cally used such institutions as a means of maintaining territorial control, selectively promoting or perverting existing indigenous offices, roles, and laws to serve their own aims. Existing social science scholarship has described such regimes and theorized about both their origins and their long-term legacies for postcolonial state-building, development, and con-flict.[5] However, because of the concept's association with colonial regimes of the past, researchers have had fewer opportunities to observe the inner workings of indirect rule as it unfolds. Perhaps for that reason, there is a shortage of explorations of how indirect rule regimes operate, what their consequences are for populations living under them, and how indigenous politicians and organizations approach local governance in such settings.

This chapter aims to establish a conceptual framework for modeling such systems of rule. Indirect rule is, in a sense, more complicated than direct modes of governance and state-building, because it requires us to define and describe those actors in the middle, situated between the dominant power and the indigenous population. The chapter also outlines several novel theo-retical predictions about which indigenous actors will engage in which tasks of governance at the local level and why. These hypotheses emerge from the analysis of the Israeli-occupied West Bank that unfolds over subsequent chapters; however, I suggest that they will most successfully apply in other cases where indirect rule is employed to secure the domination of one ethnic, religious, racial, or other identity-based group over another.

Under regimes of domination, indigenous actors' choices may not always neatly fit within the binary of cooperation versus resistance.[6] Building a theory with the potential to travel to other contexts requires the adoption of somewhat general and sterile language. However, we must not forget that the indigenous "actors" described in this chapter are real humans, with all their richness and complexity, facing political compulsions, risks, indignities, and opportunities for agency. Despite the diversity of these individual experiences, I argue that regimes of indirect rule introduce distinct pressures and opportunities for indigenous political actors attempting to govern locally. Those affiliated with the regime intermediary struggle with a reputational deficit among the indigenous population due to their connection to the dominant state or colonial power and their role in sustaining that regime. This encourages those affiliated with the regime intermediary to lessen their involvement in politically risky governance tasks (e.g., fiscal extraction or coercion) depending on which tasks are more heavily prioritized or monitored by the dominant power.

Furthermore, the empirical findings in subsequent chapters suggest that intermediaries and their local affiliates will be incentivized to compensate for their reputational deficit by increasing their capacity to distribute collective or targeted goods to the population. This distribution is often facilitated by the intermediary's relatively more privileged access to resources. On the other hand, legitimacy concerns do not pose as serious a constraint on indigenous opponents of the regime. Yet, such actors often face resource constraints, which might lead them to boost extraction or temper their distributive goals.

This argument is developed inductively from the Palestinian case over subsequent chapters, but the general form of the argument is presented here to conceptually anchor the analysis that follows. This chapter will appeal to readers seeking connections to more general political science theory or those who are seeking an answer to the question, "What is the Israeli-occupied West Bank a case of?" My approach to generalization here is to begin with a fairly narrow set of assumptions and scope conditions for answering that question.

First, I limit my attention to cases of indirect rule that are imposed with the ideological intent of domination or supremacy of one group over another. Second, I make definitional choices for the key actors within this framework—the dominant power, indigenous regime intermediaries, and indigenous regime opponents—while acknowledging that all such classifications are inevitably simplifications of reality. It is my hope that the costs of such an approach (i.e., a loss of descriptive accuracy of specific cases) do not outweigh the gains it brings (i.e., establishing portable theory). Third, I outline a theory of how such regimes of indirect rule will shape local governance strategies by those associated with regime intermediaries and those associated with their opponents. To do so, I will require four assumptions, to be described, about what governing functions dominant powers will delegate to intermediaries in these settings. Often these decisions about delegation and cooperation occur at the level of central governments; however, my theory seeks to explain how such higher-order institutional arrangements shape the decisions and capacities of political actors at the local level.

The theoretical architecture in this chapter emerges from empirical findings from the Israeli-occupied West Bank. These findings are concentrated in chapters 4 and 5. However, chapters 2 and 3 provide the historical backdrop that informs how I have positioned the Palestinian case and, thus, the scope conditions for the present theory. In other words, what are the historically rooted institutional structures of indirect rule within which Palestinian local governance takes place and to which Palestinian local governance responds? The final step, pursued in chapter 6, is to ask whether some of the causal logic underpinning the theory might operate in other settings that appear, at first blush, to meet the scope conditions of indirect rule in the service of a regime of domination. (Of course, this necessarily entails losing some of the contingencies and particularities that define the case of the Israeli-occupied West Bank.)

Next, I summarize what existing research says about governance by two of the most commonly studied organizations in political science: sovereign states and rebel movements. However, in settings where states or imperial powers seek to dominate through indirect rule, our understanding of governance must incorporate a third actor—the indigenous actor(s) serving as regime intermediary—and the institutions through which they carry out their work. Much of the political science literature has operationalized and studied such institutional arrangements as historical phenomena and subsequently inquired about their long-term effects on state-building, conflict, and development. However, an exploration of the Palestinian case calls on us to acknowledge and document cases of domination through indirect rule in the present day. As Adnan Naseemullah and Paul Staniland write, "while some forms of indirect rule arrangements were eliminated by decolonization, others have persisted and continue to structure contemporary state-society relations."[7] In fact, when the institutional mechanisms of indirect rule are paired with the ideological intent to dominate, they are arguably better described as "still colonial" rather than decolonized settings. Our attention to local politics in such contexts, I argue, has been insufficient.

EXISTING RESEARCH ON GOVERNANCE
BY STATES AND REBELS

Although the analysis in the chapters that follow focuses on local-level politics, I import a number of concepts related to the capacity to govern from the existing literature on sovereign states. However, because such theories either implicitly accept sovereignty as a scope condition or view it as the ultimate ambition of state builders, they do not sufficiently capture cases of protracted occupation, colonization, or annexation. In such settings, sovereignty is actively contested, and local institutions that we normally associate with the state become epicenters of the struggle between domination and resistance. These are not examples of state-builders developing governing capacity in a teleological fashion but, rather, cases of governance and resistance under what Mahmoud Mamdani famously called "decentralized despotism."[8] Nonetheless, the literature on state formation provides some parsimonious concepts for describing what it is that states, aspiring sovereigns, and other governing organizations actually do. As I also discuss here, the burgeoning scholarship on governance by rebel movements helpfully drops the assumption that governance is exclusively provided within a setting of sovereignty—or even exclusively by sovereignty-seeking actors—but does not necessarily theorize those relationships of delegation, cooperation, and resistance that we need for understanding settings of indirect rule.

Historical and sociological accounts from early modern Europe underpin some of the most influential theories of how sovereign states emerged.[9] Early state builders—monarchs, political leaders, and warlords—found that consolidating coercive control made it easier to defend and expand their territorial holdings. Because leaders required revenue and labor to compete in battle, they sought ways to extract those resources from local populations. Leaders who provided protection from both internal and external threats were able to extract resources—revenue and labor—with relative ease. Those rulers with moderately long time horizons chose to settle down as "stationary" rather than "roving" bandits to develop reliable relationships of extraction from local producers.[10] As Michael Mann attests, the modern state became defined in part by its infrastructural reach, which, in turn, enmeshed it further in society.[11]

According to this "war makes states" logic, state development was, first and foremost, a process of demobilizing internal rivals while expanding territory through warfare. Thus, coercive capacity, or the ability to wield violence to defend against both external and internal threats, and fiscal capacity, the ability to generate revenue, were two linked competencies of the modern state. Importantly, Charles Tilly describes how states were also called on to adopt a more prominent role in the distribution of goods and services—that is, food first and foremost, but also transportation, energy, public education, pensions, and social services, the mix of which depended on the bargaining power of key classes, the concentration of capital, and, of course, the military needs of the state.[12] Thus, even the classic bellicist theorists argued that monopolizing the means of violence was sufficient neither to sustain growth nor to allow state builders to continue extracting from their populations indefinitely. State builders had to offer production and distribution of desired goods. They also needed systems of regulation and enforcement to cultivate "quasi-voluntary compliance" with extraction.[13] Other scholars focused on the importance of representative institutions, such as parliaments, that sought to limit the executive.[14] Such institutions, in theory, ensured that taxed populations could oversee how revenues were spent and ensure that state coercion did not become overly confiscatory or repressive.[15]

A final, important set of work related to the fiscal capacity of states attests to how access to nontax revenue—for example, resource rents or foreign aid—can reduce the incentives of state builders to develop the capacity to tax their own populations. There is an active debate about whether or not this reduces state responsiveness to citizen demands or opportunities for political participation.[16]

While not all the literature just referenced focuses exclusively on European experiences with state formation, it is perhaps united by its emphasis on explaining long-term institutional outcomes. These are, largely, stories of state capacity converging over time and achieving basic uniformity across the state's territory. A distinct body of work attends to state capacity development in postcolonial contexts. These theories of postcolonial state-building in Latin America, Southeast Asia, and sub-Saharan Africa have long taken seriously subnational variation in state capacity, since in many (although not all) of these cases, formal sovereignty was achieved more recently. Factors like geography and population distributions,[17] relationships between the bureaucracy and local elites,[18] and historical elite responses to contention[19] are found to affect the circumstances under which state leaders will choose to—or be able to— project their authority. State capacity may depend, for example, on how central political leaders in the metropole decide to interact with local political organization on the ground.[20] Uneven extension of state institutions may arise from the legacies of how colonial powers balanced the motives of "greed, fear, and frugality"[21] or from their proclivities to be "standoffish" as a way of deterring challenges to their rule.[22] Nonetheless, the motivation for much of this work is to characterize the depth and reach of the state rather than to explicitly theorize about the capacities of governance developed by state intermediaries and their opponents at the local level. More importantly, one might ask: How applicable is the literature on postcolonial state-building to settings of ongoing occupation or colonization—in short, to settings that are not yet postcolonial? I argue that within such settings, we need to understand the formation of governing capacity not just for the state itself, but also for indigenous organizations that are functioning under and within the regime of domination.

A final set of work focuses on governance—coercion, extraction, and distribution—in settings of ongoing conflict. Some of the most recent work on conflict and post-conflict state-building comes, perhaps unsurprisingly, from the Middle East, including how ceasefires contribute to state formation and how foreign military intervention destabilizes internal aspects of state-building.[23] The burgeoning literature on "rebel governance" elucidates the strategies and behavior of a particular type of non-state actor: rebel organizations. This work examines interactions between rebel movements and civilian populations in conflict settings and, while careful not to impose a teleology, often notes the ways in which these interactions may approximate state-citizen dynamics.[24] Much of this work is based on detailed case studies—including examples such as the Shining Path in Peru, the National Resistance Army in Uganda, the Liberation Tigers of Tamil Eelam in northern Sri Lanka, and the Revolutionary Armed Forces of Colombia—with qualitatively rich accounts that are both hypothesis-testing and theory-building.

Like the analysis of the Palestinian case that will follow in subsequent chapters, the rebel governance literature often focuses on lower levels of variation—either geographic or temporal—in a particular rebel move-ment's structure or governance strategy. However, concept formation occurs at an aggregate level so as to facilitate cross-case comparison. Thus, concepts such as effective governance,[25] inclusive governance,[26] the extent of social order,[27] the degree of voluntary (noncoerced) compliance,[28] or the extent of revolutionary goals[29] can vary temporally or geographically within the same rebel movement. The present work is partly inspired by the rebel governance turn, which directs us away from path-dependent assumptions about state formation each time we observe an organization governing. As in the rebel governance literature, I spotlight relationships between non-state governing organizations—including some that continue to actively resist the state—and local residents. However, regions of indi-rect rule feature an extra actor layered between states and rebels—regime intermediaries. To describe how and why dominant states try to outsource authority in such settings—and the resulting investments in governance by indigenous actors—governance must be disaggregated in ways beyond what has been done in rebel governance research to date.[30]

NOT STATE-BUILDING, NOT REBEL RULE: DEFINING THE SCOPE OF ANALYSIS

Under indirect rule, there is an organized resistance movement against the incumbent state, but there is another, important set of indigenous actors that the incumbent state relies on to rule. Definitions of indirect rule vary but, at a minimum, it is described as a form of governance that features both a dominant power (sometimes referred to as the "principal") and a local, or indigenous, intermediary (whom the principal hopes to entrust as its "agent"). A highly influential formulation of the concept by Mamdani defines indirect rule as inherently "despotic," in that it entails rule over an indigenous population that is racialized and/or tribalized.[31] Accordingly, the imperial power or state's intention to dominate is what produces the indirect rule regime, which is inherently "Janus-faced, bifurcated" such that "natives" are ruled indirectly—through, in the sub-Saharan cases Mamdani explores, chiefs and customary law—while non-native colonists and settlers are given access to a separate set of civil rights and institutions.

This conceptualization of indirect rule as originating in despotic tendencies is distinct from more strictly institutional definitions of the phenomenon, which say little about the ideological or strategic intent of the indirect ruler—whether it is a colonial power or an indigenous state builder—and focus instead on the structural features of indirect rule as a decentralization of governing authority.[32] However, for our purposes, it is important to retain some substantive intent behind the indirect rule regime. The cases I speak to here are those in which indirect rule is a regime intended to impose domination or supremacy of one group (colonists, a dominant ethnic or racial group, etc.) over another. Thus, this is a more restrictive definition of indirect rule, much more grounded in its colonial origins and nature, than the purely institutional definitions.

The universe of cases for the argument to be outlined are contested territories governed under a system of indirect rule. They feature at least three actors: first, a *dominant state*, which may be a colonial, imperial, or occupying power or another kind of state featuring a regime of domination. This state maintains a coercive advantage, allowing it to rule over the territory and its population. At various times, I describe this dominant state or regime as "unpopular" with the indigenous population. While attitudes toward the dominant state or regime among the indigenous population may vary widely, I merely suggest that the legitimacy of the dominant state in the contested territory is seriously questioned and faces organized and somewhat durable forms of indigenous resistance.

As such, we can define some political actors from the indigenous population as *opponents* of, or *challengers* to, the dominant state or its regime. They can usually be described as nationalist opponents, because they hope to establish a new set of political institutions that better represents the interests of the national community they claim to represent. However, not all regime opponents seek to declare independent statehood through, for example, secession or separation; instead, they may be vying for regime change, as was the case with the anti-apartheid movement in South Africa. Frequently, some subset of these anti-colonial, anti-occupation, or anti-regime activists are armed, but this theory does not require them to be so. Most importantly, they oppose indigenous cooperation with the existing state or regime. The existence of these first two actors—the dominant state or regime and the indigenous opponents—are what allow us to describe the territory as contested.

The third set of actors in this framework are *intermediaries*. Intermediaries are those indigenous actors who fulfill some functions of governance under, and at least partially on behalf of, the dominant state or regime. Notably, I assume that intermediaries, like other actors, are goal-oriented. However, their goals are perhaps the most difficult to capture. Do intermediaries, in carrying out their work, actively seek to sustain the dominant state or regime? Or, alternatively, are they simply concerned with their individual security, career, or access to state patronage? Finally, perhaps they are motivated by a genuine desire to provide needed services or public goods to their communities. Any of these is a possibility. The minimal assumption needed is that they do not carry out their responsibilities with the intention of opposing or challenging the dominant state or regime. This is what allows us to distinguish intermediaries from regime challengers.

However, the very nature of indirect rule is such that these lines within the indigenous population—its political elite as well as the general population—are often blurry. Further, actors' intentions may be complex or evolve over time. This connects to an important undercurrent of recent historiography of cases such as India's princely states or the Bantustan governments under South Africa's apartheid regime—namely, the need to soften the seemingly sharp distinction between "resisting" the regime versus "collaborating" with it.[33] Individuals may be employed by intermediary institutions for their day jobs while supporting a resistance group during their off time. Therefore, signals such as one's party or organizational affiliation, in some settings, can be used to identify one's leanings. However, these are among the most complex and sensitive distinctions one can make between individuals living under colonial rule versus another regime of domination.

The intermediary may consist of a local political elite that predates the dominant state or occupier's control. In other cases, the colonial or state power will elevate indigenous actors who had little to no political authority prior to colonial or state intervention. Finally, a former nationalist opponent may be coopted into becoming an intermediary. This framework is flexible enough to include all these types of intermediaries. The critical feature of the intermediary for our purposes is that the dominant state or regime relies on them to fulfill some function or functions of governance.

Within comparative politics, the most relevant existing frameworks are those that explore what happens when rebels, or opponents of the dominant state, are coopted or induced into governing. For example, Paul Staniland develops a new theory for those complex situations in which states and rebels are situated somewhere between all-out conflict and lasting disarmament.[34] In Staniland's four-part typology of armed orders that can result from these interactions, two categories are of relevance here: "limited cooperation"—in which the state and rebel group have "managed boundaries of influence along functional and/or territorial lines" and may engage in "restricted sharing of information or resources"—or "alliances"—in which there is "tight, institutionalized cooperation between a state and armed group, generally involving targeting of a shared enemy, observable coordination of policies, and sharing of organizational resources."[35] At what point has the rebel group effectively transformed into an intermediary for the dominant power? In other words, when is the indigenous actor governing in cooperation with, and to some extent on behalf of, the state? Here, I suggest that either "limited cooperation" or "alliance" under Staniland's framework can be classified as forms of indirect rule, according to the definition I have provided. In both cases, the dominant state is coordinating with the indigenous actor on tactical objectives (e.g., repression of a common enemy, extraction of resources), which, in turn, feed into local governing capacities (coercive, fiscal, etc.). Thus, they are ruling in part *through* the indigenous actor as an intermediary.

The scope of cases that I define here can also be subtly distinguished from the concept of the "mediated state," defined by Ken Menkhaus and elaborated by Nora Stel to describe the relationship between the Lebanese state and the PLO in Lebanon.[36] While there may be relationships of delegation between state and non-state actors in the mediated state model, thus approximating the purely institutional features of indirect rule, I have narrowed my focus to settings where such institutional arrangements are paired with a regime of domination. Thus, while it is not a condition of the "mediated state," the intent to politically exclude an indigenous, or preexisting, population is a feature of the regimes and institutions about which I theorize here. Further, and relatedly, there is an explicit, hierarchical element to the relationship between the dominant power and the intermediary in my framework; that is not a necessary component of the mediated state model.

The framework I present here is not limited to cases in which the intermediaries are former rebels. Intermediaries may be, for example, rural chiefs or indigenous leaders who had not previously adopted overt postures of resistance toward the dominant or colonial power. In fact, there might be political actors who are eager to collaborate with the dominant or colonial power for access to patronage or resources. What is critical for my purposes is that intermediaries are those who are playing a role in carrying out some (or perhaps many) of the core functions of governance—defined in the subsequent section as extraction, coercion, and distribution.

ASSUMPTIONS ABOUT OUTSOURCED LOCAL GOVERNANCE

Contested territories feature conflicts over the nature and character of the state itself or, at the very least, the regime of rules and institutions that distribute power within the political system. Building from the literature on states reviewed earlier, we can distinguish at least four broad, functional roles that governing actors may take on, whether they represent the dominant state, indigenous intermediaries, or regime challengers. I next describe each of these while noting places where they may overlap or intersect.

- **Extracting revenue, income, or other assets from the population (*extractive capacity* or *fiscal capacity*).** In modern states, formal taxation is one of the foremost examples of extractive capacity. Private income as well as the assets of labor, land, and capital could be targets for extraction. While I often refer to fiscal capacity in the pages that follow, I leave the concept broad enough to include both monetary forms of extraction and the claiming of material or labor assets. Of course, states, governments, and even rebel movements have been implicated in extracting labor and land directly from those who live under their rule. Importantly, we are conceptually separating the actor's extractive activities from its more productive, or distributive, functions (see subsequent section).

Generally, the state-building literature has viewed extraction as intimately linked with coercion. Even Margaret Levi suggests that while states tax most effectively when citizens stand to gain from the state's use of revenues, citizen compliance is never more than "quasi-voluntary," since extraction is always backed up by the implicit threat of force.[37] This shapes how—and to what extent—I am able to delink extraction from coercion. Extractive capacity probably requires a mix of both carrots—to incentivize populations to surrender resources without the use of coercion—and sticks.

- **Wielding coercive force within and among the indigenous population for purposes other than extraction (*internal coercive capacity* or *policing capacity*).** In many settings, coercive agents carry out functions in which they do not overtly wield force, such as responding to reported thefts, assessing code violations, assisting in emergency response, and regulating traffic. For some tasks, the fact that the agent fulfilling the task is armed is highly relevant. For others, it may appear to be merely incidental. However, policing capacity captures the agent's capacity to engage in such tasks with the ability to command dominant coercive force—or to threaten dominant coercive force—while doing so. Critically, this capability is exercised *within* and *among* the native population, and it is not envisioned as defense against "external" threats (described in the next section).

  As mentioned, the ability to wield coercive force is often used to support extractive goals. Therefore, for this category of governing capacity, I am primarily concerned with what I will refer to as "noneconomic coercion"— namely, instances when actors wield or threaten coercion among the indigenous population without possessing the simultaneous goal of extracting economic value from the population against whom they are wielding or threatening force. As I will elaborate, this allows us to distinguish how extraction (which often comes with coercion, or at least the threat of it) and noneconomic coercive policing, for example, may be divided between actors in an indirect rule regime.

- **Defending against external threats (*external coercive capacity*).** It is important to clarify the distinction between internal-facing and external-facing coercion. In contested territories, the geographic borders between internal and external are often still in dispute. Further complicating the distinction between internal and external, the boundaries that are most relevant to the conflict between the dominant state and its indigenous opponents may be national or ethnic rather than geographic. As an illustration of such complexities, a rebel group's deployment of armed force within a territory could be conceptualized by the rebel group itself as externally facing—that is, defending the community against threats that emerge from outside the community—while the incumbent state may categorize it as internal to the state's geographic boundaries.

To begin, I define external coercive capacity as armed protection of what the existing state or dominant power understands to be its borders. As discussed later, this relatively restrictive definition will serve to freeze external coercive capacity as a mostly static condition of our framework. However, in the conclusion of chapter 6, I briefly invoke the consequential question of when indigenous opponents of the regime may develop their own routines and practices for defending against external threats, threats that quite often emanate from the dominant state itself.

 • **Producing and distributing, or merely distributing, goods and services to the population other than coercion (*distributive capacity*).** Distributive capacity, as defined here, incorporates a wide range of outputs that readers may informally associate with the heart of governance itself: these include regulation; dispute resolution; collective goods such as roads, schools, and health care institutions; and more targeted goods such as social spending, housing, or professional licenses. Conceptually, I collapse the production and distribution of such goods into one category, which I label distributive capacity. This is a choice that simplifies our framework; I believe it is defensible because the productive capacities of the state are not relevant for the indigenous population unless they are also distributive. For example, one may picture a state that is highly involved in economic production for export markets, but this is made relevant to domestic governance when it results in the distribution of income (e.g., social transfers), wealth (i.e. housing), or streams of future income (e.g., employment) to the population.

Distributive capacity also encapsulates a range of possible goods and services. For example, a state, governing organization, or rebel group may provide institutions or processes of dispute resolution. This would be classified as a form of distributive capacity, even if such functions sometimes require that the same actor possess a baseline level of internal coercive capacity. For example, chiefs who served as intermediaries during British colonial rule in Kenya presided over native tribunals, and the notorious warrant chiefs oversaw native courts in Igboland, then an indirectly ruled region of the British colony in southwest Nigeria.[38] Importantly, I sometimes refer to the "productive capacities" of governance to include all functional capacities of government except for extraction. Thus, both coercive capacity, as just defined, and distributive capacity are "productive."

We can define direct rule as a regime in which the dominant state, occupier, or colonial power seeks to maximize its monopoly over all four functional categories of governance described above. Under direct rule, the dominant power attempts to preclude indigenous actors from engaging in any functions of governance, particularly in a formalized or institutionalized way. Of course, rebels or regime opponents may nonetheless seek to construct their own alternative governance projects. However, under direct rule, it can be hard for them to do so. For example, Indonesia's highly repressive and omnipresent form of rule during its occupation of Timor-Leste (then referred to as East Timor) left the Revolutionary Front for an Independent Timor-Leste (FRETILIN) virtually no room for self-governance. At the beginning of the Indonesian occupation, during a brief window from 1975 until approximately 1978, FRETILIN resistance fighters were able to set up protected bases in the mountains for guerrillas and fleeing civilians. The governing capacities the movement developed at this time were primarily distributive, providing goods such as food and water. Further, using topography to their advantage, they were able to wield coercion with the aim of providing basic protection for civilians and resistance fighters.[39] However, Indonesia soon targeted these *zonas libertadas* with military force, and civilians descended from the mountains back into urban areas, where they transitioned to supporting the resistance through clandestine urban networks.[40] Thus, barring these exceptional and short-lived mountainous bases, Indonesia's occupation of Timor-Leste from 1975 to 1999 can be characterized as a largely direct style of rule that left little opportunity for rebels to develop their governing capacities.

At another extreme, indigenous opponents of an existing state or dominant power may fulfill nearly all the functions of governance I described earlier; in other words, they exercise nearly complete self-rule. Such cases approach *de facto* independent statehood.[41] There are contemporary cases that come close to this pole of comprehensive self-rule that, nonetheless, are not widely recognized as sovereign states. Somaliland, a self-governing republic that declared its independence in the wake of Somalia's civil war, is one such example, and breakaway regions controlled by separatist governments in Georgia (South Ossetia), Moldova (Transnistria), Bosnia-Herzegovina (Republika Srpska), and, until September 2023, Azerbaijan (Nagorno Karabakh) are other cases that fit this mold. While governance and control of these conflict-affected regions have varied considerably over time, we would not include them within our universe of cases of indirect rule if the dominant, sovereign state has almost entirely withdrawn from engaging in any forms of governance within the territory. Importantly, though, such forms of de facto self rule can be temporary, as Azerbaijan's 2023 military invasion of Nagorno Karabakh, and the resulting dissolution of the Republic of Artsakh, appears to demonstrate at the time of writing.

More relevant for our purposes are those cases in which governance arrangements fall somewhere between these two extremes of direct rule by the dominant state and complete self-rule for the existing population. In these settings, the dominant power retains control over some aspects of state authority, but indigenous actors will also engage in governance—extracting from, policing, and/or distributing goods to the population. Such cases do not constitute a pure form of indigenous self-rule because of the continued presence, and dominance, of the incumbent state, occupier, or colonial power, which does not permit full self-determination by the existing, or indigenous, population. The observable implications of the disproportionate power of the dominant state can be manifold. However, next I make four basic assumptions about the types of governance that dominant states will outsource to their intermediaries.

First, I assume that the dominant state or colonial or occupying power will retain relatively superior coercive capacity during the period in question. While coercive capacity may be delegated to indigenous intermediaries, it will not exceed the capacity of the dominant state itself. This ensures that the dominant state remains, in a word, dominant. It has sufficient coercive capabilities such that it could likely revoke the local governing capacities of the indigenous intermediary if incentivized to do so.

Second, I assume that the dominant state, which faces considerable indigenous resistance to its rule, will refrain from delegating external coercive capacity to the indigenous intermediary—namely, the authority and capability to defend what the dominant state views as its borders. For example, the former British protectorates in parts of the Arabian peninsula—for example, in southern Yemen and today's United Arab Emirates—are often considered among the least invasive forms of colonialism, but even these arrangements included preserving British military dominance and control over foreign policy. Nonetheless, within the geographic borders of the indirectly ruled territory, dominant powers may delegate what they characterize as internal policing to indigenous intermediaries.[42]

Third, I hold that it is unlikely that the dominant state will exclusively assign distribution to the intermediary. Thus, this theory predicts that the dominant state will try to outsource internal policing, extraction, or some combination of both to indigenous intermediaries. This assumption is derived from, first and foremost, the underlying goals of the dominant state or colonial power. Drawing on the general theories of state-building referenced earlier, the dominant power is assumed to seek control over the contested territory in question with the aim of deriving, or extracting, benefit from the territory and/or its population. In no case can we imagine, from a rationalist perspective, that a state will maintain control over territory and sustain an unpopular regime of control over the existing population with the sole purpose of distributing goods and services to that population.

Unfortunately for the dominant power, policing and extraction are inherently politically costly in a way that distribution is not and, thus, more likely to be delegated. In many cases, one of the objectives of the dominant state is to minimize the costs of maintaining the regime. Such costs can take many forms; in addition to financial costs, coercion and extraction come with reputational costs. The dominant state cannot afford to fully absorb both of those costs when it already faces active and sustained resistance to its rule.[43] Kenneth Abbott et al.'s theory of indirect governance posits a trade-off wherein the powerful state seeks to delegate tasks for which the agent, or intermediary, has greater competence and, as a result, relinquishes greater control over this task.[44] However, other explorations of indirect rule have noted that competence may not be the only benefit dominant states seek from their intermediaries—they may also delegate tasks that are unpopular to "imbue the colonial state with some modicum of legitimacy in the eyes of subject populations."[45]

While we might imagine "competence," from the perspective of the dominant power, and "legitimacy," from the perspective of the local population, are self-reinforcing in the case of distributive capacity, the two concepts might move in opposite directions when applied to extraction or coercion. In general, we can say that identifying a potential intermediary who has sufficiently high levels of one or the other (competence or legitimacy) in either extraction or policing is a necessary condition for the emergence of indirect rule regimes in the first place.

My fourth assumption is related to this last point. While dominant states may delegate both fiscal extraction and internal policing unrelated to extraction (noneconomic coercion) to the intermediary, I assume that they will rely on the intermediary relatively more heavily for one of these functions versus the other. A slightly weaker assumption that also maintains the thrust of my argument is that the dominant state may rely on the intermediary to fulfill both functions, but it will be relatively more active in monitoring the intermediary's enactment of one function compared with the other. So, while a dominant power may rely on the intermediary to both extract revenue or assets from locals and engage in some noneconomic forms of policing, it will not invest equally in monitoring the intermediary's behavior in both areas. Imperfect monitoring of agent behavior is a standard assumption in most principal-agent models; however, here I am making the additional assumption that monitoring investments will be distributed unevenly across types of tasks due to the substantive goals and preferences of the dominant state.

Critically, as noted earlier, extraction itself is often paired with the use of force, sometimes to devastating effect. However, for dominant powers that emphasize delegating extraction to intermediaries, the deliverables expected from the intermediary are the material income or assets themselves rather than a deliverable associated with policing, such as law and order. Historically, many regimes of indirect rule, from early modern Europe to the Ottoman Empire to colonial Southeast Asia, have depended on indigenous agents to engage in tax farming. In such cases, the dominant power relies on indigenous agents for fiscal extraction more intensively than they depend on such actors for noneconomic, coercive policing. By contrast, Israel's regime in the West Bank since the creation of the Palestinian Authority has emphasized the delegation of internal policing more than the delegation of extraction.

Critically, this assumption that the dominant state pursues a functionally lopsided approach to delegation means that the state retains the authority and capacity to engage in the non-delegated function themselves, without indigenous mediation. So, colonial powers that delegate extraction are, according to this theory, predicted to engage in more direct forms of internal policing with relatively less mediation by an indigenous collaborator. Dominant powers that outsource policing, on the other hand, will perform more of the extracting themselves—whether that is extraction of revenue, labor, or land.

The way that capacities are divided between the dominant state and the indigenous intermediary is best conceptualized as the result of a bargaining process but one that is asymmetrical because of the assumed coercive advantage of the dominant state, whether it is an imperial power, a military occupier, or a regime of domination, as was the case in apartheid South Africa. Labeling this as a bargaining process allows us to avoid the notion that the dominant state is able to design a flawless system of indirect rule that universally and predictably achieves its objectives. The dominant state may agree to outsource certain forms of governance to the intermediary, and this decision might ultimately backfire, causing the state to attempt to regain control.[46] Indirect rule is vulnerable to the usual tensions between the so-called principal and agent that can undermine coordination and achievement of the principal's objectives. These threats include misalignment on objectives, which could lead to agent shirking or even defection. The intermediary is an actor, and thus a complication, one does not see under more direct styles of rule.

Finally, note that our conceptualization of indirect rule here permits either a continuous or categorical typology of varieties of indirect rule. However, what distinguishes types is not how much or how little authority they delegate but, rather, what functional types of authority they prioritize in the delegative relationship. This differs from alternative formulations of the concept of indirect rule that, distinguish between, for example formal (*de jure*) versus practical (*de facto*) aspects.[47] The framework I present here is primarily concerned with *de facto*, and therefore functionalist, outcomes of interactions between the dominant state and its would-be intermediaries.

GOVERNANCE BY INDIGENOUS INTERMEDIARIES

Next, I outline a set of hypotheses regarding how such indirect rule regimes, while they are functioning, will shape local governance decisions by indigenous actors who are politically affiliated with the intermediary. These predictions are generated from the preceding conceptual and logical framework as well as my observations, contained in chapters 4 and 5, of Fatah-affiliated mayors and municipal councils operating under the Israeli-PA regime. These observations inform our understanding of regimes in which internal policing is the primary capacity assigned to the intermediary, which, in this case, is the Fatah-led PA government. In chapter 6, I extend these predictions to the case of the Bantustans under South Africa's apartheid regime, which, I argue, also emphasizes the outsourcing of coercion over extraction. My predictions about how intermediaries will behave under indirect-rule regimes that primarily out-source extraction are more deductively generated; however, in chapter 6, I apply the logic outlined here to the case of India during the period of British imperial control.

In regimes of indirect rule in which the dominant power's control of the region faces substantial indigenous opposition, the intermediary's role within the regime can come with high reputation costs. While some inter-mediaries may enjoy a certain level of popular legitimacy—for example, sources of political authority that are derived from preexisting norms and traditions—others may have weaker ties to the communities they are tasked with governing. (Intermediaries who are imposed on populations by the dominant power will tend toward the latter description.) No matter what their starting point in terms of popular legitimacy, in all cases, carry-ing out extraction or coercion on behalf of the dominant power will likely erode it. Thus, I predict that *the intermediary will reduce or minimize its investment in either extraction or noneconomic coercion, depending on which capacity is less central to its relationship with the dominant power*. If, under the indirect-rule regime, the dominant state, occupier, or colonial power relies on outsourcing extraction to the indigenous intermediary, then the intermediary will seek to minimize its involvement in forms of internal coercion (i.e., policing) that are not directly tied to its extractive function. Of course, as stated earlier, this does not preclude the use of coercion and violence to accomplish extractive tasks. However, it does mean that we could expect such intermediaries to invest less in activities associated with general, day-to-day law and order policing, and we can expect them to dedicate less coercive force to political repression that is not directly tied to extraction. Alternatively, if the dominant power prioritizes and monitors policing by the intermediary, the intermediary will minimize investments in extraction.

In a theory of how colonial (and, later, postcolonial) governments built "patchwork states" in South Asia, Naseemullah highlights how "colonial agents continuously weighed extraction against the potential for insecurity, just as they weighed the economic benefits of greater security through the application of coercion against its ongoing costs."[48] Here, the reputational considerations inherent in the nature of both extraction and coercion are made explicit.

One corollary of the prediction stated earlier is that *intermediaries will be more likely to reduce their investment in extractive (or noneconomic coercive) capacity in those areas, or among those segments of the population, where their role in noneconomic coercion (or extraction) is most intensive or most visible.* Thus, this prediction relates to local-level variation within a setting of indirect rule. As Mamdani has convincingly shown, indirect rule in some areas of a colonial territory is almost always paired with more direct forms of rule in other areas.[49] In other words, even if the dominant state or colonial power uniformly emphasizes the delegation of one function (coercion or extraction) over another, the extent of delegation is not uniform across the territory or across the colonized population. Because indirect rule often stems from the dominant power's desire to annex territory exclusive of the indigenous population, it is often paired with efforts to rule more directly over strategic land and resources or efforts to "right-people"[50] the territory through settlement. In subsequent chapters, I describe how geographic variation in the visibility of Palestinian Authority collaboration with Israel on policing produces the findings that inform this theoretical prediction.

Minimizing involvement in coercion or extraction, if it takes the form of non-enforcement of formal law, is a type of forbearance that fits within the typology developed by Alisha Holland, in which elected politicians—not unelected bureaucrats—engage in "*intentional and revocable government leniency toward violations of the law.*"[51] Unlike the precise definition of "forbearance," as Holland conceptualizes it, the indigenous intermediaries may or may not be acting in contravention of a formal law when they choose not to coerce or extract. However, some of the same logic and predictions would apply. If the theory presented here is true, politicians forbear from performing these tasks due to the reputational and legitimacy challenges they would introduce; thus, politicians would be expected to continue their passivity in these areas even if "resource constraints or competing policy demands ease."[52]

Furthermore, as with Holland's theory of forbearance, which applies to non-enforcement of law, I theorize that there is an underlying distributive, or redistributive, motivation to the intermediary's actions under indirect rule. Because local intermediaries often do not have the capacity or authority to engage in traditional tax-based redistribution, refraining from engaging in expected extraction or policing can, itself, serve as a form of targeted distribution. Intermediaries pursue such policies with the ultimate goal of maintaining political support and, thus, minimizing threats to their positions within the regime and, in some highly unpopular regimes, existential threats to their lives.

However, in the aforementioned hypothesis, I allow that the intermediary's reduced investment in noneconomic coercion also may be attributed to what Holland describes as merely weak enforcement due to institutional or material capacity constraints.[53] This is distinct from intentional forbearance. For example, imagine a case in which the intermediary is primarily engaged in extraction on behalf of the dominant power. Imagine further that they suffer from a low baseline level of popular legitimacy with the local population, and thus they face fairly prominent and identifiable political opponents. In such a setting, we can deduce that intermediaries may underinvest in repression of their political rivals due not to a strategic decision to forbear but, rather, to resource constraints. Instead, such intermediaries may be particularly likely to use extraction—for example taxation, control of land, or recruitment of labor—as a pretext, or entry point, for applying coercion to their rivals. (In a case in which such an intermediary possesses a higher baseline level of popular legitimacy, their political rivals may be less prominent and identifiable, and thus such tactics may not be necessary.)

In addition to a strategy based on forbearance, the findings from the West Bank described in the chapters that follow also suggest that *indigenous intermediaries will invest in distributive capacity when it can produce reputational benefits*. In chapter 4, for example, I find that Fatah-affiliated municipalities increase their annual spending on utilities—namely, the electricity and water sectors—significantly more than towns governed by their opponents. Because municipalities are not required to balance their budgets in the utility sector (they face a "soft" budget constraint), I argue that Fatah mayors are able to derive political benefits from such forms of distribution without bearing the political costs of extraction. In general, then, when such forms of distribution are subsidized from external sources, they are likely to be more politically beneficial than goods and services that are financed through the pure redistribution of resources within and among the indigenous population.

The literature on the politics of state distribution is vast.[54] The distribution of state resources—whether narrowly targeted, private transfers or broadly aimed public goods—is intimately connected to the specific political incentives faced by incumbents in power. Much existing research has been concerned with democratic settings, where politicians are, at least in theory, accountable to voters, but additional work has found that even non-democratically elected leaders and organizations can face strong political incentives to invest in distributive or redistributive programs.[55] Here, the general prediction that intermediaries will seek political benefits from their distributive policies is in keeping with fundamental understandings of distributive politics from work in political science. What potentially makes the situation unique in settings of indirect rule is that the dominant state also has a stake in the survival of the intermediary. Thus, we may predict that in settings where the intermediary faces a low or rapidly declining level of popular legitimacy, the dominant power may be more likely to subsidize the intermediary's distributive activities.

Overall, this framework suggests that indigenous intermediaries face political, and perhaps existential, risks to collaborating with the dominant power, because the dominant power's rule in the territory is perceived to be illegitimate by wide swaths of the indigenous population. Legitimacy is a concept with a long tradition in political theory specifically and social science more generally. In the positivist realm, Max Weber based his well-known definition of "legitimacy" on the beliefs that people had about the system of authority under which they lived.[56] As summarized by Fabienne Peter, one of the "main problem[s] that a conception of legitimacy aims to solve is how to distinguish the rightful use of political power from mere coercion."[57] Peter continues that while some normative theories of legitimacy see coercion as an exclusive right of legitimate states, others see legitimacy as epiphenomenal—in other words, the concept of "legitimate" political power is used to justify (and therefore, presumably, minimize dissent with) the use of force.

My use of the term throughout tends more toward the latter view. State-building, colonialism, and empire are inherently coercive projects that inevitably affect the populations living under them. The reader will recall that a key scope condition I have provided for my theory is that it pertains to the subset of such projects that face a low degree of legitimacy among the population whose presence in the territory predates that of the dominant state, colonizer, or empire. I root this lack of legitimacy in the dominant power's pursuit of a regime of domination. Colonial or imperial state-building projects, by definition, serve the motives and interests of actors "from ouside." Thus, they will frequently fall within our scope. This assumption contrasts somewhat with Michael Hechter, who argues that "alien" rule can achieve legitimacy if it is effective in producing collective goods and if it achieves procedural fairness.[58] By contrast, I argue that it remains very difficult to imagine that such conditions could obtain during periods of indirect rule when the intent of the regime is to promote the supremacy or domination of one group over another.

Here I do not attempt to develop a fully specified theory of how the intermediary will weigh the costs and benefits of collaboration. Dominant states can use material rewards or, perhaps, non-material incentives to attempt to maintain the cooperation of intermediaries. The intermediary may also choose the extreme method of noncooperation, which is essentially to defect from their role as an intermediary and possibly take up an active role in resistance. However, between full compliance and full defection is a range of options, such as agent drift, shirking, or foot-dragging. These outcomes are theorized in formal models of principal-agent relationships as different forms of "agency loss" due to, for example, moral hazard problems or adverse selection. Often the literature focuses on how the principal can, in equilibrium, select and reward agents such that these kinds of problems can be overcome.[59] However, existing research does not, to my knowledge, help us understand forms of indirect rule where the dominant power may enable or even encourage indigenous collaborators to reduce, or forbear from, certain functions of governance when it allows them to carry out other functions that are of greater strategic importance to the dominant power.

GOVERNANCE BY INDIGENOUS OPPONENTS

Indigenous opponents of indirect rule regime will not—at least initially—suffer the same reputational obstacles as intermediaries. However, indigenous opponents may face a variety of incentives and opportunities to develop their own governing practices. First, in some cases, they may operate as a decentralized rebel group with little practical or organizational capacity to engage in even the most informal kinds of governance. For such cases, we will likely not observe such groups governing in the traditional sense. Second, they may find an opportunity to capture some degree of governing power by working within regime institutions. Third, in settings where regime opponents are engaged in active, armed conflict over territory with the dominant state, they may have the opportunity to engage in various forms of governance within the territory they control (what is often described as "rebel governance"). In the second and third cases, local governance by regime opponents is theoretically observable. Thus, we can ask how it compares with the governing approaches used by regime intermediaries.

As chapters 4 and 5 reveal, the West Bank provides us with an example of the second type of case. In a set of important local elections, regime opponents gained unprecedented control over a number of municipalities in the West Bank. This occurred during a time when the Fatah-led Palestinian Authority's cooperation with Israel on policing was as strong as ever. Subsequently, the regime's most prominent opponent, Hamas, won a majority of seats in the PA's legislative body. Again, these elections took place within institutions that heretofore were monopolized by Israel's preferred intermediary, the Fatah leadership.

Opponents of indirect rule regimes do not always have the opportunity or incentive to enter formal political institutions. The occupied West Bank and Gaza during the period under study were unusual in this regard. However, a defining ideological feature of such groups is that they view the regime upheld by the dominant state, occupier, or colonial power to be illegitimate. Thus, they are critical of their intermediary counterparts. Therefore, I make the assumption that indigenous opponents of the regime must possess, at the very least, the *ambition* to govern. In other words, I assume that they seek to transform governance, by definition, as part of their broader aims to replace the existing regime with some form of self-rule for the indigenous population. This is a central goal for such groups that situate themselves as part of a movement for decolonization or liberation. Indigenous opponents of the regime are motivated by a desire to demonstrate that not only can they challenge the dominant state through armed force, but that they can also advance a transformation in the lives of the indigenous population, whether through regime change or new state creation. Thus, even if regime opponents do not have the chance to compete for formal office—or if they choose not to participate in such structures to avoid legitimizing regime institutions—they will nonetheless seek to credibly communicate their governing style and objectives to the indigenous population.

Because opponents of the regime are advancing a resistance project that is at direct odds with the aims of the dominant state—and because they perceive, and describe, their intermediary counterparts as illegitimate—they will likely have a number of organizational foes to contend with. Thus, both the incentives and abilities of regime challengers to develop governing capacities—coercion, extraction, and distribution—will be powerfully shaped by this context. That context is a regime of domination that employs indigenous intermediaries to maintain indirect rule and, almost by definition, aims to repress or eliminate indigenous opponents of the regime. As we saw earlier, indigenous intermediaries may repress political mobilization through traditional coercive means, or they may use their extractive capabilities to forcibly tax, expropriate, or seize resources from their challengers. Furthermore, in all cases, the dominant state itself will maintain the capability to use coercive force against opposition elements from within the indigenous population.

This logic, combined with the empirical analysis of the Palestinian case that follows, produces the intuitive proposition that absent external support, indigenous opponents of the regime will face greater resource constraints than indigenous intermediaries. Regime challengers may face obstacles such as direct repression, sanctions, propaganda, or other measures employed by the dominant state, the intermediary, or international allies. Furthermore, whether they are engaged in extraction or coercion on behalf of the regime, intermediaries will likely have access to resource privileges—a "carrot" provided by the dominant state to ensure their cooperative role within the regime. As a result, indigenous regime opponents are more likely to face a resource, rather than reputational, deficit.

Chapters 4 and 5 profile some of the strategies used by Palestinian mayors and municipal councils led by regime opponents; the following predictions flow inductively from that analysis. Panel data analysis of municipal budgets shows that Hamas-led councils were more likely than those led by Fatah, the regime intermediary, or those led by independents to increase their revenues per capita over time. Further, qualitative evidence from interviews reveals examples of how non-Fatah councils resorted to creative measures to cut costs, including by drawing on voluntary community contributions and achieving spending efficiency through creative cost-saving measures. Thus, for other settings where indigenous opponents are in a position to govern, we can form the following prediction: *absent external support, indigenous regime opponents will invest in extractive capacity.* Further, *in settings where their reputational advantage over the intermediary is relatively large, regime opponents will minimize coercive extraction in favor of extracting income or assets non-coercively.* Finally, I predict that the relative resource scarcity that indigenous opponents face will force these opponents to make tough choices. Therefore, compared with regime intermediaries, *regime opponents will need to exercise relatively more restrained or efficient spending when engaging in the productive aspects of governance.* By "productive," I am referring to those aspects of governance that require resources—namely, coercion or distribution. Here, depending on structural opportunities and the potential of generating future reputational or material benefits, regime opponents may seek to restrain their investments in either the use of armed coercion or the distribution of goods and services to the indigenous population.

Finally, it is necessary to bring this theoretical architecture back down to the level of the people who are ostensibly inhabiting these roles. As previously noted, the labels of "intermediary" and "opponent" are heuristic simplifications. Some of the most textured and evocative observations I collected while conducting field research in the West Bank pertained to the personal relationships among individuals at the local level. This is explored more in the subsequent chapters. Here, I will simply note that the sheer size of the Palestinian Authority public sector—estimated at nearly one hundred fifty thousand employees in December 2007, at the beginning of the period of analysis[60]—enmeshes Palestinians with diverse political leanings in institutions of governance. Fundamentally, it is only the central, executive branch of the PA—and the security forces it commands—that most tightly aligns with the concept of regime intermediary, as I have defined it here.

The pages that follow will focus on municipalities, a narrow slice of the PA institutional landscape but one in which, because of the open political identifications of mayors and municipal council members, politicians can be effectively sorted based on their affiliation with the intermediary political organization (Fatah) or their identification with the opposition (Hamas, smaller parties, and independents). Nonetheless, these identifications can be ambiguous and complex, and their local relevance can be context-dependent, as I describe in chapter 5. Further, the municipal staff who carry out much of the work of local governance may, and likely do, have their own political leanings, but it is nearly impossible to observe

TABLE 1.1
Predictions about local governance under indirect rule

Compared with regime opponents, regime *intermediaries* will be more likely to	Compared with regime intermediaries, regime *opponents* will be more likely to
• minimize their investment in either extractive or policing capacity, depending on which is less central to their relationship with the dominant power;	• invest in extractive capacity, absent external support;
• minimize their investment in extractive (policing) capacity in those areas, or among those segments of the population, where their role in policing (extraction) is most intensive or most visible; and	• in settings where their reputational advantage over the intermediary is relatively large, minimize coercive extraction in favor of extracting income or assets non-coercively; and
• invest in distributive capacity when it is expected to produce reputational benefits.	• exercise relatively more restrained or efficient spending when engaging in the productive aspects of governance.

On the relationship between intermediaries and opponents:
• the greater the share of the indigenous workforce employed in intermediary-controlled institutions, the more likely that boundaries between intermediary and opponent will become complex and blurred.

these political identifications since, in theory, they are not meant to shape these employees' practices.

In sum, my findings suggest that *when a sufficiently large share of the indigenous labor force is employed within institutions that are controlled by the regime intermediary, boundaries between "intermediary" and "opponent" can become increasingly complex and blurred.* As discussed in chapter 6, similar dynamics appeared within the Bantustans under South Africa's apartheid regime.

The theoretical predictions above are summarized in table 1.1.

THE FRAGILITY OF INDIRECT RULE REGIMES

Indirect rule regimes are held together by indigenous intermediaries, but these actors face a challenge in maintaining authority—or even basic governing capacity—within their own communities. If the dominant power relies on the intermediary to police the local population, the intermediary could risk losing power and possibly their very lives, if they also engage in rampant extraction. Similarly, intermediaries who extract resources from the indigenous population on behalf of the dominant power could face both resource-based and reputational challenges to increasing their investments in coercion. Thus, the glue that holds indirect rule regimes can be more or less tenuous depending on how intermediaries balance reputation costs with their ability to maintain political power.

My theory predicts that intermediaries working within unpopular regimes of indirect rule will be acutely aware of their political position vis-à-vis the indigenous population that they govern and the relative threats they face from opposition actors who arise from within it. This, along with the functional nature of the governing capacities they have already developed, will lead them to minimize or forbear from certain forms of governance. This has potential long-run consequences for the types of state-like capacity that emerges at the local level under indirect rule.

Indigenous opponents of the regime may not always have opportunities to capture local political institutions in such settings—they may be resisting authoritarian states with little to no electoral competition, for example—or they may choose to boycott existing institutions associated with the dominant regime. Nonetheless, I argue that nearly all such groups (or those that we think of as somewhat durable) will probably have, at a minimum, the opportunity to establish their own governing practices, capacities, and reputations. It is not impossible to imagine that eventually such resistance actors may use these local relationships with constituents and their burgeoning governing credentials to challenge the foundations of the indirect regime itself. However, the tactics of regime opponents will be heavily shaped by the resource constraints they face, making the productive aspects of their governance programs—for example, internal or externally facing coercion or distributive goals—a challenge. Access to external sources of support would enhance the ability of these regime opponents to fulfill their productive goals.

In the preceding theory, I have taken a relatively conservative approach in extrapolating from the case of the Israeli-occupied West Bank to additional cases. This caution has been applied in defining the scope conditions for generalization fairly narrowly—namely, regimes of domination that are paired with the institutions of indirect rule. I argue that the primary way in which this will condition the governance projects of regime intermediaries is through the reputational deficit that it creates for such actors with their own populations. On the other hand, and as inductively discovered from the case of Hamas and other regime opponents in the West Bank, regime challengers will be primarily constrained by access to resources. However, one question that remains unaddressed is whether resource constraints would play as large a role for regime opponents who gain power through the third channel described earlier—namely, militarily winning control of a defined piece of territory. As noted with the aforementioned Timorese example, it may be difficult for such forms of rebel governance to persist under direct rule, but, somewhat paradoxically, it may be precisely in these directly ruled populations where we are most likely to see such territorial challenges emerge. In any case, the resource portfolios of rebel groups in such settings may differ markedly from the oppositional actors that gain the chance to govern through formal institutional channels.

The next chapter returns to Palestine, where we will examine the institutional formations that shaped the development of local governance in the West Bank prior to the beginning of Israel's occupation.

Chapter Two

REGIMES AND LOCAL GOVERNANCE IN THE WEST BANK BEFORE 1967

Indirect rule, in its most basic form, has a long history in Palestine.[1] Since at least the Ottoman era, Palestinian notables—including landowners, politicians, religious leaders, and administrators—have navigated the complex space between the dominant empire or state of the time and local Palestinian communities. Each successive power ruled differently, generating different types of legitimacy concerns for Palestinian intermediaries enmeshed in these systems. However, indirectly ruling powers suffered some common vulnerabilities—for example, the objectives of the dominant power were not always aligned with those of their would-be "agents." Intermediaries sometimes abandoned cooperation if they felt their reputation was at risk; at times, they even defected and joined or led resistance projects. Prior to the creation of formal institutions of local government under the Ottoman Empire, Palestinian oppositional mobilization (e.g., tax revolts, rebellions, strikes) was rarely pursued through institutional channels. Subsequently, under the British Mandate, Palestinian participation in municipal institutions was increasingly shaped by nationalism and resistance to British-supported Zionist settlement and state-building.

The British Mandate came to an end with the outbreak of the 1948 war. The war, due to the hundreds of thousands of Palestinian refugees it displaced, cleaved the part of historic Palestine on which Israel declared its state from the Gaza Strip and the territory that came to be known as the

West Bank. While Egypt was left ruling Gaza, the West Bank—including the eastern portion of the city of Jerusalem, featuring the old city and its holy sites—fell under the control of the state of Jordan. This was the status quo until 1967, when Israel defeated Arab forces in the Six-Day War and begin its military occupation of the West Bank—including east Jerusalem—and Gaza, as well as the non-Palestinian territories of the Sinai Peninsula and the Golan Heights.

This chapter follows the chronological sequence of empires and states that controlled Palestine prior to 1967. In particular, our lens will increasingly focus on the West Bank, the portion of Palestine on which the empirical observations of chapters 4 and 5 are centered. As noted previously, our definition of the West Bank as a geographically delimited area is itself a product of the dramatic changes wrought by the 1948 war and the formation of the state of Israel. Thus, the West Bank's pre-1948 history is embedded in the broader political landscape that shaped Palestine as a whole.

With a particular focus on the development of modern local government institutions, I review Palestine's late Ottoman period, the British Mandate, and, finally, the 1948–1967 period, when Palestinians within postwar armistice lines in Israel were placed under military rule and those in the West Bank were partially integrated as citizens of Jordan. To be sure, Ottoman (and, for a short time, Egyptian dynastic) rulers in Palestine, British authorities, Israel, and the Jordanian monarchy had varied interests in the region; those interests changed over time and were imperfectly translated into the design of both informal and formal local governance institutions. Those institutions, in turn, collided with the interests of Palestinian landowners, religious authorities, and other local elites embedded in Palestinian communities. As such, this chapter describes how imperial and state projects to coopt indigenous, Palestinian intermediaries were variably successful.

Later chapters will focus on contemporary municipalities (*baladiyyat*). However, the first municipalities in the Ottoman Empire, and in Palestine, specifically, were not established until the mid-nineteenth century. Municipal institutions expanded gradually over time, but, even by 1967, these were limited to the larger urban areas. Thus, throughout this chapter, I situate municipalities within a broader framework of how states and other actors governed locally including, to a varying extent, in rural Palestine. I treat formal municipal institutions as one part, but not all, of this landscape.

In the later, empirical chapters on the Israeli-occupied West Bank, we will see that municipalities continue to be just one example of a local political institution in which the varied interests that emerge under indirect rule interact. This chapter places that institution in historical context.

To some extent, all dominant powers that sought to project their rule across Palestine—or, later, just the West Bank—encountered various versions of the legitimacy problem. These came into particularly sharp focus for the Ottoman and Egyptian regimes when they engaged in either the extraction of taxes or the forcible recruitment of labor—both activities associated with extractive capacity, as I have defined it in chapter 1. For British authorities, their legitimacy crisis among the Arab Palestinian majority stemmed from British support for Zionism—a movement that Palestinians experienced as extractive, with the main targeted asset this time being land—thus intensifying political mobilization by Palestinians against Jewish settlement, Palestinian displacement, and the growth of exclusivist political and economic institutions.

Jordan's more direct style of rule over the West Bank looked different from these preceding imperial projects, since the West Bank was formally annexed to the state of Jordan, and West Bank Palestinians were made citizens. Even though Jordan's governing approach did not entail the formal delegation of policing or extraction to a set of West Bank–based institutions, we see that the Hashemite monarchy depended on intermediaries for civil governance at the local level. These sheikhs and notables, in the waning years of Jordanian rule, became increasingly out of step with Palestinian nationalist currents of the time.

This chapter, with its high-level overview of certain features of local government, is crafted from the perspective of a social scientist rather than a historian. For that reason, the sources cited here may provide the reader with an abundant, if necessarily incomplete, basis for exploring each of these historical periods in more depth.

It was not until 1967, with the arrival of Israel's open-ended occupation, that Palestinians in the West Bank were subject to an outside power whose aims were neither inclusive of the Palestinian population (as, arguably, both the Ottoman and Jordanian projects had been) nor overtly temporary (as the British Mandate had been). These features of Israel's regime in the West Bank, and their close connection to Israel's settler colonial aims, shaped the strategies of indirect rule that Israel iterated over time. As described in chapter 3, this culminated in the creation of a centralized Palestinian intermediary in the 1990s that was disproportionately weighted toward internal policing and which faced inherent and increasing challenges to its legitimacy.

LATE OTTOMAN PERIOD (1830–1919)

The modern basis for indirect rule of Palestinian villages, towns, and urban areas of the West Bank was laid during the era of Ottoman control. Local elites and provincial administrators served as intermediaries between Ottoman (and Egyptian) authorities and the local population when it came to conscription and taxation. In the mid-nineteenth century, changes in class formation associated with modernization and capital accumulation, combined with Ottoman political reorganizations and administrative changes, cultivated new forms of political solidarity and competition. This period also saw the creation of increasingly institutionalized forms of local government, such as municipalities for urban areas and mukhtars (*mukhtarun*, or local chiefs) for villages.

In Jerusalem, Nablus, and Hebron—three urban areas, plus their rural peripheries, which would eventually form part of what we know today as the West Bank—the nature of Ottoman indirect rule varied. Taxation and conscription—the extractive capacities of the Ottoman state—were the most frequent triggers of rebellion, especially when paired with coercive violence. Basic security was lacking along roads between major Palestinian population centers from the coast to Jerusalem and down south through the Hebron hills, yet the Ottoman state, and the short and relatively brutal Egyptian occupation, were not afraid to wield coercive force to quell resistance. In general, though, under Ottoman rule, the relationship between the state and Palestinian society was functionally more extractive and, secondarily, distributive. Intermediaries were often tasked with filling these roles. While extraction often came with the threat, or the use, of force, the Ottoman state did not tend to outsource non-economic policing capacity. At times, actors who, in other settings, may have functioned as regime intermediaries—including religious authorities (*'ulama'*), Ottoman elite troops from among the *sipahi* land grant holders and janissaries, and rural notables—joined opposition movements, and sometimes revolts, against Ottoman or Egyptian policies.

While all of Palestine was under Ottoman control for roughly four centuries, the land of Palestine—encompassing the territory that now makes up
the modern state of Israel, the West Bank including East Jerusalem, and the
Gaza Strip—fell under several shifting administrative divisions. In the simplest terms, most of Palestine was contained within the province (*vilayet*)
of Syria, also referred to as the *vilayet* of Damascus (see map 2.1). However,
this description obscures several changes to administrative boundaries that
occurred over time, especially in the nineteenth-century period of reform.
These changes both shaped, and were shaped by, local power relations in
the Levant region in general and in Palestine in particular.

More than twenty years after the separate *mutasarrifate* of Mount Lebanon was established in 1861—in response to sectarian fighting, which
resulted in massacres of thousands of Maronite and other Christians[2]—the
larger *vilayet* of Beirut was carved out of the Syrian province. The *vilayet*
of Beirut contained some Palestinian districts (*sanjaks*) such as Acre, Safad,
and Nazareth. As for those Palestinian population centers that would later
become part of the West Bank: The district of Nablus—previously called
the *sanjak* of Balqa, and spanning east into modern-day Jordan—was
also attached to the Beirut province when it was created in the 1880s. The
Nablus *sanjak* included many of the towns and villages that are within the
present governorates (*muhafazat*) of Nablus, Salfit, Tubas, Tulkarm, and
Jenin in the northern and north-central West Bank. However, these areas
of today's West Bank also saw some shifts in their administration during
Ottoman times, often due to local political dynamics.

Ultimately, major residential communities in this area—Tulkarm, Nablus,
Jenin, Jamma'ein, and Aqraba—were assigned to four separate subdistricts
within the Nablus *sanjak*. Finally, the formally autonomous *mutasarrifate*
of Jerusalem was split off from the Syrian *vilayet* in 1872 and included the
cities of Jerusalem, Bethlehem, and Hebron, all of which later formed part
of the West Bank. This specially administered Jerusalem district, which was
governed directly by Ottoman authorities in Istanbul, also encompassed
Gaza and predominantly Arab towns such as Jaffa and Bi'r al-Sab'a (Beer-
sheba in modern-day Israel).

The creation of these complex divisions was a top-down administrative
process; it reflected the specific interests of Ottoman state elites at the center
in addition to the leverage wielded by locally prominent clans and ruling
elites to carve out their own spheres of authority. The form that indirect rule

LA SYRIE

Vilayet de SYRIE
Chef-lieu : DAMAS.

Vilayet de BEYROUTH

Province du LIBAN

Mutessariflik
DE
JÉRUSALEM

MER MÉDITERRANÉE

Vilayet d'Alep

Vilayet de l'Hedjaz

Légende

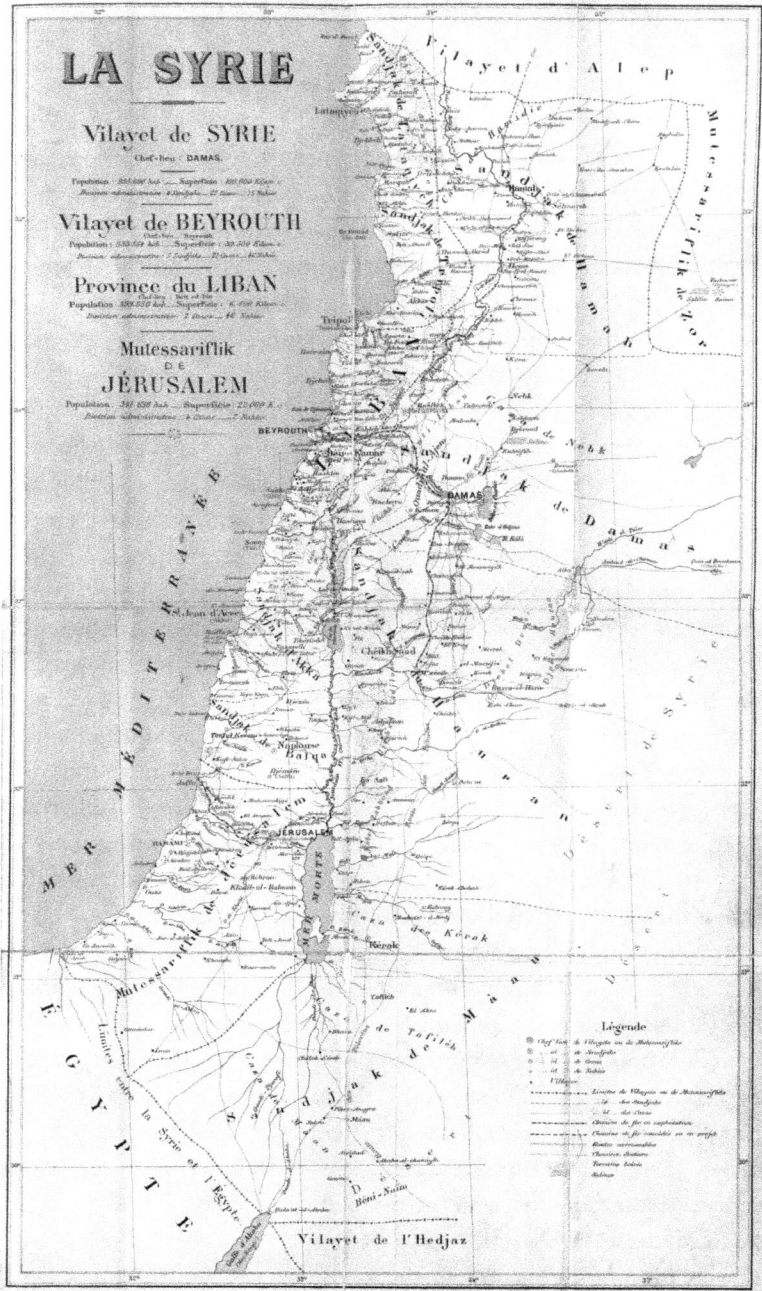

MAP 2.1. Late nineteenth-century Ottoman Palestine, within the *vilayet* of Syria, the *vilayet* of Beirut, and the *mutasarrifate* of Jerusalem. *Source*: Vital Cuinet, *Syrie, Liban et Palestine. Géographie Administrative, Statistique, Descriptive et Raisonnée* [with maps] (Paris, 1896).

took under the Ottoman Empire varied across these larger administrative regions. This meant that, for example, Jerusalem, Hebron, and Nablus— the three largest urban areas that are part of the modern occupied West Bank—each had different relationships with central authorities, and urban elites each had different relationships with their local populations and the villages in their peripheries.

Featuring the holy site of the al-Aqsa mosque, where the Islam's Prophet Muhammad is believed to have ascended to heaven, and the larger *Haram al-Sharif* (The Noble Sanctuary)—referred to by Jews as the Temple Mount, as it is believed to be the site of the First and Second Temples—Jerusalem was often the focus of special arrangements under Ottoman rule. These included an Islamic *waqf*, a religious endowment, charged with protecting the holy Muslim sites. Furthermore, before the Ottoman state began its sweeping program of bureaucratic, legal, and political reforms (*tanzimat*) in the mid-nineteenth century, there were no municipalities across the empire. Yet, in the 1860s, Jerusalem became the first town, after Istanbul, in which such a council was established.[3] In 1872, Jerusalem was split from the larger Syrian province into its own special administrative district (*mutasarrifate*).

Prior to 1872, some of the most explosive demonstrations of protest against Ottoman rule in Palestine occurred in and around Jerusalem. These occurred when rural and urban interests were able to coalesce around an overlapping set of grievances against Ottoman rule. Excessive, forcible taxation was often the catalyst. The historian 'Adel Manna' describes three revolts during the eighteenth and nineteenth centuries in Palestine, the first two of which were based in Jerusalem: the 1703–1705 *naqib al-'ashraf* rebellion and the 1825–1826 rebellion.[4] In setting the stage for the former rebellion, Manna' explains: "In the shadow of weak and ineffective Ottoman rule, local leaders emerged from among families of rural shaykhs and urban notables. It was this group that led the population when they resisted Ottoman governors who levied excessive taxes and tried to collect them by force."[5] He describes how conflicts between local leaders plagued the Jerusalem *sanjak*: "The authorities failed time and again to ensure security and stability for peasants and city dwellers. . . . The [Ottoman-appointed] governors of Jerusalem were unable to establish security, not only in Hebron and its surrounding hills, but even in rural areas around Jerusalem itself. . . . Given the overall lack of security, many people decided not to pay taxes to the governors and to rely on themselves to protect their lives and property."[6] Through a statist lens, one could explain such problems with widespread insecurity as an absence, or short-age, of state policing capacity, as defined in chapter 1, or distributive capacity, with a particular focus on dispute settlement mechanisms and institutions.

Manna' describes how 1701 brought a harsh, repressive governor to Jerusalem, Nablus, and Gaza—Muhammad Pasha Kurd Bayram, "arrived in Jerusalem at the head of a large army and doubled taxes, making it clear that money not paid willingly would be collected by force."[7] As an overly confident intermediary of the empire, Muhammad Pasha perhaps learned the lesson that ratcheting up coercive and extractive efforts at the same time was a recipe for rebellion. *Naqib al-'ashraf* refers to representatives of the descendants of Muhammad, and the positions at the provincial level in Palestine were historically occupied by members of the prominent al-Husayni family.[8] As Manna' describes,

> The *'ulama'* and notables of Jerusalem . . . advised the *wali* [governor] through the intermediary of the *qadi* [senior judge] and Muhammad Effendi Jarallah, the *mufti* [senior Muslim legal authority] of Jerusalem, to desist from his policy. When Muhammad Pasha persisted, the people of Jerusalem rose up. . . . The Janissaries and *timar* (land grant) holders (*sipahis*) joined the rebels in the city, which made it easy for the Jerusalemites to overcome the *mutasallim* [Ottoman-appointed head of Jerusalem] and his troops. Peasants from nearby villages, who had heard about the *'ulama'*'s appeal, came into Jerusalem to take part in the rebellion. . . .
>
> Once the rebels gained control of Jerusalem, they appointed the *naqib al-ashraf*, Muhammad ibn Mustafa al-Wafa'i al-Husayni, as shaykh and leader of the city. They also appointed the shaykhs of the various quarters of Jerusalem to help the *naqib* administer the city's affairs, thus beginning a period of self-rule that lasted for over two years, nearly until the end of 1705.[9]

Subsequently, as Manna' details, the rebel movement split over whether or not to accept the Ottoman authorities' offer to dismiss the *wali* as a sufficient response to their demands. The *naqib al-'ashraf* wanted to keep the rebellion active; eventually, factional violence erupted in Jerusalem, allowing the Ottoman military to reenter and retake the city. The *naqib* was later arrested and sentenced to death; a new *naqib* was appointed by the state, those who had supported the rebellion were arrested, and property was requisitioned.

The 1825–1826 rebellion, as Manna' notes, began due to excessive and forcible tax collection by an Ottoman-appointed governor, and the elimination of taxation was part of the rebels' program. In the countryside around Jerusalem and Bethlehem, peasants revolted against the *mutasallim* and his troops. Jerusalem residents seized control of the city, shutting its gates, arresting the *mutasallim*'s men, and disarming and expelling foreign troops. Two Arab officers in the Ottoman army— Yusuf 'Agha al-Ja'uni and 'Ahmad 'Agha al-'Asali—were chosen as leaders of the rebellion; they acted as "rulers of the region, rewarding the inhabitants for participating in the rebellion by exempting peasants from payment of the *miri* tax [on land use] that year and by reducing the *jizya* tax [on minorities] to be paid by the heads of the city's Christian and Jewish communities."[10]

The Ottoman-appointed governor of Acre was delegated the task of regaining control of Jerusalem. When comparing the *naqib al-'ashraf* revolt and the 1825–1826 revolt, Manna' concludes, "The main engine driving events in both cases was discontent with the policies of local governors, particularly excessive taxation and forcible tax collection. The aims of the people were similarly limited, basically amounting to no more than a change in governors and their policies. *The legitimacy of Ottoman rule under the sultan, the Islamic caliph, was not challenged.*"[11]

After the Ottoman state reform period began in the mid-nineteenth century, local government underwent some formalization, particularly in urban areas. As noted earlier, Jerusalem was one of the first cities in the entire empire to obtain a municipal council, shortly after the first Ottoman municipality law was passed in 1867. Falestin Naïli elaborates on the structure of this council in the ensuing decades:

> From the 1880s onward, the city's municipal council was composed of nine to twelve elected members (through male censitary suffrage only) for a four-year renewable mandate. The council members had to be Ottoman citizens and could not be protectees of foreign consulates. Muslims were the predominant majority on the council, but there were Christian and Jewish members always included. In addition to the elected members, there were four ex officio members: the municipality's engineer, doctor, veterinarian and head of police. The council's president (and mayor) was chosen from among the elected members by the imperial government.[12]

During this period, when Jerusalem received its special administrative status under the direct control of Istanbul, Naïli notes that it "played an 'interstitial role' between the imperial center and the provincial periphery."[13] It provided services such as street lighting and sanitation and garbage collection, and it established a municipal hospital, as Naïli explains. However, not until later, under the British Mandate, did the municipality as an institution find itself in the crosswinds of the conflict between Zionists and Palestinians. As we will see, Palestinian representation on the council vacillated across two main political currents, each represented in the municipality by one of two elite families, one of which leaned toward more accommodation of the British colonial regime and the second of which overtly challenged it.

While keen external interests in Jerusalem resulted in one set of administrative relations there, Beshara Doumani notes that Nablus, "as the capital of a hill region which enjoyed a significant degree of autonomy and self-rule and in which there were no 'foreigners' who held military or bureaucratic posts . . . remained outside the detailed supervision of the Ottoman government, at least until the mid-nineteenth century."[14] Nablus did see increasing state centralization, first piloted by the Egyptian occupiers in 1830 and taken to new levels with the Ottoman *tanzimat* reforms, as relatively autonomous subdistricts gave way to increasingly hierarchical relations between villages and city and between the cities and the center of the empire.

Doumani documents how local "native sons" in the towns and villages around Nablus often wrestled with both the central Ottoman state and one another for political control. Much of that control was secured through violence but also control of trade routes and the maintenance of urban-rural and interregional trade connections. For local notables, this tension between serving their local populations versus doing the bidding of the Ottoman authorities was always present. Further, Doumani draws our attention to the relative autonomy of rural areas prior to several turning points in the nineteenth century. For one, incipient local councils appeared during this time following the Egyptian invasion of 1830–1831. As Manna‘ also describes, these transformations—which also culminated in the bureaucratic, centralizing *tanzimat* reforms—tended to displace the traditional leaders in places like *Jabal Nablus*: "In the final decades of Ottoman rule, a new class of large landowners and bureaucratic office holders emerged. The imposition by the Ottomans of direct and centralized rule over

Palestine and the other *vilayets* [states] in the second half of the nineteenth century had undermined the independent influence belonging to the big families of the *jabals* [*jibal*, or mountains]. . . . The new social elite therefore had economic and political interests that differed from those of the traditional leaders who had led . . . popular rebellions."[15]

Hebron—the third large town in the modern West Bank that was also a significant urban area under Ottoman rule—frequently chafed under the centralizing impulses of Ottoman (and Egyptian) rule. The *waqf* constituted large swaths of land, and thus their owners wielded considerable social and economic influence. To situate Hebron in comparison with the other, major Palestinian cities, Lisa Taraki and Rita Giacaman summarize, "It is possible to piece together from different sources a 'stratified' profile of Palestinian cities during the late nineteenth and early twentieth centuries reflecting the ranking of different cities on a continuum ranging from central 'modernizing' cities to peripheral 'traditional/conservative' cities and towns."[16] While Jerusalem, Jaffa, and Haifa would be considered the former, inland Hebron was an example of the latter. The authors describe Schölch's "typology of Palestinian cities in the late nineteenth century" based on levels of European intervention: "First come Jerusalem, Bethlehem, and Nazareth (those being the abodes of Christian holy sites), followed by Jaffa and Haifa. The second category includes the more peripheral cities of 'Akka (Acre), Safad, and Tiberias, followed by the third category embracing the local economic and trade centers of Nablus, Hebron, and Gaza, which were 'indeed washed by the European flood, but were not as swamped by it' as the first group of cities."[17] Of these, only Jerusalem, Nablus, and Hebron would end up in what we now refer to as the West Bank.

However, on the distinctiveness of Hebron (*al-Khalil* in Arabic) Taraki and Giacaman, citing Karmon, describe that the town itself did not exercise hegemonic social or political control over its surrounding villages or hinterlands: "This is attributed to what [Karmon] assumes is the lack of regional interdependence between town and village in a subsistence economy; the absence of a proper regional administration under the Ottomans and thus the predominance of local tax farmers; and the constant danger of attacks by bedouins, which created coalitions of villages whose combined population was much greater than that of Hebron."[18] That corresponds to the pre-nineteenth-century picture of Ottoman Palestine described earlier, whereby the metropole relies on indirect rule, outsourcing extractive capacity to tax-farming intermediaries; and yet we see an absence of anything akin to "policing" capacity, thus deepening the threat of raids.

Further, according to Taraki and Giacaman, Suad Amiry theorizes that "because much of the land in Jabal al-Khalil was *waqf* land and thus not subject to taxation, a 'feudal' landlord class was not allowed to develop in this area."[19] Without large, taxable properties, the imperial center faced little incentive to provide security. The picture that emerges mirrors some of the theoretical intuitions described in the preceding chapter, whereby there is a political trade-off for regime intermediaries to invest too much in both fiscal and coercive capacity, each of which can elicit resistance threatening the intermediary's position and perhaps the regime itself.

Despite, or perhaps because of, its peripheral status, Hebron was not immune from revolt against centralized rule. A peasant rebellion broke out in 1834 in response to policies of the newly occupying Egyptian authorities; in this case, rebels were supported by Ottoman rulers who had recently lost a large swath of territory to the khedival dynasty of Muhammad 'Ali. The rebellion incorporated a wide range of Palestinian notable families, peasants, and Bedouin tribes from "from Galilee in the north to Hebron and Gaza in the south."[20] Manna' explains that 'Ali's centralizing policies, including "the imposition of military conscription and the disarming of the population, were seen as detrimental to wide sectors of the people. In addition, the Ottoman state was constantly inciting the population to rebel: Ottoman decrees repeatedly stressed the illegitimacy of the Egyptian occupation, endowing the 1834 rebellion with an ideological character transcending limited demands concerning matters of taxation and specific measures and amounting to *a challenge to the legitimacy of government itself.*"[21]

The 1834 rebellion was put down ruthlessly, but it was notable for its wide geographic reach and the role of rural religious leaders and notables, many of whom were executed or exiled after Muhammad 'Ali regained control. This period was one of economic decline for Hebron and its surroundings. By 1855, the Ottoman Empire had regained control of the region after Ibrahim Pasha's defeat, appointing their own *nazir* (administrator) and subduing the remaining rebels.

BRITISH MANDATE (1920–1948)

With the establishment of the British Mandate after World War I and the collapse of the Ottoman Empire, some Ottoman-era institutions were preserved while others were abolished. Palestinian nationalist sentiment and organizational cohesion were on the rise in response to British rule and British support for Zionist settlement and land expropriation. In the 1920s and 1930s, lines hardened between Palestinian nationalists and Palestinians who either worked within British institutions or were viewed as collaborating with the Zionist cause. Municipal leadership of the major urban areas became a central focus of this competition. Municipal functions, however, were controlled and surveilled in many ways by the British authorities. Furthermore, the prominence of some local rural sheikhs and notables continued to decline—a trend that began under late Ottoman rule—but the rural sphere was complex. Often, rural notables chose how to position themselves vis-à-vis three other collectives: the largely urban nationalist elite, the British (who, in many ways, seemed to ignore the rural periphery), and the Zionists, who continued to pursue the purchase or forcible acquisition of Palestinian lands and sometimes relied on rural leaders to do so. Once again, we see that leaders at the local level—whether in the urban centers or the villages of the periphery—played important roles as intermediaries between the Palestinian population and the overlapping state-building entities that occupied their land: namely, the British Mandatory state and the budding Zionist state.

As the mandate introduced its own formal laws and institutions, municipalities were brought into its fold. For example, while many historians have focused on institutions such as the Supreme Muslim Council, led by al-Hajj Muhammad 'Amin al-Husayni, the Grand Mufti of Jerusalem, as a central ground for organized Palestinian nationalism, local government was also pertinent to these political struggles. Sherene Seikaly describes two of the most prominent political families in Jerusalem, the Husaynis and the Nashashibis, and the attention they devoted to local institutions using "municipal elections, competition for mayoral posts, and control of institutions like the Supreme Muslim Council to jockey for power and create alliances."[22]

Rami Zeedan summarizes the somewhat passive British approach to municipal governance in the early years of the mandate: "From 1918 to 1920, the British military administration in Palestine mainly maintained the status quo without changing the Ottoman laws that were in effect until the end of the First World War. . . . The administrative structure of districts and sub-districts was changed; however, the local government structure remained the same. Except for a few, those Mayors holding appointments from the Ottoman period were allowed to continue in their positions."[23]

However, in subsequent years, three municipal elections were held under British mandatory rule: in 1927, 1934, and 1946–47, as noted by Zeedan. This contrasts with the single national electoral event of 1923, in which the British attempted to form a legislative council consisting of Muslim and Christian Palestinians, members of the Druze minority, and Jewish residents. The Palestine Arab Congress boycotted the vote, and the results of this election were soon declared void. Consistent with other narratives, Zeedan documents how the first municipal elections of 1927 in many cities essentially amounted to a competition between the Husaynis, who advocated for nationalist opposition to the mandate, and the Nashashibis, whose approach was more conservative, while the majority of Palestinians still lived in villages and rural areas that were exempt from the vote. The Palestinian Arab Executive in the 1920s, under the leadership of Musa Kazim al-Husayni, refused to participate in British institutions.[24]

The Palestine general strike of 1936 and ensuing revolt was a major turning point in the relationship between Palestinians and their British occupiers. Throughout the mandate, but especially after the revolt, Palestinians' interactions with the British mandatory state were inherently shaped by their continued displacement at the hands of British-supported Zionist immigration, their exclusion from critical institutions of power, and the violent repression that many of them faced in the wake of the revolt. In addition to coercive capacity, though, Palestinians business owners were distrustful of their presumed role in the fiscal architecture of the state. For example, Seikaly documents Palestinian urban capitalists' perspectives on the introduction of a general income tax during the 1941 to 1943 period, a time of world war and heightened inequality and scarcity in Palestinian society. Seikaly writes that Shibli Jamal, a business representative at the Jerusalem Arab Chamber of Commerce,

> responded with perhaps the clearest summary of what the world looked like in the 1940s: The 'Arabs are not comfortable about their future after the war.' The 'people' would comply if 'a clear, honest policy on the future of the state was articulated.' . . . Thus, these Palestinians supported the 'equity principal of fiscalism' precisely because they understood themselves as equal members of one Palestine. They were able to envision, if begrudgingly, Jews, European and otherwise, as members of that Palestine. Their most pressing fear was the lack of clarity on what sort of state would rule it.[25]

This discussion is centered on a national-level institution—the income tax to be introduced throughout mandate Palestine. Yet, it highlights how the imposition of new taxes by an occupying power cannot be divorced from the national liberation struggle of the occupied. The "men of capital" of the 1940s whom Seikaly profiles were different figures from the urban dwellers or rural notables who facilitated the rebellions against excessive taxation and coercion in the eighteenth and nineteenth centuries. It is not possible to draw a line between the tax rebellions against the Ottoman Empire during the latter periods and Jerusalem's businessmen of the twentieth century. However, each group resisted, in one way or another, coercion or extraction by agents of a far-off state and thus called into question the legitimacy of the state-building projects to which Palestinians were being expected to contribute. What was new was a settlement project backed by a major Western power and the displacement and sense of vulnerability about the future that it created.

On the distributive side of governance, municipalities were integrated into British wartime strategies of control and rationing. Furthermore, in the period after the general strike and revolt, municipalities were also more integrated into the coercive aims of the British authorities. One example of this intersection between distribution and policing was a "'municipal market' scheme in which local authorities would oversee the direct contact between producers and consumers" under the supervision of the British colonial Palestinian Control Authority.[26] Under one iteration of the British system to tightly regulate food production, pricing, and distribution, a colonial food control office "moved vegetables from producers, at times by force, into the main municipal areas. Municipalities were then responsible for marketing, selling, and distributing the vegetables," according to Seikaly. Municipalities that did not comply with their role in supplying these markets under British watch were threatened with "either withdrawing grants-in-aid or replacing the municipal council altogether."[27]

In this case, it is abundantly clear that the distributive capacity of municipalities was tightly bound to their compliance with the British regime. However, this cooptation of distributive channels apparently required a coercive presence as well. Seikaly goes on to describe how this scheme for the regulation food production and distribution "depended almost completely on the cooperation of the police in checking the movement of produce. . . . A Haifa district commissioner report provides a glimpse of the heavy police presence in the vegetable scheme's implementation on 11 October 1943. The police set up posts surrounding the city and inspected all incoming lorries. . . . In the Galilee district, municipal authorities and Food Control inspectors joined forces to oversee prices in the markets; the police made rounds in residential areas and reportedly stopped 'house to house hawking.' "[28] The mandate also outsourced certain aspects of justice provision to the mayors, allowing, in 1941, "for mayors to preside over the municipal tribunal, which had all the powers of a magistrate with regard to the summoning of witnesses, the arrest of accused persons, and any other matter concerned with the trial of a criminal case."[29]

On the Jerusalem municipality under the mandate, Naïli demonstrates that some of its roles atrophied or were weakened, including in urban planning and tax collection. However, the municipality's importance for the distribution of water—a role that many West Bank municipalities continued to fill in the Israeli occupation years, analyzed in subsequent chapters—maintained its continued relevance. As a result, the municipality "became a theatre for and a stake in the conflict between Palestinian nationalists and the Zionist movement which militated for a stronger representation of Jews at all levels of the institution."[30] Further, the Jerusalem municipality, in particular, was still viewed by the British as important enough to justify continued intervention as tensions rose between Zionist immigrants and Palestinian nationalists. Again, turning to Naïli,

> British mandate authorities intervened repeatedly in municipal affairs, starting with the dismissal of Mayor Musa Kazim al-Husayni for participating in an anti-Zionist demonstration during the Nabi al-Musa festival in 1920 . . . In 1937, the city's mayor—Husayn Fakhri al-Khalidi (elected in 1934)—was exiled for having played an active role in the Arab Revolt that had begun in 1936. Finally, in 1945, conflicts within the municipality became so paralyzing that the British High Commissioner decided to dissolve the municipal council and appoint a municipal commission to replace it.[31]

Naïli concludes that in weakening the municipality and undermining its elected leadership, the mandatory authorities aimed "to reduce the margins of political mobilization of the Arab population."[32] Palestinians would never regain representation on any government institutions that shaped urban planning in Jerusalem.

The mandate period also saw forms of Palestinian collaboration, with either British authorities or Zionists, that some would describe as treacherous. In many cases, this collaboration took the form of Palestinians selling land to Zionist settlers, resulting in the mass displacement of peasants and workers. Hillel Cohen describes some of these collaborators as nonetheless commanding a loyal set of followers. He introduces an anecdote about Sheikh 'Abd al-Fattah Darwish, who was the chief of a *nahiya* in al-Maliha, south of Jerusalem. Cohen writes that according to the stories told by residents in the 1970s, "Arab rebels besieged [his] house in 1938" and he "repelled the attackers," while his son, a police officer serving the British Mandate, "was executed by the rebels that same year."[33] Figures like 'Abd al-Fattah were immensely polarizing, especially in the years during and following the revolt. The political trajectories of such figures often spanned multiple phases of Palestine's history of foreign or external rule. Cohen notes that after the 1948 war, with Jordan in control of the West Bank at the end of the fighting, Darwish eventually ended up as an elected member of the Jordanian parliament. He was by then a refugee in Beit Jala, and, Cohen writes, "when he died, his son Hasan took his parliamentary seat."[34]

At times, these tensions were between urban nationalists and rural sheikhs who possessed authority over *nawahi*, or regional collections of villages. When faced with exclusion on multiple levels—exclusion from nationalist institutions emerging in Palestinian cities and exclusion by the colonial forces of the British and the Zionists—these rural leaders were placed in a difficult position. As Cohen describes, these village leaders "had three options: try to fight the urban [Palestinian nationalist] elite on their own; support the national urban leadership and derive power from whatever legitimacy the leadership would grant them; or unite forces with the major enemy of the national elite—the Zionists. The choice was not easy, and there were village leaders, like the *nahiya* sheikhs in the Jerusalem area, who shifted back and forth."[35]

Collaboration was not limited to rural leaders; a number of mayors of cities and towns in Mandate Palestine cooperated with the Zionists as a means of personal advancement. For example, according to Cohen, the mayor of Haifa at the time of British conquest, Hasan Shukri, was viewed by Jewish settlers as "a symbol of coexistence, an Arab who was willing to live with Jews. To Arab nationalists, however, Shukri was a collaborator and traitor."[36] He was reelected mayor in 1927 with the support of Jewish voters after "the disciples of Sheikh Izz al-Din al-Qassam [a nationalist leader who had planned militant attacks against Zionist and British targets] tried to assassinate him."[37] Also mentioned is a former mayor of Tulkarm, 'Abd al-Rahman al-Hajj Ibrahim, who, along with members of his family, "worked alongside Zionist land purchasers from the Mandate's first days through the establishment of the state of Israel, sometimes at great personal risk. . . . As mayor, [al-Hajj Ibrahim] was able to achieve a lot—sell his own land and persuade others to sell theirs."[38] Of course, such "achievements" were castigated by Palestinian nationalists. However, they point to the influential role that municipal politicians had, even in the urban areas, in shaping the nature of the colonial regime—both the British-controlled regime within which they operated and the emerging Zionist regime that would decisively gain political power in 1948.

In summary, these accounts all point to the critical role of local rural and urban Palestinian indigenous leaders in establishing their position vis-à-vis the British-supported occupation and whether and how they might support nationalist resistance. Overall, as Zeedan concludes, municipal office was an arena "of competition between the families of the urban elite" and excluded wide segments of the nonurban Palestinian population.[39] Furthermore, with many municipal positions directly appointed by the British High Commissioner, and with sweeping powers granted to British representatives such as the district governor, "some mayors were merely representatives of the mandate government more than representatives of their people."[40] Municipalities again, perhaps unexpectedly, became arenas for competition under Israeli occupation.

After the United Nations vote on the resolution to partition Palestine on November 29, 1947, war broke out in Palestine. In May 1948, after the British Mandate was terminated, Israel declared its independence and Egypt, Syria, and the Transjordanian and Iraqi armies entered the war. The 1947–1949 war resulted in the mass displacement of more than seven hundred thousand Palestinians from their homeland. Some left as conflict broke out, some fled in fear, and many were forcibly displaced at gunpoint. The towns of Lydde (also known as *al-Lidd* in Arabic and now Lod in Hebrew) and Ramla were ethnically cleansed after a small contingent from the Arab Legion in Transjordan combined with hundreds of civilian volunteers could not hold the towns, sending tens of thousands of residents on foot to East Jerusalem and Ramallah where, if they survived (hundreds did not), they would begin a new phase of their lives as refugees.[41] The military operation that saw the newly anointed Israel Defense Forces (initially formed from the Zionist paramilitary organizations such as the Haganah and the Irgun) enter Lydde and Ramla resulted in the expulsion of an estimated eighty thousand Palestinians from at least twenty-five depopulated villages.[42]

PALESTINIANS UNDER ISRAELI AND
JORDANIAN RULE (1948-1967)

Many of the Palestinians who stayed within the territory that became Israel's *de facto* borders in 1949 had also endured being displaced from their towns and villages. As Mark Tessler states, "although they had not left the country, they, too, abandoned their homes during or immediately after the war, and then either were prevented from returning, allegedly for security reasons, or found that their dwellings had been razed or occupied by Jews. As a result, they either resettled in neighboring Arab villages or were obliged to occupy the homes of others who had fled."[43] At the conclusion of the war, the Palestinian population within Israel's armistice boundaries were placed under military rule through the application of the 1945 British Mandate's emergency laws and subsequent emergency regulations issued by the new government in 1949, resulting in "roughly 90 percent" of Palestinians living under military rule by May 1949, notes Shira Robinson.[44] With the 1950 Absentee Property Law, the property of Palestinians who had left or fled was expropriated by the state of Israel. Some form of military rule over Palestinian citizens of Israel, including the liberal use of administrative detention and strict permit regimes for traveling outside one's immediate place of residence, continued until 1966.

The focus of the empirical analysis in the chapters that follow is the West Bank, which fell under Jordanian rule after the war. However, it is worth noting that before the last vestiges of military rule were eliminated in 1966, Israel's treatment of the Palestinians who stayed within the state's new borders included experimentation with indirect modes of control, perhaps shaping how it would approach the West Bank later. For example, under military rule in the south, with Bedouin populations concentrated on what was, in effect, a reserve, Israel worked through and empowered tribal leaders in an early experimentation with indirect rule.[45] On the other hand, in more concentrated and urban Palestinian population centers in the Galilee and the "Little Triangle," Israel did attempt to coopt municipal leaders. However, even after the period of military rule, when we can say that full Israeli annexation and so-called direct rule had been achieved, the municipalities were still not disconnected from the broader Palestinian nationalist struggle. Palestinian participation in formal institutions was limited primarily to the Communist Party, which later split into Jewish- and Palestinian-led factions.[46] Tawfiq Zayyad, then mayor of Nazareth with the successor to the Arab-led Communist Party, Rakah, played a key leadership role in organizing protests and strikes on what became known as "Land Day" in 1976 to protest Israeli expropriations.[47] (Notably, this was the same year in which municipal elections were held in the West Bank, and oppositional mayors such as Bassam Shaka'a, Karim Khalaf, and Ibrahim Tawil swept into power.)

However, if we return to the period prior to Israel's 1967 occupation of the territory west of the Jordan River—what is now the West Bank—the political structures for Palestinians looked different.[48] After the 1948 war, Jordan extended citizenship to the hundreds of thousands of Palestinians living in the West Bank and refugees who had fled into the East Bank. The Jordanian monarchy formally annexed the West Bank in 1950. A trend toward centralization within the Jordanian state was, according to Janine Clark, felt in the West Bank, too, especially "with the integration of the National Guard (heavily recruited from the West Bank) into the army in 1956."[49] Drawing on the work of Laurie Brand,[50] Clark describes how, after Jordan's annexation of the West Bank, the state strove for "a policy that would integrate the two peoples on either side of the Jordan River," creating a "hybrid Jordanian identity for the two communities, one that would focus on the monarchy in general and the king in particular as the central symbol of Jordan."[51]

Through the institutional legacies that Jordan inherited from previous powers and also due to the monarchy's own strategic preferences, the Jordanian approach to governance did include elements of indirect rule. Clark notes, "the centrality of the Bedouin tribes to the state-building process in Jordan cannot be overstated.[52] This carried from the Ottoman era through the British Mandate period and into independence. British policy, through some trial and error, integrated tribes into the state during the mandate period. Clark provides this quote from Yoav Alon: "The government ruled through the shakyhs, not in place of them, and continued to delegate responsibility for maintaining law and order, tax collection, dispute settlement, and distributing state largesse. Shaykhs remained the main link between the central government and the population, maintaining and even increasing their status as important political actors even as the powers of the central government increased."[53]

This state of affairs persisted under Jordanian rule in the villages and more rural parts of the West Bank. In the municipalities, the monarchy allowed for the formation of municipal councils. However, against the opposition of mayors in newly annexed West Bank cities such as Hebron and Nablus, the Jordanian Ministry of the Interior retained control over appointing mayors, altering municipal council composition, and recommending dismissal of councilors.[54] Moshe Ma'oz describes in depth the way that a centralized, hierarchical system of control over municipalities emanated from the center of the Jordanian state, with much control vested in the office of the minister of the interior.[55] Thus, at the risk of oversimplification, it is accurate to say that Jordanian rule in the West Bank consisted of a more indirect form of rule in the countryside, with rural shaykhs playing an important intermediary role, and a more direct style of rule in the urban areas.

The Palestinian Liberation Organization (PLO) was not formed until 1964, and in those early years, it was largely viewed as a project spearheaded by Egypt and the Arab League to coopt Palestinian nationalism. Thus, municipal councils did not feature a strong Palestinian nationalist voice during most of the Jordanian period. Due to the centralized control of the Jordanian state in urban areas at least, most mayors and council members were reliably conservative and loyal to the Hashemite monarchy in Jordan. This approach toward West Bank elites was replicated through all levels of the Jordanian government. As Glenn Robinson notes, "it was precisely those notables who had tacitly renounced their national Palestinian aspirations who were chosen for positions in the Jordanian state."[56]

In such a context, municipal offices did not become a staging ground for any kind of resistance to the Jordanian state, even as mayors under Jordanian rule were increasingly at odds with growing Palestinian nationalist sentiment. Not until Israel began its occupation of the West Bank did a Palestinian presence in Jordan and its militant activity became a threat to the Hashemite monarchy. In 1967, Jordan lost control of the West Bank, including East Jerusalem and its holy sites, to Israeli forces. Israel moved to immediately annex the eastern half of Jerusalem, but not the rest of the

West Bank, which it assigned to a more ambiguous form of military occupation. Menachem Klein provides the following backdrop to the changes this entailed in the waning moments of the 1967 war.

> Even before the Israeli government decided officially to annex East Jerusalem, the Israeli part of the capital had penetrated the Jordanian city. It took less than six days for municipal workers, under the direction of Mayor Teddy Kollek, to bury the Palestinian and Jordanian dead who lay in the streets and to connect the two water systems. Telephone wires that had been damaged in the war were repaired, and the police put up street signs on Jordanian streets. Israeli municipal officials perused the records of the Jordanian municipality and met with their East Jerusalem counterparts to fill in information that was not contained in those documents.[57]

Among major Palestinian population centers, though, Jerusalem proved the exception. Israeli military rule in the rest of the West Bank after 1967—documented in more detail in the following chapters—did not come along with municipal absorption. Instead, Israel imposed military rule over Palestinian villages, towns, and cities in the West Bank and Gaza Strip. Without the intent to absorb the Palestinian population in the occupied territories into the Israeli state, Israel would at first attempt to continue a form of indirect rule built on the Jordanian model, wherein Israel would continue to depend on less overtly nationalist leaders who had been supportive of the Hashemite regime to mediate its occupation.

Meanwhile, the influx of a new wave of Palestinian refugees in 1967 and increasing PLO militant activities "fueled resentments," eventually resulting in the PLO's expulsion from Jordan in 1970.[58] Jordan continued to provide financial assistance to Palestinian municipalities under Israeli occupation, even to those that, after 1976, were led by pro-PLO mayors.[59] Indeed, after 1976, Israel learned that it would not succeed in cultivating mayors as reliable local-level intermediaries in the service of its regime. Eventually, Israeli objectives and on-the-ground realities—pushed along by the outbreak of the first Palestinian intifada in 1987—would culminate in a new, highly institutionalized form of indirect rule in which a newly created Palestinian Authority was to serve as the most well-endowed and institutionally developed intermediary that any occupying or foreign power had ever established in the territory.

The subsequent chapter paints a picture of how this specific form of indirect rule came to be, describing how the bounded ideological space within which successive Israeli governments operated resulted in an intermediary that was heavy on policing—namely, coercion that faced inward, toward Palestinian communities—while Israeli actors would retain responsibility for extraction (in this case, primarily of land). Ultimately, the introduction of this newly upgraded and institutionalized indirect rule regime would dramatically refashion the political context in which Palestinian mayors and municipal councils operated.

Chapter Three

THE ORIGINS AND DEVELOPMENT OF ISRAEL'S INDIRECT RULE REGIME

The theoretical argument presented in chapter 1 is focused on understanding the effects of indirect rule on local governments in indigenous communities. Chapters 4 and 5 will use variation in the relative visibility of Israeli-PA collaboration—with some Palestinian towns facing a form of Israeli military rule that is consistently unmediated while others are more regularly subjected to policing by the Palestinian intermediary—and differences in the local power of regime opponents to explain governance outcomes. However, before considering an analysis of Palestinian local governance in the West Bank on such a granular level, it is worthwhile to reflect on the origins of the indirect rule regime. Why would a state such as Israel, which possesses superior coercive control over a contested territory, seek to outsource governance to an indigenous intermediary such as the Fatah-controlled Palestinian Authority (PA)? How did the aims of Israel, the dominant state, shape which functions of governance were prioritized for delegation to the indigenous intermediary?

This chapter provides contextual, qualitative analysis on the Israeli state's approach toward the West Bank after 1967 and how Israel's approach to annexation and territorial control resulted in the creation of a Palestinian intermediary with specific functional limitations and restricted geographic reach. Thus, this chapter is written with a particular focus on the perspectives and goals of Israeli decision-makers, with an eye toward understanding how these objectives shaped the political institutions under which Palestinians in the West Bank would live following the Oslo Accords.

With the basic assumption that actors—including the leaders and decision-makers in such states—are goal-oriented, we can logically deduce that states that predominantly aim to absorb the contested territory itself but are opposed to politically incorporating the territory's population are most likely to adopt strategies of indirect rule. In this chapter, I show that, first, Israel's objectives toward the West Bank in the period leading up to the signing of the Oslo Accords fit this description—in other words, the Israeli state and its decision-makers sought to annex the West Bank exclusive of its Palestinian population. To demonstrate this, I use evidence from Israeli political discourse following the state's victory in the June 1967 war, which, while representing a variety of opinions, is consistent with an overall approach that values control of the contested territory—either as a permanent feature of the Israeli state or a bargaining chip in future negotiations—more than absorption of the territory's population. Inclusion of the Palestinian population in the West Bank under the purview of Israeli political institutions was never a position that gained serious consideration or elaboration within the Israeli political establishment.

Second, I use qualitative evidence to demonstrate that the criteria for Palestinian self-rule were all but guaranteed by the nature of arguments made on both the Israeli left and the right about the future political status of the West Bank.[1] While many on the far right—often referred to as "territorial maximalists"—were insistent on annexing the territory to the Israeli state and eliminating any sense of difference between pre-1967 Israel and the post-1967 occupied territories, even those who sought the most aggressive forms of state expansion into the West Bank did not advocate for political incorporation of the Palestinian population. While successive Israeli governments varied in the extent to which they pursued *de facto* territorial annexation, even the most avid proponents of territorial annexation did not advance a plan to extend any Israeli political institutions to the Palestinians in the West Bank and Gaza Strip. This contrasted somewhat with the official policy toward Palestinians in East Jerusalem, who were granted a residency status within Israel that conferred some rights but fell short of full citizenship. No such status was seriously contemplated for Palestinian residents of the West Bank and Gaza after 1967. The Palestinian population of the West Bank would not have access to Israeli institutions of civil governance, according to this discourse on the right; if anything, annexation would proceed with Palestinian areas carved out in a way explicitly comparable with the Bantustans of apartheid-era South Africa.

However, the maximal potential of Palestinian self-rule was also guaranteed by limits in the discourse on the left. While many on the left advocated for eventual separation from the West Bank along what was to be known as a "land for peace" formula, the potential for a Palestinian state to develop outward-facing coercive institutions was always an Achilles' heel in such arguments. The prime concern of critics of the land-for-peace argument was, in sum, the security of Israel's Jewish citizens. Thus, external coercive capacity in the hands of Palestinians, with whom Israel had not yet made peace, was not something to be seriously contemplated. This limitation has proceeded to characterize Israeli left-wing positions in the decades since.

Israel's approach to ruling Palestinians in the West Bank was iterated over time, and when reliable intermediaries could not be found at the local level in the 1970s and 1980s, the idea of a centralized agent disproportionately weighted toward internal policing began to emerge. While observers may not have predicted the exact type and nature of Palestinian intermediary institutions that would result from the Oslo Accords, I argue that three features of the accords—which defined the capacities delegated to the new PA—would not have occurred without Israel's motivating goal of exclusive annexation. First, responsibility for externally facing coercive capacity was maintained within the Israeli military, and no Palestinian actors were to play a role in its provision. Second, the introduction of *de jure* and *de facto* geographic variation in PA policing capacity was a result of Israel's entwined goals of facilitating the entrenchment of Jewish Israeli settlements, as a tool to promote *de facto* annexation, while maintaining stability and order in Palestinian towns. While the functional restrictions of the PA are uniform across the entire sample of towns that I analyze in subsequent chapters, the geographic fragmentation of PA rule—as it was eventually defined in the Interim Agreement ("Oslo II")—generated differences, sometimes subtle, in the lived experiences of Palestinians across localities and their exposure to these functionally restricted PA institutions.

Finally, authority over (and responsibility for) local distributive capacity—including the provision to end users of certain collective goods such as electricity, water, education, health care, and sanitation within Palestinian communities—was outsourced to PA central and local institutions, with other organizations such as the United Nations Relief and Works Agency and foreign donors also playing important roles. Thus, while the particular institutional complexities of the PA that emerged in 1994 and 1995 were not predetermined, they were bound within a certain range of possibilities given the positions and preferences of the Israeli political leadership at any given time.

Because the positions of Israeli decision-makers are the consequential area of focus here, subsequent sections of this chapter are divided chronologically to review the nature of Israel's political approach to the West Bank over time as governments changed. The subsequent sections cover, first, important historical context from the creation of Israel in 1948 until June 1967 and, subsequently, the periods of 1967 to 1977, 1977 to 1984, 1984 to 1993, the period of the Oslo negotiations and agreements between 1993 and 1995, and the collapse of further peace negotiations from 1995 to 2005. Within each period, I discuss the ways in which the political status of the West Bank was imagined by Israeli political actors across the spectrum of beliefs from territorial minimalism to maximalism.

1967–1977: THE FIRST DECADE OF OCCUPATION

The establishment of the state of Israel in 1948 was a celebrated moment for the Zionist movement, following a long history of persecution and discrimination in Europe and the horrors of the Holocaust. While chapter 2 described the overwhelmingly negative effects of the 1947-1949 war on the Palestinian people, the reverberations of the war were almost the polar opposite for Zionists, as it culminated in the creation of a national homeland for the Jewish people. Israel and its neighbors continued in a state of belligerence between 1948 and 1967, when frictions exploded into open conflict once again. Following escalating tensions with Egypt and Syria, Israel struck Egyptian airfields on June 5 and pushed ground troops into Gaza, Sinai, East Jerusalem, and the West Bank. The swift conflict generated a second wave of hundreds of thousands of Palestinian refugees. At its conclusion, Israel had captured the West Bank and East Jerusalem from Jordan, the Gaza Strip and Sinai Peninsula from Egypt, and the Golan Heights from Syria (see map 3.1). Along with the territory, Israel found itself with more than one million people now under its rule: roughly 600,000 residents of the West Bank, 350,000 residents of the Gaza Strip—each of which

MAP 3.1. Israel and the territories captured in 1967. *Source*: Author. The author thanks Neil Ketchley for the Sinai Peninsula shape files.

featured large populations made up of refugees from the 1947–49 conflict—and an estimated 65,000 residents of East Jerusalem.[2] The Sinai Peninsula was relatively sparsely populated—Tessler estimates 45,000 to 50,000 in 1967[3]—and was returned to Egypt following the 1979 Camp David Accords and associated peace treaty.

The new territory under Israeli occupation after 1967 comprised three contiguous blocks of land but five distinct territories in terms of the strategic calculus they presented to Israel's leadership. First, was the Sinai Peninsula, a large, sparsely populated stretch of land between Egypt and

Israel that had been part of Egypt. Second, directly northeast of the peninsula along the Mediterranean, was the Gaza Strip. Gaza was a far more densely populated strip of territory, only one hundred forty square miles, with a population largely comprising Palestinian refugees who had fled or departed Israel in the 1948–49 war.[4] Third, at the end of the 1967 war, Israel came to control the eastern half of the city of Jerusalem, including the site holiest to the Jewish people, the Temple Mount (*Haram al-Sharif*), where the second Jewish temple was believed to have stood before it was destroyed by the Romans. Fourth, to the east of Jerusalem was the West Bank, which also contained a number of sites of biblical significance to the Jewish people. Finally, Israel won the Golan Heights from Syria, in which several thousand Syrians remained at the end of the war, only a small fraction of the pre-war population.[5]

While the Sinai Peninsula and Golan Heights were never part of historic Palestine—and the former was returned to the Egyptian state after 1979—the West Bank, Gaza Strip, and East Jerusalem came to form an increasingly central focus of the Israeli-Palestinian conflict after 1967. Almost immediately after the war, Israel enlarged the municipal boundaries of Jerusalem to effectively annex the eastern half of the city, explicitly signaling its intention to secure the holy sites on the Temple Mount as part of the Jewish state.[6] The Israeli military maintained control of the West Bank, Gaza Strip, and, initially, the Sinai Peninsula. In particular, the status of the West Bank and Gaza Strip became one of open-ended military occupation.

The West Bank presented a unique dilemma: on one hand, religious and symbolic attachments to the territory ran deep in Israeli society. Further, the territory's fertile Jordan Valley and the inner hills and mountains provided strategic and economic benefits. Yet, full absorption of the territory would dilute the Jewish demographic advantage in Israel, not to mention that guerrilla attacks against Israel were already emanating from PLO bases in nearby Jordan. As Ariella Azoulay and Adi Ophir describe, the Israeli military and intelligence apparatus were more ready for this moment than may have first appeared.[7] Two years before the war, a set of military training courses was convened "for reservists who had served in the military administration ruling Palestinian citizens inside Israel, as well as for [intelligence] agents."[8] Revealing that Israel acknowledged the importance of local Palestinian political actors in the success or failure of the occupation, the course included pragmatic steps for "the immediate activation of local institutions and services, location of local leadership that would help return life to its normal course and handling possible religious strife."[9] From 1967 until 1977, left-wing parties, which united to form the Labor Party in 1968, controlled the Israeli government. In the 1969 elections, the Labor-led Alignment list demonstrated its dominance in Israel's multiparty system by almost obtaining an outright majority of seats.

The mood in Israel following the 1967 war has been described as euphoric. While Labor Zionists had historically attached themselves to maximalist conceptions of the whole "Land of Israel" (to the Jordan River in the east and, before that, even the East Bank), the movement had evolved, according to Nadav Shelef, to accept the 1949 armistice lines as Israel's stable borders, within which a Jewish majority could be maintained. Shelef explains,

> For the Labor movement, the result of the 1967 war disrupted whatever process of routinization and adaptation to the 1949 borders might have been taking place. Labor Zionists now came face to face with the trade-off between maintaining control of the entire land of Israel that they aspired to and the cherished Zionist goal of a Jewish majority state. The ideal outcome for most within the movement was control of the land without integrating the Arabs there into the Israeli population. As Golda Meir put it, 'Every one of us' wants 'the dowry without the bride'."[10]

While Jewish settlement of the newly occupied West Bank began under the post-1967 Labor governments, the party eventually staked out a position that opposed annexation and defended the 1949 boundaries, which, it was argued, could best sustain a Jewish and democratic state. However, in the early years after the 1967 conquests, Gershom Gorenberg describes the ruling coalition as painfully divided.[11] As he recounts, just one day after the war, Defense Minister Moshe Dayan went on record to declare his support for keeping Gaza and the West Bank under Israeli control with some form of "autonomy" for West Bank Palestinians. Yisrael Galili from the United Kibbutz Party concurred that Palestinians in the West Bank should not be given citizenship, while Dayan proposed that Israel retain control over defense and foreign affairs. Predictably, Menachem Begin, then part of the unity government but representing the right-wing Gahal party, favored annexation of the territories "while putting off the inconvenient decision on the status of its Arab residents."[13] Yet another plan emerged from Yigal Allon, which was unique in proposing partition of the West Bank into a Palestinian state in the northern West Bank, with Israel retaining control of the Jordan Valley and southern Hebron, which would be rapidly settled.[13]

Diana Buttu critiques Gorenberg's contention that the approach of Israel's government in 1967 was "accidental," as the title of his book suggests, rather than the result of a planned strategy.[14] Indeed, as the Israeli settlements grew and Israel contemplated future negotiations on a peace deal with Egypt, Labor leaders often refused to openly embrace the country's pre-1967 borders. For example, in a 1972 interview, Prime Minister Golda Meir stated unambiguously, "One basic article in Israel's policy is that the borders of the fourth of June [the prewar, 1949 boundaries] cannot be re-established in the peace agreement. There must be changes in the border. We want changes in borders, on all our borders, for security's sake."[15]

Ultimately, the majority of government ministers coalesced around a position of maintaining the territories while postponing any decisions on "autonomy" or any other form of political concession to the vexing Palestinian population in the West Bank. Jewish settlement in the territories gained in 1967 began almost immediately under Prime Minister Levi Eshkol. While some of the first establishments in the West Bank were military bases in the Jordan Valley that were presumably defensive in nature, Israeli military personnel came along with these establishments. Etzion Bloc, just south of Jerusalem, was another area of early settlement, "redeemed" by the second-generation descendants of those who had been killed or displaced there in confrontations with Arab armies in 1948, but the settlement was packaged by the government as another military installation to minimize alarm.[16] The Eshkol government's framing of even those early settlements, which were clearly residential in nature, as "outposts" or as part of a larger military strategy may have been done as much to convince themselves of the impermanency of the settlements and their limited nature as it was to convince international audiences.

In sum, it was a Labor government that came to militarily control the territories, and thus it was a Labor government that deployed its military and state resources toward managing the new territory along with its Palestinian population. This was done, primarily and almost entirely, through the military itself. On June 7, 1967, on gaining full control of the territory, the Israeli commander of the West Bank campaign issued its first proclamation, declaring military rule over the region in the name of "security and public order."[17] Thus, under Labor, the occupation of the West Bank proceeded via martial law.

The occupation was almost entirely unmediated—and thus we could characterize Israel's initial approach as a largely direct form of rule; however, it was important for Israel to maintain Palestinian-run municipalities from the beginning. As Moshe Ma'oz states, "according to Israeli official thinking, the major *non-political* institution in the West Bank which could serve as an infrastructure for social, economic, and administrative activity and could facilitate *normalization* of life was municipal government."[18] The emphasis I added here demonstrates the underlying logic of the occupation, wherein municipal governance could be divorced from national resistance.

It is notable that Israel did not seek to abolish municipal councils—as it did with the Jordanian city council in East Jerusalem shortly after the war—although it did repeatedly attempt to coopt institutions of local governance in the West Bank. In any event, there is no evidence that Israeli political or military leaders ever advocated for incorporating these municipal institutions more wholly into the Israeli state or for supplanting these institutions with new, more "Israeli" ones. Initially, the Israeli administration in the West Bank sought to maintain allegiances with the traditional, pro-Jordanian rulers. Because Israeli bureaucratic presence in areas of civil governance was limited, Palestinian municipal institutions in the West Bank began to fill some of the gaps. Municipalities were responsible for providing basic services; however, with regard to the centrality of land and territory in the conflict, their role in zoning, planning, and development was limited.[19] Municipalities in these first years of occupation were sometimes venues that bred political polarization and infighting. While some mayors were dogged by accusations of corruption and inappropriate use of municipal resources, Ma'oz also reveals how the municipality's role as a mediating institution between the Israeli occupation and the Palestinian population introduced tensions, often between mayors and their fellow municipal council members, breeding distrust.[20]

As the Palestinian nationalist movement gained ground in the occupied territories, municipal governments became a base on which the Palestinian resistance movement could coalesce. Following the war, the PLO had emerged as the most prominent organization advocating for liberation of Palestine. Beginning in 1969, the organization was headed by Yasser Arafat and his Fatah party. Under Arafat, the Palestinian national movement both inspired and mirrored other nationalist movements of the time throughout Latin America, Africa, and Asia. Following the Cuban Revolution and the Algerian War of independence, these movements drew on the revolutionary philosophies and tactics of Mao Tse-tung, Che Guevara, Frantz Fanon, and others in the fight for decolonization and national liberation. The transformation of Palestinian national identity that started to occur toward the end of Jordanian rule in the West Bank is aptly summarized by Rashid Khalidi: "The ascendancy in the 1950s and 1960s of the leaders of Fateh [sic], along with the rise of other competing militant groups, represented a thoroughgoing generational change and a striking alteration in the image presented by those who represented the Palestinians. It involved a shift from the domination of Palestinian politics by sober men in their fifties and sixties wearing suits and red tarbushes . . . to the leadership of militants in their twenties and thirties wearing short-sleeved shirts and military fatigues."[21]

In 1976, Israel permitted local elections in the West Bank, and many Palestinian nationalist candidates affiliated with the PLO swept into victory, advocating resistance against the Israeli occupation and continued struggle for national self-determination. This new cohort of mayors—including Bassam Shaka'a, who was profiled in the introduction to this volume—positioned themselves confidently as political figures, not depoliticized service providers. Ma'oz attributes the reduction in conflict between municipal council members to the ascent of this new generation of nationalist mayors: "It is true that rifts and rivalries continued to occur in town councils even after the 1976 elections. . . . Yet in comparison with the previous years, the number of such internal conflicts was significantly low. The major reason for this improvement was the emergence of a new young town leadership with a cohesive ideological basis converting the town councils into *political* power centers in order to fulfill important *national* goals."[22]

The 1976 municipal elections experiment demonstrated that mayors chosen by the Palestinian people themselves would not serve as reliable intermediaries in Israel's occupation regime. The empowerment of these local nationalist leaders—like Shaka'a, Karim Khalaf of Ramallah, and Ibrahim Tawil of Al-Bireh—did not last long. As described in the introductory chapter, several of these elected mayors were targeted in assassination attempts by the Jewish Underground in 1980. By 1982, all elected mayors had been replaced by appointed leaders amid a climate of increasing Israeli repression of Palestinian nationalists. In 1984, Israel's High Court of Justice upheld a decision by the military administration to ban local elections in the West Bank.

Israel's policies in the territories—its settlement policies, its construction of roads and infrastructure, and the restrictions it put in place to limit Palestinian access to Israeli labor markets—meant that Palestinian areas became geographically and, over time, increasingly economically isolated from Israeli areas. Practically, this meant that the systems of local governance of the Palestinian- and Israeli-populated areas also functioned as relatively distinct from each other. What the experiments such as the 1976 municipal elections show is that Israel was willing to pilot strategies in which Palestinians were granted some degree of local self-governance, and these experiments, while risky, were seen at the time as preferable to direct rule by the Israeli civil apparatus at the local level. Another component of this strategy, the largely unsuccessful "Village Leagues," will be discussed in the following sections.

1977–1984: TERRITORIAL MAXIMALISM

The year 1977 brought a dramatic shift in Israeli politics, with a right-wing, non-Labor government coming to power for the first time, soon under the leadership of Likud. This represented the ascendance of a revisionist Zionist conception that was territorially maximalist and resulted in a far more detailed and aggressive settlement promotion policy in the West Bank than had been seen previously. Settlement of the West Bank evolved from small-scale strategic and religious establishments to a state-directed strategy of altering the demographic landscape and increasing Jewish Israeli claims on the territory through outright expropriation, purchase, and "legal redefinitions."[23] While there were just over one thousand settlers in 1972,[24] there were more than twenty thousand by the end of 1982, with much of this growth occurring after 1977.[25] Prime Minister Menachem Begin's government also expanded the geographic reach of settlements into areas abutting Palestinian towns and villages, thus making security and resource distribution to these settler populations more complex.[26] The steady growth in the Jewish settler population in the West Bank was an intentional policy of the government itself; in turn, it shaped the government's calculus vis-à-vis the territories with each passing day and consequently what the relationship was to be between the Israeli state and the occupied Palestinian population.

Much has been written about, and ascribed to, the central role of Begin, the former leader of the Revisionist Irgun who assumed the office of prime minister in 1977. It is not possible to recapitulate the entirety of his biography here. What seems uncontroversial to assert is that Likud was motivated by a different "national ethos"[27] regarding the relative importance of the territorial versus the ethnic imperative—a return to the territory of the greater Land of Israel was paramount. In December 1977, Begin put forward a Palestinian autonomy plan in negotiations with Egyptian president Anwar Sadat that was ultimately incorporated into the Camp David Accords; that plan included a component that dealt specifically with the fate of the Palestinian territories, which vaguely called for the establishment of a Palestinian self-governing entity that would achieve "full autonomy" within a five-year transitional period.

Consensus is reflected in the scholarship on Begin's plan that "autonomy as conceived by Likud applies only to the people of the occupied territories and not to the land."[28] Similarly, Tessler notes that "Likud and its supporters pointed out that the language agreed to at Camp David offered autonomy not to the West Bank and Gaza but rather to their inhabitants, which meant, these Israelis insisted, that the 'full autonomy' promised to the Palestinians was personal and local rather than territorial."[29] Interestingly, the interpretation of Camp David from the left was that it granted too much room for Palestinian self-determination and ultimately would leave Israel no choice but to permit the creation of a Palestinian nation-state, which the Labor party still did not support.[30]

Additional evidence can be found in the Camp David Accords that no matter the form of Palestinian autonomy that might result from future negotiations, the foremost priority of any governance arrangement would be the security of "Israel and its neighbors," and a Palestinian police force, constructed by the future self-governing authority, was to "maintain liaison on internal security matters with the designated Israeli, Jordanian, and Egyptian officers."[31] It is telling that Israel saw its security interests in the territories as overlapping to a sufficient degree with Egypt's own security interests that they could agree to some common language on this topic. On the other hand, the security concerns of the Palestinian self-governing authority—or, more importantly, of Palestinians themselves—was not believed to merit formal recognition in this preliminary agreement. This fundamental orientation of the "security" discourse—emphasizing the security of Israel and Israelis while neglecting the security of Palestinians—reappeared in subsequent direct Israeli-Palestinian negotiations and the final documents at Oslo. That had important implications for those Palestinian coercive institutions that did and did not emerge.

In the absence of any discussion of Palestinian territorial autonomy, Israel implemented a bureaucratic reform to its institutions in the West Bank in 1981, which, while it did not dramatically alter facts on the ground for Palestinians or for Israeli settlers, was notable at least for its rhetorical implications. At this time, Israel created the Civil Administration (CIVAD) as a separate branch, still under Israeli military and ultimately the portfolio of the Minister of Defense, but meant to represent the Israeli state in matters of "civil" governance within the Palestinian communities of the West Bank and Gaza. The changes proved to be largely cosmetic: CIVAD did not entail an extension of Israeli political institutions to the Palestinian population; in fact, Palestinians simply saw it as occupation by another name. As described by Ian Lustick, CIVAD was subsumed within the command structure of the Israel Defense Forces.[32] While some of those Israelis interacting with Palestinians in the West Bank may have worn a different uniform, the Israeli state's structures of control in the territory did not demonstrably change.

In 1983, just over two years after elections that saw a divided electorate give Likud a narrow plurality, Begin retired from public life and Yitzhak Shamir took over as prime minister. The talks on Palestinian autonomy that ensued after Camp David fell apart, with the Israeli war against the PLO in Lebanon absorbing relatively more attention. In an interview by Shamir with *Ma'ariv* after his 1992 electoral loss, he revealed what many have interpreted to be his insincerity in his approach to the idea of Palestinian autonomy in the West Bank: "I would have carried on autonomy talks for ten years . . . and meanwhile we would have reached half a million people in Judea and Samaria."[33] Lustick marks the 1982–1984 period as a critical transformation in discourse surrounding Israel's incorporation of the occupied territories, noting that treatment of the topic passed the "regime threshold" at this point, such that any discussion of relinquishing the territories was met not just with concern by political incumbents about their or their coalition's fate but also with the threat of a total breakdown in the rule of law and descent into possibly violent civil conflict.[34]

Note that the focus of Israeli policies was shaping Israeli, not Palestinian, beliefs. According to Lustick, the intent was "to reshape the cognitive map of Israeli[s] to conform with an image of the country which included the territories as no different from other regions of the state."[35] To do so, an infrastructure was developed that minimized contact or integration with Palestinian Arabs. In some cases, the right-wing maximalists did give at least symbolic nods to a more civic conception of governance in the territories; for example, in 1983 Hannan Porat of the ultranationalist Tehiya party—which was part of Prime Minister Begin's ruling coalition from 1981 to 1984—proposed citizenship for Palestinian Arabs, but only with the admitted assumption that it would never be accepted.[36] In any case, citizenship was never advanced as the government's primary position. Instead, what was more often discussed as an option in this period was annexation with specific reference to the territories of Judea and Samaria, not its population.

While the position of the ruling Likud party under first Begin and then Shamir is now clear, it is also worth emphasizing that the Israeli left, as represented by Labor, did not successfully articulate any inclusive conceptions of annexation. Shelef provides a rich and nuanced discussion of varied conceptions of Israeli, or Zionist, nationalism across three movements—the Labor, Revisionist, and Religious wings of Zionism.[37] While his account offers a powerful argument of how conceptions of the homeland and its membership changed according to an evolutionary dynamic over time, his examination of nationalist discourse vis-à-vis the Palestinians reveals that the latter's membership in the Israeli nation-state never became an ideologically institutionalized view. Importantly, he argues that integration of Palestinians into the territories acquired in 1967 was never seriously promoted within Labor. Somewhat contrary to Mark Tessler's interpretation above, Shelef finds that, on the left, Begin's "autonomy plan" was vociferously "castigated as fostering a binational state because it opened the door for the naturalization of Arabs living in the territories and therefore undermined Israel's Jewish majority."[38] Thus, somewhat unexpectedly, we are left with an image of the right-wing leaders coming closest to articulating a version of political inclusion for Palestinians east of the so-called Green Line (the 1949 armistice line separating Israel and the West Bank). However, even if the label "citizenship" was floated at some point—as surprising as this is—the right wing was careful to never articulate a plan wherein Israeli political institutions would play a central role in serving the Palestinian population.

In the occupied territories themselves, Israel was doing everything it could to repress Palestinian nationalism while maintaining a general state of security and calm for its Jewish residents. While Israel experimented in 1976 with local elections in the territories, as discussed earlier, it pursued a slightly different strategy to maintain compliance in the smaller towns and villages. Israel attempted to divide the rural Palestinian population from the urban nationalists with the creation of the so-called Village Leagues in the early 1980s. These puppet leaderships were largely seen as a failure and often were causes of violence themselves, as they were armed. Tessler writes, "In practice . . . the village leagues were unable to strike roots; aside from gaining the support of some members of their immediate families and clans, the leagues could not claim any substantial constituency."[39]

Thus, in the end, while Israel did delegate—or foist—some governing responsibilities onto local Palestinian actors in the occupied West Bank and Gaza, CIVAD, under the Ministry of Defense still had *de facto* final authority over resources and governance. And while the vast majority of rank-and-file employees of CIVAD were Palestinians, almost all senior positions in the organization were held by Israeli citizens.[40] By the mid-1980s, local elections had been banned in the municipalities and the village leagues were starting to collapse. Israel tried to maintain its tenuous policy toward localities in the West Bank and Gaza. This can be described in general terms as the selective empowerment of Palestinian elites who were willing to work within and/or under the military regime. Popular grievances associated with this process, among other things, fed into the first intifada.

1984–1992: ANNEXATION HITS A WALL

The 1984 elections gave Shamir his official mandate as prime minister, and Likud continued to control the government. Jewish settlement had expanded rapidly in the 1982–1984 period as part of the Likud's suburban settlement drive. The late 1980s were a time of dramatic transformation in both the events on the ground in the Palestinian territories and in the political discourse surrounding them. While Palestinians experienced limited economic benefits in the early years of occupation,[41] ongoing military rule, settlement growth, and economic stagnation fueled frustrations with the lack of progress toward a Palestinian state. Amid this environment, the first intifada, or uprising, broke out in 1987. An estimated twelve hundred

Palestinians were killed, while the Palestinian side maintained a largely unarmed resistance strategy using tactics such as throwing stones as well as staging boycotts, strikes, roadblocks, and nonviolent protests.[42] Despite Israeli rule being fairly direct in nature during the period, it is worth noting that Palestinians were employed in institutions of the occupation, including CIVAD. A prominent activist from the town of Beit Sahour described the decisions that Palestinians had to make at this time amid the national uprising: "People continued working in education and health. . . . The ones who started resigning were the ones working with the police and the finance department. The ones who actually work for the benefit of the government rather than for the benefit of the people."[43]

While the intifada demonstrated the costs of continued occupation to Israel's leadership, no Palestinian organization existed to which Israel could confidently delegate governing responsibility while maintaining its control of the territories. In 1988, Jordan officially relinquished all claims to the West Bank. Israelis' distrust of Palestinian nationalists, such as Fatah and the other groups subsumed under the PLO, was great. Finally, Hamas was formally established in 1988, just as the uprising was getting under way. The organization, discussed in more detail in subsequent chapters, had evolved from a branch of the Muslim Brotherhood based in Gaza—an organization that Israel had initially supported—into the newest front in the Palestinian liberation struggle. (Hamas did not openly compete with Fatah during the intifada, but it would later emerge as its most important rival.) While Hamas was not yet carrying out armed resistance against the occupation, Israel certainly had no intention of delegating formal governing responsibilities to the organization.

In a July 1989 interview with the *Jerusalem Post*, Yossi Ben-Aharon, Prime Minister Shamir's director-general, tellingly described the alternative to Palestinian self-rule that made its way into the discourse of the time—the idea of apartheid-style Bantustans.[44] As far as the Israeli government was concerned, should the Palestinian public throw its support behind the PLO, this segregationist option might be all that remained. Ben-Aharon stated, "I don't want to be patronizing, I don't want to be their guardian and I don't want a Bantustan here. However, I am not willing to chop off my own head in order to prevent the creation of a Bantustan." The full political absorption of Palestinians in the West Bank and Gaza under Israeli rule was not conceived as an alternative strategy for achieving security and control.

The early 1990s were a volatile time for Israeli politics, first with the formation of a narrow right-wing coalition under Shamir in 1990 and, subsequently, the formation of a narrow, left-wing government in 1992.[45] Poll data from 1990 and 1991 show that a plurality of Israeli Jews preferred some kind of federal solution (featuring autonomy, a confederation, or a Jordanian-Palestinian state) or a return of territory via compromise with Jordan.[46] In addition, 12 to 18 percent of respondents preferred the "dovish" approach of separation via the establishment of a Palestinian state, while 10 to 16 percent preferred hawkish annexation. Of those preferring a hawkish approach, at least twice as many preferred annexation with transfer, or expulsion, of Palestinians (6.8 vs. 11.2 percent) as those who preferred full annexation without forced transfer (3.6 vs. 5.1 percent). According to these data, annexation with the full incorporation of Palestinians was a position held by a very small share of Israelis.

1992–1995: CREATING THE PALESTINIAN INTERMEDIARY

During the waning years of the intifada, international powers made a renewed push to bring about a resolution of the broader Arab-Israeli conflict. The multilateral Madrid Conference was launched in 1991, co-convened by the United States and the Soviet Union. This was a time of hardship for Palestinians due to the consequences of the PLO's support for Saddam Hussein in the First Gulf War and the subsequent impact on remittances and aid, as well as high unemployment in the territories.[47] The Madrid process launched unprecedented face-to-face talks between an Israeli and joint Jordanian-Palestinian delegation. These talks were begun under the Shamir government but continued after the 1992 elections saw Prime Minister Yitzhak Rabin come to power on a Labor ticket.

It was not the Madrid process but, rather, the secret negotiations that began the following year in Oslo that precipitated joint recognition between Israel and the PLO and, subsequently, the creation of the PA. The outcomes of the Oslo negotiations—central to the empirical analysis that follows—will be discussed in more detail in chapter 4. However, Israeli discourse from the preceding talks that were part of the Madrid process provide a window into the strategic approach of both Israel and the Palestinians as they began discussing a future for the West Bank and Gaza. For example, as late as December 1992, Ehud Ya'ari, an Israeli journalist and commentator who was present at the Madrid talks, was penning an op-ed titled "It Just Won't Work." One key reason he cites is failure to agree on where the functional authority of the Israeli military and the Palestinian police in the West Bank would begin and end: "Israeli negotiating chief Elyakim Rubinstein has already been asked, but has not answered, this provocative question: 'An armed man is reported to be moving suspiciously at a certain place; it is not known if he is a Jew or an Arab, criminal or terrorist. Who will give chase?'"[48] Further, Rabin was reportedly "heckled by opposition members in parliament . . . when he said it would be up to the Palestinian police force to suppress violence in the occupied territories."[49] In addition to the consistent distrust of autonomous Palestinian coercive agents, territorial delineations of authority also continued to present important challenges to the negotiators. One interesting example was the lasting dispute over the size of the town of Jericho—even after the town was included in the earliest agreement ("Gaza-Jericho First")—about where the PA should be able to exercise its rule.[50] In sum, due to Israel's territorial aims, the issue of Palestinian coercive capacity and questions about the geographic reach of Palestinian authority continued to be important constraints on negotiations over Palestinian self-governance.

While different sets of negotiators were present for the Oslo Accords— indeed, distinct teams negotiated the two components of the accords themselves—the early discussions that occurred as part of the Madrid talks shed light on the maximal acceptable position that the left-leaning Israeli government was able to adopt as far as self-rule for Palestinians in the West Bank. Notably, securitizing Palestinian communities was key—as it had been earlier in the Camp David Accords—and the possibility of externally facing (i.e., defensive) institutions for the Palestinians was all but precluded given the starting point of the Israeli delegation.

The Oslo Accords established the main institutional features of the new regime of indirect rule. The first of the two agreements signed ("Oslo I," or the Declaration of Principles) was formally celebrated with Israeli Prime Minister Rabin and PLO Chairman Arafat shaking hands on the White House lawn. It included mutual recognition between Israel and the PLO while also calling for the establishment of a "Palestinian interim self-government" in the West Bank and Gaza Strip, which would last for a transitional period "not exceeding five years." During this time, Israel and the PLO were meant to settle areas of continued dispute, such as final borders, security, the status of Jerusalem, the future of Israeli settlements, and the status of Palestinian refugees.

As a result of the agreements, the Palestinian Authority was formed in 1994–95 to assume some governing authority in Palestinian communities under Israeli occupation, moving first into the West Bank city of Jericho and then the Gaza Strip. Functionally, the PA was constrained according to the letter of the agreements. For example, while the PA was allowed to set its own tax rates on certain quantities of imported goods from specific countries, most other customs taxes, purchase taxes, value-added taxes, and gasoline prices could not fall below Israeli rates. Furthermore, because no geographic borders were established, Israel was tasked with collecting trade and sales taxes on goods destined for the Palestinian territories and transferring those revenues to the PA, minus a fee that Israel extracted. The Israeli currency (the New Israeli Shekel, NIS) was established as required legal tender in the territories and thus continued to be the *de facto* currency (although the Jordanian dinar was still used for certain legal transactions in the West Bank, and the Egyptian pound played a similar, secondary role in Gaza). The PA was prohibited from introducing its own currency without mutual agreement with Israel.

Most importantly for the analysis here, Israel's exclusive annexation strategy, combined with the geographic proximity of Palestinian communities to Israeli settlements, military bases, and state-appropriated land, meant that the PA's geographic authority was also not uniform. Article 12 of the Interim Agreement stresses that "Israel shall continue to carry the responsibility for defense against external threats . . . as well as the responsibility for overall security of Israelis and Settlements."[51] The PA was barred from developing any externally facing armed forces. In the West Bank in particular, the second formal agreement to come out of these accords ("Oslo II") introduced complex geographic variation in the authority of the Palestinian security forces over Palestinian territory. The PA was given more policing authority in some localities, while in others Palestinian police presence had to be coordinated with Israel or was effectively prohibited. In the latter portions of the West Bank, the coercive authorities and actions of the Israel Defense Forces, Border Police, intelligence apparatus, and security contractors was unmediated.

Oslo II assigned all territory in the West Bank to one of three noncontiguous zones. The zones, depicted in map 4.1, can be summarized as follows:

- Area A, where the PA has authority over civil governance and internal security;
- Area B, where the PA has authority over civil governance, but authority over internal security is shared with Israel; and
- Area C, where Israel has full authority over civil governance and internal security.

According to Oslo II, Area C, subject to continued negotiations as a "permanent status" issue, was to be "gradually transferred to Palestinian jurisdiction." Following the Oslo Accords, Israel made several small transfers of land from Area C to Area B and from Area B to Area A, but additional transfers were halted with the outbreak of the second intifada. Thus, by 2000, Area A constituted 18 percent of the territory of the West Bank and includes most of what had been the geographic footprint of the built-up areas of major Palestinian cities, in addition to a number of small- and medium-sized towns. Area B made up approximately 22 percent of the West Bank and includes many additional small- and medium-sized Palestinian towns and many villages. Finally, 60 percent of the territory of the West Bank falls into Area C; it contains the Jordan valley, hundreds of thousands of Palestinians living in villages and Bedouin encampments, and the extant Israeli settlements and land designated for settlement expansion.[52]

The accords codified a nominally transitional arrangement. However, in the years that followed, Palestinians won no greater authority over territory, while the geographic footprints of both Palestinian populated areas and Israeli settlements continued to expand, placing them in ever closer proximity to one another.

1995-2005: DESCENT INTO VIOLENCE

After the signing of the Oslo Accords, official-level Israeli-Palestinian relations gradually degraded, as no additional territory was ceded to the PA and settlements grew unabated, protected by Israel's military regime. In November 1995, Prime Minister Yitzhak Rabin was assassinated by a Jewish extremist who opposed the agreements signed with the Palestinians. Benjamin Netanyahu was chosen as prime minister in 1996 after Likud emerged as the dominant party from the Knesset elections; he had run on a campaign that had been highly critical of the accords.

The late 1990s saw an increase in violent attacks by Palestinians against Israeli targets. Prime Minister Ehud Barak and PLO Chairman Arafat failed to reach a deal at the Camp David Summit of 2000. The second intifada—also known as the *al-Aqsa Intifada*—erupted in September 2000 following a highly politicized visit to Jerusalem's holy Temple Mount by Likud Party leader Ariel Sharon, which resulted in widespread protests. Sharon then became prime minister in 2001 amid an uprising that engulfed major cities in Israel, Jerusalem, the West Bank, and Gaza.

The second intifada was a devastating period for both Israelis and Palestinians, with a number of suicide attacks against Israeli civilian targets, including clubs, restaurants, and public buses, that killed hundreds of Israelis, and with major Israeli military incursions into Palestinian cities. Israeli combat forces used tanks, heavy artillery, and military helicopters in the West Bank and Gaza, which resulted in the deaths of more than three thousand Palestinian civilians. During this time, Israel also began construction of its barrier separating Palestinian communities in the West Bank from Israel. The barrier—in some places a thirty-foot-high concrete wall and in others, a nest of barbed wire fencing—tracks east of the Green Line, thus trapping sections of the occupied West Bank on the Israeli side of the wall.

During the uprising, the geographic divisions that had granted the PA some autonomy and limited self-rule within Palestinian populated areas of the West Bank evaporated with the Israeli reoccupation of major Area A cities, including Ramallah, Nablus, Bethlehem, and Jenin. In Jenin, which had reportedly been a site of Palestinian militant planning, Israel's military used infantry, helicopters, and bulldozers to decimate large sections of the city's refugee camp, killing scores of Palestinian civilians.

As such, the period of the second intifada (2000–5) can be viewed as one in which Israel's indirect-rule regime—wherein Israel relied on delegating governance and certain security tasks to the new PA—broke down. During this time, PA offices and ministries were targeted by Israel, Israel laid siege to PA President Arafat's compound in Ramallah, and PA security personnel joined in gunfights against the Israeli military.

The uprising and ensuing conflict also took an immense toll on the Palestinian economy. Economic conditions were poor before the second intifada; Salem Ajluni quotes International Monetary Fund (IMF) estimates showing that "by the year 2000, after seven years of the Oslo process and more than five years after the establishment of the PA, per capita income levels in the OPT [occupied Palestinian Territories] were estimated to be about 10 percent below their pre-Oslo level."[53] The author further notes, "per capita income declined by about 23 percent in the first fifteen months of the crisis," while he estimates, based on IMF growth expectations and population growth rates, "in constant 1997 prices, the cumulative lost income-earning opportunities in the OPT during twenty-seven months [were] estimated at $4.8 billion, or more than 70 percent of what the GNI might have been in 2002 in the no crisis scenario. In other words, the loss [was] nearly equal to the Palestinian GDP in 1999."[54] (69). That does not include the costs of infrastructure damage, estimated to be in the hundreds of millions of dollars, due to Israeli incursions.

During this period, daily realities for Palestinians in the West Bank versus those living in the Gaza Strip began to diverge dramatically. In 2005, under Prime Minister Sharon, Israel began a unilateral withdrawal of its settlements from Gaza. Hamas and other groups that embraced armed struggle as an alternative to negotiations portrayed this as a victory.

Following the 2004 death of PA president and PLO chairman Arafat, Palestinians in the occupied territories turned a new page as they readied for elections for their new leadership. On the heels of several years of traumatic violence, repression, and closure, Palestinians prepared for municipal-level elections—to be held in several rounds, beginning in December 2004 and concluding in December 2005—and presidential and legislative elections in 2005 and 2006, respectively. The legislative elections resulted in a conclusive victory for Hamas, a major and dramatic reorientation of Palestinian politics, and the violent separation of what would become a Hamas-ruled Gaza Strip and a Fatah-ruled West Bank. It is in this environment that we will study how indirect rule was reconstituted in the West Bank and what opportunities and challenges it provided for Palestinian opponents of the status quo regime.

The preceding historical review shows that successive Israeli governments adopted strikingly different rhetoric toward the West Bank and were motivated by fundamentally different strands of Zionist ideology in their views of what the optimal future would hold. Nonetheless, within this fraught and divisive discourse, the contours of what would be possible for governing institutions in the West Bank were established. In particular, the upper bound on what autonomy would look like should the Israelis maintain their comparatively greater leverage in future talks was set by Labor Zionism and leftists' inability to advocate for a full Palestinian state or even a Palestinian entity that involved an autonomous Palestinian military or police force. The lower bound, on the other hand, was protected by the position of Likud and both secular and religious Zionists on the right, who—somewhat ironically—produced the more detailed picture of what autonomy could look like but who thus restricted the concept to something personal, or local, rather than territorial.

The lack of a territorial basis for autonomy continued to preoccupy Palestinian negotiators throughout the Madrid process. The territorial agreement that was ultimately reached with Oslo II in 1995 surprised many of the negotiators who were involved in earlier rounds of talks. The delineation of zones of authority in the West Bank—Areas A, B, and C—represented a new twist on the discussions, and the variation in Palestinian policing capacity that was introduced across these zones was a complexity that has no parallel in any other modern self-determination conflict. Yet, as we can see from the discussion in this chapter, it is clear that both functional and geographic restrictions on Palestinian coercive authority were a high priority for Israeli delegations and that this concern, or fear, is rooted in earlier positions adopted by Israeli governments from both ends of the political spectrum. Furthermore, the second intifada and its aftermath demonstrated that the Israeli military and coercive apparatus was able to fully reoccupy Palestinian localities the West Bank when the incentives were great enough, including overriding the PA's territorial autonomy in major Palestinian cities. After the second intifada, opponents of the indirect rule regime in the West Bank found other ways to advance their programs. One critical, understudied avenue was that of municipal government.

Chapter Four

PALESTINIAN LOCAL GOVERNMENT UNDER ISRAELI INDIRECT RULE

Quantitative Findings

As the second intifada receded and Palestinians in the occupied territories began to pick up the pieces and rebuild, a fundamentally different political reality began to take shape. First, following the death of the iconic PLO and PA leader Yasser Arafat in November 2004, a set of local and national elections in the occupied territories revealed the sharpening ideological divisions between Fatah—the party that Arafat built—and its opponents. The latter included, most prominently, the Islamic resistance group Hamas but also secular leftists, smaller Islamist parties, and independent activists and politicians. Second, Israel began to transform its coercive regime across the occupied territories as the uprising came to an end. In the Gaza Strip, Israel evacuated all its settlers in August and September 2005, inviting political upheaval in Israel; yet, that action ultimately resulted in a reformulation of Israeli military control over the 1.3 million Palestinians living in the densely packed enclave.

In the West Bank, Israel reconstituted features of the indirect rule regime, with a renewed emphasis on a disciplined and restructured PA internal security apparatus. Israel's security coordination with the Fatah-led PA was slowly revived. European donors worked closely with the civil police, while the PA security and intelligence apparatus was overhauled under the watchful guidance of a new U.S.-led team. In the words of the U.S. security coordinator at the time, Lieutenant General Keith Dayton, the goals of the reform program were "to allay *Israeli fears* about the nature and capabilities of the Palestinian security forces" and to "make them accountable to the leadership of the Palestinian people whom they serve."[1]

Thus, the historical and political context of this chapter is one that witnessed a deepening of collaboration—particularly in the realm of policing and security—between Israel (the "principal") and the Fatah-affiliated PA leadership (Israel's desired "agent") in the West Bank. At the same time, the post-uprising period was one in which Fatah faced increasingly prominent political opposition, which undermined its popular legitimacy. Between December 2004 and December 2005, during this time of enhanced collaboration with Israel and tenuous political support for Fatah, the Palestinian Authority held competitive multiparty elections for local offices across the West Bank and Gaza. For the first time, local politicians who did not identify with Fatah—and who, in many cases, vocally opposed its rule— were elected to municipal councils and into mayorships in cities and towns across the West Bank.

While the local polls passed without much international attention, the PA presidential and parliamentary elections in 2005 and 2006, respectively, were seen as ground-shifting. In January 2005, presidential elections brought Mahmoud Abbas into power as successor to Arafat. Abbas, long associated with Fatah's more moderate wing, was sometimes critical of Palestinian armed struggle. Thus, Israel and Western donors expected that he might be easier to work with than his predecessor. However, Abbas's ability to maintain the PA's alignment with Israel's objectives became much more complicated when, in the January 2006 elections for the Palestinian Legislative Council, Hamas won a majority of seats.

The elections commanded international attention. Hamas's victory precipitated a temporary freeze in international donor support for the PA, a period of armed conflict between Fatah and Hamas, and Hamas's seizure of Gaza in June 2007, cementing a new level of both political and geographic division in Palestinian politics.[2] The fractures within the national movement had been evident for some time, but the series of elections between December 2004 and January 2006 and, ultimately, the violent split in Palestinian institutions between Gaza and the West Bank (*al-Inqisam*), thrust them into the spotlight.

Therefore, the two macro-level conditions just described—increasing top-down investments in Israel's coercive intermediary in the West Bank, combined with rising bottom-up political challenges to Fatah, the Palestinian party engaged in this collaboration—capture a colonial indirect rule regime at a particular political crossroads. Using an inductive approach, in the present chapter and the one that follows, I develop theoretical propositions of how local politicians govern their communities in such a setting. One of the first questions I address with my dataset is: Where were opponents of Fatah more likely to win control? Subsequently, both here and in chapter 5 I ask: Once in office, did mayors affiliated with Fatah, the regime intermediary, govern differently than those mayors who had challenged them?

In the present chapter, I introduce a municipal-level dataset featuring originally coded results of the 2004–5 elections, capturing where Fatah versus its challengers (Hamas, small parties, and independents) won control of local office across the West Bank. I find, among other things, that Hamas was more likely to win more populated towns that were more economically marginalized, as reflected in employment rates and housing supply. After the elections, some opposition mayors were able to serve their entire terms, while others were incrementally pressured to resign or ousted. Thus, the dataset also captures this variation over time in the duration of opposition mayors' terms.

To facilitate the study of how intermediaries and opponents governed locally, the dataset includes detailed budgetary variables from 107 municipalities between 2006 and 2012, representing the fiscal and distributive capacities of local governments. It also includes geo-referenced variables to measure the policing capacity of the Palestinian Authority, a key feature of the indirect rule regime. I provide motivation for considering this variation in PA coercive capacity as local-level differences in the visibility of the indirect rule regime—and Fatah's essential role in it—to Palestinian constituents. In addition, a set of variables capture some basic socioeconomic characteristics of the municipalities.

I find that greater PA policing capacity is associated with increased local revenue collection and revenue growth, but these fiscal benefits are concentrated in towns governed by regime opponents. In areas of greater PA coercive authority, Fatah's control of local government results in *less* revenue collection than if the opposition were in control. These findings suggest that the regime's delegation of policing to Fatah, as the Palestinian intermediary, has not spurred Fatah, as an organization, to build local fiscal capacity.

Additionally, while overall revenue collection from punitive fines is low across municipalities, I find that, averaging over the seven-year period, Fatah-led towns mobilize *less* revenue per capita from fines than towns under opposition control. Looking at change over time, municipality-years with mayors affiliated with Hamas, in particular, appear to exhibit *greater* year-to-year revenue growth than their Fatah-governed or independently governed counterparts. Finally, on spending, Fatah-led towns are more likely to run deficits driven by spending on utilities (electricity and water). This distributive spending is concentrated in towns where Fatah's role as regime intermediary is least visible (as captured by the share of the municipality's land located in Area C).

The empirical material from this chapter (quantitative) and the next chapter (qualitative) are used to develop the overarching theory of this manuscript: Namely, that indirect rule introduces reputation costs for regime intermediaries, which condition how they and their affiliates approach governance at the local level. For example, it may mean forbearing from unpopular governing tasks (e.g., revenue collection) that are not prioritized by the dominant power while attempting to sustain political support through certain forms of distributive spending. Opponents of the regime, on the other hand, may face greater resource constraints, requiring them to increase their efforts to generate revenues locally. My findings suggest that these efforts are most successful where the intermediary's collaboration with the dominant power is most visible and, thus, where the opponent's legitimacy advantage over the intermediary is greatest. Further, these results suggest that, absent external support, regime opponents may be required to exercise more discipline over distributive spending.

Chapter 5 will integrate field-based insights from present and former mayors, municipal council members, and municipal staff from across the West Bank. As will be shown in the next chapter, testimonials from interviews support the proposition that (a) raising revenue from constituents is controversial under military occupation, (b) regime intermediaries are more likely to exercise forbearance in areas where they have more functional autonomy, and (c) opposition actors have to resort to creative measures to mobilize and conserve resources. However, the conversations documented in chapter 5 demonstrate the complications and nuances inherent in local relationships between "intermediaries" and "opponents", as I have defined them. In fact, these labels can be more blurry and ambiguous than the empirical categorization in this chapter suggests.

The rest of the present chapter is structured as follows. First, I describe my dataset in some detail. I begin with the two main independent variables in my analysis: the extent of Palestinian policing capacity possessed by Fatah, the regime intermediary, and the political affiliation of the municipal government. My theoretical expectation is that these two variables—because they are intimately tied to the nature of the indirect rule regime and Israel-PA cooperation—may causally impact the activities and priorities of Palestinian municipal governments. Next, I introduce the dependent variables, which measure various types of revenues and expenditures and, thus, provide a fairly detailed picture of the activities and outputs of municipal governments. Subsequently, I briefly describe several additional variables used to capture the socioeconomic profile of the towns and cities in my dataset. I then employ multivariate regression analysis to produce the chapter's main findings regarding the correlations and possible causal relationships between Palestinian policing capacity, which roughly captures the visibility of the Israel-PA indirect rule regime, the political affiliation of municipal leaders, and municipal governance outcomes in the towns and cities of the West Bank. The concluding section summarizes these insights, setting the stage for the qualitative exploration of these relationships in chapter 5.

POLICING CAPACITY

Policing capacity—what I have also referred to as noneconomic internal coercive capacity—is the primary area of cooperation between Israel and the central Palestinian Authority government based in Ramallah. As described in chapter 1, by internal coercive capacity, I mean the *de facto* ability of authorities to display and use dominant coercive force within territory and among populations under their control. This often takes the form of policing populated areas, but it also includes related capacities such as intelligence gathering and projecting coercive presence over territory. The dominant coercive power throughout the occupied Palestinian Territories is Israel. However, the selective allocation of responsibility for policing, security, and intelligence within populated Palestinian areas of the West Bank is a central plank of the regime of indirect rule, and new energy was invested in this collaborative relationship following the second intifada and the 2006 Palestinian legislative elections.

As described in chapter 3, the Oslo Accords restricted Palestinian policing capacity both geographically and functionally. The PA was not permitted to possess a military; all its coercive capacity was directed internally, toward Palestinian towns and cities. Furthermore, the Interim Agreement (Oslo II) divided the West Bank into three areas: Area A, approximately 18 percent of the territory of the West Bank, where the PA had the greatest (in relative terms) amount of authority over internal policing; Area B, approximately 22 percent of the territory, where the PA was required to formally coordinate policing and security matters with Israel; and Area C, about 60 percent of the territory, where the PA was not permitted to project any coercive authority. Among other things, these divisions meant that Palestinians living in some parts of the West Bank would regularly encounter Palestinian police, while Palestinians in other areas would rarely see any coercive agents other than the Israeli military, police, or security contractors in their communities.

While the entirety of the West Bank is under military occupation, the restrictions on PA policing outside Area A represented *de jure* and *de facto* limitations on the PA's policing capacity during the period of analysis. Entrances to Area A are clearly marked (see figure 4.1). Importantly, the Israeli military does enter Area A to conduct home raids and arrests, often in the middle of the night or very early in the morning. During the second intifada, preceding the period of my analysis, Israeli forces reinvaded major Palestinian cities in Area A. Thus, these area designations do not necessarily signify a large difference in Palestinians' lived experiences with Israeli coercion. However, a crucial component of the occupation during the 2006–2012 period was that day-to-day policing of Palestinian communities in Area A was conducted by the PA. Although the PA has a number of police stations in Area B, police units based at these stations must coordinate with Israeli authorities to deploy outside a restricted radius, which can sometimes take hours.[3] Thus, for example, confrontations between Israeli settlers and Palestinian residents in these areas are handled, if at all, by Israeli authorities. Outside Area A, the authority of the Palestinian security apparatus is more contingent and readily restricted by Israel.[4]

Survey data from more recent years than the period of analysis support the inference that Palestinian populations in Area A experience security differently from those outside it. Interestingly, a set of polls carried out in 2016 found that Palestinians living outside Area A—particularly those in the portion of the city of Hebron fully controlled by Israel ("H2") and those in the neighborhoods of Jerusalem that are severed from the city by

FIGURE 4.1. Sign showing the entrance to Area A. *Source*: David McWilliam.

the separation barrier—had lower overall perceptions of personal security than those in Area A.[5] These polls also demonstrate that 11 percent or less of respondents residing outside Area A believe that the PA police provides protection from Israeli settler attacks or army incursions. Further, less than 50 percent of respondents outside Area A reported seeing Palestinian police officers in the two months preceding the surveys.[6]

Israeli and PA coercive institutions in the West Bank operate at the central government level; Israeli coercive actors that operate in the West Bank are under the authority of the Israeli Ministries of Defense and Public Security, while the Palestinian Authority central government, based in the West Bank city of Ramallah, oversees the PA security forces. However, while these are central government institutions, the territorial divisions described earlier produce local-level differences in coercive force on the ground. Local-level geographic differences in PA policing capacity, I argue, capture the relative visibility of the indirect rule regime to Palestinian constituents. In the analysis that follows, I create a few variables measuring these local-level differences. These variables require measuring the proportion of each town located in Areas A, B, and C. In addition, I quantify the distance of each town's center to the nearest PA police station along roads accessible to Palestinians.[7]

I measure the policing capacity of the PA in each municipality in three ways. I use geo-referenced boundaries of Areas A, B, and C obtained from the Israeli human rights organization, B'Tselem; data on the geolocation of PA police stations obtained from the United Nations Office for the Coordination of Humanitarian Affairs (UNOCHA) in Palestine and an online map published by the Palestinian Authority; and geocoded files depicting Palestinian-accessible roads in the West Bank Road network data, courtesy of UNOCHA.[8]

For my first measure, I use geocoded data on building cover from the Palestinian Ministry of Local Government (MOLG) geodatabase to capture an approximate footprint of the built-up areas in Palestinian towns and cities as of 2007. Thus, my first measure captures the share of a municipality's built-up area that is located in Area A (*shareabuilt*).[9] In my second measure, I rely on MOLG data on the administrative land borders of each municipality, which are exhaustive of the entire territory of the West Bank (exclusive of the portion of Israeli-occupied East Jerusalem that Israel claims). The second variable measures the share of a municipality's total land that is located in Area C (*sharecland*).[10] My final measure of PA policing capacity is the logged distance along Palestinian-accessible roads (in meters) to the nearest PA police station from the geographic center of each municipality's largest built-up area (*log_routepolice*).[11]

Palestinian built-up areas, municipal boundaries, and Areas A, B, and C can be seen in map 4.1.[12] Israeli settlements and the separation barrier between the West Bank and Israel are not depicted on this map for ease of presentation. The map inset shows a zoomed-in portion of the north-central West Bank between the cities of Tulkarm and Nablus. The Palestinian towns in between sometimes fall primarily into Area A and sometimes into Area B.

Because the analysis here probes the possible causal effects of this variation in internal coercive capacity on local governance, it is important to explore how Areas A, B, and C were determined in the first place. Interested readers will find more discussion of the assignment of the West Bank's

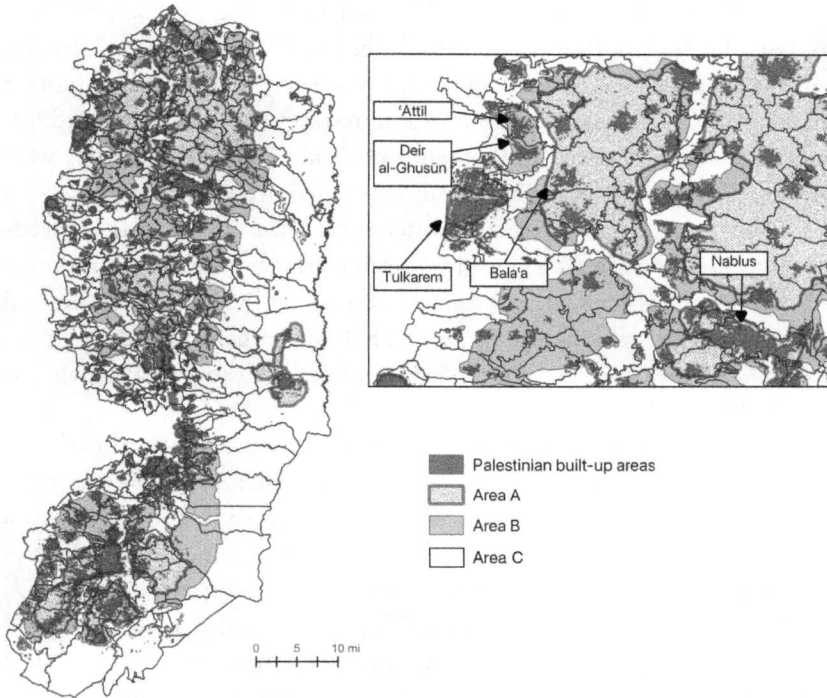

MAP 4.1. Map of the West Bank showing Palestinian built-up communities as of 2007 and Areas A, B, and C. *Sources*: Boundaries of Area A and Area B are from B'Tselem. Boundaries of municipalities and Palestinian built-up areas are from the Palestinian Ministry of Local Government.

security zones in the appendix at the end of this volume. In summary, both observed factors (e.g., population size) and unobserved factors (e.g., possibly unknown or opaque Israeli security considerations) contributed to the assignment of policing zones in small and medium-size Palestinian towns along urban peripheries. These factors must be taken into account in advancing causal inferences.

LOCAL PARTY IN POWER

The diverging political paths of Fatah and its opponents dates from at least the beginning of direct negotiations with Israel in the early 1990s, which drove a wedge in the Palestinian national movement. Nearly all major opposition groups—including Hamas, Palestinian Islamic Jihad, the

Popular Front for the Liberation of Palestine, and the Democratic Front for the Liberation of Palestine—rejected the Oslo Accords. The subsequent centralization of PA institutions under one-party rule fueled persistent grievances.[13] Palestinian control over internal security in the occupied territories was concentrated in the hands of Fatah. Opposition parties were prevented from developing an organized, armed presence, and those who were not Fatah loyalists were most often excluded from the new PA security force. Hamas, which had evolved from a branch of the Muslim Brotherhood into Fatah's most important rival, was, by the time of the second intifada, repeatedly using deadly suicide bombings against Israeli civilians. This adoption of militant tactics illustrates the increasingly stark divisions within the national movement.

The 2004–5 municipal elections—the first competitive local elections held since the PA's creation—occurred amid this environment of insecurity and polarization. The first local councils were appointed in 1996, and a subsequent Local Authorities Law was passed in 1997, outlining the roles and responsibilities of municipalities vis-à-vis the central government.[14] When local elections were finally held, it was revealed that the PA-led proliferation of municipalities had created many new arenas for political competition. Individual candidates and those on lists that challenged Fatah performed strongly. Thus, across much of the West Bank, politicians who opposed the status quo were in the unprecedented position to govern for the first time at the local level.

In some ways, it is understandable that many observers missed the signs of significant discontent with Fatah, because the results of the 2004–5 local elections were not straightforward. Mohsen Mohammad Saleh triangulates between sources to estimate how each faction performed across all municipalities and villages that held elections across both the West Bank and the Gaza Strip.[15] Overall, he finds that Fatah obtained 1,164 seats (42.7 percent), Hamas obtained 862 seats (31.6 percent), and independents and/or smaller parties obtained 701 seats (25.7 percent), although he cautions that these results remain "an approximation given the sometimes-huge inconsistencies between different sources."[16]

The local elections took place over four rounds between December 23, 2004, and December 15, 2005, with the last round cut short by cancellation of the vote in seven West Bank municipalities.[17] In the first two rounds, councils were elected according to a block voting system that allowed voters to select multiple candidates. Between the second and third rounds, President Mahmoud Abbas ushered through a new law that switched the system to closed-list proportional representation, likely because the winner-take-all outcomes under the previous rules were seen as disadvantaging Fatah.

In theory, following the elections, mayors are selected by a majority vote from council members. If no candidate obtains a majority, a run-off election is held with the two candidates with the largest number of votes on the council. In reality, post-election negotiations across factions often takes place behind closed doors. Thus, the partisan affiliation of the mayor does not always match that of the party that won a majority, or even plurality, of votes in the election.

With the help of two Palestinian research assistants, I worked to fill gaps in the official, published election results to determine the partisan makeup of elected municipal councils and the partisan affiliation of those selected as mayor. The Palestinian Central Election Commission's published results of the 2004–5 municipal elections do not list the party affiliation of all candidates who ran individually in the first and second rounds, or the affiliation of local lists of candidates who ran in the third and fourth rounds. While some of them are best categorized as independent, others had informal party affinities that were known locally. For example, some candidates and lists affiliated with Hamas did not run on the party's official list. Finally, the set of candidates who won seats in the municipal council does not always reveal what the partisan affiliation of the mayor would be or what the makeup of their coalition would look like.[18] Follow-up research on the partisan affiliation of the mayors for each municipality year was needed, especially in those municipalities that Hamas won. To my knowledge, this is the first dataset that attempts to code not just the election results but also the partisan affiliation of mayors following the 2004–5 elections.

Winning candidates from Hamas faced specific challenges. Following the elections, Hamas-affiliated mayors did not always take office in towns where a Hamas-affiliated list won a plurality or majority of seats. Further, some Hamas-affiliated mayors and council members were arrested and detained by either the PA or Israel during their terms. Some were released and returned to office, while others were forced to resign their posts and replaced with ruling party appointees. At least one independent mayor also resigned due to political pressure. Acquiring detailed information about the fate of local opposition politicians was difficult due to political sensitivities. This process required both online and field-based research to determine who was ultimately selected as mayor following the elections and how long they stayed in office.[19]

For these reasons, I created several variables. First, I created a three-category measure—Fatah, Hamas, or "independent"—for which party won a plurality of seats in the elections (*partyplur*). This variable does not vary over time.[20] For the 100 West Bank municipalities in my dataset that held elections, I find that Hamas-affiliated lists or politicians won a plurality of municipal council seats in 44 municipalities, Fatah-affiliated lists or politicians won a plurality in 40 municipalities, and lists that were independent or unaffiliated with a major party won a plurality of seats in 16 municipalities. Most of the candidates coded as independent are those who ran as unaffiliated with any party, but I also place those politicians and lists associated with smaller parties—for example, a smaller number of candidates maintained affiliations with the secular, Marxist-Leninist Popular Front for the Liberation of Palestine (PFLP)—in this category. Seven municipalities in the dataset did not hold an election.

A second set of variables measure the partisan affiliation of the mayor in office (*Fatah* dummy, *Hamas* dummy, *independent* dummy, or a trichotomous variable with categories for all three); this does vary from year to year. According to this measure, 449 (64 percent) municipality-years had Fatah mayors, 114 (16 percent) had Hamas mayors, and 137 (20 percent) had independent mayors. From this, I also created a variable for each municipality measuring the number of years spent under Fatah rule (*fatahsum*), which ranges from 0 to 7.

Figure 4.2 depicts the share of mayoralties led by each political faction over time, showing that Fatah gradually regains control over former Hamas-led municipalities. In 2012, new municipal elections were held, but the main opposition parties, including Hamas, did not formally participate. Thus, during this time, the last vestiges of Hamas's formal representation in local political offices across the West Bank was nearly eliminated. However, during my field research, I found that a few politicians from Hamas lists remained active on municipal councils, and Hamas-appointed staff sometimes stayed on. These nuances are discussed in the next chapter.

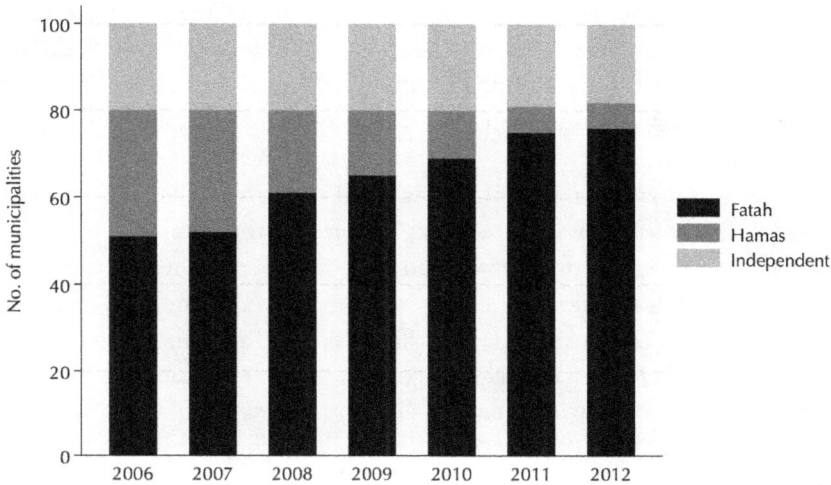

FIGURE 4.2. Partisan affiliation of mayors by year, 2006–2012. *Source:* Author.

REVENUES AND SPENDING

Ultimately, I aim to understand how the coercive regime and the political allegiances of Palestinian localities—each described earlier—may influence the concrete work of local governments. The municipal budget data used in the subsequent analysis were obtained from the Palestinian Ministry of Local Government. Revenue and expenditure data were extracted from approximately 750 detailed budget files in Arabic—one file for each municipality-year—and manually entered into a clean dataset in English. This study represents the first analysis conducted with these data.[21]

Municipal taxing and spending are shaped by the functions that municipalities carry out, and most are defined in the 1997 Local Authorities Law. Among other tasks, West Bank municipal councils issue building permits, manage sewage and waste systems, monitor public health, rehabilitate roads and sidewalks, manage public parks and markets, regulate select industries, and, in some cases, directly supply water and electricity.[22] Municipalities obtain revenue from a variety of sources, including revenue they collect on their own, taxes that are collected by the central government and transferred to the municipalities, project-based funding that they raise from outside donors or the Palestinian diaspora, and returns on municipal investments. Their spending corresponds to many of the responsibilities mentioned earlier, in addition to salaries and other forms of overhead. The municipal budget files submitted to MOLG do not always categorize these revenues and expenditures in a consistent way. I next describe how I organize these data.

First, I use revenues to capture the fiscal capacity of the local government. I do not assume that revenues generated by the municipality necessarily capture a social contract between the local government and taxpayers. When analyzing actual revenues per capita mobilized at the local level, we are looking at a composite outcome that is likely a function of three broad factors: first, the ability of the local government to generate revenue; second, its incentives, or will, to do so; and, third, the extent of compliance by the population. Similarly, spending data are likely shaped by both the ability of the municipality to execute spending and its incentives to do so, with the latter potentially shaped by popular demands for spending. Therefore, in a very broad sense, the revenue variables described below measure how active the local government is and, when examined in tandem with data on spending, how central a role the municipal government takes in (re) distribution.

My preferred operationalization of fiscal capacity incorporates those revenues that the municipality assesses and collects itself; thus, I created a measure of municipal self-generated revenues per capita (rpc_{it}).[23] For this variable, I include only those sources of revenue that are common to all municipalities. In other words, all municipalities have the authority and capacity to collect these revenues. The revenues come from three sources, each of which I divide by the town's population to obtain per capita estimates: fees for permits provided by the municipality (e.g., building permits, professional licenses; ppc), punitive fines collected by the municipality (fpc), and fees for nonutility services (e.g., garbage collection, parking fees, proceeds from public markets or slaughterhouses; spc).[24] These revenues, while small in magnitude, require municipal action to assess, collect, and enforce. While I do not have direct observations of enforcement, weak compliance would manifest in Palestinian residents and businesses building without the appropriate permit, engaging in professional activities without the required license, or using services (garbage collection, sewage and sanitation systems, public facilities, etc.) without paying.

A second variable captures any revenues municipalities collect from electricity and water provision (upc_{it}). For those municipalities that collect these utility revenues, those funds make up a large share of the overall budget. However, not all municipalities distribute and sell electricity or water.[25] Regarding electricity—a particularly complex sector—some municipalities have surrendered the authority to distribute electricity to one of a number of public-private utilities across the West Bank. For example, municipalities in the districts of Jerusalem, Ramallah/Al-Bireh, Bethlehem, and Jericho do not provide electricity themselves and thus do not charge for its provision; instead, power is supplied by a regional utility, Jerusalem District Electricity Company (JDECO).[26] However, while JDECO is a near-monopoly provider in the central West Bank, many municipalities in the north and south have opted out of joining similar regional utilities or resisted pressure to do so. As such, they have maintained responsibility for distributing electricity within their municipalities and for collecting fees. These municipalities' choices may have been political, in the sense that they depended on the political risks and rewards that mayors perceived from maintaining control over this utility.[27] In addition, often under the directives of the central PA government, some municipalities have formed joint services councils with neighboring municipalities to collectively handle their water provision.

Due to the severe power imbalance between Israel, the occupying state, and Palestinians and their leadership, most local utility revenues—whether collected by the municipalities or the regional utilities—represent liabilities to Israel. Much of the West Bank's drinking water supply is purchased in bulk from Israel's water company, Mekorot, and the vast majority of its electricity supply is purchased from the Israel Electric Corporation.[28] Israel sometimes deducts the unpaid fraction of utility liabilities from its revenue transfers to the central PA government. Subsequently, the collection of this debt can become subject to a politicized bargaining process involving the central PA government, municipalities, and, ultimately, Palestinian consumers.[29] In summary, electricity and water provision in the West Bank is complex—embodying both moral hazard problems and the extractive qualities of military occupation. Below I return to how the political affiliation of the municipal council is associated with electricity debt.

A third type of revenue, transfers per capita from the central PA government, is captured separately as tpc_{it}. Transfers involve several types of revenue that, according to the Local Authorities Law, the central PA government collects and subsequently transfers to localities.[30] They primarily include vehicle registration fees and fines for traffic violations that occur within the municipality's borders. In some cases, *tpc* also includes property tax revenue. When these data were collected, official surveys and assessments had not been conducted in all municipalities, so not all municipalities received property tax revenue transfers. In addition, transfers from the central government are frequently delayed due "a lack of accountability and transparency in intergovernmental relations."[31] Thus, transfers can vary substantially across municipalities, and within the same municipality, from year to year.

Interestingly, there is a strong positive correlation between average self-generated municipal revenues $(\overline{rpc_i})$ and average transfers from the central government $(\overline{tpc_i}, r = 0.80)$, implying that transfers do not depress incentives for municipalities to collect their own revenue. Perhaps that is because transfers from the central government are viewed as unpredictable. Finally, some municipalities generate revenues from investments, property sales, and, less frequently, loans. I capture these with a separate measure of other revenues per capita (opc_{it}).[32]

The units of all variables are nominal New Israeli Shekels (NIS).[33] Descriptive statistics for each of these revenue categories averaged over the seven-year period are shown in the appendix. In general, utility revenue is the largest source of revenue for those towns that have access to it.[34] Furthermore, self-generated revenues, transfers, and other revenues exhibit strong positive correlations with one another—bivariate correlation statistics range from 0.77 to 0.80—whereas utility revenues are essentially uncorrelated with the other three.

The last set of variables are those capturing municipal governments' spending patterns. The categories of spending found in regular municipal budgets are as follows, with each divided by the estimated yearly municipal population to obtain per capita estimates: general administration (*apc*), public health (*hepc*), engineering and public works (*pwpc*), security and firefighting (*secfirepc*), education (*edpc*), cultural and societal projects (*cusopc*), community planning and development (*planpc*), spending on public markets and slaughterhouses (*markpc*), and other spending (*otherpc*).[35] Separately, municipalities that oversee electricity or water provision document spending related to those utilities (*uepc*). I created separate variables of spending per capita on each of the aforementioned substantive areas. Descriptive statistics of spending data are also provided in the appendix.

As with the collection of revenues, we can think of spending, in its broadest sense, as a measure of the level of activity of the local government. Our emphasis will be on regular forms of spending, often including infrastructure maintenance and upkeep but excluding large new capital projects. The largest line items within each of the spending categories are often the salaries of staff in the relevant department. Other typical line items may include things like "heating expenses" (under administration), "sanitation supplies" (under health expenditures), "maintenance of cemetery" or "valley dredging and aerial photography" (under public works), "school maintenance" (under education expenditures), and "buying books, newspapers, and periodicals for the library" (under cultural and societal projects).

For municipalities that maintain control over electricity and water provision, the utility sector forms the largest share of expenditures. Averaging across municipalities, administration, public works, and health care form the next three largest spending categories.[36] It is notable how little, on average, municipalities spend on education. Municipalities are not the main entities charged with the provision and management of primary and secondary schools in Palestine. Public schools are provided by two main sources—the central PA government and the United Nations Relief and Works Agency (UNRWA), the special agency established to serve Palestinian refugees, which manages its own network of primary schools. However, municipalities do spend on school maintenance and, further, are sometimes involved in cofinancing the development and rehabilitation of private schools with outside donors. The latter type of capital development projects, funded partially or wholly by outside donors, are not included in my dataset.[37]

ADDITIONAL VARIABLES

I now introduce some additional control variables to capture socioeconomic and demographic characteristics of the municipalities. For population data, I use the 1997 and 2007 Palestinian censuses to derive population estimates for each municipality in 1997 and for each year between 2006 and 2012. In some estimations, I also include dummy variables to indicate the district (also referred to as "governorate") in which a municipality is located.[38] I match Alexei Abrahams' neighborhood-level employment rate variable, which is derived from the Palestinian Central Bureau of Statistics (PCBS)

2007 census, to the municipalities in my dataset.[39] This is captured in the variable *emprate*. PCBS also publishes some municipal-level aggregates of their census data, two of which are included here. One variable captures the number of operating business establishments in the municipality per 1,000 residents (*est*), and a second measures the number of occupied housing units in the municipality per 1,000 residents (*houseunits*).[40] Finally, a measure of the number of municipal employees per 1,000 residents (*munemp*) is drawn from the World Bank.[41]

There are limitations to these variables. First, they capture static realities in 2007, after the local elections took place. Nonetheless, I assume that these variables can still proxy for the socioeconomic situation in each municipality on the eve of the polls. Importantly, that means these variables should not have evolved differently across municipalities after the elections in a way that is correlated with election outcomes. Because it is unlikely that local elections altered the economic situation in the municipality so soon after voting took place, concerns about reverse causality are minor. A second disadvantage is that *est* is not available for the ten municipalities in the Jerusalem district. Thus, specifications that use these variables drop those Jerusalem observations.

The dataset also includes a dichotomous variable capturing whether a municipality has a refugee camp within its borders (*camp*). Palestinian refugees who reside in the camps include those who fled and were displaced from the 1948 and 1967 wars and their descendants. There are nineteen camps across the West Bank located in twelve municipalities in the West Bank. Because UNRWA provides education, health care, and sanitation services in the camps, this is an important factor that may shape financing and spending by municipalities.

Two final variables measure the logged distance along roads (in meters) to the nearest district capital (*log_routecap*) and to the nearest Israeli settlement, outpost, or military base (*log_routesettle*).[42] Descriptive statistics of all control variables are included in the appendix.

WHERE DID REGIME OPPONENTS WIN?

What led some towns to be governed by Fatah while others fell under the control of the opposition? Qualitative accounts describe how Hamas, in particular, campaigned on an anti-corruption platform in the 2004–5 local elections and the 2006 national elections, drawing on perceptions that Fatah unfairly rewarded its supporters. As Tareq Baconi notes, "Hamas ran under the banner of 'Change and Reform.' Without being overtly political, this message leveraged widespread disapproval with the long-standing and pervasive corruption within the Palestinian Authority, long dominated by Fatah, and offered Palestinians the option of changing their leaders to opt for a new beginning."[43]

In the four quarterly polls carried out by the Palestinian Center for Policy and Survey Research in the year prior to the first round of local elections, there was consensus among Palestinians in the West Bank that corruption was a problem: 84.5 percent (March 2004), 86.6 percent (June 2004), 86.8 percent (September 2004), and 87.8 percent (December 2004) of West Bank respondents said there was corruption in PA institutions.[44]

Unfortunately, such survey samples are designed to be representative of the overall West Bank and Gaza population, not populations at the district—much less municipal—level. That means we cannot use these data to reliably determine how perceptions of PA corruption may have varied across West Bank localities. Nonetheless, we can use some of the socioeconomic variables described earlier to understand which factors may have increased the chances that Palestinians in the West Bank would vote Fatah, Hamas, or independent/small party politicians into power. To do so, I estimate multinomial logit regressions for the three-category dependent variable (*party-plur*) for the one hundred municipalities that conducted elections in 2004–5. In these models, Fatah is the base category.

These estimations, shown in table 4.1, demonstrate a robust correlation between a town's population size in 2006 (logged in the regressions) and the likelihood of Hamas candidates obtaining a plurality of seats.[45] In columns 2–11, I sequentially add each of the previously mentioned static variables that could plausibly capture the economic, social, and geographic conditions prior to the elections. These include the employment rate; the number of business establishments per 1,000 residents; the number of housing units per 1,000 residents; the three variables proxying for PA policing capacity (*shareabuilt*, *sharecland*, and *log_routepolice*); the distances to the nearest governorate capital; the distance to the nearest Israeli settlement, outpost, or military base; the presence of at least one refugee camp within municipal borders; and fixed effects at the governorate level.[46]

TABLE 4.1
Multinomial logit regressions of plurality-winning party on control variables

Hamas	(1)	(2)	(3)	(4)	(5)	(6)	(7)	(8)	(9)	(10)	(11)	(12)
constant	-8.195**	-0.441	-10.382**	-3.136	-9.323**	-7.672*	-12.204**	-9.808*	-11.164*	-7.521*	-6.461+	4.184
	(3.165)	(4.917)	(3.524)	(3.848)	(3.406)	(3.281)	(4.317)	(4.122)	(4.658)	(3.236)	(3.690)	(5.804)
log_pop06	0.925**	0.954**	1.207**	0.944**	1.072**	0.896*	1.123**	1.048**	0.920**	0.843*	0.694+	0.945*
	(0.353)	(0.364)	(0.402)	(0.355)	(0.388)	(0.358)	(0.390)	(0.404)	(0.352)	(0.363)	(0.412)	(0.458)
emprate		-9.491*										-10.948+
		(4.626)										(5.781)
est			-0.008									
			(0.018)									
houseunits				-0.030*								-0.017
				(0.014)								(0.019)
shareabuilt					-0.562							
					(0.566)							
shareland						-0.519						
						(0.787)						
log_routepolice							0.291					
							(0.200)					
log_routecap								0.060				
								(0.102)				
log_routesettle									0.354			
									(0.401)			
camp										0.791		
										(0.910)		
governorate FE											Y	Y

Independent

Independent												
constant	−2.803	−9.962	−4.621	1.643	−2.886	−2.945	−1.820	−1.560	−3.322	−2.833	−0.715	−4.114
	(4.030)	(7.071)	(4.311)	(5.223)	(4.171)	(4.204)	(4.861)	(5.094)	(5.947)	(4.124)	(4.399)	(8.775)
log_pop06	0.214	0.223	0.332	0.190	0.227	0.223	0.170	0.118	0.210	0.217	0.0180	0.0533
	(0.456)	(0.425)	(0.498)	(0.462)	(0.480)	(0.461)	(0.471)	(0.507)	(0.452)	(0.467)	(0.504)	(0.485)
emprate		8.219										3.906
		(6.521)										(8.088)
est			0.019									
			(0.021)									
houseunits				−0.024								−0.001
				(0.018)								(0.022)
shareabuilt					−0.068							
					(0.703)							
shareland						0.126						
						(1.039)						
log_routepolice							−0.079					
							(0.222)					
log_routecap								−0.047				
								(0.127)				
log_routesettle									0.066			
									(0.530)			
camp										0.176		
										(1.277)		
governorate FE											Y	Y
N	100	99	90	100	100	100	100	100	100	100	100	99

Note: Standard errors in parentheses. FE = fixed effect. $^{+}$ $p < 0.10$, * $p < 0.05$, ** $p < 0.01$, *** $p < 0.001$.

These estimations show that compared with the likelihood of Fatah winning a plurality of seats, both a lower employment rate (*emprate*, column 2) and greater housing scarcity (*houseunits*, column 4) is associated with a greater chance of Hamas victory at a 95 percent confidence level. Column 12 retains all four covariates that were significant in the prior estimations. These results show that the town's population size maintains its significantly positive association with Hamas victory ($p < 0.05$). The employment rate's association with Hamas victory is still negative at a lower level of statistical significance ($p < 0.1$), and the number of housing units per 1,000 residents retains its negative coefficient, but it is no longer statistically significant.

Interestingly, these models do not give us a clear sense of which factors predicted a stronger performance for independent or smaller party candidates. That may be because our independent category contains politicians and lists representing a wide variety of ideologies and/or local, familial affinities. However, in the online appendix, I estimate binomial logit models using dichotomized dependent variables for whether Fatah, Hamas, or independents won a plurality of seats.[47] In these models, I find that both a smaller population and a larger relative housing supply are associated with Fatah victory ($p < 0.05$); higher employment rates are associated with a greater likelihood of independents winning a plurality ($p < 0.05$); and the estimations with the binary *hamaswin* variable confirm that larger population size ($p < 0.05$ or $p < 0.01$) and a lower employment rate ($p < 0.01$) are positively correlated with Hamas's performance at the polls. (*Houseunits* shows a negative correlation, and *log_routepolice* a positive correlation, with Hamas victory. Both are significant only at the lower, 90 percent confidence level.)

In summary, we can take away several fairly confident assertions about the outcomes of the 2004–5 local elections. First, Hamas candidates tended to prevail in larger (more populated) towns and cities, while candidates affiliated with the ruling Fatah party were more successful in less populated towns. This echoes claims by Saleh and Palestinian news media at the time, including from outlets sympathetic to Fatah.[48] These findings are not sensitive to the exclusion of the city of Nablus, which is the second-largest municipality by population size and where a Hamas-affiliated list won a plurality of seats in the election.

Second, while there is some sensitivity to model specification, residents of municipalities experiencing relative economic exclusion—as exemplified by lower employment rates and lower housing supply—were more likely to vote for Hamas. On the other hand, in areas that were less economically marginalized, either Fatah or independent/small party politicians seemed more likely to win. This conclusion depends on how we conceptualize economic marginalization—a greater housing supply is associated with Fatah candidates' victory, while higher employment rates are associated with independents' victory.

Notably, none of the measures of the policing capacity of the PA—the share of the built-up area in Area A, the share of land in Area C, and the log of the distance to the nearest PA police station—is a robust predictor of election outcomes. This means that in the analysis of revenue and spending outcomes to be discussed, we can include these measures as independent predictors with the knowledge that they did not also influence the selection of towns into Fatah or opposition rule.

INTERMEDIARIES, OPPONENTS, AND APPROACHES TO LOCAL GOVERNANCE

Following the elections, mayors were selected from among the newly elected municipal councils. In councils in which multiple factions were represented, negotiations sometimes occurred behind closed doors to arrive at majority support for a mayor. Once in office, did mayors affiliated with Fatah govern differently from their opposition counterparts? Municipal budget data allow us to ask whether or not the political orientation of local governments shaped their actions and priorities in Palestinian communities across the West Bank.

First, I examine differences in revenue mobilization. In brief, I find evidence consistent with the theory that municipalities led by Fatah mayors were more likely to forbear from revenue mobilization, whereas towns under Hamas mayors, in particular, were more likely to increase revenue mobilization. This helps explain lower overall collection of revenues from punitive fines by Fatah-led councils, as well as greater year-to-year growth in revenues per capita by Hamas-led councils compared with their Fatah- and independent-led counterparts. Surprisingly, though, I do not find evidence of political favoritism in revenue transfers to municipalities from the central, Fatah-led government. I also find that greater Palestinian coercive authority—captured by the distinctions among Areas A, B, and C—is associated with revenue gains only in towns governed by Fatah's challengers. In areas of greater PA policing authority, local governments controlled by Fatah collect relatively *less* revenue than localities controlled by the opposition.

These findings suggest that the outsourcing of internal policing to Fatah, as the intermediary in Israel's indirect rule regime, has not enhanced the fiscal capacity of Fatah on a local level. While there are a number of possible explanations for this finding, the theory I develop here and in chapter 5, through the iterative incorporation of quantitative and qualitative evidence, suggests that Fatah may be even more likely to forbear from revenue collection in areas where its policing role is most visible. Due to the nature of its functional collaboration with Israel on coercion, I argue that its reputational deficit with the Palestinian public will be greatest in these areas.

Second, I incorporate data on municipal spending across substantive areas, like health, public works, administration, and the electricity and water sectors. Turning again to the panel data, I show that municipalities under Fatah rule demonstrate greater increases in annual spending per capita on electricity and water when compared their opposition counterparts. Further, this growth is concentrated in towns where PA policing capacity is weaker—as captured by the share of the municipality's land in Area C—and it is not matched by similar year-to-year increases in revenue collection.

These results imply that Fatah mayors are more likely to leverage soft budget constraints in the utility sector to engage in distributive spending, and I suggest this could be a strategy to secure political support. The absence of PA policing in Area C communities means, among other things, that Palestinian residents in these areas face more direct and unmediated threats from the Israeli military and settler violence. In such areas, Fatah-led councils may invest relatively more in essential collective goods such as electricity and water to substitute for their coercive weakness. Thus, I use these findings to further develop my theory of how Fatah-affiliated municipal leaders cope with the organization's subordinated status within the indirect rule regime and its associated legitimacy problems with the Palestinian public.

Revenue Generation by Fatah Versus Its Opponents

First, I ask whether the number of years a town spent under a Fatah-affiliated mayor (*fatahsum*) shaped average revenue mobilization over the seven-year period. In trying to isolate the possible effect of the local party in power on revenue mobilization, we must control for other features of Palestinian towns and cities that may influence their fiscal positions. General economic factors like the level of employment, the housing supply, and the number of business establishments for a given population size would be expected to affect the size of the tax base. These three variables in particular are fairly strongly correlated, so, following exploratory factor analysis, I combine them into a single index variable (*econ_index*), which ranges from 0 to 5.[49] Indeed, the bivariate correlation of a town's self-generated revenues per capita over the seven-year period ($\overline{rpc_i}$) and this index variable is large: 0.69.

However, earlier we found that some of these same economic variables were correlated with the election results. If economic features of the municipality influenced the partisan affiliation of the municipal council that took office, then the main independent variable of interest in our models of revenue collection—the partisan affiliation of the mayor—could be "on the causal path" between economic features and municipal revenue collection.[50] To address this, I regress *fatahsum* on the two variables that were significant in predicting Fatah victory at the polls—*log_pop06* and *houseunits*—and preserve the residuals. These residuals should capture any unobserved factors that shaped the number of years Fatah-affiliated mayors held office in a given municipality. Subsequently, I estimate ordinary least squares regressions of our revenue variables ($\overline{rpc_i}$, $\overline{ppc_i}$, $\overline{spc_i}$, $\overline{fpc_i}$, $\overline{tpc_i}$, $\overline{upc_i}$, and $\overline{opc_i}$) on three variables: the logged mean population, the economic index variable, and, alternatively, the number of years a municipality spent under Fatah rule (*fatahsum*) or the residuals from the preceding regression (*resid_fs*). The results are presented in table 4.2.

While the number of years under Fatah rule has a negative coefficient in all models, it only appears to have a significant relationship with average revenues raised via fines; when the *fatahsum* measure is used (column 7), it is only weakly significant.[51] However, when we use the residual variable (*resid_fs*)—which captures variation across towns in years spent under Fatah rule, washed of those economic factors that may have led to Fatah's electoral victory in the first place—it is a significant predictor of fines per capita at the 5 percent level (column 8). At the weaker 10 percent threshold, we also see that years spent under Fatah rule is associated with lower revenues in the "other" category (columns 13 and 14).

TABLE 4.2
Cross-sectional regressions of mean revenue per capita on years under Fatah control

	(1) rpc	(2) rpc	(3) ppc	(4) ppc	(5) spc	(6) spc	(7) fpc	(8) fpc	(9) tpc	(10) tpc	(11) upc	(12) upc	(13) opc	(14) opc
constant	-212.8***	-229.0***	-139.4***	-149.8***	-58.91*	-63.24*	-14.96***	-16.30***	-378.1***	-400.4***	232.5	228.0	-562.6**	-639.6***
	(52.65)	(51.25)	(37.13)	(36.17)	(24.97)	(24.30)	(3.218)	(3.132)	(75.73)	(73.75)	(298.0)	(290.1)	(184.6)	(179.9)
log_meanpop	18.07**	19.07***	10.96**	11.60**	5.617*	5.886*	1.522***	1.605***	35.30***	36.66***	-8.270	-7.944	48.15*	52.87**
	(5.628)	(5.588)	(3.969)	(3.943)	(2.669)	(2.649)	(0.344)	(0.341)	(8.094)	(8.040)	(31.85)	(31.63)	(19.73)	(19.61)
econ_index	54.91***	54.05***	35.21***	34.67***	18.50***	18.26***	1.265***	1.195***	56.47***	55.32***	50.32	49.75	101.8***	97.86***
	(5.662)	(5.682)	(3.993)	(4.010)	(2.685)	(2.694)	(0.346)	(0.347)	(8.143)	(8.176)	(32.04)	(32.17)	(19.85)	(19.95)
fatahsum	-2.010		-1.287		-0.540		-0.167+		-2.761		-0.619		-9.536+	
	(1.388)		(0.979)		(0.658)		(0.0848)		(1.996)		(7.853)		(4.865)	
resid_fs		-2.067		-1.283		-0.598		-0.170*		-2.776		-1.492		-9.463+
		(1.403)		(0.990)		(0.665)		(0.0857)		(2.019)		(7.942)		(4.925)
N	100	100	100	100	100	100	100	100	100	100	100	100	100	100
R^2	0.540	0.541	0.490	0.489	0.366	0.367	0.303	0.304	0.440	0.440	0.025	0.026	0.291	0.289

Note: Standard errors in parentheses. FE = fixed effect. $^+ p < 0.10$, $^* p < 0.05$, $^{**} p < 0.01$, $^{***} p < 0.001$.

It is important to note that these results are sensitive to the exclusion of outliers. Al-Bireh, the neighboring town to Ramallah, was governed by a Hamas-affiliated mayor, Jamal al-Tawil, during the full seven-year period, and it is a positive outlier on fee collection. Dropping Al-Bireh from the estimations in columns 7 and 8 causes the coefficients on the Fatah variables to fall just below the weaker 10 percent threshold for statistical significance. Further, Ramallah, the *de facto* capital of the PA, was governed by an independent mayor, Janet Mikhail, during the entirety of this period. Ramallah is a positive outlier on revenue generation, presumably due to the much higher levels of foreign investment, construction, and employment in the city. If we drop Ramallah from the regressions of other revenues, the coefficient on *fatahsum* falls below the 10 percent threshold in column 13; however, the coefficient on the residual term in column 14 remains weakly significant.

In summary, for those West Bank towns that are less connected to the economically developed, relatively capital-rich city of Ramallah, we cannot say that the duration of Fatah rule negatively shaped average revenue collection from fines or other sources over the seven-year period of our dataset. Nonetheless, we should not dismiss the observations from these two cities, which are important because of their disproportionate contribution to the West Bank's overall economy, their political centrality, and the size of their populations. (If summed together, they form the West Bank's third-largest city, after Hebron and Nablus.)

Two final observations stand out from table 4.2. First, it is somewhat surprising to note that, while not statistically significant, time spent under Fatah's control has a negative association with revenue transfers from the central government (columns 9 and 10). One of the most important drivers of total transfers from the central government is whether or not a municipality has a property tax system in place, a factor not accounted for in these models. In any case, though, this result challenges the intuition that the central PA government in Ramallah practiced political favoritism and delivered greater fiscal transfers to Fatah-led municipalities. That does not appear to have occurred, at least as a general trend. Second, no variables in our models are significantly correlated with average revenues generated from the utilities of electricity and water provision (columns 11 and 12), demonstrating that demographic, economic, and even political factors may not play much of a role in which municipalities have access to this revenue source.

To gain a more fine-grained look at revenue mobilization over time, we can leverage the fact that the party in power changed over the seven-year period of the dataset. As noted previously, this occurred due to the resignation or removal of a number of non-Fatah mayors, primarily those from Hamas. Thus, the party in power for a particular year in a particular town is a complex combination of many factors, including how parties performed in the elections and, in towns where Hamas performed strongly, whether Fatah had the will or capacity to push them out of office or whether the Hamas mayor made the individual choice to resign. These dynamics are explored more in chapter 5.

For the present analysis, I estimate one-way fixed-effect models that, because they include a lagged dependent variable, estimate year-to-year change in revenues across municipalities:

$$Y_{it} = \alpha + \beta_1 y_{i(t-1)} + \beta_2 party_{it} + X_i\Gamma + \zeta_t + \epsilon_{it}.$$

I include year-fixed effects (ζ_t), which capture features of year t that are constant across municipalities and potentially correlated with the outcome.[52] Thus, this model asks, "What explains differences in the amount of revenue per capita growth (or decline) from the previous year across municipalities?" The model focuses on identifying cross-sectional variation across the towns and cities of the West Bank.[53] The key independent variable of interest is the local party in power, depicted above as $party_{it}$, which is either a trichotomous variable or a dummy variable capturing the partisan affiliation of the mayor in town i in year t.

Table 4.3 shows the results for the estimations with the Hamas dummy variable (columns 2–6), thus allowing us to compare municipality-years under Hamas mayors with those under non-Hamas (Fatah or independent) mayors. By the same logic used in the cross-sectional regressions, I also generate residuals from a first-stage regression of the Hamas dummy on the three variables that predicted Hamas victory (*houseunits*, *emprate*, and the municipality's population) and substitute it (*resid_h*) for the Hamas variable in columns 7–11 of table 4.3.

I successively add four time-invariant control variables (X_i): the economic index, the share of built-up area in Area A, and the number of municipal employees per 1,000 residents.[54] Because these capture conditions in 2007, we can think of them as baseline factors that might shape each municipality's year-to-year growth (or decline) in revenues.[55] Finally, I also include the log of the town's population in year t.

Municipality-years featuring a Hamas-led government generate significantly more revenue growth from the previous year compared with municipality-years with Fatah- or independent-led governments in columns 2 and 4 ($p < 0.05$), and the relationship is significant at a weaker threshold in columns 3, 5, 7, 8, and 9 ($p < 0.1$).[56] Including the variable measuring the size of municipal staff in 2007 (*munemp*) seems to dampen the relationship, and the same is true when fixed effects at the governorate level are included.

The effect sizes are small: Hamas-run municipalities are expected to grow revenues by approximately 5 NIS per capita (approximately $1.34 in constant 2010 U.S. dollars) more than Fatah-run municipalities. For a municipality with a population of 14,218 residents—the mean population in our sample for 2010—this would result in an additional 68,361 NIS (approximately US$18,376) per year for the municipality. Average income per capita in the West Bank and Gaza Strip was roughly US$2,500 to US$3,200 during this period; thus, this additional revenue could potentially cover the salaries of a few more employees, for example, or other material costs.[57] In the online appendix, I also estimate the models using panel-corrected standard errors, which causes some of the specifications featuring *resid_h* to fall below the 10 percent significance threshold and others featuring *hamas* to fall to $p < 0.1$.

In general, these results are consistent with qualitative reporting that Hamas mayors had to exert more fiscal effort while in office. For example, in 2006 reporting that draws on in-person interviews with municipal council members and residents, the International Crisis Group notes,

> Hamas councils have sought to cut expenditures, raise taxes, and lease or sell municipal assets. In Qalqilya, Hashim Masri claimed office expenses and petrol allowances had been substantially reduced, while Hamas councillors in Bethlehem said they had cut the mayor's salary, though not their own. Councillors also offered incentives for up-front payment of local fees in an attempt to boost revenues. Khalid Saada, a Bethlehem councillor and veteran Hamas member, said he canvassed markets and shops for payment: "I went to collect the taxes personally from the markets. I said—look you've voted for me, and for this municipality to succeed you have to pay your fees."[58]

In another segment of the same report, a dissatisfied resident of Qalqilya critiques his Hamas-led municipal government: "'Hamas hasn't provided compensation to the victims of the [Israeli separation] wall despite election promises. I don't see any difference between the old and new administrations, other than an increase in local fees.'"[59] Additional evidence on the greater fiscal demands on Hamas-led municipalities and how mayors approached these challenges is provided in the subsequent chapter.

It is worth noting that Hamas was no longer a significant predictor of revenue growth in the specifications including governorate-fixed effects. The individual governorate dummy variables are not shown in the table for ease of presentation, but the coefficients on the Jerusalem, Jericho, and Hebron governorates are significant ($p < 0.05$, with the Hebron coefficient dropping to $p < 0.1$ in column 11). That means municipalities in these governorates, *ceteris paribus*, raised less self-generated revenue per capita than municipalities in the Ramallah governorate (the excluded category). The Jericho governorate contains only three municipalities; thus, the small town of al-Auja, with its low levels of revenue collection, has a large impact on this estimate. Hebron is a generally poorer region of the West Bank, so it is not surprising that its municipal revenue collection suffers.

The Jerusalem governorate consists of ten towns located on the West Bank side of the separation barrier. These municipalities are under PA control; they are not within the part of East Jerusalem that Israel unilaterally annexed. Nonetheless, these towns tend to have more depressed economies because of the wall, which impedes travel, business, health care access, and access to land. While Hamas won a plurality of seats in three of the ten towns in this governorate, only one ended up with a Hamas mayor (three were independent and six were Fatah). If Jerusalem's depressed economy was to explain the relatively poorer performance of non-Hamas municipalities, it would be reasonable to expect our economic index variable to pick this up. Still, we shouldn't discount the possibility that some omitted governorate-level factors are correlated with both who ends up in office and how much revenue they generate from year to year.

Of course, it is still possible that it is not Hamas governance per se but some other characteristic of municipalities that is affiliated with partisan differences in mayors and also shaped revenue collection. However, the omitted variable would also need to be something that wasn't captured in

TABLE 4.3
One-way fixed-effect lagged dependent variable regressions of mean self-generated revenues per capita on Hamas control

	(1)	(2)	(3)	(4)	(5)	(6)	(7)	(8)	(9)	(10)	(11)
constant	-19.59***	-22.60***	-51.94**	-43.16*	-66.70**	-108.2**	-20.95***	-52.82**	-44.11*	-68.78*	-109.1**
	(4.552)	(4.917)	(17.32)	(16.82)	(24.76)	(33.90)	(4.794)	(17.65)	(17.59)	(26.22)	(33.99)
lag_rpc	0.943***	0.944***	0.930***	0.926***	0.894***	0.854***	0.945***	0.929***	0.927***	0.894***	0.855***
	(0.0721)	(0.0748)	(0.0753)	(0.0755)	(0.0800)	(0.0740)	(0.0747)	(0.0752)	(0.0753)	(0.0800)	(0.0740)
econ_index	8.154***	8.510***	9.034***	8.735***	8.799***	6.894***	8.208***	8.911***	8.506***	8.627***	6.687**
	(2.256)	(2.411)	(2.555)	(2.417)	(2.434)	(1.987)	(2.385)	(2.591)	(2.459)	(2.527)	(2.082)
hamas		5.279*	4.239+	4.529*	4.502+	2.808					
		(2.359)	(2.243)	(2.269)	(2.428)	(2.658)					
resid_h							1.876+	1.612+	1.664+	1.622	0.892
							(0.967)	(0.925)	(0.931)	(1.010)	(1.123)
log_pop			3.252*	2.205	4.434+	9.551*		3.471*	2.476	4.816+	9.723*
			(1.602)	(1.588)	(2.390)	(3.752)		(1.620)	(1.645)	(2.502)	(3.740)
shareabuilt				4.476*	4.463*	4.530			4.120+	3.880	4.168
				(1.964)	(2.227)	(3.220)			(2.033)	(2.342)	(3.760)
munemp					1.979	4.843**				2.010	4.904**
					(1.339)	(1.640)				(1.356)	(1.604)
governorate FE						Y					Y
year FE	Y	Y	Y	Y	Y	Y	Y	Y	Y	Y	Y
N	575	543	543	543	490	490	537	537	537	484	484
R²	0.860	0.864	0.866	0.866	0.868	0.874	0.864	0.866	0.867	0.869	0.874

Note: Robust standard errors clustered by municipality in parentheses. FE = fixed effect. $^+$ $p < 0.10$, * $p < 0.05$, ** $p < 0.01$, *** $p < 0.001$.

the set of unmeasured variables (*resid_h*) that may have brought Hamas into office in the first place. Without a strong theory of what that omitted factor might be, it appears that Hamas-led municipalities did indeed emphasize revenue growth more than their counterparts under either Fatah or independent rule.

The Coercive Regime and Local Fiscal Capacity

Drawing on existing theories of governance and state-building, there are reasons to expect that an organization's fiscal capacity—or its ability to extract revenue from constituents—may be conditional on the nature of coercive authority and control. The geographic variation in *de facto* Palestinian coercive capacity captures the relative visibility of the Palestinian Authority's specific role as an intermediary within Israel's regime that is responsible for internal policing of Palestinian population centers. In this section, I seek to address the following question: Did Palestinian policing capacity—a variable which is associated with the visibility, presence, and level of activity of Palestinian police forces—affect local governance outcomes differently depending on the party in power? Or, to emphasize a different aspect of the causal relationship, did the party in power shape local governance outcomes differently depending on the extent of policing capacity held by the Fatah-dominated PA?

First, it is noteworthy that towns located in areas of greater Palestinian policing authority tend to exhibit greater municipal fiscal capacity. On average, municipalities that fall under greater PA police authority—defined as those with more than 50 percent of their built-up area in Area A—raise more self-generated revenues per capita ($t = -3.08$, $p < 0.01$), receive more central government transfers per capita ($t = -2.36$, $p < 0.05$), and also mobilize more revenues per capita in the other category ($t = -2.63$, $p < 0.01$).[60] This is unsurprising in some ways because, as noted previously, larger population centers are more likely to fall into Area A. Larger towns and cities may generate more revenue on a per-capita basis due to the higher average incomes of their residents or the relative ease and economies of scale that come with taxing denser urban areas.

However, the results presented next suggest that the local fiscal benefits of PA policing capacity are concentrated not in municipalities controlled by Fatah but, rather, in those governed by its opponents. In table 4.4, I estimate

TABLE 4.4
One-way fixed-effect regressions of mean revenues per capita on interaction of policing capacity and party in power

	(1)	(2)	(3)	(4)
constant	−16.71	0.290	−17.82	−58.76**
	(12.90)	(21.80)	(12.90)	(21.46)
lag_rpc	0.989***	0.998***	1.001***	0.909***
	(0.0582)	(0.0555)	(0.0557)	(0.0633)
log_pop	0.881	1.857	2.439	2.797+
	(1.390)	(1.404)	(1.502)	(1.677)
shareabuilt	14.88*			
	(5.891)			
fatah	1.899	−25.24	−13.57*	19.59
	(2.225)	(22.03)	(5.928)	(12.28)
fatah*shareabuilt	−12.99*			
	(6.105)			
log_routepolice		−2.878		
		(2.662)		
fatah*log_routepolice		3.053		
		(2.778)		
sharecland			−19.31*	
			(8.028)	
fatah*sharecland			23.33*	
			(9.033)	
econ_index				16.28**
				(5.999)
fatah*econ_index				−10.62+
				(6.229)
year FE	Y	Y	Y	Y
N	543	543	543	543
R^2	0.862	0.860	0.862	0.869

Note: Robust standard errors clustered by municipality in parentheses. FE = fixed effect. $^+ p < 0.10$, $^* p < 0.05$, $^{**} p < 0.01$, $^{***} p < 0.001$.

a reduced-form model similar to the lagged dependent variable model above, but I include only logged population and year-fixed effects as controls across all specifications. In addition, I include an interaction term, which allows the relationship between policing capacity (*shareabuilt* here but alternatively operationalized as *sharecland* or *log_routepolice*) and revenues per capita (y_{it}) to be conditional on the party in power at the local level (*party*$_{it}$, for which I plug in the three dichotomized variables for Fatah, Hamas, and independent control, respectively):

$$y_{it} = \alpha + \beta_1 y_{i(t-1)} + \beta_2 log(pop)_{it} + \beta_3 shareabuilt_i + \beta_4 party_{it} + \beta_5 shareabuilt_i * party_{it} + \gamma_t + \epsilon_{it}.$$

In general, these estimations demonstrate that policing capacity has no discernible effect on revenue growth for towns governed by Fatah, whereas it appears to be associated with increased revenue collection for towns governed by the opposition.[61] To understand the relationship between Palestinian policing capacity and revenues in towns governed by regime opponents, we can turn to the coefficients on *shareabuilt, sharecland,* and *log_routepolice* in columns 1–3, respectively. Each coefficient estimates the marginal change in revenues per capita associated with a one-unit increase in policing capacity if the opposition is in power. Because our first two measures range from 0 to 1 and the second measure is on a log scale, a one-unit change is not very meaningful. Instead, we can use these coefficients to calculate the change in revenues associated with an increase of one standard deviation.

Accordingly, an increase in the share of a municipality's built-up area that falls in Area A (column 1) by one standard deviation produces a 6.63 NIS ($1.78 constant 2010 U.S. dollar) increase in revenues per capita from the preceding year in opposition-held towns. For a municipality with a population of 14,218 residents (the 2010 sample mean), this would result in an additional 94,345 NIS (approximately US$25,362) per year for the municipality. Further, the more of a municipality's land that is located in Area C (column 3), the less revenue per capita generated in opposition-led towns.[62]

Overall, these results imply that among towns held by the opposition, greater PA policing authority is associated with increased revenue collection. We do not see a significant relationship between the distance to the closest PA police station and revenues in opposition-held towns.

What about towns governed by Fatah? To calculate the estimated association between policing capacity and revenues for such towns, we must use both the coefficients on policing capacity ($\widehat{\beta_3}$ in the aforementioned model) and the interaction term ($\widehat{\beta_5}$). This analysis reveals that PA policing capacity does not have a significant relationship with revenue mobilization in

Fatah-led municipalities.[63] That is true across all three measures of policing capacity (columns 1–3).

In summary, these results imply that opposition-led towns are more effective at raising revenue in areas of higher Palestinian policing capacity— as captured by *shareabuilt* and *sharecland*—while they are less effective at raising revenue in towns that have more land fully controlled by Israel. In Fatah-run localities, however, these variations in coercive capacity have no observable relation to local revenue generation.

Did the party in power at the local level shape local governance outcomes differently, depending on the extent of Palestinian policing capacity? We can use these models to compare the estimated marginal effect of Fatah versus opposition rule in municipalities with similar levels of PA coercive capacity. To perform this kind of comparison, we must use both the coefficients on *fatah* $(\widehat{\beta}_4)$ and the coefficient on the interaction term $(\widehat{\beta}_5)$.

Figure 4.3 plots the estimated marginal effect of Fatah rule on revenues per capita at various levels of policing capacity using the estimates from columns 1 and 3 of table 4.4. The figure shows that, compared with opposition rule, Fatah rule at the local level begins to have a negative association with revenue performance at the very highest levels of PA policing capacity—in

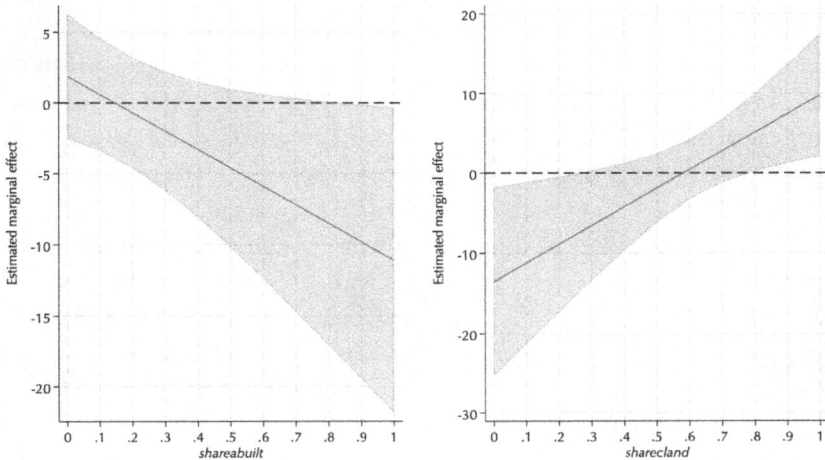

FIGURE 4.3. Marginal effect of Fatah rule on revenues per capita at various levels of policing capacity (measured as *shareabuilt* or *sharecland*). *Source*: Author.

other words, where the share of the town's built-up area located in Area A is above 90 percent (left panel of figure 4.3), or where the share of the town's land in Area C is 20 percent or less (right panel of figure 4.3). In towns where the Palestinian Authority has the greatest amount of policing presence and capacity, local Fatah governments are raising *less* revenue than their opposition counterparts. The opposite is true in areas of less coercive control, as captured in the share of land in Area C. In the latter case, Fatah-led municipalities mobilize relatively *more* revenue than their opposition counterparts. The interactive relationship between Fatah rule and the share of land in Area C is robust to the exclusion of the outlier cities of Ramallah, Al-Bireh, and Nablus. (The *shareabuilt* estimations, on the other hand, are somewhat sensitive to the exclusion of Ramallah and Al-Bireh.)

Finally, how do we know that *shareabuilt* and *sharecland*, first and foremost, are capturing the PA's internal coercive capacity rather than some other underlying feature of municipalities? In short, the limited availability of data on the selection process that drove the assignment of Palestinian populations and lands to Areas A, B, and C means that we cannot entirely rule out omitted variable bias. However, I perform a couple of checks to attempt to isolate the concept of interest—Palestinian policing authority— in these variables.

First, what did these towns look like before they were assigned to Areas A, B, and C in 1995? Data from the pre-Oslo period are scarce. Further, Israel recognized fewer than one-quarter of the 107 municipalities in our dataset as municipalities at the time—many others were village councils or did not even exist as local government units. Nonetheless, in the appendix at the end of this volume, I use observations from Israeli statistics bureau yearbooks produced between 1982 and 1994, before the Oslo Accords and creation of the PA, to analyze revenue data from a small subset of municipalities. I compare revenue collection in four municipalities, most of whose built-up area was later assigned to Area B, with seven municipalities, most of whose built-up area was later designated as Area A. Average self-generated revenues from this earlier period were not statistically different across these two sets of municipalities.

Further, in column 4 of table 4.4, I use my economic index variable (*econ_index*) as a placebo check. Is policing capacity the only variable whose association with revenue collection would condition (and be conditional on) the local party in power? These results show that the marginal effect of an increase in the level of economic development of the town is positive and significant for both municipalities governed by Fatah and those governed by the opposition. Further, while the marginal effect of Fatah rule appears to decrease and become negative as the level of economic development of the municipality increases, these effects are not statistically significant at the conventional 5 percent threshold. Thus, the local party in power does not appear to condition the effect of economic development—nor does a town's level of economic development appear to condition the effect of the local party in power—on revenue collection in the way that policing capacity does. This increases our confidence that it is the coercive arrangements embodied in Areas A, B, and C that are, in conjunction with the local party in power, shaping local governance outcomes in these towns.

SPENDING BY FATAH VERSUS OPPONENTS

To conclude the analysis, we turn to the relationship between the local ruling party and spending. I estimate models using, first, nonutility spending per capita—a variable I call epc_{it}, which includes all forms of spending except upc_{it}—and, subsequently, each of the disaggregated types of spending per capita listed earlier. I use the same lagged dependent variable model, but, in addition to controlling for the previous year's spending, I also include the current year's total revenues per capita in the regressions.[64] For other right-hand-side variables, I include the same as in the revenue regressions: logged population, the index of economic variables, the share of total built-up area in Area A, and municipal employees per 1,000 residents.

Importantly, the dependent variables we use for spending capture financial allocations made from the regular municipal budget. As mentioned earlier, capital development projects that are partially or fully donor funded are excluded from both our revenue and expenditure variables. Thus, in general, our disaggregated spending variables capture how municipalities decide to allocate their regular, day-to-day budgets across different sectors (administration, public works, education, health, etc.). As such, these variables approximate our conceptual understanding of spending as the capacity to distribute—spending that is wholly carried out within the institution of the municipality and includes spending on the human and material resources needed to accomplish a particular distributive goal. However, importantly, these forms of spending may be targeted more narrowly—for example, in the form of noncontingent, targeted spending or political patronage—or more broadly—such as in the form of collectively supplied club or public goods.[65]

This analysis shows that towns controlled by the ruling party, Fatah, tend to spend more than their opposition counterparts on the water and electricity sectors ($p < 0.05$), and this holds when, instead of Fatah, I substitute the residuals (*resid_f*), which capture any unmeasured factors—other than population and housing supply, which were correlated with Fatah victory in the elections—that may have made Fatah more likely to be in office in municipality *i* in year *t*.[66] These estimations are shown in table 4.5.

These findings do not change substantially when panel-corrected standard errors are used, although the estimated coefficients in column 5 on *fatah* and columns 7, 10, and 11 on *resid_f* drop to the weaker 10 percent significance level (see the online appendix). Furthermore, in considering which municipalities from our sample are more likely to see this "Fatah effect" on utilities spending, I estimate an interactive model, specified identically to our model for revenues, where the Fatah effect is allowed to vary by levels of internal coercive capacity (see the online appendix). Here, we see that the share of a municipality's land in Area C exercises a conditioning effect: it is in those towns with larger shares of land in Area C where Fatah establishes its spending advantage in the electricity and/or water sectors.

Fatah's greater spending in the utility sector is not matched by greater revenue collection. When restricting our attention to only municipalities that have responsibility for water and/or electricity—and, thus, have utility revenues and expenditures greater than zero—municipality years under Hamas mayors were significantly more likely to have a positive budget balance for their utilities sector than municipality years under non-Hamas mayors ($X^2 = 4.74$, $p = 0.03$). Fatah- and independent-run towns were more likely to run deficits in their utilities sectors. Further, we showed earlier that the duration that a town spent under Fatah rule appeared to be associated with lower self-generated revenues.

If we estimate using the same models from table 4.2 but employ the municipality's overall budget balance as the dependent variable—incorporating all revenues and expenditures, including utilities—the sum of years spent under Fatah rule becomes a significant negative predictor of budget balance ($p < 0.01$). These results still pass the 5 percent significance threshold when the outlier cities of Nablus and Ramallah are excluded

TABLE 4.5
One-way fixed-effect lagged dependent variable regressions of mean utility expenditures per capita on Fatah control

	(1)	(2)	(3)	(4)	(5)	(6)	(7)	(8)	(9)	(10)	(11)
constant	22.88+ (13.26)	12.88 (12.88)	101.3* (50.56)	74.60 (49.94)	112.9* (52.58)	99.61 (59.98)	22.52 (13.65)	120.8* (53.58)	95.33+ (53.08)	129.1* (53.12)	116.4+ (59.51)
totrpc	0.105 (0.0720)	0.102 (0.0690)	0.106 (0.0712)	0.108 (0.0725)	0.0961 (0.0698)	0.0991 (0.0653)	0.101 (0.0688)	0.106 (0.0711)	0.108 (0.0724)	0.0960 (0.0699)	0.0910 (0.0652)
lag_uepc	0.858*** (0.0979)	0.873*** (0.0907)	0.868*** (0.0927)	0.869*** (0.0933)	0.872*** (0.0885)	0.737*** (0.100)	0.874*** (0.0906)	0.868*** (0.0927)	0.869*** (0.0932)	0.872*** (0.0886)	0.737*** (0.100)
econ_index	-25.16** (7.688)	-26.17*** (7.717)	-26.76** (8.022)	-25.82** (7.786)	-21.60*** (6.079)	-15.94* (6.153)	-25.28* (7.579)	-25.98** (7.937)	-25.03** (7.709)	-20.88*** (5.994)	-15.18* (6.045)
fatah		18.90* (7.464)	17.88* (7.165)	18.51* (7.074)	15.69* (7.606)	17.38* (8.121)					
resid_f							7.040* (3.018)	7.252* (3.034)	7.460* (2.985)	6.447* (3.214)	7.289* (3.426)
log_pop			-9.729+ (5.362)	-6.645 (5.292)	-10.68+ (5.441)	-13.78* (6.936)		-10.87+ (5.553)	-7.894 (5.506)	-11.59* (5.481)	-14.67* (6.893)
shareabuilt				-13.17 (9.420)	-13.33 (9.763)	-14.42 (13.75)			-12.86 (9.444)	-13.03 (9.768)	-14.32 (13.77)
munemp					-3.615 (3.694)	-2.984 (5.097)				-3.634 (3.695)	-2.972 (5.104)
governorate FE						Y					Y
year FE	Y	Y	Y	Y	Y	Y	Y	Y	Y	Y	Y
N	575	543	543	543	490	490	543	543	543	490	490
R^2	0.777	0.789	0.790	0.791	0.760	0.777	0.788	0.790	0.790	0.759	0.777

Note: Robust standard errors clustered by municipality in parentheses. FE = fixed effect. $^+$ $p < 0.10$, * $p < 0.05$, ** $p < 0.01$, *** $p < 0.001$.

or, alternatively, when a winsorized version of the dependent variable is used.[67] These estimations are all provided in the online appendix.[68] The other categories of spending—for example, health care, administration, or public works—do not reveal robust differences across party in the lagged dependent variable models.[69]

Regarding municipal spending by Hamas mayors in particular, it is important to note that Hamas is known to be affiliated with some *zakat* (Islamic charitable) organizations in the West Bank that invest considerably in certain social sectors, such as health care.[70] Thus, we must consider the possibility that Hamas-led municipal councils adapted—and perhaps attenuated—their spending in this sector because the political movement has historically been able to associate itself with this form of spending via institutions that operate outside the municipality. While I did not question respondents in depth about their associations with specific welfare institutions due to political sensitivities, the different spending and cost-saving measures pursued by opposition mayors is discussed more in chapter 5.

In conclusion, we can summarize and develop the findings from this chapter into more generalizable propositions. First, the results lead us to identify some conditions under which indigenous actors serving as intermediaries in an indirect rule regime may forbear from developing a controversial form of governing capacity, such as fiscal extraction. The analysis suggested that Fatah-led towns may have refrained from enforcing fines on Palestinian taxpayers relatively more than their opposition-governed counterparts, while Hamas-led towns outperformed their Fatah- and independent-led counterparts in municipal revenue growth.

One possible explanation for these findings is that raising revenue from the Palestinian population may be harder for Fatah than for its opponents. In this and the next chapter, I develop a theory that this is related to the form of indirect rule we observe in the occupied West Bank, wherein Israel, the dominant state, places special emphasis on the delegation of internal policing to the PA. Because of the perception among Palestinians that Fatah's policing is conducted on behalf of Israel rather than the Palestinian population, Fatah's reputational challenges may shape its approach to local governance. These challenges could increase the incentives of Fatah-led town councils to forbear from revenue collection. Among towns where the

PA wielded greater policing capacity in particular, we found evidence that Fatah rule was associated with lower revenue collection than was opposition rule. While there could be numerous explanations for these findings, they are broadly consistent with the aforementioned theory, because it is precisely those towns where the Palestinian internal policing presence is most visible where we expect that Fatah's reputation would be weakest.

Intriguingly, greater PA policing capacity produced opposite results in municipalities controlled by regime challengers—in these cases, it was associated with greater revenue collection relative to areas that were more directly ruled by Israel. Why might this be the case? The next chapter explores the relationship between opposition politicians and the Fatah-dominated police in more detail. It also elucidates some reasons that, especially following the 2006 legislative elections, regime opponents faced incentives to increase their revenue mobilization efforts. It is possible that these efforts were more heavily concentrated in Area A towns, or perhaps that is simply where these efforts paid off the most. Some of these questions cannot be fully answered with the data available.

Furthermore, the conditions in 2006 in the West Bank following Hamas's legislative victory were somewhat unique. Outside this very specific context, when else might regime opponents face greater external constraints? The theory-building hypothesis here, in its general form, is that indigenous challengers to the indirect rule regime face greater externally imposed constraints on their local governance programs. In some cases, these challengers may develop resource-building capacities—in this case, revenue mobilization—as a substitute or response.

Our analysis of Fatah-run locality spending also suggests that regime intermediaries might exploit resource advantages to engage in distributive spending. The empirical analysis suggests that Fatah is likely to engage in more spending on the utility sector than its opposition counterparts. This is particularly the case in towns where Palestinian coercive capacity is weaker, and thus Fatah-led councils may seek to compensate for this institutional weakness. As described earlier, water and electricity provision to Palestinian communities in the West Bank is thoroughly enmeshed in the military occupation. The utilities sector in general is one in which municipalities can and do accrue debt. Most of this debt for both electricity and water ultimately shows up on the balance sheets of the central PA government's arrears due to Israel. The PA has attempted to, but not always succeeded in, collecting these debts from the municipalities. Chapter 5 delves further into this issue.

Electricity and water debt may represent a type of "moral hazard" problem, wherein municipalities can supply these basic services without balancing their books. Municipalities, public-private utilities, and joint service councils in the West Bank are responsible for collecting payments from Palestinian families and businesses. However, for municipalities that control this revenue stream, the budget is somewhat elastic. Municipalities are able to become increasingly indebted on water and electricity provision without the central PA government enforcing debt collection. Here, I hypothesize that the soft constraint on municipal utility budgets provides Fatah-run municipalities with an opportunity to engage in spending more flexibly without necessarily recouping the revenues from their constituents. This lends some support to the proposition that Fatah may be using this relatively "costless" form of spending to bolster political support. While the data do not allow us to probe the political nature of this access to deficit spending, it is possible that the central PA government permitted such a practice to a greater degree in towns governed by Fatah. We did not see political favoritism in our analysis when examining the PA central government's direct revenue transfers to municipalities, but it would be a possible alternative venue in which such favoritism could emerge.

A final caveat is that examining spending on electricity and water provision does not necessarily mean improved access for residents. As noted, this spending includes salaries for municipal workers, for example, in addition to more brick-and-mortar forms of infrastructure. A more detailed analysis would be needed to examine possible partisan differences in consumption and access to these critical services across municipalities.

Other than being relatively less likely to boost utility-sector spending, the preceding analysis did not uncover many other ways in which spending by Hamas- or independent-run municipalities (the opposition) differed from spending in those governed by Fatah (the regime intermediary). The conversations reflected in the following chapter help us flesh out the individualized strategies used by opposition-affiliated municipal councils to govern given the resource challenges they faced.

Chapter Five

PALESTINIAN LOCAL GOVERNMENT UNDER ISRAELI INDIRECT RULE

Qualitative Findings

In this chapter, I use qualitative evidence from field-based interviews to understand potential causal relationships among the indirect rule regime, the political affiliation of local governments, and local fiscal and distributive outcomes. The intention is to probe some of the correlations observed in the quantitative analysis in the preceding chapter, while also exploring additional granular relationships that emerge between indigenous intermediaries and their adversaries under indirect rule regimes.

The insights from this chapter reveal support for some of the propositions from the preceding chapter. First, evidence from interviews and additional secondary sources suggests that Fatah, as the Palestinian intermediary, faces greater reputational costs to enforcing revenue collection and thus fewer incentives to develop local fiscal capacity compared with regime opponents. Overall, the qualitative evidence is consistent with an explanation based on a form of forbearance by Fatah-led councils due to the political sensitivities they face in extracting from the Palestinian population.

Second, the preceding chapter demonstrated that greater Palestinian coercive capacity resulted in increased local revenue collection in towns governed by the opposition. The conversations in this chapter convincingly rule out the possibility that this was due to opposition-led municipalities relying on the police for enforcement. While Fatah mayors and some bureaucrats in Area B towns—areas where the Palestinian Authority police have less capacity and presence—express a desire for the PA police to have better access to their towns, independent and opposition politicians in such areas struck a different note, describing how they adopted more creative, and sometimes confrontational, strategies to encourage tax and fee payment. Further, these conversations reveal that Hamas-affiliated mayors and municipal councils featuring Hamas members faced both financial challenges and overt repression. Interview respondents from these municipalities spoke of strategies they used to reduce the costs of their operations, including by relying on voluntary contributions from residents. This suggests that regime opponents may develop alternative modes of distribution that do not rely as heavily on spending through institutional channels.

Finally, my interviews, which took place after most opposition mayors had left office and Fatah had reconsolidated nominal control over most municipal councils, reveal complex relationships between regime intermediaries such as Fatah and their opponents at the local level. Hints of nostalgia for opposition rule appeared in some of my interviews with local bureaucrats, while in other cases, politicians acknowledged the importance of family linkages, and even friendships, across the political divides.

Interviews were conducted with more than fifty respondents over the course of several visits between 2014 and 2019.[1] Some of these conversations were conducted with academics, national-level politicians, bureaucrats, and activists; however, the majority of respondents were current or former mayors, municipal council members, and staff. These individuals were chosen to represent diverse political affiliations; municipalities of varying size, with variation in their assignment to Areas A, B, and C; and both small and large towns in eight of the West Bank's eleven governorates (also referred to as "districts"). To preserve respondents' anonymity, district rather than municipality names are referenced in the text and in the list of interviews provided in table A.3 of the appendix.

PARTISAN DIFFERENCES IN REVENUE MOBILIZATION

We must consider, beyond the informational, administrative, and bureaucratic capacity to assess, mobilize, and collect revenue, the incentives of the municipal government to engage in revenue mobilization. An encompassing definition of fiscal capacity captures not only the ability to generate revenue for the municipal government but also the will to do so. One theme that emerged from my conversations was that local governments that included Hamas mayors or Hamas-affiliated council members—the latter including those with nominally independent mayors—faced a greater demand for revenue, especially after 2006. Following Hamas's victory in the January 2006 legislative elections, the central PA government experienced a negative budgetary shock, as funding from donors and revenue transfers from Israel were temporarily frozen. Several interlocutors suggested that the costs of the donor freeze that targeted Hamas, as a political movement, were passed on to Hamas-run localities. Further, opposition politicians spoke in general about the fiscal hardships they encountered while in office, which necessitated additional effort to increase revenue (and resource) mobilization locally. Conversely, conversations with Fatah politicians— and some bureaucrats who serve under them—reveal that Fatah-led councils exerted less effort overall to mobilize revenue from constituents.

Municipalities with Hamas mayors—or even those that featured Hamas municipal council members in multiparty coalitions—struggled due to the 2006–7 funding freeze implemented by Israel and international donors. On the donor financing side, one mayor who was elected on a Hamas-affiliated list recounted, "In 2005, [we] had a project to build a school, and it was 90 percent completed, but then [the United States Agency for International Development] realized the elected municipal council was mainly made up of Hamas members. This shouldn't [affect] municipal projects, but they stopped the funding for the school" (Interview 2014.7). Still others suggested that they were penalized by the PA government for their affiliation with the opposition. Another former mayor who was elected on a multiparty list that included Hamas described the effects of the political crisis on municipal finances:

Before the legislative elections, challenges had already started. . . . Even, unfortunately, the [Ministry of Local Government] . . . practiced favoritism when the mayor was not Fatah. . . . After the legislative elections, there were limitations and closure on a larger scale and we were one of the councils targeted by these forced limitations. . . .

The boycott was comprehensive so to speak. . . . The situation, if I can put it in a metaphor, felt like we were swallowing a knife. The local council is expected to stand tall, yet it is asked to do so without any support. (Interview 2019.8)

We did not find evidence of any political bias in transfer revenues in the preceding chapter. However, municipalities had uneven access to transfers, since not all municipalities benefited from a property tax system. If, for example, opposition candidates were more likely to be elected in towns that did assess property taxes, those revenue transfers could possibly obscure evidence of political bias against such municipalities that were hidden in the non-property-tax component of transfers. Alternatively, it is possible that this respondent's perceptions of favoritism by the central PA government did not appear in the form of reduced central government transfers but cropped up in other places.

The data analyzed in chapter 4, for example, did not allow us to analyze the central government's willingness to approve municipal projects before they even got off the ground. A former mayor affiliated with Hamas described it this way in 2019:

> In 2005, there were elections. These are lived experiences that we are discussing, it is not yet history. These are recent events. Hamas achieved political advancement during these elections. Political gains during these elections were advanced over the best interest of our country. This is my opinion. It was evident and clear. There was a division between the parties, especially between Hamas and Fatah. This of course was reflected in the municipalities. To be brief, the impact of the division on international relations had a very negative impact on the municipalities. . . . Events even happened to me on a personal level. Of course, I am affiliated with Hamas. This of course meant that the municipality was affiliated with Hamas. As a result, support to the municipality would either be reduced or completely cut." (Interview 2019.5)

Even a Fatah-affiliated mayor spoke of discrimination by PA leadership against the Hamas-led mayor who preceded them.

MAYOR: [Name of former mayor] represented Hamas. During the time that [they were] in office, as I heard, there was a lack of funds.
RESEARCH ASSISTANT: So, the difficulty in funds was due to the political affiliation of the council not because of the [second] intifada?
MAYOR: Yes, this is what I heard. I heard that the PA was punishing [the former mayor] because [they] represented opposition. So, funds during that time from the PA were less generous. There were some projects, but they were

smaller and not many. . . . I do not belong to [name of former mayor's] party. I speak in objectivity. This is what I heard during that time. [Name of former Hamas mayor] is my colleague and friend. I heard that they were not generous in project allocation during [their] time. . . . They did some work . . . the council. They had projects and worked enthusiastically through the self-financing of the municipality. Their best project, was a junction road that they excavated here in the town. . . . (Interview 2019.14)

Among other reasons, this account is notable for the way in which the Fatah-affiliated mayor amicably refers to the former Hamas mayor as a friend. In an environment defined by bitter political polarization at the national level, it is important to acknowledge that local relationships are often more complex and, in some ways, intimate.

Even if there was no discrimination in the transfer of revenues from the central, Fatah-controlled government to Hamas-affiliated municipalities, opposition mayors and councils sometimes faced yet another form of financial pressure: on their first day as mayor, they found empty bank accounts. One former mayor from Hamas describes the municipal debt they faced when they took office in 2005 and how they perceived the financial pressure to be politically motivated.

When I came to office, the municipality fund was also almost empty. The total of everything we counted was approximately 33,000 [New Israeli] shekels only. I took office on October 23, which meant that employee payroll was due within one week. It was also 'eid time, when employees receive [a holiday] bonus. In addition, I had to pay outstanding bills. The total that was due at the end of that month amounted to 350,000 shekels. Only 10 percent of that was available, if we added the money at the municipality with that at the bank. [My] opponents were, of course, happy about this, and were waiting to see how I would handle the people who were waiting to be paid. People with bouncing checks from the municipality were knocking on our door for money . . . although the checks bounced many months before, . . . six months ago and sometimes even a year ago. The value of these checks was over 100,000 shekels. Some people were coming at this time due to incitement by other parties advising them to take up their issue with the new mayor. Some were coming because they wanted to corner me so that I give up and ask Fatah to come take over. Pardon my honesty. . . . I am speaking with complete transparency here. (Interview 2019.13)

There is also evidence to suggest that opposition-run towns were forced to mobilize nonfinancial resources in more innovative ways than their Fatah counterparts due to financial pressures. For example, the Hamas-affiliated respondent mentioned earlier also described how popular support for municipal projects—either financial or in kind, that is, in the form of volunteer labor—helped them overcome the financial blockade. They described how townspeople contributed to projects, such as road excavations, and residents of the town also assisted in using personal relationships with PA offices and ministries to connect the municipality to resources.

In general, opposition-affiliated municipalities perceived an urgent need to mobilize revenues to support municipal operations in the wake of the 2006–7 political crisis between Fatah and Hamas. Further, factors other than immediate financial pressure may have led opposition municipal councils to invest more effort in tax and fee collection. Hamas had campaigned—both in the local elections and, more overtly, in national elections—on a platform of fighting corruption and with pledges to more equitably enforce laws. Their electoral list, "Change and Reform" (al-'Islah wal-Taghayyur), did not explicitly refer to their Islamist credentials. Independent candidates and lists in the local elections also emphasized fairness in their campaigns (and in at least one of the interviews to come). Once they were in office, this may have translated into enforcing municipal revenue collection more regularly than Fatah had done in the past.

Qualitative sources suggest that the ruling party, Fatah, adopted progressive forms of forbearance at the local level, refraining from fee collection in cases where constituents had less ability to pay. A documentary from a local election campaign in the town of Beit Ummar in 2012—the period following the time span reflected in chapter 4's analysis—is illustrative. A supporter of the Fatah-supported candidate, Nasri Sabarna, who had previously served as mayor for an abbreviated term, suggests that Sabarna is distinctive from the current, Hamas-affiliated mayor because during Sabarna's previous time in office, he did not enforce electricity bill collection on small taxpayers.[2] The interviewer asks the supporter, "Some people are talking about the electricity situation, saying [Sabarna] shouldn't have forgiven people that didn't have money." The supporter replies, "He [was] the mayor of a town—you don't want the mayor to help people? . . . Sometimes you have to help, whether you like it or not."

As Alisha Holland describes, forbearance as a means of redistribution is an especially attractive strategy in developing countries and other settings where politicians' capacity to improve the social welfare of their constituents is limited.[3] Operating under military occupation, Palestinian politicians face many such constraints. In the West Bank, forbearance by Palestinian officials can be a powerful tool to either enact redistributive welfare or cultivate targeted political support.[4] If Fatah did, indeed, exert less effort in collecting revenues, this would reinforce the findings revealed in chapter 4.

After 2012, nearly all municipalities were dominated by Fatah or affiliated politicians. Elections had been held again that year, but Hamas and most opposition parties refused to participate under allegations that the polls were not being conducted fairly. Thus, Fatah was able to regain uncontested control across many towns and cities. Political sensitivities thus introduced complications during my interviews, since they occurred after nearly all Hamas-affiliated mayors and many independent mayors had been removed from office or left on their own. Yet, subtle moments could be revealing. In a group interview with a Fatah-affiliated mayor who took office in 2017 and a couple of staff members, I asked, "Have the municipality's sources of revenue changed over time? Is there anything you are doing differently than past mayors?" One employee in the room responded, "of course, there is a difference." The mayor deferred the question to another employee, the general director of the municipality, who had been employed in the municipality for a longer period. They responded, "From the 1990s until about 2005, there was not a lot of emphasis on enforcement for people to pay for water, electricity, and services. . . . Before 2005, there were only about 300 people in the town who could pay. . . . The municipality was weak. . . . After 2005 to 2006, with the elections [which Hamas won locally], the municipality began to organize itself as an institution, not simply as an appointed council and not simply one person." (Interview 2018.4)

At this point, the first employee, the one the mayor had interrupted previously, chimed in again to emphasize that at this time, "there were elected councils." In addition to suggesting that Hamas organized the municipality differently, these quotations allude to Hamas's commitment to tax and fee enforcement, unlike the previous, Fatah-affiliated council. Perhaps it is no coincidence that the mayor sought to partially silence this particular employee.

This anecdote also highlights the political complexities that can shape relationships within the municipality itself and how even a municipality where Fatah had reasserted control might still contain vestigial support for the opposition among staff. A budget director with whom I met in 2018 worked under a Fatah-affiliated mayor at the time of our interview, but they had been in their position since 2003. In 2005, Hamas had won a majority of seats in the municipality's elections, but Fatah soon ousted the winning candidates and regained control of the council. In response to a generic opening question about the most important roles for local government, the general director—who had served throughout this period—was quick to emphasize the importance of competitive elections for municipal office. Such elections had not been conducted for more than thirteen years at the time we spoke.

ME: Now, I have just a very general question on your perspective on the role of local governance, what you think is the most important role of local governance as compared to district, regional, national government?

BUDGET DIRECTOR: . . . Universally, there are three different roles for local governance. The roles set out for local governance here in Palestine are a reflection of those universal roles. The roles are, number one, service provision. . . . The second universal role [of local government] is democracy. It should indeed be its first role. Local governance should encourage democracy through local elections of municipal councils. Local governance should have an effective role in promoting democracy across all local governance units. This will allow a fair rotation of power and authority and allows citizens to express their opinions freely, and will reserve their right to select their representatives. (Interview 2018.2)

It is notable that an unelected bureaucrat would emphasize elections in such a direct way, especially given the increasingly authoritarian context in which they worked and lived. In a separate question about revenue collection, this staff member alluded to the leniency with which the current municipal council enforced (or did not enforce) fee payment.

ME: What if [the municipality] see[s] a building that is built without a permit? What do they do?

BUDGET DIRECTOR: The right thing to do is to stop that building from being completed if it is erected without a permit. However, right now the municipality employees are overlooking such issues. Everyone is building without a permit. [Laughs] . . .

Revenue is increasing on paper . . . because there is an increase in population size. The services are more diverse now and fees have increased. So, naturally, revenue increases. However, not in the rate that it should. The problem is in collection.

Based on their prior comment on the importance of elections, I was curious to know this staff member's own political leanings, if any. Of course, it was too politically sensitive for me to ask. We cannot know if this employee attributed the lax enforcement of revenue collection to Fatah's control of the municipal council, but their statements nonetheless provide evidence of leniency.

In another interview, an energetic, Fatah-affiliated mayor spoke openly about the challenges they faced in collecting fees from residents.

ME: Obviously support from donors and support from the central government is important. But what about the fees they raise from the residents here from water, garbage collection . . . etc. [Do you] see any possibility of increasing these sources of revenue over time?

RESPONDENT: Yes, I think so. Current fees are not sufficient, and also people are not committing to the payment of these fees. This is our main problem with residents. Residents see that they are under the occupation, and they deem that we should help them and that we should not be collecting these fees from them. This creates an embarrassment between us and the residents, because we cannot keep providing services without receiving payment. . . .

Residents here would not easily accept an increase of fees. A lot of effort should be invested in convincing the people, before we are able to increase any fees. There is a lot to be done before a decision can be taken to increase the fees. This applies to all towns, not just [name of town]. (Interview 2018.6)

This mayor connected residents' reticence to pay municipal fees to how they view the occupation. Further, by referencing the "embarrassment" it creates for the municipality, the mayor seemed to acknowledge the legitimacy problem this creates for the municipal council and perhaps, in particular, those affiliated with Fatah. Later, when I asked if the mayor had observed any changes over their years working in the municipality, they returned to the topic of fee collection, suggesting a relatively incremental and tentative approach. Subsequently, perhaps indicating some insecurity around their popular legitimacy, the respondent refocused the discussion on how popular they (claimed they) were with the residents. "In my opinion, I have to be good with the residents, to listen to them and to try to provide whatever they want, and then I can ask them to pay. That is my policy. I don't say 'have to' or 'must'! These are heavy words to use sometimes. When I am in contact with them on Facebook for example, I feel that they are comfortable. I don't want to talk about myself, but the people here love me. I am a hero in their eyes. They respect me a lot." (Interview 2018.6)

Some background on how this particular individual reached office is pertinent to our understanding of their potential legitimacy—or lack thereof—in the eyes of their constituents. At the beginning of the interview with this mayor, they provided some background information, including that they "became mayor" in 2009. As an ice-breaker, I asked what led them to begin a career in local governance: "I was an accountant here at the municipality from 1998 to 2002. For five years I was here as an accountant and then I went to the U.S and got my two master's degrees and when I returned, they, I mean the people of [name of town], announced me as mayor." (Interview 2018.6)

In fact, this individual was not freely elected, so "the people" had very little role in their ascent to the office of mayor. The town was subjected to Israeli raids as early as June 2006, following Hamas's victory in the local election.[5] The elected mayor, a sheikh at a local mosque and member of Hamas's Change and Reform list, was seized by Israeli occupation forces in October that year.[6] As of April 2007, this individual was still detained, and then the deputy mayor was also arrested.[7] By 2009, the Fatah loyalist—my interview respondent, who described themselves as a hero in the eyes of their constituents—was installed as mayor.

PARTISAN DIFFERENCES IN SPENDING

The quantitative analysis in chapter 4 did not find that Hamas distinguished itself from its Fatah or independent counterparts in terms of spending. An interview with a former mayor affiliated with Hamas adds some complexity to our understanding of how opposition-affiliated councils approached distribution and the implications for our analysis of formal spending. Does more spending always signify greater distributive capacity? This former mayor, for example, explains how they were able to do more with less.

> I consider good management and the proper use of human resources, whether in terms of municipality employees or the town people, as one of our main strengths. For example, [name of a Palestinian telecommunications company] wanted to erect a telecommunication tower in [name of town]. We agreed, with the condition that they would donate the money for a road excavation project. They calculated the cost and it was 80,000 shekels. So, we told them, you will pay 80,000 shekels; however, the management of the project will be through the municipality. The 80,000 shekels were allocated for the paving of a 150-meters-long road at 3 meters wide. Nevertheless, through our proper management, we were able to complete the road with a width of 6 meters. How? Through the smart use of resources.
>
> Another example, we built a retention wall here in the village. Instead of buying new equipment for its construction, we used refurbished equipment in order to work within our budget. Thus, from this example we see that we can increase revenue through the proper management of resources and through good project management.
>
> Additionally, [name of school] was also another success story. The budget for this school was 1,200,000 USD. Instead, we spent 800,000 to 900,000. We saved at least 400,000 USD . . . [Residents of the town] donated not only money, but also people were offering to complete parts of the construction themselves. One of the citizens has health issues and owns a small café in the town. He does not have a lot of money, but he wanted to participate and to be part of this project. He offered to provide breakfast to the workers every day until the construction was complete. Another one owns a bee farm. He offered to contribute to the breakfast by providing honey. Other people were working for days in the construction site, lifting steel and bricks, for free. This saved us a lot of money. One-third of the school was built through the effort of the people. Moreover, instead of building a one-story school, we built a two-story school building. Other people also, through their external relations with traders from Hebron, were able to bring in external donations in the form of school doors, for example. The municipality thus became an institution that reduced the cost of providing its services, instead of being an institution of corruption and overpriced services. (Interview 2019.5)

The preceding narrative draws attention to the nuance behind formal figures on revenues and spending. For some municipal councils, distributive aims were achieved by leveraging volunteers, donated resources, and other savings that would be invisible in official budget files. The precipitous drop in donor funding meant that Hamas and Hamas-affiliated municipal councils faced specific incentives to reduce costs and increase revenues. As one Hamas-affiliated former mayor has described, municipalities were sometimes in dire financial shape when winning opposition lists took office. This may have both constrained the spending ambitions of opposition-affiliated councils and encouraged them to mobilize lower-cost, informal alternatives.

MUNICIPAL AUTONOMY OVER "SOFT BUDGETS"

Another factor that shapes the fiscal outlook for West Bank municipalities is whether or not they distribute electricity, water, or both to their residents or are part of a regional company or council that does so. While some municipalities manage the revenues themselves and others pass them on to a regional utility or council, for the most part, these revenues are ultimately liabilities that are due to Israel. From a technocratic perspective, the question is, "Should these debts be borne by the central PA government, the municipalities, or the end users of the service?" From a legal perspective, international humanitarian law on occupied territories implies that Israel is responsible for ensuring access to basic services for the Palestinian population.[8]

The vast majority of electricity in the West Bank is imported from Israel. The municipalities of the central West Bank—those located near Jerusalem, Ramallah/Al-Bireh, Jericho, and Bethlehem—do not provide electricity, because this authority was granted to JDECO, a public-private company that dates from the British colonial period. While there are similar companies in the north (serving parts of Jenin, Tulkarm, Tubas, and Nablus) and the south (serving the Hebron area), these companies were established later, and municipalities had greater leverage to choose whether to join the companies or continue collecting electricity on their own. The process by which these outcomes were determined is relatively opaque, but, in general, my interviews suggest that some mayors were more proactive in maintaining this form of autonomy for the municipality.

For example, this respondent—a municipal employee whose own political leanings are unknown—expressed the municipality's desire to control electricity fee collection without the public-private regional utility as a kind of middleman: "Today, the [PA central] government is working on a national [electricity] transfer plant. They want us to join, but we have refused. . . . They bought from the Israelis a plant in [name of nearby town]. They expanded the network to reach our town. But we refused. They want to control us, but we told them we will pay directly to the Israelis." (Interview 2019.12)

We cannot say with any degree of certainty whether such examples are correlated with the political affiliation of municipal mayors or councils, particularly because many of these decisions were made prior to the time of my interviews. However, this excerpt is illuminating in that it reinforces the politicized nature of electricity provision in the context of Israel's occupation.

Despite respondents from diverse political affiliations and professional roles reporting challenges with electricity and water revenue collection, some interview subjects from opposition parties lent credence to the proposition from chapter 4 that Fatah-run municipalities used electricity spending to garner political support. One former Hamas mayor recounted this to me:

In making the simplest decisions, we had to go through political battles. There was this . . . factory that had opened . . . in an illegal place. He opened it in a residential neighborhood. The [PA] did not force him to close. When he applied to join the electricity network, he faced an issue with me. I received a direct threat from the [PA Preventive] Security Forces because I refused to connect him. When I turned to the [PA] Ministry of Local Government, they said that they cannot support me if I am facing the [Preventive] Security Forces. I told them, the security forces can hold me accountable for any political work they deem unsuitable, but they cannot intervene in my work as mayor. This incident went on for multiple months. In the end, a delegation from the ministry came [to me] with instructions to connect this business to the network. I think he was able to bribe them. Otherwise, why would a delegation come with these orders? The same day the delegation came, I received two orders from the Preventive Security Forces and [PA] Intelligence to report to them for investigation. (Interview 2019.11)

To the extent that this respondent's narrative is an accurate reflection of events, it strengthens our confidence in the proposition that Fatah—in this case, the Fatah-dominated central government rather than a Fatah-affiliated municipality—sees potential political gain from providing key services such as electricity. While the theory that emerged from the preceding chapter suggested that such service provision may be to bolster Fatah's support, this respondent suggested, instead, it was due to outright corruption in the form of bribe-taking.

Another subject, also affiliated with Hamas, described their efforts to reduce municipal debt on taking office. "I needed to control municipality revenue. I needed to make sure that revenue is properly collected. I found it bizarre that the electricity bill was 1 million [New Israeli] shekels, while the municipality was only collecting 500,000 [NIS]! This meant that there was an issue here. People were not paying for the services. And this was encouraged by the previous council." (Interview 2019.13) This respondent thus substantiates our hunch that Fatah-led councils are predisposed to building debt in their utility sectors—namely, not collecting enough revenue to cover their spending.

Regarding water, Israel, again, possesses disproportionate control over the Palestinian water supply. Many municipalities sell and distribute water directly to their residents, whereas other towns are part of so-called joint services councils that represent several towns banded together and operate as their own institutions. A number of respondents pointed out that when municipalities controlled water provision, they also accumulated debts. For example, this independent mayor noted,

> The Municipal Lending and Development Fund [a semipublic institution] used to grant small amounts to the municipalities. Then, they tried to bargain with us to use these grants to deduct from our water debts. When we entered office, the municipality was already in debt for water services. These debts were never settled, not even during our time. We remained in debt. It is difficult to cut water services from people if they do not pay. So, we always continued to postpone the payment due to the [central] government because the people are not paying . . . and we would tell the government: we cannot cut water services from people's homes. (Interview 2019.8)

Indeed, an independent mayor of a municipality that maintained authority over both electricity and water spoke about the revenue surplus generated by the former and the deficit generated by the latter:

MAYOR: To this day, the municipality is responsible for water and electricity service provision.

ME: In your view, is this a good thing?

MAYOR: Yes, it is better if the municipality is responsible for these services. This way, the employees are from within the town. They know the people and know how to deal with them. Electricity service provision creates revenue for the municipality, but the water does not. It loses. It is cheap, one cup is four shekels, whereas, if the network is damaged, we pay thousands of shekels in maintenance. If we join a private company, we will lose this source of revenue from the electricity. The municipality will be destroyed, especially since we are in debt! Israel provides water and electricity to us directly. (Interview 2018.3)

A head of a budget department in a municipality outside Ramallah noted how their municipality did not collect electricity or water revenues, since these were under the control of JDECO and a regional water council. However, they noted that from their perspective, it would be preferable if the municipality controlled these revenue sources themselves.

ME: Compared with some other towns that collect electricity revenue, does this make it harder for [name of town]?

BUDGET DIRECTOR: Yes, it is harder, because if there were water and electricity services and revenue is collected by the municipality, then we make money. Especially now that these bills are [collected through] prepaid [meters]. . . . This increases revenue, and collection becomes better. (Interview 2018.2)

And a mayor from a small party—representing neither Fatah nor Hamas—notes that collecting payments from constituents for water was a struggle because it is ultimately Israel that restricts the water supply to the Palestinian Authority and, subsequently, the PA that restricts the amount going to each municipality.

MAYOR: [We have a] semigovernmental company for water and electricity, and this gives us a lot of relief because collecting money for fees is the main obstacle we face here at the municipality. We used to have our own water network, and it was a disaster for the municipality. . . .

ME: So, the water was difficult. Was the municipality previously losing money?

MAYOR: Yes, because we don't control the sources for the water. We can't control how to give people their share. . . . [As] if the pressure is not enough, the neighborhoods in the highest [elevation] areas will not receive water until the week after! We need 10,000 [cubic meters] each day. They give us 15,000 [cubic meters] per week!

ME: Israel?

MAYOR: The [PA water] company, but the Israelis . . . they give the company for the whole of the [district] area 35,000 [cubic meters] per day. We need 100,000 to cover the need of this same area. . . . We take one-third of our need. . . . This is occupation. They take our resources. In the settlements, you don't see any tanks on the rooftops, that's because they take water directly from the network. This is the main obstacle and why we can't really develop agriculture; we can't develop our resources. (Interview 2019.6)

Israel's rationing of water to Palestinians living under military occupation was a common complaint of local leaders. Further, grievances about the Palestinian Authority—or the utility companies it supports—impairing municipal fiscal capacity were not limited to anti-Fatah politicians. In an example not related to electricity or water, a Fatah mayor described the problems they faced in encouraging residents to pay taxes and fees, but then they were quick to criticize the central PA government for failing to transfer property tax revenues to the municipality that had already been collected from the town's residents.

ME: Has [the mayor] seen, over the years, other challenges with getting people to pay for, like, a permit for buildings, for example? Do they have challenges in collecting revenue from people? Or for the most part, do people pay willingly?

MAYOR: We have a culture of not paying. People don't like to pay tax. . . . Since January 1st, the PA owes us just over 200 thousand Jordanian dinars of property tax that people have paid through banks. The Ministry of Finance is supposed to deduct 10 percent and then transfer the rest to us. We still have not received this payment. There is a total of 500 thousand Jordanian dinars of property tax that has not been paid, 80 percent of which is for property owned by our people who live in the U.S. With this money, we can [complete] many projects! Despite the financial situation, I was able to open roads, build a water network, . . . and we will build a new electricity network. Without this money, how can we continue with our projects? (Interview 2019.14)

These conversations with interview respondents illuminate complexities that are not captured in the empirical analysis in the preceding chapter. For example, partisan affiliation does not appear to fully explain levels of skepticism toward central PA institutions that we see in municipal offices. Even Fatah-affiliated mayors and municipal councils resent the government in Ramallah at times. Municipalities that have had greater flexibility often mention the benefits of maintaining autonomy over electricity provision specifically and sometimes water as well. For those who did not want to be responsible for their own water networks, the problem comes down to the ability of residents to pay and the willingness of municipalities to collect. While some of these observations transcended political divisions, the testimonies highlighted in this section suggest that Fatah was more lenient with revenue collection and more likely to extend electricity networks as a form of political favoritism.

GEOGRAPHIC FRAGMENTATION: AREAS A, B, AND C

Towns differ in the amount of their populated area is located in Area A (areas where the Palestinian police have relatively greater freedom to operate) as opposed to Area B (where the Palestinian police must coordinate directly with Israel on most of their movements). They also differ in how much of their land is designated as Area C—the portion of the West Bank that not only is off-limits to PA police forces but also restricts nearly all forms of Palestinian development. Israel regularly demolishes housing and structures serving the populations living in Area C, which consist of small Palestinian villages and Bedouin communities. Residents of Area C are also subject to greater direct threats of Israeli settler violence. Thus, while the *de jure* distinction between Area A and Area B in the Oslo Accords is primarily about internal policing capacity, the absence of Palestinian Authority institutions in Area C underlies a much broader set of challenges and existential threats to Palestinians. I discuss each of these in turn.

Palestinian Policing Capacity

When respondents were asked if they thought the Area A versus Area B distinction shaped other aspects of local governance, their responses were mixed. Some suggested that it did not. A typical response of the sort was as follows, in this case with a general director—a high-level municipal employee—of an Area A town:

> I think for us, because we are close to [Area A district capital] and are away from borders, we do not face many issues. A few days ago, however, they attacked a resident. But because we are away from tension areas, we do not face so much trouble. The zones are irrelevant, or are not the main factor. But it is different from town to town depending on where they are located. For example, [Area] A towns in [other district] and [other district] have more issues because they are close to the separation wall. (Interview 2019.1)

However, when respondents answered in the affirmative, the difference often boiled down to the ability of the PA police to enter their town, respond to incidents, and help with code enforcement. In particular, Fatah-affiliated councils and unelected bureaucrats express, in the discussions quoted here, a greater inclination to use the police to assist the municipality with enforcement. On the other hand, opposition-led councils often described alternative forms of enforcement. It is worth quoting a lengthy conversation with two staff members of a municipality in Hebron governorate whose populated area is primarily in Area B, meaning the PA police cannot act without coordinating with Israel. While discussing the challenges the municipality faced with controlling its land in Area C and urban planning, one of the employees (Employee 1) suddenly began discussing the situation with the police.

EMPLOYEE 1: Also, today for example, there are seventy security police from [the Palestinian Authority] present in [name of municipality]. They are camped in a school here. We requested them because we have over six thousand unlawful cars in the town.

EMPLOYEE 2: They are here through coordination with the Israelis.

RESEARCH ASSISTANT: How long will they stay?

EMPLOYEE 1: One or two weeks.

EMPLOYEE 2: It depends on how long they received permission to stay from the Israelis. They also have the authority to kick them out early. They might ask them to leave three days after they have arrived for example. It is up to the Israelis how long they stay. . . .

EMPLOYEE 1: We cannot live without security. Without security, life cannot go on. In [name of municipality] we do not have security, we do not have a police station or anything like that. They are not allowed to be here, to help us maintain the laws in this area. Whose responsibility is this? The occupation. They prevented them from controlling this area. I could use these security forces, if they were available, to enforce laws related to construction. For example, I could have prevented people from building on agricultural land. But we can't do that without any forces. My authorities as a municipality employee are limited.

RESEARCH ASSISTANT: How far is the closest police station from [name of municipality]?

EMPLOYEE 1: Six kilometers.

RESEARCH ASSISTANT: And they cannot come without security coordination with the Israelis?

EMPLOYEE 1: Of course not. If there is a fight in the town, and I call them. They need two to three hours to coordinate with the Israelis before they are allowed to come. They also can't take the main road to arrive here. They need to take all the back roads. This factor is important as to why the economic situation is bad here. We live in anarchy today. People are buying cars from the black market for 1,000 shekels. This is why many households have multiple cars. All of them are purchased illegally.

EMPLOYEE 2: Also, people who have money, they invest in [name of nearest city]. They do not invest here. It is much easier to invest there. There is security and services there. Why would they invest here? Even people from this town who live abroad, when they come back, they invest in [name of nearest city] . . . not here.

EMPLOYEE 1: The security forces need two hours on the backroads to arrive here from [nearby town]. Two hours instead of five minutes.

EMPLOYEE 2: By the time they arrive, the fight would be over.

RESEARCH ASSISTANT: If there was a police station, would this have impacted the construction here? Permits?

EMPLOYEE 1: Yes, of course. (Interview 2019.12)

Note that these are two employees of the municipality, not elected politicians with partisan affiliations. The depiction they provide is that areas outside PA policing control face enforcement problems when it comes to illegal vehicles, construction permits, and even criminal altercations such as fights. The employees make a straightforward link between these gaps in security and the revenue base of the municipality.

A Fatah-affiliated mayor described the challenges of being outside the accessible range of the Palestinian police and how that influenced revenue collection.

ME: I heard a lot about the problems in Area C, but does the mayor think that being in Area B also puts the municipality at a disadvantage compared to if they were in Area A? In terms of operation or revenue?

RESPONDENT: Sure. Yes! . . . I see the difference between a mayor in Area A or one in an area that is completely B, how things are easier for them compared to us. If I face any issue here that require immediate police intervention, although I have a police station, they still need to refer back to headquarters in Area A before they can make a move. If I need an officer in Area C, we have to wait for Israeli coordination and this can sometimes take up to three to five hours! By that time, for example, if someone was building over municipality road borders, they would have completed their construction by the time I can receive police backup. I consider Area B and C divisions as a huge obstacle for service provision. (Interview 2018.6)

In a separate interview with a Fatah-affiliated mayor, the respondent mentioned that the municipality "does not have the authority to stop illegal building" because they do not have a police station in their Area B town. They noted that a police station would help the municipality enforce construction permits, since illegal building can progress over time and police response times were slow. (Interview 2019.9) By contrast, municipal leaders who were affiliated with the opposition sought greater autonomy from police-assisted enforcement. The former, Hamas-affiliated mayor in the same town described how they aimed to increase local revenue collection in ways that did not depend on police enforcement.

During our first week [on the] council, we noticed issues with construction. Construction is random and shops are operating without permits. So . . .

I invited the contractors to a meeting. We told them that any construction site that you work at must already have a permit from the municipality. . . . They must abide by construction rules—[such as] distance between buildings and from the road—as well as fee payments. . . .

Of course, it is against the law to be lenient with fee payment or to allow installments. According to the law, you need to pay the fees in full at the time of your application. But no one [was] abiding, no one [was] paying the fees, . . . so we had to allow installments. We called . . . factories and we told them, you cannot supply . . . construction sites that do not have a permit. We threatened that we will disconnect their water and other services as a punishment if they supply any construction site without a permit. This has forced people to completely abide and apply to receive permits. . . . Of course, this was reflected positively on the municipality and increased its income through permit application fees. (Interview 2019.11)

Even if this town had a police station, the Hamas-affiliated mayor noted that their political affiliation made turning to the police for assistance with enforcement less feasible. Instead, they used their control of a distributive service (utilities) to pressure compliance with revenue collection.

RESPONDENT: The smart way to deal with this, is to reduce your need for police support. So, you start thinking of mechanisms, of other alternatives. For example in the case of the permits, instead of sending them a notice to stop building and to send the police over if they ignore the notice, I found the solution to threaten [them] through cutting off water and electricity services. In this way, I eliminated my need for a police force. . . .

ME: In general, did you need to cooperate with the police at all in the municipality? In your work?

RESPONDENT: Yes, we needed them. But bear in mind we [had] an issue. . . . There is corruption and favoritism. We [Hamas] are considered a new party. . . . Sometimes when the issue reaches the police, there is no cooperation because they have received recommendations not to cooperate. They would ignore our issue. . . . It was a battle. (Interview 2019.11)

While the former mayor just quoted points to the Fatah-Hamas rivalry as one reason they did not cooperate with the Fatah-led police, another Hamas-affiliated former mayor recalled a generally cooperative relationship with the PA police even though they did not seek police assistance with enforcement.

ME: Some of the municipalities we talked to about enforcing payments to get people to pay their taxes or fees, they talked about not having a police station. That it would be easier to get people to pay if they had police, a Palestinian police station. Is that something that could have helped you, for example, collect the debt from these people . . . that had not paid over twenty thousand shekels? Or because of the political situation, maybe it would not help?

RESPONDENT: I did not need the police to enforce payments because I used the approach of persuasion and transparency, which I think are better approaches than police force. During my term, I participated in the Friday preaching at the mosque on a monthly basis. During this sermon, I would update the people on the work of the municipality during the past month, including our future plans. . . . When people saw that we were asking everyone to pay their debt without any discrimination, they realized that it was fair and that it was based on the amount of debt everyone had. . . .

The police and the judiciary system were cooperative during that time, I have to be honest. . . . Anytime there was vandalism of public property, I would file a lawsuit at the court and they would handle it professionally. . . . On another occasion, I needed the police during road excavation work, and they cooperated. (Interview 2019.13)

Finally, one former mayor affiliated with Hamas expressed skepticism about the PA police and the supposed limitations it faced in Area B, where a majority of the mayor's municipality's population was located.

ME: The final question is about the issue of the police. If [the respondent] thinks not having a Palestinian police station in [name of town] affected [their] work? Or was it something [they] didn't feel the municipality needed to cooperate with the police much for their work?

RESPONDENT: There was a need, yes. But the question is, if there was one, would they cooperate?

RESEARCH ASSISTANT: And the reason for that being?

RESPONDENT: The political affiliation of the municipality, and also they do not want to work.

RESEARCH ASSISTANT: You mean even if the [municipal council] was Fatah, they do not want to work?

RESPONDENT: It's relative. When we need them and we call them, they say we do not have [permission through] coordination with the Israelis. But when they want to imprison someone for being religious and praying in the mosque, they know how to coordinate to travel and conduct their work here. . .

In the end, they could if they wanted to, travel in a civil car and arrive in the town in their capacity as police officers and practice the law. It is not a big deal. If they wanted to, they can find solutions. If they really wanted to work, they can find alternatives. (Interview 2019.15)

In summary, the preceding excerpts show that even if relationships with the police were not uniformly antagonistic, opposition politicians appeared more likely to develop forms of tax collection effort and enforcement that were autonomous from the police. On the other hand, politicians affiliated with Fatah, the ruling party—in addition to select municipal staff with whom I spoke—tended to observe the lack of police authority in Area B as a greater challenge to enforcement and revenue collection than politicians affiliated with the opposition.

Interestingly, the findings in chapter 4 suggest that access to PA police would not, in fact, have improved enforcement and revenue collection in the way that some Fatah-affiliated politicians argued in the foregoing excerpts. Among towns governed by Fatah-affiliated mayors, we found that greater policing capacity—as captured, for example, by a greater share of the municipality's built-up area in Area A—did nothing to improve revenue collection. Further, while greater Palestinian policing authority was associated with revenue gains for towns governed by Fatah's opponents, these conversations demonstrate that this was not due to greater collaboration between opposition-affiliated mayors and the Fatah-controlled police. Instead, the interviews suggest that greater overall fiscal effort by opposition-led councils may have been concentrated—or particularly successful—in areas of greater PA policing capacity.

Area C and the Broader Issue of Territorial Control

My conversations with local Palestinian politicians and staff in the West Bank revealed that the Oslo regime's geographic fragmentation took on meaning beyond simply distinguishing (and limiting) the policing capacity of the Palestinian government. Especially when referring to Area C—the over 60 percent of the West Bank's territory over which the Palestinian Authority has no jurisdiction—territorial control, in its most basic sense, is important for the development of Palestinian municipalities and, thus, their fiscal and distributive capacities as well. I could not help but wonder how things might have looked different if Palestinian policing institutions possessed *de jure* and *de facto* authority to operate in Area C. In such a counterfactual world, the activities of mayors, municipal councils, and their staff may appear more similar to what occurs in Area A.

As the quantitative analysis in the preceding chapter showed, this type of security setting could provide opportunities for opposition-led councils to boost their fiscal capacity. Furthermore, the Fatah-led councils' advantages in distributing utilities like electricity and water might diminish, since these partisan differences were starkest in towns with large portions of their land in Area C—namely, areas where Palestinian coercive authority is complete lack.

One municipal general director described to me how, because their town is located mostly in Area A, they face fewer problems in expanding the geographic footprint of the town

> They are limited, for example, in [name of another town] in terms of construction expansion. They cannot expand beyond certain borders. For us, for example, we have full authority over our masterplans. We are the ones creating them in collaboration with relevant ministries who need to certify these plans. Our recent plan is almost approved, it includes an expansion of 5,000 dunums [approximately 1,236 acres]. In previous years it did not exceed 861 dunums [approximately 213 acres]. We need this expansion area to organize the town and provide the best services. Expansion for us is into area A still, so it is easier than other towns. As long as you have jurisdiction over your area, you can do what is needed for the residents. (Interview 2019.1)

Restrictions of access to land in Area C formed a central theme of the conversations I had with current and former municipal politicians and staff. These restrictions included Israeli interference in development, municipal service provision, taxation, road maintenance, and water infrastructure development, to name a few. During a group interview with independent and Hamas-affiliated politicians, the respondents discussed the extra effort of having to travel much farther to dispose of garbage due to the threat that their equipment might be confiscated by the Israeli military in Area C.

EMPLOYEE 1: Last year the occupation army confiscated our garbage collection vehicles while they were in a garbage landfill near [name of other town] in Area C.

EMPLOYEE 2: When we operate anything in Area C, they give us problems because they consider some of the lands in Area C as a red line that cannot be crossed. Once, we excavated a road in Area C and we found that there were some rocks that were marked in red paint indicating a security area, which we cannot pass. . . . When we asked the contractor, he confirmed that they would confiscate our equipment if we go further. The confiscation lasts for a month or two before they return the vehicles. So, even Area C, it is not all dealt with by the Israelis in the same way.

EMPLOYEE 2: [My colleague] mentioned an important point. The landfill is close to us, however, we have to travel seventy kilometers to [another town] to reach the landfill we are allowed to use. This of course is more expensive. We do not have a permit to use the one in [closer town] because it is in Area C. This is why they confiscated our vehicles. (Interview 2019.5)

Further, a Fatah-supported mayor of a town in the Bethlehem district located primarily in Area B was asked whether the municipality might find it harder to collect revenues in areas where residents experienced insecurity. The mayor did not really observe this link in Area B, but it was Area C that came up again—the area where Palestinians' homes and buildings are at risk of demolition by occupation authorities.

ME: Another thing I am interested in is how people's perception of safety and security affects their willingness to pay for governance and services. I know we are mostly in Area B, does that mean that there is a strong Israeli military and civil administration presence in [name of town] a lot of the time? Is there a Palestinian police station here?

MAYOR: No, there is no Palestinian police station here. I think that [name of town] is considerably safe. People here do not connect these two things [security and paying for government services] together. Some of the areas in C, especially the ones close to the alternative highways, and the area in C to the east of the town, think in this way that you describe because there is no housing security in this area. Their houses are at risk of demolition at any minute. They are located at the outskirts of the town. Inside [name of town], it is safe. (Interview 2018.7)

Interestingly, the analysis in chapter 4 revealed that Fatah-led municipalities were able to mobilize more revenue than their opposition counterparts in municipalities with a large concentration of land in Area C. Furthermore, the annual growth in utility spending, in particular, that was observed in Fatah-governed municipalities was significant in towns with large sections of Area C land.

Drawing on the interviews excerpted in this section, we can only tentatively suggest a possible explanation for these partisan differences as they relate to local governance in Area C. If, in keeping with the theory I have proposed thus far, Fatah's legitimacy challenges with the Palestinian population are most acute in areas where it possesses greater policing capacity—policing capacity that is delegated by Israel with the intent of preserving its overall regime of domination—then Area C may be where its political reputation faces relatively fewer challenges. If so, without the capacity to provide any form of protection or policing for Palestinian populations in these regions, Fatah-led councils may face incentives to engage in relatively greater effort—and at greater expense—to achieve their distributive goals.

PARTISAN AND NONPARTISAN IDENTITIES

Fatah exercises power in an authoritarian manner in the West Bank. As a result, in some ways, the fault line between Fatah loyalists and everyone else is the major organizing feature of local politics in the West Bank. However, my interviews revealed that the collection of candidates, lists, and councils that formed Fatah's opposition organized and identified itself differently across towns depending on the strength of partisan or ideological affiliations, polarization across these lines, and the relative strength of other, nonpartisan forms of identification (e.g., family or clan). In some cases, Hamas or the PFLP, for example, were strongly organized and rooted parties. In other towns, the salient axes of identification may be family-based.

Furthermore, in some municipalities, diverse segments of the non-Fatah parties and politicians were able to collaborate and form multiparty coalitions, whereas in others, party lines were more rigid. For those that featured more collaboration, sometimes it occurred before the election, allowing politicians to join forces and form an "independent" but ideologically diverse list of candidates, whereas in other municipalities, this opportunity for coalition formation followed after the election results were in and it was time to choose a mayor and begin governing.

The formal political affiliation of municipal politicians—Fatah, Hamas, PFLP, independent, or a smaller party—carries more weight in some areas than others. In some towns, it is one's connection to a particular family or clan that is the salient identity for electoral campaigning and voting. However, despite such connections, the division between Fatah and non-Fatah parties is fairly clear. Note this quote on the importance of familial representation in one town: "On a familial level, there was a diversity in familial representation amongst the people who were elected from [name of village]. Even if a person was from Fatah, he was first and foremost part of the family. Or even if he was from the Popular Front Party [al-Jabhah al-Sha'biyya li-Tahrir Filastin, PFLP]. . . . So, he was part of the family and this is what mattered. I believe that this played a role in maintaining the unity of the municipality, despite the diverse political representation of its council." (Interview 2019.8)

By contrast, on another municipal council, partisan identification shaped the formation of a kind of non-Fatah coalition list that, perhaps in part due to its ideological diversity, performed very strongly in the elections. One interlocutor, a former mayor, discusses the period preceding the election when they and fellow politicians were forming electoral lists.

> To help the city, we should have a coalition. This was my thinking. We tried to have a coalition of 28 members, but at that time Fatah refused because they said, we can win 10 or 12 seats . . . why should we join you?! So, there were 5 lists and I [formed] a coalition with Hamas's list. It was called the Reform and Change Coalition. It contained some [non-Hamas] people and [some] Hamas. We received 73 percent of the votes. 33,000 people voted. That was a lot of people at that time. So, we received about 26,000 votes [imprecise estimate]. We got 13 seats and [Fatah] listed 2 seats. (Interview 2019.4)

On the relative advantage of nonpartisan or multiparty coalitions, another independent mayor noted, "When someone is independent, it is easy for them to access all political parties. I am not Fatah, not Hamas, nor Jabhah [PFLP], so it is easier for all of them to deal with me. But the coalition that happened, which caused me to become mayor, was between the council members from Hamas, Jabhah, and the one who ran independently." (Interview 2019.8)

Another independent mayor discussed their own electoral campaign and how transparency and fairness from the government might cultivate more voluntary forms of compliance.

> In the past, political parties would impose their agendas. They did not treat people equally. I decided to create a list to run for elections. It was an independent list. We were strong because of the support from the local community, especially those who were also independent and not following political affiliations. In the past, there was never transparency at the municipality when dealing with the residents. So, we wanted to change service provision, we wanted to preserve the dignity of residents. We wanted to deal with residents in a respectful way when they come to pay fees or complete paperwork. I was encouraged to run for elections also because people used to see the municipality as their foe. They viewed it as an entity that takes their money and imposes punishments. We wanted to change this. We wanted people to feel engaged in the decisions being made. Residents should see the municipality as a transparent entity. They should see what the municipality does, understand its role, and be convinced that they need to pay their dues and contribute. If the people understand what roles and responsibilities the municipality has, what its budget is, they will become responsible and will pay what is due. (Interview 2018.3)

In discussing one municipality's transition from the period of direct Israeli rule to the period of governance under the Palestinian Authority in 1994, one Hamas-affiliated mayor and his colleague transitioned to discussing the 2005 elections, when they were elected into office.

MAYOR: Before 1994, the municipality depended on rainwater wells . . . the Israeli occupation didn't build any schools. After 1994, foreign donors provided funding for building schools. For example, the first garbage collection truck came from a donation by the Spanish government. The first car for the municipality came from Kuwait. Afterward they had their own accounts in the bank, and they started following a more systematic approach. For example, they began requiring signatures for three different people to make an expenditure. . . .

The first municipal council was appointed by the PA, but three years later [in 1997] they had an election.

EMPLOYEE: The major change came in 2005, when they came to office. . . . [Laughs]

MAYOR: After 2005 the municipality started having real, effective projects, because 2005 was the first, actual election.

ME: The first actual election in what sense?

MAYOR: In the first election [1997], the families campaign each chose their own representative, and the families. . . . [inaudible]. But this one, no. There were laws, observers. . . .

Research Assistant: So it wasn't controlled by families?

EMPLOYEE: No, no, no, like elections. Real elections. Like in America, in Chicago, or in the European or American way.

ME: The elections in Chicago aren't that great. [Laughter.] (Interview 2014.7)

In summary, the importance of familial versus party representation in municipal office seems to vary by municipality. In some cases, familial or clan-based identities align with partisan ones, and in others, they supersede them. This variation, particularly in the small- and medium-size towns of the West Bank, is an area deserving of additional research.

REPRESSION AND INTIMIDATION OF ELECTED HAMAS POLITICIANS

Mayors from Hamas were treated differently; especially as their five-year term in office approached, mayors were pressured to resign, even though the central PA government chose not to hold new elections. In three interviews, former mayors from Hamas told me they were told they would lose the public-sector job they had before becoming mayor if they did not resign. This usually happened after four to six years on the job; that is, in the 2008–10 period. This was perceived by Hamas mayors as a tactic for Fatah to remove them from office.

One Hamas-affiliated former mayor, like some of their counterparts in other towns, was an employee in the PA civil service.[9] They described how a policy granted civil servants up to four years of leave, after which time the PA ministry threatened them with losing their job if they stayed in office.

RESPONDENT: I received four letters threatening of service termination from the Ministry of [redacted].

RESEARCH ASSISTANT: Because you stayed in the municipality? What happened? Did you sue?

RESPONDENT: Yes, I stayed. No, I did not sue. I believed that I was fighting for what is right. The ministry's position was that I had to return because my leave duration was only four years. I told them, yes, true, and the election period is also four years. Hold elections to end my term. There were exceptional circumstances at the time that prevented the elections. These circumstances affected the law on elections; they should likewise affect any laws that impact mayors who work in government institutions. If the elections were postponed, then so should the leave period [be extended]. Especially since the legislative council [elected in 2006] was annulled. The situation required a decision from the minister's council. The first time they decided to extend, and the second the same. The third, Salam Fayyad was the prime minister then, . . . we talked to him about this, and he took the decision to extend leave until elections are held.

ME: I am surprised that more [mayors] did not try this approach.

RESPONDENT: Yes, even some people in this municipality finished the term and did not want to extend beyond it because municipality work is tedious. I remember that some mayors . . . the PA wanted these people who were elected to leave . . . for many reasons . . . especially because they were from other political parties, or because they wanted to show people that [those] whom they elected were eager to leave office. This was one of the main reasons I did not want to leave. I was willing to sacrifice my job at the ministry and not let the people down. I wanted to stay until the end. (Interview 2019.15)

The uniquely challenging context facing those mayors who overtly identified with Hamas was revealed through interviews and provides an important contextual elaboration on the analysis from the preceding chapter. A number of local Hamas-affiliated politicians were arrested by not only the Israeli forces while in office but also the Palestinian Authority. One mayor relays how they were fired by the PA while in an Israeli prison. They were imprisoned by Israel under "administrative detention," a method used by Israel to incarcerate Palestinians without charge. "The accusation was serving as mayor" (Interview 2019.13):

FORMER MAYOR: My struggle with the [Palestinian Authority] continues to this day.

RESEARCH ASSISTANT: How?

FORMER MAYOR: They did not pay my end of service compensation, nor the salaries I was due from the time between when I was arrested [by Israel] to when I was removed from office [by the PA]. They orchestrated the coup against me when I was in prison. When I came out, I took the matter to the [PA] Supreme Court in Ramallah and I received the order to return to my position as mayor. But the minister could not implement the decision, and I never received my payment. I have been fighting them in court since 2010.

I addressed the Goldstone committee [the 2008–2009 United Nations Fact Finding Mission on the Gaza Conflict, which was charged with investigating Israeli violations of international law in the occupied territories] to report the violation of my rights as a mayor by the PA. They interviewed me and produced a report. . . . However, nothing happened.

ME: We've visited several towns, and in some towns a mayor from Hamas stayed until 2010 or 2012 and some left early.

FORMER MAYOR: The reason behind this variation is due to the weight of Fatah in that area. The mayor before me was from Fatah, so he took it personally when I became mayor. He said that very clearly to my face. . . . He said, I will not forget that you are sitting on my chair! I told him this is not your chair nor is it mine. It belongs to [name of municipality]. There was a mayor before you and there will be a mayor after me. So, he considered it personal vengeance against me. That is why I faced such issues. I was arrested by the Israelis six times. When I was mayor, I was arrested twice. The first time . . . I was arrested eight months after being in office. The reason was that they were expanding the settlement opposite to our town and they wanted to keep me in until they finished this expansion. They wanted to keep me because I filed for a lawsuit at the Israeli court against this decision to expand and I received an order stopping them from expanding for one month. On the morning after the end of that month, I was arrested. My son was five years old. He was sick that night, and when he woke up that morning asking where

I was, his mother told him that I was arrested by the army but he would not believe her. He went outside crying, and then he noticed the tractors had resumed their work. He went back in and told her, "now, I know why they arrested my dad." . . . I was arrested that time for fifteen days. When I came out, they were done.

The second time I was arrested was May 24, 2007. The accusation was: Mayor of [name of municipality] under the list "Reform and Change." The judge ruled for my release. The army appealed, and he again ruled for my release. The moment I was about to go free, I received notice that I had been transferred to administrative detention. The reason they gave: my activities as mayor threaten the security of the area and of the Israelis. I was arrested for eleven months then. The first order was an arrest for five months, then it was extended for another five months. The second five months were reduced to four, so, a total of nine now. Then I received a ruling from the Israeli Supreme Court prohibiting a second extension. However, a few days before leaving, I nonetheless received a two-month extension. At the same time, I was still being prosecuted for the first accusation, which was initially overruled: Mayor of [name of municipality] under the list "Reform and Change." I was released on bail. I was probably the first person being prosecuted in both courts, the administrative and the other one, both for being a mayor. According to the [Israeli] Supreme Court, I was supposed to be released from jail on February 21. The municipal council was dissolved by a decree from the [Palestinian Authority] on February 12, and that was when the new mayor took over: one week before my due date to become free. On that day, I received the decision of another two-month extension [to my detention]. Palestinian law allows you sixty days to object to a decision to dissolve the municipal council. So, they kept me until the objection period was over.

RESEARCH ASSISTANT: No one else could have objected?

FORMER MAYOR: I thought it was only me that had to do it. When I consulted a lawyer after I came out, . . . he told me that anyone from [name of municipality] could have objected. He based his consultation on the fact that I was in prison and the decision was taken while I was absentee. So, we appealed, and the case was in court for fourteen months. In the end, the judge read the verdict to rescind the decision of the minister. Nothing was done, though.

This particular story illustrates the regime of indirect rule in action and how the Palestinian Authority, under the guise of self-rule and with the veneer of legality, promotes and prolongs authoritarian governance that serves Israel's objectives. What is unique, and perhaps most telling, about this case is that being elected mayor on the Hamas list was not initially sufficient grounds for this individual's arrest by the Israeli army, according to the ruling of Israel's justice system. So the military simply transferred the individual to administrative detention, where no specific charge was needed other than that the elected mayor allegedly posed a threat to Israel's security.

These conversations generate numerous insights. The following summary points draw on the statistical analysis in the preceding chapter as well as the discussions with interview subjects profiled in this chapter.

First, regime opponents may face increased demand for revenue and resources due to the challenges of operating under the regime. That may encourage them to develop greater local fiscal capacity (via increased tax collection effort) or find creative ways to accomplish their distributive goals without increasing spending through institutional channels. Interview respondents—including mayors affiliated with Hamas and independent mayors who oversaw multiparty opposition councils—frequently mentioned the suspension of aid from U.S. and other international donors after Hamas won the 2006 legislative election. While this funding freeze was temporary, other non-Fatah respondents relayed that the Fatah-controlled PA ministries practiced political favoritism with municipalities. Thus, opposition-affiliated municipal councils drew on voluntary labor and in-kind contributions from residents, for example, and faced pressure to maximize the efficiency of their spending.

The interviews documented here demonstrate that opposition politicians (Hamas, independents, and smaller parties) had subjective and complex relationships with the Fatah-controlled Palestinian police force on the ground. Surprisingly, relationships between opposition politicians and the Fatah police were not universally antagonistic, even after the violent unrest that led Hamas and Fatah to take up arms against each other in 2007. However, in general, these politicians did not express a reliance on police for enforcement of revenue collection.

What, then, might account for the opposition's relatively stronger revenue performance in areas of greater PA policing capacity, a finding reported in the preceding chapter? One observation that our interviews confirm is that raising revenue from local constituents is controversial under occupation and is particularly delicate for any Palestinian actors who might be perceived as being an intermediary between the Israeli occupying authorities and the occupied Palestinian public. These sensitivities may be particularly acute for local politicians affiliated with Fatah, the ruling autocratic party in the PA. However, non-Fatah politicians also spoke about the hesitant and piecemeal ways in which they needed to approach fiscal extraction from Palestinian residents. While some blamed the unwillingness to pay on culture, others highlighted the particular hardships faced by poor residents and ways they sought to lessen the burden for such constituents.

Despite these complexities, we can theorize that greater fiscal effort by the opposition was relatively more successful in areas of higher Palestinian coercive capacity, because these are the areas where their reputational advantage over the intermediary is greatest. According to this argument, it is those areas where Palestinian policing is most visible—where Israel's reliance on its Palestinian intermediary is most overt—that the Palestinian opposition is able to develop more effective fiscal relationships with the public. On the other hand, in towns with large shares of their land designated as Area C and thus subjected to the unmediated, coercive rule of Israel's occupation and, frequently, Israeli settler aggression, Fatah-led councils appear to be more active in mobilizing overall revenue and spending on utilities, in particular, than their opposition-led counterparts.

Respondents who emphasized the importance of police access to their town were primarily Fatah-affiliated politicians or municipal employees who directly managed and oversaw these interactions with residents. However, despite what these respondents suggested, the analysis in chapter 4 shows that greater policing capacity in Fatah-run municipalities would likely not boost local revenue collection. This shows that enforcement is relatively inelastic to increases in coercive capacity.[10] Interview respondents—either Fatah-affiliated politicians or municipal staff—need not have been disingenuous in suggesting that greater policing capacity would allow them to increase revenue collection. It is possible that the reputational problems faced specifically by Fatah-run municipalities would not fully reveal themselves until such individuals were presented with that counterfactual condition on the ground: they had the theoretical ability to call on the police to assist with enforcement. In any case, the interviews provided reasons to doubt that enforcement actions would actually be carried out and completed with the help of Palestinian police.

The interviews in this chapter reveal the multilayered indirect rule regime in stark detail through the firsthand accounts of local Hamas-affiliated politicians. For example, some Hamas politicians faced repression and intimidation from both Israeli and PA authorities. The anecdotes from these interviews suggest that the Israeli-PA regime was required to resort to convoluted, autocratic tactics to remove Hamas mayors from office as expeditiously as possible without eliciting excessive backlash. These tactics included arresting politicians and holding them without charge, dissolving municipal councils by executive order, and threatening elected politicians with forced resignation from their full-time jobs. These firsthand testimonies make it all the more surprising that we don't observe substantial differences in revenue and spending patterns, on the whole, across Fatah- versus opposition-run towns. In many respects, the opposition-run towns were able to maintain a level of normalcy despite rampant repression.

A further, surprising, insight from this chapter—especially given the coercive environment just described—is that interactions between the indigenous intermediary and opponents on the ground are complex and not always hostile. Indirect rule creates adversaries between those within the indigenous population who cooperate with the regime (i.e., Fatah) and those who oppose it (Hamas, independents, and smaller parties). However, political conflict may not always translate into personal conflict, especially at the local level. Because indirect rule generates these divisions in small towns and villages—and even within families—it can produce intricate and nuanced effects on the social fabric of occupied societies. Individual-level relationships are not always as sharply polarized as outside observers might assume.

Finally, the strength of partisan identification as an organizing principle of local politics varies, but the distinction between Fatah and non-Fatah is fairly consistent. Towns and municipalities vary, though, in the importance of family- or clan-based identification and the likelihood that diverse opposition parties and independents will cooperate in a governing coalition. (Sometimes this form of cooperation takes place prior to the election and sometimes afterward, when the newly elected council is negotiating about who should become mayor.) A Fatah-affiliated mayor might refer to a former Hamas-affiliated mayor as a friend; in other cases, these relationships might be very strained.

The next chapter concludes the book by extending some of these accumulated observations to other settings featuring regimes of domination, with brief illustrative comparisons to indirectly ruled parts of British colonial India and South Africa's apartheid regime. In those settings, did regime intermediaries leverage what autonomy they had to minimize politically risky tasks of governance (e.g., policing or extraction)? Did regime intermediaries spend on distributive goods as a strategy to enhance their reputations with the indigenous population? These are some of the questions that the final chapter will consider.

Chapter Six

HISTORIES AND FUTURES OF INDIRECT RULE
Situating the Palestinian Case
in Comparative Context

National liberation movements are, at their core, about constructing, or reconstructing, the state into a new form and reconstituting governance within it. Such movements have waged their campaigns against both imperial powers and nominally postcolonial states. Opportunities for political liberation are shaped by the nature of the regime that activists, fighters, politicians, peasants, professionals, and other movement participants are confronting. Regimes of domination—by virtue of the fact that they seek to uphold the domination of one ethnic, racial, religious, or other identity-based group over another—will likely face continued resistance over their life span. However, they may also delegate some forms of authority to indigenous actors as part of an overall strategy of regime maintenance. Dominant states and empires are particularly likely to pursue such an approach—namely, indirect rule—when they are seeking to politically exclude the population in the territory they covet. Indirect rule is one way in which regimes of domination, and the conflicts they produce, can settle into more enduring equilibria.

What forms of governance do indigenous actors provide under indirect rule? How do those who are integrated into the regime as intermediaries approach governing at the local level? Do regime opponents develop their own capacities to govern locally, and if so, what sorts of capabilities do they develop? These questions reflect some of the broad concerns that have motivated the preceding investigation of Palestinian local governance in the West Bank. Fatah was born as a militant political movement to advance Palestinian liberation and resist Israeli occupation. Yet, after the creation of the Palestinian Authority in the mid-1990s, the organization found itself, instead, governing *under* occupation. While some Palestinian nationalists had hoped the Oslo Accords would pave a path for Palestinian statehood, it became increasingly clear that the PA served to sustain, more than challenge, Israel's rule.

The preceding chapters have revealed how the Israeli-PA regime and Palestinian political dynamics have shaped local governance in such a setting. The analysis showed that while the loyalties of local Palestinian politicians can be complex, fluid, and sensitive, mayors and councils affiliated with Fatah versus those affiliated with its challengers faced distinct incentives, opportunities, and obstacles in pursuing local governance. Fatah-affiliated mayors were encumbered with reputational costs, leading their municipalities to moderate politically risky tasks while exploiting resource advantages to distribute collective goods. Mayors from the opposition, on the other hand, grappled with resource constraints. Thus, they responded by exerting greater effort to generate resources—through both *de jure* extraction and the mobilization of voluntary contributions—and restraining spending.

In this final chapter, I have three primary goals. The first is to engage with what I believe is the most viable counterargument to explain my empirical findings. This is, in essence, an explanation for Fatah's negative reputation that is grounded in its own policies and practices rather than its position within the occupation regime. The second objective is to carefully begin to widen the analytical scope beyond the Palestinian case to understand whether the logic underlying my theory extends to two other historical settings of indirect rule. The first setting includes those parts of India that were indirectly ruled under the British Empire, and the second consists of the Bantustans under the apartheid regime in both South Africa and what is now Namibia.

Admittedly, this analysis merely scratches the surface of the massive amount of scholarship that has been produced on each case. This preliminary research exercise reveals a rich body of work on institutions and governance in each setting, but the practices of day-to-day local government remains less prominent in the literature that I have been able to survey. Nonetheless, we can still broadly classify these cases based on which functional aspects of governance—extraction or noneconomic coercion, as I define them in chapter 1—are more central to the delegative relationship between the dominant power (the British imperial state and the central government under apartheid) and their would-be intermediaries (landlords, estate holders, and princely rulers in India, and the Bantustan chiefs in South Africa and Namibia). Furthermore, while neither setting of indirect rule featured electoral opportunities for regime opponents at the local level akin to what we observed in the occupied West Bank, we can still seek answers to some basic questions about what oppositional mobilization looked like in each setting—even if it did not qualify as "governance"—and how intermediary and opponent relationships played out at a subnational, if not entirely local, level.

The final purpose of this chapter is to conclude the volume by providing an update on the trajectory of municipal politics in the West Bank in the most recent few years as Israeli governments have shifted closer to enforcing *de jure* annexation of the West Bank, as settler-backed attempts to ethnically cleanse Palestinians from certain areas of the West Bank have intensified, and as political competition at both the local and national levels in the West Bank and Gaza has atrophied. I identify some questions that remain unanswered about the future of indirect rule in Palestine in light of this volatile environment.

POLITICAL FAVORITISM AND CORRUPTION WITHIN FATAH: A RIVAL ARGUMENT

The argument I make in the preceding pages relies on the idea that Fatah suffers from a reputational crisis with the Palestinian public in the West Bank due to its role as an intermediary within Israel's indirect rule regime and, specifically, its robust cooperation with Israel on policing Palestinians. However, my empirical findings do not rule out a possible alternative explanation for Fatah's legitimacy problem: that it is due not to the party's collaboration with the occupying power but, rather, to the widespread belief that Fatah uses its political clout to engage in political favoritism and outright corruption.

Indeed, survey data consistently demonstrate that Palestinian residents of the occupied territories view corruption as a major problem within PA institutions. For example, in twenty-two polls conducted between March

2006 and December 2012, corresponding to the period of the data set analyzed in chapter 4, an average of 76 percent of West Bank Palestinian respondents replied in the affirmative when asked if they believed there was corruption in PA institutions.[1] In fact, a staggering 86 to 88 percent of respondents agreed with this statement in the five preceding polls, carried out between December 2004 and December 2005, during the period of the local elections.

The Coalition for Integrity and Accountability (AMAN), an independent civil society organization and member of Transparency International, regularly reports on manifestations of corruption in the West Bank and Gaza. In its 2008 report, for example, in the midst of the period analyzed in chapter 4, AMAN noted the prevalence of favoritism and nepotism in public-sector recruitment, misappropriation of public funds, bribe-taking, and money laundering.[2] Tariq Dana characterizes dynamics between Palestinian political and business elites as "crony capitalism" and documents how the Oslo framework, Israeli and donor interests, and Fatah's own economic conservatism, which empowered and relied on close ties with the nationalist bourgeoisie, have all contributed to market monopolization, rent-seeking, patron-client dynamics, and corruption in the Palestinian economy.[3]

Given these perceptions and some well-documented research and evidence that such forms of favoritism and corruption exist, it is highly likely that those conditions play a role in how constituents view Fatah-affiliated municipal politicians, especially those who were appointed rather than elected to their positions. This situation may hold whether or not the individual mayor or municipal council members in question have themselves engaged in political favoritism or corruption. Further, it is important to recall that Hamas, rather than boasting its Islamist credentials in the lead-up to the local elections, ran on a platform that explicitly sought to distinguish itself from Fatah on these matters.

Here, I wish to suggest that rather than being an independent cause of Fatah's legitimacy and reputational challenges, favoritism and corruption are themselves epiphenomenal of the regime of indirect rule. First, since the 2007 split in governance between the Fatah-led authority in the West Bank and the Hamas-led authority in Gaza, the Palestinian legislature has been inactive. That has removed a major institutional vehicle for accountability. The effective dissolution of the legislature and the broader issue of the division between Fatah and Hamas have been seen as major factors reinforcing a lack of accountability in the PA. Of course, what Palestinian governance in the West Bank would resemble without the occupation and the associated indirect rule regime is a question that is impossible to answer definitively. However, the sequence of events that led to the Fatah-Hamas split following the relatively free and fair legislative elections of January 2006 cannot be explained without understanding the subordination of Palestinian Authority institutions to the interests of Israel and its allies, and thus the hierarchical nature of the relationship between Israel and the PA. Thus, one can speculate that one of the main institutional drivers of corruption—the absence of an elected legislature—is an outgrowth of this particular regime.

When Hamas won a majority of seats in the Palestinian Legislative Council in 2006, the movement's leader, Ismail Haniyeh, was appointed prime minister and sworn in by President Abbas. Because of Hamas's refusal to officially recognize Israel and concede what it views as its right to militarized resistance, this appointment precipitated a comprehensive boycott of the PA by U.S. and European donors and a freeze on Israeli-collected tax revenue transfers. The dire financial situation created by this months-long funding freeze preceded the outbreak of fighting between Hamas and Fatah loyalists in Gaza and the West Bank, which eventually resulted in the fracturing of PA institutions, with Hamas seizing control in Gaza and Fatah maintaining authority exclusively in the West Bank. Furthermore, following the 2006 elections, Israel pursued a campaign of arrests against newly elected Hamas representatives, which, in turn, prevented the legislature from obtaining a quorum. Thus, the legislature was effectively made defunct. Since the PA's creation, we have not had the opportunity to observe an opposition-dominated legislature in action, so we cannot know with certainty how the Fatah-led executive branch would behave under such conditions.

Second, even after the events of 2006–2007, there is the question of whether Fatah would have the opportunity to engage in favoritism and corruption in the West Bank if the indirect rule regime were not present. Research shows that levels of economic development, rather than political institutions, are more reliable predictors of levels of corruption.[4] Yet, as evidenced in some of the literature reviewed here on colonial India and apartheid South Africa, qualitative accounts suggest that the institutions of indirect rule can play a role in at least enabling predatory rent-seeking by intermediary elites. In the Palestinian case in particular, Leila Farsakh argues that the neoliberal development discourse in the occupied territories has "led to the rise of new loci of power, in particular the PA and a whole new class of private investors and international donors, to the detriment of other forces such as the Palestinian Liberation Organization . . . workers, and/or refugees."[5]

Further, Dan Sobovitz finds that, when using cross-national regressions to estimate the relationship between variables accounting for sixteen theories about the causes of corruption, observations for the Palestinian Authority consistently fall below the regression line, meaning the PA has higher-than-predicted levels of corruption.[6] That raises the distinct possibility that unobserved factors related to the occupation, the lack of territorial control, the lack of a functioning parliament, and the Fatah-Hamas rivalry may help explain the PA's deviation from theoretical predictions.

Third, it is worth considering whether or not the outcomes we observed in the preceding chapters would have obtained if the story was instead about corruption undermining Fatah's legitimacy. If political favoritism and corruption primarily take the form of misuse of public funds, then it might be surprising to see that Fatah-led municipalities were more likely than opposition-led municipalities to increase funding to the electricity and water sectors. Furthermore, the empirical results in chapter 4 also did not strongly support the idea that the Fatah-led central government was systematically favoring Fatah-led municipalities in revenue transfers (although interview subjects in chapter 5 spoke about other ways in which they perceived discrimination from the PA central authorities). On the other hand, I argue that Fatah does engage in forbearance in enforcing tax and fee collection as a means of securing political support. If true, this could indeed constitute a form of political favoritism. Our data do not as yet enable us to fully disentangle the possible motivations for Fatah mayors to engage in such forbearance. In the words of one of the interview subjects profiled in chapter 5, it appears that the occupation is at least partly responsible for generating "embarrassment" for Fatah politicians in raising revenue from their constituents.

Finally, while we cannot observe the counterfactual of what Fatah's governance would look like absent the indirect rule regime, we can glean some insights from another setting where Fatah played a leading role in supplying governance: in Lebanon, through its role in the PLO. As Nora Stel describes, PLO governance in Lebanon can be divided into two phases: first, during the lead-up to and outbreak of Lebanon's civil war, prior to the PLO's expulsion after Israel's 1982 invasion, and, second, after the war concluded, when the PLO, in the form of popular committees, reclaimed an active role over governance in the Palestinian refugee camps.[7]

After the PLO's ousting from Jordan in 1970, it relocated its military and political base to Lebanon. During this time, the PLO also operated what some have called a "state within a state" inside Lebanon—or what Stel refers to as a "mediated state"—at times in surprising cooperation with the Lebanese state. That entailed providing governance in the camps and other areas where Palestinians lived, such that, as Sarah E. Parkinson notes, "areas of West Beirut and South Lebanon became near autonomous regions."[8] Furthermore, after the war ended, the PLO reclaimed a more modest role in providing governance through the popular committees, which function as *de facto* municipalities in the refugee camps.

Nadya Hajj, for example, details Fatah's role in establishing and governing a new property rights regime within the camps after its arrival in 1970.[9] This is distinct from the West Bank's setting of indirect rule, in which Fatah serves as an intermediary for a regime of ethnic, racial, or religious domination. Nonetheless, we see some common threads in how it approached governance—for example, in its focus on cultivating political loyalty, not relying on taxation of camp residents for its revenue base, and weakly enforcing the payment of utilities such as electricity and water.[10] In a conclusion remarkably reminiscent of one of the Hamas-affiliated mayor's testimonials provided in chapter 5, Hajj finds that "Fatah agreed to quietly and systematically ignore the exploitative practices of heavy energy and water guzzling businesses like ice cream, chocolate, and cement manufacturing."[11] In chapter 5, the interview subject I reference earlier described how he was threatened by the PA security forces when he initially refused to supply an electricity connection to a factory that was built illegally on partially residential property.

To fully capture how political favoritism, corruption, and legitimacy informed Fatah's shifting role in local governance in Lebanon is beyond the scope of this book. Lebanon provides an example of Fatah participation in governance during both active conflict and an ostensibly post-conflict environment. Parkinson highlights, for example, how the discourse adopted by "Old Fatah" members who were active in Lebanon during the revolutionary period of the 1970s and early 1980s evinced the generational, ideological, and subjective ways in which the morality of money is understood.

"Members of Old Fatah felt that money in [the revolutionary period] gave them 'power' to: fund scholarships overseas, staff a massive social service apparatus, buy weaponry and train soldiers. 'Saudi' money [on which Fatah in Lebanon increasingly relied beginning in the mid-1980s], in contrast, put a price tag on what long-term militants saw as a sacrosanct national project. In their eyes, Saudi money did not simply turn them into mercenaries; the very act of putting a monetary value on the resistance profaned it."[12]

In summary, it is clear that Fatah—even when operating outside direct Israeli occupation—does not hesitate to commandeer resource distribution as a source of political patronage, nor are its practices of non-enforcement, or forbearance, limited to the context of the West Bank. However, the reputational costs and benefits of these policies appear to be contingent on underlying perceptions of Fatah itself. These relate to its ability to, as the title of Hajj's book aptly puts it, provide "protection amid [the] chaos" that characterized refugees' lives. Further, as we might infer from some of Parkinson's informants, these costs and benefits also related to how immersed it was in the struggle for national liberation. Palestinian populations looked to basic security—of property and lives—and ongoing national struggle as values by which they judged Fatah's governance decisions, and this, in turn, appeared to shape Fatah's practices. These examples from Lebanon highlight additional ways in which the experience of Palestinian dispossession and displacement have structured Fatah's governance approach. Indirect rule may not be the only institutional framework in which such reputational concerns are relevant. Nonetheless, we still have not—and cannot, to date—observe Fatah, Hamas, or any other Palestinian political party governing in conditions of true sovereignty. Thus, our ability to disentangle the prevalence of political favoritism and corruption within Fatah from the environments in which it has governed—environments characterized by Palestinian statelessness, insecurity, disenfranchisement, and displacement—remains elusive.

SELECTING COMPARISON CASES

I expect the Palestinian context to be most immediately comparable with other regimes of domination that deploy indirect rule to exclude or otherwise divide the indigenous population from a smaller, favored ethnic, racial, national, or religious group. These are settings where the dominant power is broadly unpopular with the indigenous population, which is most easily observed when such powers face organized popular or militant resistance to their rule. This scope condition generates the logical basis for a key causal mechanism in my argument: namely, that by collaborating with the dominant power, unlike indigenous opponents of the regime, intermediaries face a reputational deficit with the indigenous population. However, in analyzing the comparison cases to follow, it is important to consider that some intermediaries may possess extant sources of "traditional" or "customary" legitimacy prior to their incorporation into the indirect rule regime. Thus, we might theorize that even if cooperation with the dominant power introduces political costs for intermediaries, these different sociopolitical starting points might matter, too.

In India, the literature generally focuses on two forms of indirect rule that the British deployed after 1858: first, the use of landlords and tax farmers as fiscal and sometimes coercive intermediaries; and, second, signed agreements with semiautonomous rulers in the so-called princely states. I will summarize how existing literature from social scientists and historians has described and defined both of these layers of indirect rule. Subsequently, I dedicate special attention to the princely state of Jammu and Kashmir, where legitimacy problems appear to be particularly prominent for the ruling class. India's semiautonomous princely states during the British colonial period varied considerably in terms of the degree to which their rulers benefited from some form of historic, precolonial legitimacy, and undoubtedly there were dynamic changes over time in how populations living under princely rule viewed these leaders and particularly their partial incorporation into the British imperial project. However, the rule of the princely state in the Kashmir valley is one for which existing scholarly sources suggest that the legitimacy problem was acute.

Apartheid was an overt regime of racial supremacy, astonishing in its level of institutional refinement and in how long it endured. It was also born at a time when, following World War II, the international orientation toward decolonization and a renewed emphasis on collective security seemed to some to make the apartheid regime an anachronistic outlier. As such, it is almost hard to consider the word "legitimacy" and apartheid in the same sentence. The collective antipathy of Black South Africans, in addition to the Coloured and Indian populations, toward white minority rule as it was inscribed in the apartheid regime hardly needs further scholarly justification. It is also the case that, as Mahmood Mamdani has argued, the apartheid regime constitute[d] a contemporary perfection of indirect rule.[13]

In addition to identifying settings of institutional indirect rule and weak regime legitimacy, another way to seek comparative cases for the West Bank is to identify national territorial maps that are intricately carved into regions of indigenous autonomy as opposed to regions of external, or colonial, control, akin to what is shown in the West Bank in map 4.1. Doing so shows that the case of the Bantustans (or "homelands") under the apartheid regime in South Africa and modern-day Namibia seems particularly appropriate, while one form of indirect rule practiced in British colonial India—the princely states—also contains such geographic fragmentation (see maps 6.1 and 6.2).

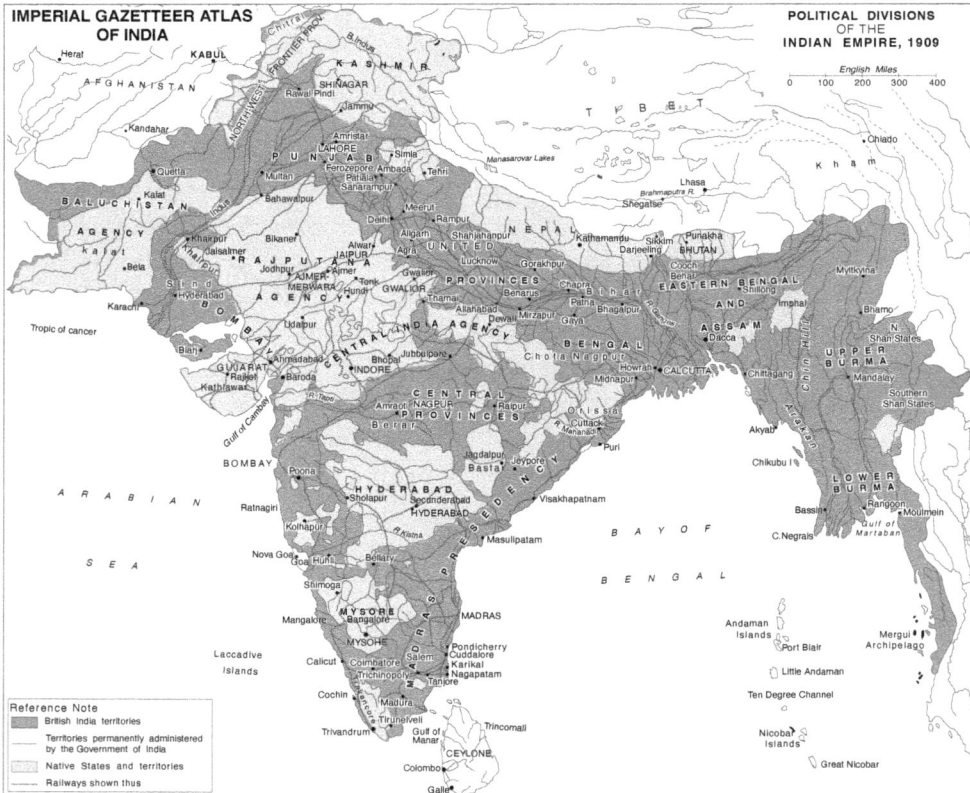

MAP 6.1. Map of the British Empire in India, 1909. *Sources*: Edinburgh Geographical Institute, "Political Divisions of the Indian Empire [map]," *Imperial Gazetteer Atlas of India* 26 (1909): 20; modified for Shivaji Mukherjee, *Colonial Institutions and Civil War: Indirect Rule and Maoist Insurgency in India* (Cambridge: Cambridge University Press, 2021), 64.

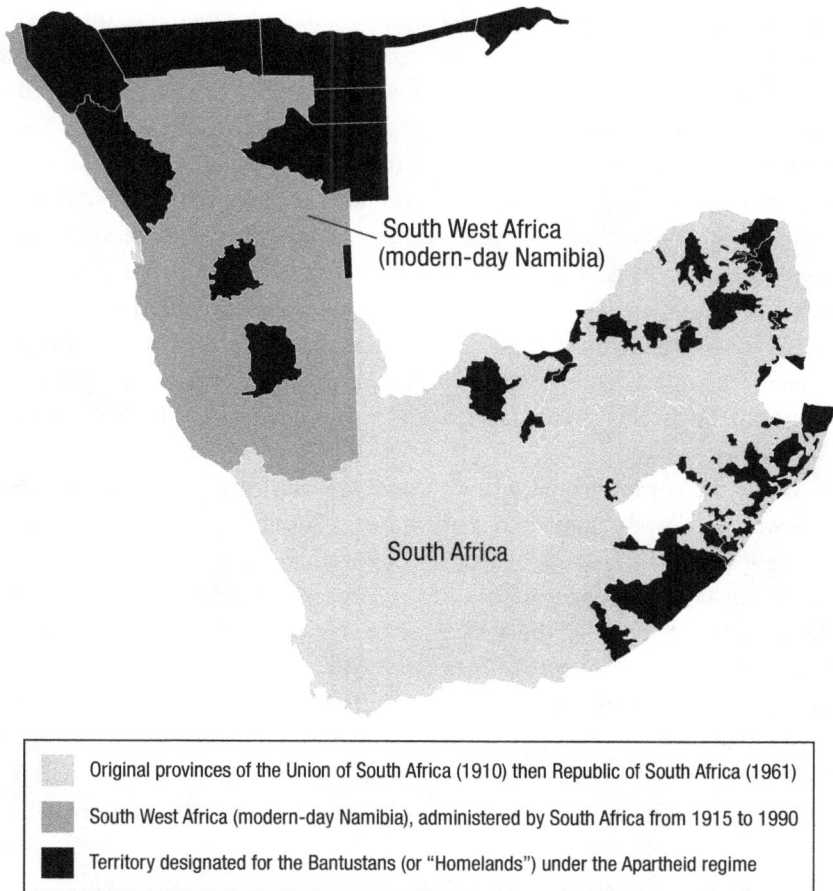

South West Africa
(modern-day Namibia)

South Africa

Original provinces of the Union of South Africa (1910) then Republic of South Africa (1961)

South West Africa (modern-day Namibia), administered by South Africa from 1915 to 1990

Territory designated for the Bantustans (or "Homelands") under the Apartheid regime

MAP 6.2. Map of the Bantustans in apartheid South Africa and South West Africa. *Source*: Author-modified version of DrRandomFactor, "South Africa & South West Africa Bantustans Map," Wikimedia Commons, April 29, 2017, https://commons.wikimedia.org/wiki/File:South_Africa_%26_South_West_Africa_Bantustans _Map.svg.

In recent work, Mamdani defines the princely states as an "individual" form of indirect rule, because tributary relationships were designed between the colonizing power and individual princes, versus "territorial" indirect rule, a label he applies to the case of the Bantustans under South Africa's apartheid regime.[14] In any case, the British and the Indian rulers with whom they entered into agreement shared an interest in delineating geographic zones of control that could be demarcated on a map. An important historically prior example is the creation of reservations for Native

Americans in North America; indeed, Mamdani has argued that this practice introduced "the paradigm of territorial indirect rule."[15]

A few caveats are in order. The evidence and conclusions I present below, as a non-specialist of either case, should be considered a preliminary exploration. I have learned a great deal from the sources cited here, but, undoubtedly, they merely scratch the surface of the scholarly literature on how political institutions functioned in each setting. Further, the treatment of each case is necessarily brief in this final chapter; thus, I am not able to comprehensively test each of the hypotheses presented earlier. So, to the extent that this exercise raises more questions than it definitively answers, I hope it does go some way toward de-exceptionalizing Palestine and the Israeli occupation, opening up avenues for future fruitful comparisons.

While the comparisons in this chapter are illustrative and leave plenty of room for further inquiry, I find that the South African case matches the case of the West Bank more closely because the primary purpose of the Bantustans, as concerned the central apartheid government based in Pretoria, was to uphold the system of race-based territorial segregation, which ultimately relied on the Bantustan governments' ability to use coercion more than taxation or revenue extraction. I also find accounts suggestive of support for one of my hypotheses about regime intermediaries: that Bantustan leaders, like some of the intermediary-affiliated local councils in Palestine, also frequently engaged in deficit-financed distribution to shore up their rule.

The case of British colonial India, which I begin with next, cultivated intermediaries whose primary role within the regime, at least at first, was to extract revenue. That dovetailed with Britain's primary aim in the territory, which was not to settle and seize land but, rather, to extract capital, natural resources, and labor. The princely states featured delegation that was ultimately conditional on the transfer of revenues, although, while there was variation across the princely states and over time, revenue extraction entailed a good deal of coercion to maintain. In the annexed portions of India (not the princely states), landlords (*zamindars*) served as intermediaries with, again, the emphasis on revenue mobilization. In both India and South Africa, there are indications that intermediary actors weighed their tenuous legitimacy to rule against their ability to engage in politically unpopular tasks such as either coercion or extraction.

INDIRECT RULE IN INDIA UNDER THE BRITISH EMPIRE

The British colonial enterprise in India had its roots in the early expeditions of the East India Company in the early seventeenth century and lasted until independence and partition in 1947. As of 1871–72, British colonial authorities estimated the territory—including the princely states—to be nearly 1.5 million square miles containing more than 230 million people.[16] Thus, due to issues of sheer scale, any comparison to the Israeli occupation in Palestine would likely benefit from a much finer-grained geographic focus. For that reason, the observations provided here are best viewed as a collection of snapshots rather than a presentation of a generalized picture of what governance looked like across the subcontinent.

Existing scholarship has operationalized indirect rule in two primary ways in relation to colonial India. Each has implications for the geographic scale of variation across directly and indirectly ruled areas. One typical application of the concept is in distinguishing between the portions of India that Great Britain annexed versus those referred to as the princely states. In 1858, following a major revolt led by Indian military officers, the British Crown claimed imperial sovereignty over the Indian subcontinent from the British East India Company, which until then had been the main arm of British colonial intervention.[17] Some portions of the territory and population were annexed to Great Britain, while for others, the British maintained control over foreign policy, military affairs, and trade through formal agreements with ruling Indian princes. The latter constituted the so-called princely states.

After 1858, it is clear that higher-order variation existed between directly annexed provinces and indirectly ruled princely states. Existing social science literature exploits this geographic variation to compare directly ruled India—the annexed provinces—with the indirectly ruled princely states.[18] However, additional research has offered a second, important operationalization of the (in)directness of British rule by focusing on land tenure institutions—comparing, for example, areas where landlords and estate holders engaged in taxation on behalf of the British versus areas where British officials directly taxed cultivators.[19] In empirical research, these measures are most frequently applied to the British-annexed parts of India. However, variation in land tenure systems also distinguished princely states from one another, thus suggesting that indirect rule in India during the period of British control was multilayered and complex.[20]

Below, I focus most of my attention on the princely states. I find that despite diversity across the princely states, they differ from the Palestinian case in three, general ways. First, the princes possessed considerable authority over both policing and taxation, but the British relied more heavily on cooperation from the princes in the realm of revenue extraction. Second, many, though perhaps not all, the princes began with a higher stock of so-called traditional legitimacy than did the leaders of the Palestinian Authority. This—along with, of course, the backing of the British Empire—delayed the creation of coherent bases of political opposition. Third, because of the autocratic nature of princely states, oppositional mobilization often occurred outside state institutions. Nonetheless, in some cases, even local government employees within the princely states were able to join these efforts. While some of this opposition did not, at least initially, present itself as regime-challenging, one example of "nonstate governance" during the Telangana rebellion deserves further analysis.

Before transitioning to this analysis, I offer a brief preview of how one could apply the hypotheses generated from the Palestinian case to the operationalization of indirect rule in India, which is based on land tenure and taxation. In both annexed provinces and the princely states, *zamindars* and *jagirdars* (estate holders) served an intermediary role in their function of extracting revenue. For example, Abhijit Banerjee and Lakshmi Iyer describe how these systems were instituted in the British-annexed provinces: "In the landlord areas, the revenue liability for a village or a group of villages lay with a single landlord. The landlord was free to set the revenue terms for the peasants under his jurisdiction and to dispossess any peasants who did not pay the landlord what they owed him. Whatever remained after paying the British revenue demand was for the landlord to keep."[21] In the princely states, Barbara Ramusack notes that the *jagirdars* were often the favored intermediaries for revenue collection in "tracts beyond the control of the [princely] state administration," and, at an even more local level, the princely states also variously relied on cooperative "village headmen (*patels*), accountants (*patwaris*), and councils."[22]

In line with the theoretical predictions from chapter 1, this arrangement would suggest that landlords and estate holders in, for example, the British-annexed provinces would minimize their investment in traditional forms of policing and noneconomic coercion, due to the reputational costs they would incur from collaborating with the imperial state. They would be expected to do that particularly in areas where their role in extraction on behalf of the British state is most visible or impactful. Furthermore, they would be expected to invest in distributive capacity in areas they controlled if it could bring them reputational benefits. Their opponents, on the other hand, would be expected to develop less coercive forms of revenue mobilization in settings where their reputational advantage over the *zamindars* and *jagirdars* is greatest. Further, due to resource constraints, regime opponents might be required to spend less, or more efficiently, to achieve their productive or distributive goals.

The relationships among land, class politics, and regime opposition in Indian colonial history surely constitute far too large a topic for a non-specialist to cover here; thus, I cannot present a test of each of these hypotheses. However, in his research on the effects of land tenure systems on state capacity and long-run economic development, Alexander Lee notes that, in fact, *zamindars* did historically maintain their own police forces. This legacy from the times of Mughal rule carried into the British colonial period, and "even after these obligations were removed, landlords remained the most important force in law enforcement, as they appointed and paid the village watchmen (chaukidars)."[23] Lee describes how these village police were used, noting that "zamindars were often able to use them as a tool against recalcitrant tenants and avoid prosecution for crimes of their own."[24] The first example demonstrates that at least some of this coercive capacity was directly tied to extraction, while the latter example suggests, perhaps, a use of these village watchmen as a personal defense force for the *zamindar* against the state.

Note that these are not examples of noneconomic coercive capacity as I have defined it in chapter 1. In other words, this excerpt does not provide evidence that landlords developed policing capacity that was divorced from material extraction, or that coercive capacity was used explicitly to repress political rivals. Further, both Lee and Mukherjee have suggested that areas featuring *zamindar*-based revenue collection featured lower long-run levels of state capacity than areas where British authorities engaged in revenue collection more directly, but neither uses policing capacity specifically to make this argument.[25] In short, the amount of non-extractive policing capacity—whether used to produce a form of public order or to engage in political repression—developed by *zamindars* and *jagirdars* appears to be limited. Their main role—and the emphasis of their use of coercion—was extraction.

When addressing the hypotheses on oppositional governance, there is also the question of which actors in the anti-regime Indian nationalist landscape to focus on. Thus, if we were to define the extraction-based "regime"—in this case, as one co-constituted by the British Raj and the landlord and estate-holding classes—then the Indian National Congress (INC), under the leadership of Mahatma Gandhi, did not, at least initially, structure its opposition as such. As Walter Hauser describes, "so long as peasant interests were adversely and directly affected by government, the Congress . . . defended peasant interests with vigor. But where peasant interests were circumscribed by landed interests, the Congress under Gandhi counseled mutual trust and understanding. Pressure from the Left [within Congress] would force a deviation in this policy, but for the 1920's the non-payment of land taxes to the government was one thing, the regulation of excesses between zamindar and peasant, another."[26] However, Hauser proceeds to document how these tensions became a major flashpoint of disagreement between leftist and conservative elements of the Congress, with Jawaharlal Nehru advancing the more progressive position of radical changes in existing land tenure systems to advance peasants' rights.

The *zamindari* system ultimately was abolished under Nehru's leadership after India's independence. However, writing in 1963, Hauser concluded of the *zamindars* that "the political economic, and social influence of the privileged intermediary group on the land, legislative change notwithstanding, is still very great."[27] The trajectory of postindependence land reform and economic transformation in India, Adnan Naseemullah argues, was another way in which the "patchwork" state emerged.[28] Would an "abolition" of the West Bank's intermediaries—whose capacity is much more focused on policing than extraction—even be thinkable, and, if so, would the process share any parallels with the trajectory of India's *zamindari* system? Because of the very different foci of these institutions, profitable extrapolations from this aspect of the Indian experience to a potential Palestinian future should be applied with caution. In short, giving up land and taxation rights may look very different from giving up guns and armor.

Princes as Intermediaries

Indirect rule is a controversial and contested term to describe the role of Indian princely states in the British imperial context. For example, Karen

Leonard writes, "Hyderabad State was technically under British indirect rule, but this status was one of the least significant things about it."[29] Going further, Hira Singh argues that the concept of indirect rule should be abolished, claiming it "is in fact a conceptual tool of the colonial mode of historiography and misrepresents the history of colonial rule and resistance."[30] Furthermore, "the alliance between the colonial state and the landed aristocracy in India was a two-way process of compromise and accommodation, which the colonial state entered in the face of resistance by the latter. . . .While privileging the metropolis [the concept of indirect rule] denies Indian subjects their agency, excepting as instruments or 'puppets' of the supreme power."[31]

I believe the conceptual definition of indirect rule, and the theory we have deployed throughout the preceding chapters, takes Singh's critique seriously. Indirect rule should not—in either the Palestinian case or the Indian one—imply a unidirectional structure of domination in which intermediaries have no agency. For example, the labels of "principal" and "agent," while they may describe a status quo, at a minimum merely reflect what the dominant power *aims* to achieve as a stable equilibrium.[32] In the case of India's princely states, we might characterize the bargaining power brought to the table by the British imperial authorities and the princes as unequal, but not quite as asymmetrical as what was seen in other versions of indirect rule in the British Empire.

The princes (or *rajas*) who came to lead the princely states after 1858 were rulers with varied levels of geographic and popular reach; their prominence predated British intervention. While at one point there were more than five hundred such princes, Ramusack counts just over one hundred who survived "into the twentieth century," at which point the map separating British annexed provinces from the princely states had become fairly static.[33] The creation of what are now commonly referred to as the princely states derived largely from treaties that the British signed with the princes to delineate their autonomy, territorially circumscribe their rule, and secure their recognition of British paramount authority.[34]

Further, while there is great variation both across and within the princely states, many of their rulers were generally viewed as possessing preexisting sources of political legitimacy due to traditional forms of kingship and aristocracy and the battlefield successes of rulers who emerged from the ruins of the Mughal Empire.[35] This variation distinguishes the princely states from, for example, the Palestinian Authority, which was created *de novo* via an agreement between the Palestinians and Israel and which, as an institution, was fairly unmoored from other social institutions of authority in Palestinian society. However, without access to archival records that reflect the perspectives of various populations living under the rule of the princes, it is nearly impossible to reconstruct a full picture of the precolonial political reputations of these rulers.

While it is impossible to summarize the diverse sets of contingencies that shaped the formation and trajectory of the princely states, the general nature of British imperial intervention in South Asia focused on the mobilization of profits (for the British East India Company) or revenues (for the British imperial state). This was particularly the case at the beginning. As described by Ramusack, the treaties signed by princely rulers with the British dramatically shaped their political roles and their futures. "These agreements defined territorial boundaries, rendering them compact or diffuse but generally more restricted; they regulated relationships with both stronger or weaker neighbors, and to varying degrees modified relationships within a state between a ruler and his or her kinspeople, administrators, merchant groups and peasants. *Most importantly*, the treaties appropriated resources of Indian states, including revenues in the form of subsidies or tribute, subjects as soldiers, and commercial goods, for the benefit of the English East India Company."[36]

Without too much loss of specificity, we can say that the overarching aim of extraction continued to motivate British colonial policy into the late nineteenth century, although the experience of the 1857 rebellion clearly elevated matters of security as well. It is critical to recall that our theoretical framework does not require the dominant power (the British, in this case) to have a greater interest in either extraction or coercion. Rather, it simply assumes that one of these functions is more definitively emphasized in the set of capacities that the dominant state outsources to the intermediary.

When it came to the princely rulers, the cost of their protection by the British came in the form of revenues, or tribute, that they had to transfer to the empire. Thus, they were certainly delegated extensive authority over taxation and extraction within their territories. In this sense, their functional focus was not dissimilar from that of the landlord-based form of indirect rule discussed earlier. However, the level of autonomy granted to the princes was much wider in scope; the treaties they signed with the British defined the extent of their geographic authority, and they were allowed to raise and control their own armed forces. Thus, the princely states represented a functionally more extensive outsourcing of authority than what we observe in either the Israel-PA case or the case of the landlord-based systems in, for example, the British-annexed portions of India. The princes had much more room to govern as they saw fit, as long as they remained at peace with the British and paid tribute.

As such, while the emphasis was on extraction, it appears that princes did mobilize internal policing capacity for ends other than extraction. However, importantly, the agreements signed with the British imperial state usually restricted the forces to internal policing purposes, and the imperial authorities shunned the establishment of "unnecessary armies."[37] Initially, the princely rulers were endowed with forces "for which they paid but could not command," because those forces consisted of armed men supplied by the *jagirdars* and "British-trained and equipped subsidiary forces."[38] Thus, a number of states began centralizing reforms in the nineteenth century. The princes' insecurities about their hold on power also played a role. As Ramusack describes, "in the twentieth century some ruler such as the maharaja of Patiala reorganized their police departments as educated elites, jagirdars and peasants *challenged princely autocracy.*"[39] Ramusack also notes that while the British were hesitant to deploy their own military force in the princely states, they sometimes used their leverage to try to reduce what they saw as excessive forms of coercive punishment employed by the princes.

In summary, it does not seem that the princes tended to forbear from exercising force and violence due to legitimacy challenges; and in general, the British were inclined to delegate both functions to the princes. However, when examining the strategy underlying Britain's policies, we might argue that its subcontracting of authority to the princely states ensured that princes could primarily coerce in order to extract rather than extract in order to coerce. For example, in a review of the patterns of agrarian settlement and revenue collection in the princely state of Jammu and Kashmir, Shakti Kak summarizes, "The primary interest of the colonial administration was to generate revenues, and intervention in state administration and the system of tax assessment and collection was designed to ensure this."[40] Ultimately, though, it is notable that the ability of British officers to transform landownership and revenue-collecting institutions in the state was limited. Princely states such as Jammu and Kashmir had been incorporated into the regime as extractive intermediaries. Paradoxically, that sometimes meant preserving existing institutions and practices that had their own momentum.

Opposition to British Rule from the Princely States

Perhaps the first major demonstration of difference between the princely states and the directly ruled territories in India occurred during the 1857 rebellion, which, Fisher notes, "had been confined primarily to areas under direct British control. Princely states like Hyderabad had been held out of the conflict by their rulers and Residents. *Even in the areas where the populace had risen against the British, the princes had exerted authority*, an authority which the British sought after 1858 to harness to their own purposes. . . . Indeed, British policy depended on the princes as the 'natural leaders' who would hold the people of their states in loyalty to the British crown."[41] This quote demonstrates that the populations living under princely rule did not wholly refrain from participating in the sepoy-initiated rebellion. Fisher nonetheless hypothesizes that if restive regions, such as Awadh and Jhansi, that were officially annexed to British India had instead "continued under indirect rule, it is quite probable that [directly ruled areas] would have remained quiet as did the other princely states. The British Empire after 1858 relied upon the loyalty of the areas under indirect rule as its cornerstone."[42]

Indeed, overtly nationalist mobilization was late to arrive to the princely states. Popular activism in the princely states did not immediately challenge the princes' legitimacy to rule, and the reach of such mobilizations were sometimes limited due to urban-rural, caste, and religious divisions. Ramusack notes that the Indian National Congress "consciously distanced itself from political mobilization in the princely states" in the late nineteenth and early twentieth centuries, concentrating its efforts on the provinces that had been annexed by Great Britain.[43] The author argues that this was due in part to the INC's sympathies—and Gandhi's in particular— "[toward] the princes as sources of legitimation and models of the Indian capacity to govern."[44]

However, this dynamic began to shift in the 1920s and 1930s, as certain class-based movements allied themselves with the independence movement. For example, the *praja mandal* (loosely, "people's organizations") movements began in places such as the tributary princely states of western Orissa and in Baroda state. In the tributary states of Orissa, this movement took the form of a series of peasant, tenant, student, and civil rights mobilizations against excessively extractive land revenue settlements and tyrannical princely rule.[45] In a study of the broader labor movement in Baroda state, Pravin Patel describes how, as the state industrialized, many economically and socially disadvantaged migrant workers came to work in the cotton mills, where they were exposed to highly exploitative and sometimes dangerous working conditions for unreliable wages.[46]

It is relevant to our present study that some of the earliest examples of labor militancy in Baroda state were organized among municipal workers in transportation and sanitation. Patel describes how a prolonged strike of the street sweepers of Baroda municipality forced higher-level "municipal officers to take brooms in their hands to clean the streets of the city."[47] Thus we see oppositional politics entering municipal governance through a path that contrasts with the Palestinian case. Whereas municipal workers in this example from Baroda state became political challengers as part of a broader-based labor movement, in Palestine, mobilization was channeled through political parties—some of which were hybrid political-militant movements—into municipal elections.

The *praja mandals* and related political movements across the princely states eventually consolidated into an institution called the All India States People's Conference (AISPC) in the 1920s. Not until the late 1930s was it openly supported by the Indian National Congress, since until then, the INC had avoided political involvement in the princely states.[48] The evolving relationship between the Congress—which emerged out of the more directly ruled British-annexed portions of India—and the princely states is a topic deserving a far lengthier analysis than can be addressed here. The relationship was refracted through the differing perspectives within the INC on the extent to which the nationalist movement should attempt to overcome rather than embrace class struggle.

A turning point of sorts came at the Haripura Congress in 1938, when the Congress made its entry into princely state politics official.[49] Writing about the trade union movement in Baroda state, Patel notes how it "grew in strength and legitimacy" when it affiliated with a newly invigorated *praja mandal* led by INC leader Sardar Vallabhbhai Patel.[50] Importantly, though, not all the labor mobilization in Baroda state was as moderate as the type that was supported by the Congress; Patel details the divisions between the more hardline communist organizations and those that hewed more closely to "Gandhi's ideology of industrial harmony, class amity and willingness to accept arbitration in industrial disputes."[51]

As a general phenomenon, the tenants, workers, peasants, and other groups who came together under the *praja mandals*, and later in the AISPC, came closest, as a broad-based movement, to articulating a coherent challenge to the indirect rule regime in which the rulers of India's princely states served. However, this cursory survey of work written on the topic in the English language does not suggest that these movements sought or were able to build their own oppositional local governance programs in the princely states. Instead, without suggesting that it was a one-way transmission of ideas and resources from British-annexed India to the princely states, we can still say that currents of exchange, learning, and information transmission between the British-annexed provinces and the indirectly ruled princely states played a role in "nationalizing" these movements.

Ramusack discusses the divergent legacies of some of the popular movements and communal activism across the princely states. She noted that the INC was "able to lay the groundwork for later dominance" in states such as Mysore, Rajkot, Rajputana, and Tehri Garhwal, while in Travancore and Patiala states, "communist and communal parties were such strong antagonists that they would emerge as major rivals in the post-colonial era."[52]

The princely states of Jammu and Kashmir and Hyderabad are both settings where the rulers who assumed their positions as intermediaries within the British Empire were encumbered from the first day with basic challenges to their popular legitimacy. The princely state of Jammu and Kashmir was created in 1846 under the rule of Dogras, a linguistically based ethnic group of the Hindu faith, through a treaty with the British East India Company. The British gained territory in the wake of the Anglo-Sikh war and subsequently sold Jammu and Kashmir to Gulab Singh, who became the ruler of the new princely state. In *Hindu Rulers, Muslim Subjects*, Mridu Rai writes that the initiation of Gulab Singh's dynasty

> ushered in a critical break—in terms of a vital change in the nature of arrangements of power inaugurated at the same time as the state of Jammu and Kashmir was founded by the colonial government of India. This shift endowed the individual ruler with a personalized form of sovereignty,

erasing earlier traditions of layered authority shared simultaneously by various levels in Kashmiri society. As a result of changes inaugurated at the moment of transition to "indirect" colonial influence, Kashmiris, the vast majority of whom happened to be Muslim, found themselves unrepresented in an enterprise of Dogra domination without legitimacy.[53]

Indeed, according to Rai, "a fundamental distinction to bear in mind is not simply that [the Dogra regime] entailed rule by Hindus but that it had become a Hindu state,"[54] language that aligns with one of our theoretical scope conditions that the indirect rule regime must be in the service of a regime of domination, with religious identity being one potential axis along which groups are organized.

Due to its sheer size, the princely state of Jammu and Kashmir may also provide supporting evidence for the hypothesis I present in chapter 1: namely, that the greater the share of the indigenous workforce employed in intermediary institutions, the more likely that boundaries between intermediary and opponent will become complex and blurred. For example, Rai describes how in the first decades of the twentieth century, challenges emerged from both nonstate social institutions—primarily Islamic and other religiously affiliated institutions—and institutions founded "under the aegis" of the state itself, such as the Dogra Sabha, an assembly that, despite its name, came to represent not just Dogra elites but also Kashmiri Pandits (Hindu Brahmins from Kashmir) and Kashmiri Muslims.[55] In addition, Rai documents how Muslim subjects also began mobilizing for greater educational access and representation within state institutions, and how even municipalities—such as the local government of the city of Srinagar—found themselves caught in the middle at times.[56] Thus, through perhaps the 1920s, it is difficult to disentangle intermediary from oppositional actors and, thus, the governance programs they pursued.

However, there does appear to be a trajectory whereby the opposition began to challenge not just policies but also the regime itself. Ramusack describes an initial phase of mobilization in 1931 sparked by a "trial of a Muslim servant arrested for making an allegedly anti-Hindu and seditious speech during a public protest against discriminatory state policies toward Muslims."[57] Organized Muslim groups from the British-annexed Punjab province "soon contended as champions of the Kashmiri Muslims," but "in the process Kashmiris acquired substantial experience of agitational politics and incarceration in state jails for political activity. When repressive policies failed to quell the public demonstrations, the first phase ended with Maharaja Hari Singh appealing to the British for military force. . . . As would continue to happen after independence, the [British government of India] became the last resort for an embattled state administration in Kashmir."[58]

A rural front in the mobilization soon began in the form of protests against land taxation, and eventually this mobilization was channeled into the political arena. Importantly, when considering comparisons with the case of the West Bank, the 1931 agitations transformed into a political movement and party under the leadership of Sheikh Mohammad Abdullah, first known as the Jammu and Kashmir Muslim Conference and then formed as the Jammu and Kashmir National Conference. Sheikh Abdullah's movement and its approach to both resistance and "oppositional governance" before partition provide fertile ground for future study. After 1948, he was officially appointed to a leadership role in a new regime when he became prime minister of the state of Jammu and Kashmir. The violence that has afflicted the region since partition is now all too well known.

A final case of resistance from within a princely state deserves mention here: the Telangana peasant rebellion against the *nizam* (or ruler) of Hyderabad state in the waning years of British imperial control. Over the course of this uprising, a commune-based "rebel governance" system was established and existed for a short time. This conflict also fed into the Maoist insurgency after independence and later experiments with Marxist-inspired forms of communal governance by insurgents.[59]

How would our predictions about governance by the indigenous opposition fit here? We would expect the communes to emphasize less coercive forms of extraction. We would also expect them to face resource challenges due to their position as regime challengers and thus to exercise restraint in the productive features of governance (e.g., the provision of coercion or security or the distribution of other collective goods and services). An important question in testing these theoretical propositions in such a case is how the functionalist, resource-driven predictions of our theory might interact with ideological goals.[60]

Another important question—not just in the case of the Telangana rebellion—is whether the context of an ongoing violent conflict and insurgency is a factor powerful enough to shape and disrupt the governance decisions of regime challengers in ways that are not predicted by the theory I have presented thus far. Of particular interest in the case of the rebellion against Hyderabad state is how the rebels balanced their productive (including the production of coercion), distributive, and redistributive goals given the resources at their disposal. These are potential avenues for additional research.

SOUTH AFRICA'S APARTHEID REGIME

The history of apartheid in South Africa is entwined with the country's history of settler colonization—first by the Dutch and subsequently by Great Britain—and the anticolonial resistance it engendered from the indigenous Khoesan and other Black South African populations; the emergence of the mining and manufacturing economies; and ideologies of racial, cultural, and religious supremacy.[61] These factors shaped the means by which the British in particular sought to govern the first colonies they established on the southwest cape and in the colony of Natal on the country's southeastern coast.

Following the creation of the Union of South Africa as a dominion of the British Empire, and subsequently the Commonwealth, the vast majority of the Black South African population and nonwhite (e.g., "Coloured" and Indian) minorities remained disenfranchised. The 1948 elections brought to power the National Party, a radical white supremacist and Afrikaner-nationalist party. At that point, the apartheid regime began implementing systematic policies of social control and legal segregation to prevent racial mixing, escalated forced removals of Black South Africans from urban areas, and intensified a system of pass laws and restrictions on movement that buttressed a migrant labor economy to feed white-owned capital, agriculture, and industry. This was apartheid (a term meaning "separateness" or "apartness" in Afrikaans).

Mamdani argues that the apartheid regime instituted in South Africa and what was then South West Africa (now Namibia) between 1948 and the transition to democracy in the early 1990s represented a kind of culmination of colonial domination through indirect rule, or what he terms "decentralized despotism."[62] While many of the well-known inflection points in the anti-apartheid struggle—the Sharpeville massacre in 1960, the 1973 mass labor strikes in Durban, the Soweto uprising in 1976—occurred in cities and townships, which were subject to a more direct form of rule from the government's capital of Pretoria, those less well versed in apartheid's history may not know as much about the politics in the indirectly ruled Bantustans. Many of these areas had already been designated as native "reserves" under colonial rule and the subsequent Union of South Africa.

Following a series of laws—including the Group Areas Act of 1950, the Bantu Authorities Act of 1951, and the Promotion of Bantu Self-Government Act of 1959—the apartheid regime forcibly removed millions of Black South Africans to these regions, which at first were predominantly rural but also included some peri-urban townships, while also dispossessing Coloured and Indian populations. Mamdani cites an estimate that more than 3.5 million, or more than 10 percent of the country's population, was forcibly removed between 1960 and 1985.[63] This transformed millions of Black South Africans into migrant workers and criminalized their existence in the urban areas of the Republic of South Africa (as the rest of the state was known) except as workers. Many migrants ended up camping out in hostels in the urban periphery, but a predominantly rural peasantry and, in fact, a disproportionate share of women and children stayed in the Bantustans.

The Bantustan governments consisted of chiefs who were invested with some traditional bases of authority and legitimacy but who were elevated into new roles of intermediaries within the apartheid regime.[64] Under these chiefs, Bantustan "states" contained large administrations, with public employment reaching nearly 200,000 by 1980.[65] The Bantustans were also highly dependent on fiscal transfers from the government in Pretoria. Interestingly, in light of the earlier discussion of corruption within the Palestinian Authority, Bertil Egerö notes that "the corruption that goes with these subsidies may for Pretoria be an inevitable part of the costs of the bantustan strategy. However, it also serves the function of tying local interests to the bantustan administrations."[66] Indeed, in the Palestinian case, the outsized public sector and its disproportionate contribution to the Palestinian economy in the West Bank might, through its relationships of dependency, contribute to PA corruption in a similar way.

The Bantustans were thus a territorialized and highly institutionalized form of indirect rule under apartheid. Research on politics in the Bantustans is a rich but perhaps underemphasized area of scholarship in the historiography of apartheid. Having established that the they fit our conceptualization of indirect rule and thus the scope conditions for the theoretical intervention I aim to make, we can subsequently ask a few general questions about the nature of indirect rule in the Bantustans and the ways it might have compared and contrasted with the example of the Israeli-PA regime in the West Bank. What forms of governance did the apartheid regime, based in Pretoria, seek to offload on to the Bantustan leadership? Did the central government depend on the Bantustan governments primarily to engage in direct extraction, or did the relationship prioritize noneconomic coercion and policing? Further, did anti-apartheid opposition actors develop any capacities related to governance within the Bantustans?

The South African government's primary goal in outsourcing authority to Bantustan leaders was undoubtedly to territorially segregate Black South Africans from whites while controlling their movement and harnessing them for cheap labor. Thus, when asking what functional capacities were most important from the view of the government in Pretoria, here it seems, as in the Palestinian case, that the delegation of coercive control was emphasized over extraction. Extraction was, of course, inherent to apartheid—Black South Africans were dispossessed of their property and land, and the economy of South Africa's mines, industrial factories, and farms depended on ruthless labor exploitation. Extractive functions were central to the political interests represented in the central government and were thus processes managed by Pretoria, to say nothing of the complicity of various economic and political actors in the country.

Importantly, as Holmes notes, there was variation across the Bantustans in their "autonomy, funding, resource endowments, governing capacity, and territorial fragmentation," all of which, we can conclude, shaped the functional capacities of their governments.[67] However, without loss of too much precision, we can propose that the apartheid regime's intermediaries— the Bantustan governments—were not deputized by the government in Pretoria with extraction as their primary purpose. In addition to the direct coercion of the South African police and security forces in the cities and townships, Bantustan authorities were entrusted to a relatively greater degree with securing the territories and populations under their control through everyday coercion.

Examples of how coercion was used by these authorities to buttress the apartheid project include not only the Bophuthatswana Bantustan's suppression of political opponents of the Bantustan president, Lucas Mangope, but also his government's campaign to forcibly incorporate villages into the

Bantustan at the behest of the apartheid regime.[68] Further examples can be found in the ruthless suppression of anti-apartheid activism and militancy that relied on close cooperation between the Pretoria government and Bantustan institutions, including the Transkei Defence Force. The latter would itself foster the collapse of the Bantustan government due to a revolt led by one of its own brigadiers, Bantu Holomisa.[69]

Coercion by bantustan authorities did, indeed, enable them, in their role as regime intermediaries, to tax and extract from their own populations. However, in the context of the apartheid regime, such coercion was carried out largely to enable extraction by the central government and actors who politically supported them. This took the form of violent policing and repression, deportations, and other human rights violations, which have at times been neglected or overshadowed by the dramatic violence of the apartheid state in the cities and townships.

Bantustan states also pursued distribution, like the PA government in the West Bank, and the new histories of these so-called homeland governments, reflected in Shireen Ally and Arianna Lissoni's volume, for example, have focused attention on these distributive programs in areas such as health and education.[70] Laura Evans argues for greater scholarly attention to the "networks of patronage" that Bantustan leaders and rural elites developed and how "the distribution of state resources (pensions, education, land, housing, labour contracts, for example) . . . is central to any discussion of power in the bantustans."[71]

Bantustan distributive capacity development was also, it seems, a learning process. The notorious rural "betterment" schemes were often disastrous, uprooting communities and failing to achieve the agricultural efficiency improvements they were supposedly seeking, and thus they faced resistance.[72] This finding presents a potential challenge to my theoretical assumption that coercive and fiscal capacities will be the most politically controversial for intermediaries, since the distributive programs of the Bantustan state were often politicized and potentially played a role in aggravating the inherent legitimacy crisis that the chiefs and their administrations faced as intermediaries.

However, there is also evidence that Bantustan authorities learned from these risks, spending on distributive items—such as, for example, livestock veterinary services—that "provided an increasingly important social welfare function," according to Timothy Gibbs.[73] In another telling example,

Gibbs relays how the Transkei Bantustan authorities were castigated—even, surprisingly, by "ANC-linked dissidents"—in their own efforts to outsource management of cattle dipping to lower-level tribal authorities. When live-stock disease began spreading through communities in the mid-1970s, the authorities stepped in to reclaim control over this service (and the associated budget). "Within a year the number of livestock deaths caused by tick-borne diseases declined by 40 percent."[74]

Nonetheless, similarly to the Fatah local authorities I profiled, Bantustan governments spent their way into increasingly large deficits in the 1970s, and it was a proposed livestock tax that sent the rural regions in Transkei close to revolt. As Eliphas Mukonoweshuro wrote in 1991, "the fiscal crisis in the Bantustans has made it impossible to meet some of the homelands' people's most basic demands, such as the need for clean water, electricity, and health and educational facilities."[75] While the Bantustans did have the capacity to raise their own taxes, it appears that their disproportionate tilt toward both policing and distributive capacity meant that they were finan-cially reliant on the central government. (A parallel can be drawn to the soft budgets on which Palestinian municipalities can draw in the utilities sectors, in which the municipalities are not held fully accountable for set-tling their debts with the Fatah-led central government; as the findings in chapters 4 and 5 suggested, Fatah-affiliated municipalities might have used this tactic to their political advantage.) Gibbs concludes that despite the willingness of Kaiser Matanzima, the head of the Transkei Bantustan, to use "the full force of the state" to repress and expel rivals, the "second, smoth-ered Mpondo revolt of the late 1970s suggests that despite the increasing reach of the state into rural communities, the Bantustan government did not hold the whip hand."[76] Why not? Gibbs reveals that despite the appar-ent failure of the revolt, Matanzima agreed to scale back the proposed livestock tax that had spurred opposition and increase spending directed toward Transkei's poverty-stricken communities, despite the mounting fis-cal imbalances this produced. This logic suggests that, as in the Palestinian case, the intermediary's use of disproportionate coercion to maintain both the broader indirect rule regime and their own hold on power introduced reputational trade-offs. As a result, fiscal extraction was reduced while dis-tributive spending was increased.

Did the ANC or other anti-apartheid groups build any local govern-ing capacity—even, for example, "rebel governance" institutions—in the

Bantustans? It is clear that the Bantustans were sometimes used by anti-apartheid activists for underground or guerrilla organizing, as was the case with the uMkhonto we Sizwe (MK) militant wing of the ANC under leaders like Chris Hani, who was born in Transkei and cultivated recruitment and connections there.[77] Further, as detailed by Nicholas Rush Smith, oppositional institutions seeking revolutionary justice—which we might consider a productive aspect of governance but which was inherently buttressed by violence and, thus, coercive capacity—developed in the more urban parts of the KwaZulu Bantustan.[78] There, the Bantustan government, dominated by the Inkatha Freedom Party, armed youth gangs and collaborated with them to suppress and violently target their common adversary, the youth "Comrades," who were affiliated with the United Democratic Front, an anti-apartheid umbrella group. Smith identifies the Comrades' informal "popular justice" institutions as one among a number of antecedents of contemporary vigilantism in post-apartheid South Africa.

Furthermore, while the anti-apartheid resistance did not make a point to thoroughly infiltrate formal political institutions in the Bantustans, anti-regime activities nonetheless seeped into Bantustan governance. Thus, to try to characterize the range of oppositional governance projects that emerged in the Bantustans, one would need to take account of both informal capacities developed by underground and insurgent groups and the capacities within formal Bantustan institutions that may have been coopted, or partially captured, by resistance actors. In one fascinating example, Vha-Musanda Vho-Shandukani Mudzunga recalls his experience working for the Venda Bantustan government in its Consulate General, as some Bantustans were declared independent from South Africa and thus had their own foreign affairs apparatuses. "In 1983, I was promoted to the position of Vice-Consul. It was in this period that I began to operate in a dual capacity as government employee and underground political activist."[79] The author then describes how they played an instrumental role in issuing passports and providing permission for ANC revolutionaries and activists to travel. Despite the "stop lists" that the South African and Bantustan governments shared with the goal of restricting the travel and movement of these individuals, the author was able to take advantage of the supposed independence of the Bantustan to assert the rights to travel documents in opposition to the directives of the apartheid government. Mudzunga writes, "Many activists approached me for documents to travel out of the country, and I provided them. Cyril Ramaphosa [president of South Africa at the time of writing]—my old friend from BECO [the Bold Evangelical Christian Organization, a faith-based youth group that organized against apartheid]—was one of them, and I became a small but significant cog in the struggle wheel, operating from within the very system we were fighting to overthrow."[80]

This case is different from that of Hamas, for example, formally participating in PA local and national elections; it is not an organized wing of the anti-apartheid movement (say, the ANC) running for office or pursuing the concerted capture of the Bantustan bureaucracy. However, it still points to the way in which the creation of indirect rule institutions also generates new potential roles for diverse elements of the indigenous population, including regime opponents.

In summary, the central apartheid regime depended on the Bantustan intermediaries not so much for direct extractive capacity as for "containerizing," in Mamdani's words, the Black South African population and thus wielding force and coercion to do so. That was the nature of delegation inherent in the Bantustan project, along with, importantly, distributive capacities that, we might assume, were supported cynically by the regime to maintain a sustainable supply of migrant labor but were also likely used by Bantustan authorities to shore up their legitimacy and maintain popular quiescence as much as possible. Those actions were not, of course, entirely successful, and anti-apartheid resistance actors were also able to use the territorial bases of the Bantustans—along with, at times, their formal political institutions—to begin to practice their own forms of governance. These efforts were sporadic and context dependent. However, in many cases, these resistance projects emphasized the development of their own forms of coercive capacity—both externally facing, in the way that guerrilla activities sought to project force on to and against the apartheid regime, and, in some cases, internal forms of community policing and "popular justice." As yet, the scholarship does not seem to suggest that regime opponents—whether ANC, MK, or other revolutionary or anti-apartheid groups—had the incentives or opportunities to develop fiscal capacity within the indirectly ruled Bantustans. Thus, the comparison with regime opponents in Palestine, such as Hamas and other smaller parties, is not a seamless one.

CONCLUDING THOUGHTS AND AVENUES
FOR FUTURE RESEARCH

The theory I developed in the preceding chapters argues that regimes of domination that settle on a strategy of indirect rule will generate various risks, constraints, and opportunities for indigenous populations as they seek to govern their communities locally. In particular, because such regimes rely on indigenous actors to fulfill some politically risky forms of governance—such as extraction or the use of coercive violence— indigenous individuals and organizations at the local level are often forced to choose between affiliating themselves with the regime intermediaries or positioning themselves as regime opponents. Despite the fact that these identities can be fluid, ambiguous, and nuanced across different geographical, temporal, and individual contexts, I find, through detailed examination of the Palestinian case, that local actors associated with the regime and its intermediaries face a different set of constraints and opportunities to provide governance than those associated with the regime's challengers. Indirect rule introduces reputational challenges for regime intermediaries, a condition that will encourage them to forbear from certain politically risky governing tasks at the local level, depending on which tasks are less essential to their relationship with the dominant state or regime at the center.

Furthermore, I argue that, in an effort to compensate for their reputational deficit, and because of the relative resource advantages they have over regime opponents, intermediaries are more likely to invest in distributive capacity to deliver either patronage or collective goods. The opportunities and challenges facing regime opponents who seek to develop governance projects at the local level are more context-dependent. However, in general, I argue that opponents will not be hamstrung by the reputational and legitimacy problems that plague regime intermediaries. Nonetheless, they are more likely to face resource constraints due to their disadvantaged position as opponents of a dominant state, ruling power, or colonial regime. Thus, opponents may be required to develop greater fiscal, or extractive, capacity at the local level. Where they have a greater legitimacy advantage over their intermediary counterparts, that extraction can be carried out with relatively little coercion. However, their relative resource deficit may still require them to moderate the productive and distributive aspects of their governance program or find opportunities to pursue them in a more cost-efficient manner.

I conclude this volume with some thoughts on avenues for future research. The first question is whether, or how, indigenous local governance would look different under a regime pursuing inclusive rather than exclusive state-building and thus under an institutional structure that looks more like direct rule. These cases are outside the scope conditions that I outline in chapter 1, but we can still make some tentative predictions. Because direct rule does not generate a formal role for indigenous intermediaries, it is more likely to pit the dominant state or regime against its opponents in an unmediated fashion. The example of East Timor (now the independent Democratic Republic of Timor-Leste) under Indonesian occupation is discussed briefly in chapter 1. In addition, Israeli occupation of the West Bank until 1994 was, somewhat begrudgingly on Israel's part, a more direct form of rule, despite Israel's continual effort to find reliable Palestinian intermediaries at the local level. Furthermore, while the Hashemite monarchy in Jordan did not face quite as severe a legitimacy crisis in the West Bank during its rule from 1950 to 1967, its style of rule was more inclusive and direct.

The speculation that could be tested in future research is that, because direct rule does not tend to divide the indigenous population as harshly between those who are embedded within the regime and those who are resisting it, the governance projects of regime challengers will be more bimodally distributed—in essence, functionally they will be "all or nothing." Challengers might begin to take on fiscal, distributive, and coercive roles in an effort to cultivate their own mini-states, or they will face such severe repression that they will be able to develop little by way of functional local governance. Accordingly, in future research, we can ask whether these settings generate different institutional trajectories for the opposition—one, under indirect rule, in which they are attempting to distinguish themselves not just from the dominant state but also from their indigenous intermediary counterparts, and a second, under direct rule, whereby they seek to build anti-regime governance wholly outside of existing state structures.

While this book has focused entirely on the situation in the Israeli-occupied West Bank, a more empirically rich account could incorporate observations of local governance from the other region of occupied Palestine: the Gaza Strip. From 2007 until the moment of writing—the fateful fall of

2023—Hamas had governed the Palestinian population of Gaza while Israel had maintained control over the territory's sea and skies, and, in cooperation with Egypt, imposed a partial blockade, restricting the movement of all people and goods that try to enter or exit the territory. In a series of successive wars, Israel has continued to militarily target Hamas and other armed groups that are active in the territory, such as Palestinian Islamic Jihad.[81] Even before 2023, the economic and humanitarian toll of these wars had devastated the population in Gaza, killing thousands of Palestinians, decimating critical infrastructure, including desalination and sewage treatment facilities, and leaving tens of thousands scarred with lifelong injuries and enduring consequences for mental health.[82]

In some ways, Gaza from 2007 until 2023 was an example of the second trajectory mentioned earlier, since Israel's domination of the Gaza Strip was more direct and less mediated than its form of governance in the West Bank. However, the institutional footprints of the Palestinian Authority as a vehicle of indirect rule—even in Gaza—remain. Somdeep Sen describes how Hamas's strategy of legitimation rested on its position as a fierce opponent of Israel rather than its intermediary: The movement "appropriated that which was meant to dismantle the resistance [PA institutions], reconstituted it to serve as a means of facilitating the resistance, and subsequently, inducted the role of government and all that it administers into the path of the national struggle."[83] Yet, as Sen's work illuminates, even if Hamas had, somewhat paradoxically, been able to assert a postcolonial state-building project in this still colonial condition, it was not without its legitimacy challenges either. These might emerge because of individuals' overt political allegiances to Fatah or, for example, perceptions of favoritism and discrimination in Hamas's policing, taxing, or spending practices. Additional research could seek to understand if these reputation costs shaped the Hamas government's behavior—did it strategically forbear from, or minimize, certain forms of coercion or extraction? Or did Hamas pursue a more functionally uniform type of state building—investing evenly in extractive, coercive, and distributive capacities—hoping that its adoption of resistance rhetoric and tactics would shield it from the reputational challenges that its rival, Fatah, faced in the West Bank?

As this manuscript was going to press, thousands of Hamas militants—mostly young men—broke through the barrier separating the besieged enclave from Israel and, in the largest terror attack in Israel's history, killed some 1,200 Israelis and seized approximately 240 hostages, including men, women, and children, and transported them back into Gaza. The ensuing war that Israel has launched on the land, infrastructure, and 2.2 million people of Gaza—ostensibly to eradicate Hamas—has been unlike anything Palestinians have experienced in recent memory. By the end of January 2023, the war had claimed the lives of more 26,000 Palestinians—more than one out of every one hundred people in the territory—denying the surviving population of critical fuel, food, water, and medical supplies, destroying over seventy-three thousand housing units, forcibly displacing some 1.7 million people, and leveling the northern part of the territory to the ground.[84] These dynamics continue to involve moment by moment, and, by the time this book is in the hands of readers, I am not sure what will remain of Gaza or its people. While many are wondering what is next for governance of the population, the current view is obscured by the dark clouds of a war that seems to have no end date in mind. Prime Minister Netanyahu has stated his government aims for Israel to maintain security control over Gaza while "demilitarizing" it and placing the responsibility for governance in the hands of some unnamed civilian authority that is neither Hamas nor the PA.[85] Thus, after an incomprehensible level of destruction, Israel will be faced with a familiar problem—it seeks to control territory without governing the surviving population. However, this time, no Palestinian intermediary is likely to emerge from the ruins.

A second set of questions that deserve additional attention, beyond what I have provided here, relate to the concept of legitimacy. The brief overview of scholarship on India's ruling princes, landlords, and estate owners who are described as the intermediaries in the British imperial project raised a number of questions about when and how we can ascertain that these intermediaries do, in fact, face a reputational deficit, or even crisis, with the populations they are seeking to govern. In chapter 1, I acknowledged the variation in preexisting sources of legitimacy that intermediaries bring to their positions. This variation most likely matters, but one could argue that the longer intermediaries derive benefits, authority, and power from serving within the regime of domination on behalf of the dominant state, the more these preexisting sources of legitimacy may wane.

Subsequently, we could ask whether these mounting reputational deficits may nonetheless fail to shape the calculus of intermediaries if their willingness to use repression is high enough. In such cases, intermediaries may not view extraction and coercion as trade-offs but—in the formula all too familiar in despotic regimes; they may regularly and unapologetically employ them hand in hand, to brutal results. On this point, I will make only a tentative suggestion: I believe the geographic scale and local rootedness of the intermediary might shape these outcomes. If the interviews documented in chapter 5 revealed nothing else, they showed that Palestinian politicians at the highly local level—in this case, those serving within municipalities—were clearly a part of the communities they served. The decisions they made about, for example, whether to pave a road, penalize a building code violation, or rehabilitate an electricity line were decisions that impacted their own acquaintances, friends, neighbors, colleagues, and sometimes family members. Thus, one might imagine that this relatively low degree of insulation from the community they governed might have increased their time horizons, allowing them to govern for the future in a way that would be less likely for an intermediary functioning in a remote regional capital. As a result, these Palestinian mayors, like India's princes under colonial rule, were more sensitive to the trade-offs between the use of coercion and extraction and their legitimation with their publics.

Another avenue for future research is how urban versus rural dynamics might interact with, or condition, the effects of indirect rule. Israeli rule in the West Bank is most direct in the rural and transitional areas, while it is most indirect in Palestinian urban centers, where, from at least the end of the second intifada around 2005, Israel attempted to rely on the PA more for internal policing. However, the example of the Bantustans versus the cities in apartheid South Africa demonstrates the opposite configuration, even though some Bantustans did incorporate urban areas, and the transformation of Bantustan economies (and class structures) over time belie the myth that Bantustans were monolithically rural.[86] Nonetheless, I have observed elsewhere that the degree of urbanization in indirectly ruled areas may shape both the short- and long-term impacts of the regime on local governance.[87] However, this is a complex set of possible causal relationships to unpack, since the initial political formations of indigenous political actors—whether later classified as intermediaries or opponents—will likely be shaped by existing levels of urbanization.

One finding that both the South African and Palestinian cases appeared to share was the intermediary's emphasis on distributive spending in nonurban areas. This may be partly because it is relatively easier to cultivate relationships of patronage and dependency with nonurban populations whose access to public goods is often more tenuous and whose bargaining position with political authorities may be weaker due to the relatively immobile nature of their assets.[88] However, as the example of the Bantustans revealed, intermediaries do not shield themselves from challenges indefinitely through their distributive capacity alone. Further, even if done inadvertently, such spending may itself bring about more opportunities for collective action, mobilization, and oppositional activity challenging the indirect rule regime. The way in which urban and rural dynamics shape these outcomes deserves continued study.

What should not be lost in any of this analysis are the experiences and perspectives of everyday citizens. In post-Oslo Palestine, Dana El Kurd extensively documents how the Palestinian Authority—and particularly its reliance on international donors and patrons—has fractured the elites working within this system from the broader Palestinian public.[89] Rather than drawing an elite-public distinction, my analysis of municipal governance has shown that both regime intermediaries and their opponents may find themselves working within institutions that are formally a part of the regime. However, like that of El Kurd, my research reveals how the fault lines created by the Oslo regime can cut across society in deeply harmful ways that are challenging to fully document. It is profoundly difficult to imagine that these societal wounds will heal as soon as these institutions are replaced with something new.

A final underexplored area for research in the Palestinian context relates to the relative importance (or unimportance) of Islamist ideology in local governance. Readers will note that in the preceding chapters, I did not dedicate a lot of attention to Hamas's identity as an Islamist group. A robust existing literature explores how Islamist groups that are out of power can use social service provision to win support.[90] Interestingly, I find that the level and nature of Hamas-run municipalities' spending from within formal municipal institutions did not distinguish them from those run by Fatah or independent or smaller party mayors during the period of our analysis. I suggest that may be because Hamas, with its established connections to social service and *zakat* committees in the West Bank, may have substitute channels for delivering such programs. If so, this could have important implications for how such groups might engage in formal governance in the future. Would they continue to use these alternative channels, or would they be more formally integrated into government institutions?

Furthermore, because organizations such as Hamas appeared to be relatively successful at enhancing local revenue collection while in office, we did not obtain a clear picture of how different types of spending or saving may have been prioritized. Would, for example, Islamist groups be more likely to spend on administrative capacity—staff, administrative resources, and so on—rather than distributive goods if the latter are already provided through nongovernmental organizations with which they can claim an affiliation? These are questions that fit squarely within the literature on Islamist politics and deserve further exploration. Scholarship on the Gaza Strip from 2007 to 2023, when Hamas began to exercise control of the government under ongoing Israeli and Egyptian blockade, is perhaps best suited to address these questions in contemporary Palestine.

I conclude by noting that there have been a number of worrying transformations in Israel's regime in the West Bank since the period covered in the preceding chapters. Local elections in the West Bank have become less competitive, and municipal councils have been seemingly plagued with resignations. In 2012, despite the indefinite postponement of Palestinian presidential and legislative elections since the 2007 *Inqisam*—the fracture between the Fatah-led West Bank and the Hamas-led Gaza Strip—President Abbas authorized the holding of municipal elections in the West Bank. Hamas rejected the vote for violating an earlier accord it had signed with Fatah to advance a national reconciliation government that would have been responsible for supervising local elections. Thus, it boycotted the election in the West Bank and did not permit elections to take place in Gaza.[91] Candidates endorsed by the ruling party performed well in Hebron and Bethlehem but not in Nablus, Ramallah, or Jenin. Local elections were held once again in 2017 and 2021, but Fatah-affiliated or seemingly apolitical family lists were able to regain control of many municipalities in the absence of any competitive alternatives.

Despite the bleak picture for electoral competition within the PA at the moment, the former opposition mayors and municipal council who ran for and won office in the 2004–5 elections have not disappeared from local politics or their communities. Some have even run as independents in subsequent elections, and many, as I have noted elsewhere, are still active in socially prominent positions in their communities as educators, preachers, and active commenters on local political affairs.[92] Thus, if and when electoral competition does return to the West Bank, whether at the local or central government level, it is hard to imagine that these individuals will refrain from participating even if they face Israeli, PA, or joint forms of repression for doing so. Furthermore, in the event of the PA's total dissolution, the alternative roles these erstwhile opposition leaders play within society may become even more important to Palestine's future.

The inauguration of a new Israeli government at the end of 2022 brought a far-right coalition into power, led by Prime Minister Benjamin Netanyahu. Religious Zionist and more secular-leaning parties have seemingly united around the mission of *de jure* Israeli annexation of the West Bank while maintaining a discriminatory regime that fits the international definition of apartheid. Thus far, 2022 and 2023 have demonstrated a spike in Palestinian fatalities at the hands of Israeli forces as they reentered and directly occupied parts of Nablus, Jenin, and other Area A cities in recent months. Settler and military violence then escalated even more sharply since the October 7 attacks and ensuing war on Gaza. Depending on the stability of the current Israeli governing coalition, this could mean a gravitation back toward a form of direct rule over the West Bank, with a withering away of the PA as a central intermediary between the occupation and Palestinian towns and cities. Under such conditions, I would suggest, we might see the next generation of Bassam Shaka'a's emerge again—wherein the *baladiyya* is pushed back to the front line between a military regime practicing apartheid and the Palestinian population living within it.

With increasingly bold Israeli incursions into West Bank Palestinian cities in Area A, such as Nablus and Jenin, the past couple of years have seen Palestinian militias rearming and reorganizing their projection of external coercive capacity at a highly local level. Palestinian Authority security forces have engaged in selective arrests, but the coercive basis of Israel's indirect rule regime in the West Bank feels at least as fragile as it did during the second intifada, if not more so. In reading about apartheid's collapse, two quotes from scholars of South Africa stand out to me. First, Egerö writes, "The bantustan strategy as such would turn out to be self-defeating for the apartheid government because the necessary vesting of power and financial resources in reactionary local leaderships prepared to accept the patronage of Pretoria, with no reforms in the structural conditions of bantustan subordination, could only intensify the contradictions of the system to the level where local defence against repression widened into a general anti-apartheid position."[93] Second, Gibbs notes that "the Bantustans were a peculiarly rickety type of indirect rule: as soon as apartheid waned, Bantustan government crumbled. Paradoxically, the expansion of the Bantustan state created new forms of dissent within its interstices."[94]

These two quotes raise important questions about when, how, and if such regimes collapse under the weight of their own "contradictions" and paradoxes. Due to the centrality of internal coercive violence to both the original apartheid regime and today's occupied Palestine, the moment when such structures become "peculiarly rickety" can be filled with both great excitement and, justifiably, an enormous amount of fear. Former regime intermediaries may, when the timing is right, transform into some of that regime's harshest critics.[95] Others may hold fast to their guns, as we saw with the PA's suppression of Palestinian protests against the June 2021 murder of the West Bank activist and critic Nizar Banat. As Antonio Gramsci reminds us, when the "old is dying and the new cannot be born: in this interregnum, morbid phenomena of the most varied kind come to pass."[96]

While it is probably impossible to identify a set of shared normative goals across Palestinians, Israelis, and the wide array of observers, analysts, and activists who feel connected to the fate of these populations on the ground, I believe I can clearly state mine. They are as follows: securing meaningful freedom, justice, full civil and political rights, and existential security for all who live between the Jordan River and the Mediterranean Sea. It may be that events outside Israel and Palestine will ultimately determine the fate of the regime in the Israeli-occupied West Bank. Previous waves of decolonization have been shaped by global transformations, wars, and transitions from unipolarity. The present work simply asks that we consider the role that existing local institutions in the West Bank—whether they are abolished, sustained, or transformed—could play in achieving these or other normative objectives under various sovereignty arrangements that might ensue. When the new might finally be born.

METHODOLOGICAL APPENDIX
Additional Notes for Chapter 4

As noted in chapter 4, additional robustness checks for the regression analysis are available in an online appendix on the author's website at www .dianabgreenwald.com/mayors-in-the-middle.

The Origins of the West Bank's Security Zones

Almost all the populated centers of Palestinian towns and cities were assigned to Area A or Area B. Area A comprises fourteen noncontiguous regions (see map 4.1). The most developed Palestinian cities and larger towns in the West Bank were frequently assigned to these Area A regions. However, on the immediate urban outskirts—and among the small- and medium-size Palestinian towns that surrounded these cities—the designations were less predictable. The majority of the populated area of some of those small- and medium-sized towns located in the close periphery of the major Palestinian cities were assigned to Area A, within the *de jure* jurisdiction of the new Palestinian police, while others were designated as primarily Area B, where the PA's role in internal security was formally subordinated to the Israeli military.

The creation of the Oslo security zones was not random—in the sense that it was not driven by a completely stochastic process.[1] However, towns in the close urban periphery faced unpredictability in terms of how authority over policing and security was to be distributed. For example, as shown in the inset of map 4.1, northeast of the city of Tulkarm in the northern West Bank, most of the developed area of the town of Bala'a (2007 population 6,545) is in Area A, yet two towns that are almost equidistant to Tulkarm on its northern side, Deir al-Ghusun (2007 population 8,168) and 'Attil (2007 population 8,957), find that most of their populated areas are designated as Area B. With no Israeli settlements in the immediate vicinity, the rationale for these designations is opaque. Deir al-Ghusun and 'Attil are closer to the Israel-West Bank separation barrier than Bala'a, suggesting that Israeli security-based motives may have played a role. However, the city of Tulkarm itself also nearly abuts the barrier; yet, since it is a major Palestinian population center, it falls primarily within Area A.[2]

The developed portion of these populated centers was generally well known to negotiators as they drew the Oslo II maps. Nonetheless, towns were often divided in uncomfortable ways. The city of Hebron is perhaps the best-known example; its status was not decided until a special agreement in 1997 due to the presence of Israeli Jewish settlements in the city center. In other cases, the Oslo boundaries of Areas A, B, and C cut awkwardly through Palestinian residential areas or, even more commonly, their surrounding land, much of which was used for agricultural purposes. Some of the most haphazard and disruptive effects of the security zone designations were felt at an extremely local level.

While chapter 5 is focused on insights gleaned from field-based interviews, a couple of brief observations demonstrate local perceptions of the security zone divisions. On the distinction between Area B and Area C, for instance, one mayor explained: "As you know, the border between the areas A, B, and C are a mere line! So, one house can be located in one area and its neighbor in another area." (Interview 2018.6) A municipal employee in another town relayed, "I have two brothers living next to each other. One street apart. One is in Area B and one is in Area C. These areas are this close! The one living in Area B has no problems. The one in Area C has no [building] permit. He received a notice for the demolition of his home." (Interview 2019.12)

How Security Zones Intersect with Municipalities

To understand how these divisions are imposed on Palestinian towns and cities and, thus, local governance, we must also understand how the municipalities themselves are defined. The land boundaries of Palestinian municipalities were defined by the PA in the years that followed the Oslo Accords. In some cases, these borders were historic in nature and did not change in the post-Oslo period. In other cases, municipalities were formed from what were formerly classified as villages, or from a combined set of villages, so the boundaries of municipalities were created anew. In general, the PA's incentives at this time were to maximize Palestinian claims to all the land and to ensure thereby that all the West Bank and all Palestinian population centers were fully incorporated into an official municipality if possible or a village if not. The number of municipal units sharply proliferated after the Oslo Accords were signed.

In sum, the share of a municipality's territory located in Area A, B, or C is the result of two processes: the 1995 creation of the three areas and the almost simultaneous drawing of municipal boundaries by the PA. To be sure, this latter process was likely subject to intra-Palestinian political pressures and negotiations between national and local elites. While there are no known studies of this process, there is no *prima facie* evidence that Palestinian planners systematically distributed town boundaries to privilege some local Palestinian actors and punish others. It appears that the extent of PA policing capacity in each town was overarchingly determined by the Oslo II mapmaking process, not by subsequent Palestinian municipal planning.

Municipality Sample Size

My data set includes 107 municipalities. Where does this total come from? For example, the data set in Rafeef Abdelrazek's 2017 report for the World Bank includes 116 municipalities.[3] Two municipalities in my data set are not included in Abdelrazek's report: Al Newe'ima (Jericho district) and Beit Awwa (Hebron district). Ten of the eleven municipalities included in Abdelrazek that are not included in my data set were upgraded from village to municipality between 2013 and 2016, and thus they did not qualify as municipalities during the period analyzed here. The final municipality that Abdelrazek includes was upgraded in 2011 and thus is omitted from my data set since it qualified as a municipality for only a single year (2012) during the period of analysis.

Descriptive Statistics

Descriptive statistics of the revenue and spending variables used in chapter 4 can be found in table A.1.

TABLE A.1
Descriptive statistics of dependent and independent variables

Variable	Type of revenue/expenditure	N	Mean	SD	Min	Max
$\overline{rpc_i}$	Self-generated revenues (service fees, permit fees, fines)	107	60.22	57.93	6.73	472.61
$\overline{tpc_i}$	Revenue transfers from the central government	107	49.19	74.57	2.40	564.24
$\overline{opc_i}$	Other revenues	107	51.64	163.31	0.00	1585.17
$\overline{upc_i}$	Utility revenues (electricity/water)	107	256.10	230.26	0.00	914.18
$\overline{apc_i}$	Administrative expenditures	107	60.95	39.37	12.97	230.72
$\overline{hepc_i}$	Health care expenditures	107	35.91	38.71	2.33	307.06
$\overline{pwpc_i}$	Public works expenditures	107	53.90	46.34	0.00	219.58
$\overline{secfirepc_i}$	Security and firefighting expenditures	107	1.62	6.81	0.00	49.06
$\overline{edpc_i}$	Education expenditures	107	2.77	4.09	0.00	23.98
$\overline{cusopc_i}$	Culture and society expenditures	107	3.04	7.51	0.00	55.20
$\overline{planpc_i}$	Planning and development expenditures	107	0.89	4.13	0.00	34.47
$\overline{markpc_i}$	Market and slaughterhouse expenditures	107	1.28	5.08	0.00	27.58
$\overline{otherpc_i}$	Other expenditures	107	19.25	96.88	0.00	926.76
$\overline{uepc_i}$	Utility expenditures (electricity/water)	107	181.82	176.48	0.00	728.39
$\overline{bal_i}$	Overall budget balance (total revenues minus expenditures)	107	867,362.80	3,359,842	−6,778,503	27,900,000

$\overline{bal\_w_i}$	Winsorized budget balance (total revenues minus expenditures)	107	807,216.70	2,485,109	−1,736,318	16,500,000
$\overline{balpc_i}$	Overall budget balance per capita	107	−23.15	109.09	−232.09	941.94
shareabuilt	Share of built-up area in Area A	107	0.37	0.45	0.00	1.00
sharecland	Share of land in Area C	107	0.49	0.29	0.00	0.97
log_routpolice	Log of the distance to the nearest PA police station	107	7.62	1.27	3.99	9.85
$\overline{pop_i}$	Average population (2006–2012)	107	13,855	21,700	1,302	172,011
emprate	Employment rate	106	0.85	0.06	0.64	0.98
est	Business establishments per 1,000 residents	97	35.96	15.52	9.72	113.54
houseunits	Housing units per 1,000 residents	107	176.96	17.41	143.90	223.70
econ_index	Index variable combining emprate, est, and houseunits	107	2.14	0.72	0.21	4.54
munemp	Municipal employees per 1,000 residents	95	2.81	1.65	0.97	12.76
log_routecap	Log of the distance to the nearest district capital	107	8.35	2.89	0.00	10.42
log_routesettle	Log of the distance to the nearest settlement	107	8.53	0.57	6.97	10.11

Municipal Revenue Collection Before the Creation of the PA

It is possible that underlying differences between towns that were later granted different levels of Palestinian policing capacity—differences that predate the creation of these security zones in the 1990s—might affect long-term patterns in local governance. If so, these underlying differences, rather than policing capacity itself, might explain differences in revenue collection in later years.

To address this concern, I seek information on local governance prior to the PA period: during the period of unmediated Israeli rule. For this, I consult Israel's Central Bureau of Statistics *Judea, Samaria and Gaza Area Statistics* (JSGAS) publications.[4] JSGAS reports provide municipal revenue data from 1982 to 1994. The publications were released either annually or biannually, and each year, one volume contained an appendix titled "Financing of Local Authorities," which provided detailed budget data for twenty-five West Bank municipalities, including total revenues and revenues by source. Print copies of the JSGAS publications were acquired from the Central Bureau of Statistics office in Jerusalem. The tables on local government financing are in Hebrew and were translated with the help of a native speaker.

With the creation of the PA, many localities that were designated previously as villages were upgraded to municipalities. Because Israel collected regular local budget data only from municipalities, not villages, early data for many of these smaller towns are unavailable. However, for a simplified comparison, I create a subsample of eleven municipalities—seven of which later had the majority of their built-up area designated as Area A, and four of which would have the majority of their built-up area assigned to Area B—and look at revenue mobilization patterns across these two groups.

While JSGAS publications provide the revenue figures, some very approximate estimation is required to get the population figures for municipalities. I use two sources: the 1967 Census of the West Bank and Gaza Strip, conducted by the Israeli statistics bureau,[5] and the 1997 census estimates from the Palestinian Central Bureau of Statistics (PCBS).[6] Then I take an average of one set of population estimates that extrapolates forward from 1967 and another set of estimates that interpolates backward from 1997.[7] Table A.2 shows the matched subsample of municipalities with their estimated average population over the thirteen-year period (1982–1994).

TABLE A.2
Subsample of pre-Oslo municipalities with comparable populations

Higher coercive capacity			Lower coercive capacity		
Area A			Area B		
Municipality	District	Population	Municipality	District	Population
Bani Zeid	Ramallah	2,967	Birzeit	Ramallah	3,244
'Anabta	Tulkarm	4,453	Silwad	Ramallah	3,678
Beitunia	Ramallah	4,694	Deir Dibwan	Ramallah	3,861
Salfit	Tulkarm	4,825	Ya'bad	Jenin	7,344
Beit Sahour	Bethlehem	7,901			
Tubas	Jenin (now Tubas)	7,992			
Dura	Hebron	9,028			

The JSGAS data provide an estimate of ordinary revenue per capita and the subset that is transferred from the Israeli Civil Administration to the municipalities. Thus, by taking ordinary revenue per capita and subtracting that portion that is transferred, we have a measure of the direct revenue per capita raised by the municipality itself.

Comparing across the four future Area B towns and the seven future Area A towns in our sample, a Welch two-sample t-test shows no statistically distinguishable difference between the average municipal revenue per capita mobilized in the Area A (27.9 NIS/capita) and Area B (25.9 NIS/capita) towns ($p = 0.78$). Thus, when examining this restricted subset of existing municipalities, we see that the ones that were eventually designated as Area A (high coercive capacity) did not differ considerably in their revenue-generating capacity from those that were designated as Area B (low coercive capacity) before the intervention of the Oslo Accords. This analysis suggests that the subsequent assignment of these eleven municipalities to Areas A and B does not appear to have been correlated with existing fiscal capacity.

ADDITIONAL NOTES FOR CHAPTER 5

This research draws on field-based, semi-structured interviews conducted by the author in the West Bank from 2014 to 2019 and a smaller set of interviews conducted in 2011 for a related research project. A total of forty-six individual or, occasionally, small-group interviews were conducted with fifty-three respondents, each of whom provided verbal or written consent to participate. Interlocutors were chosen to achieve a sample reflecting diverse political affiliations, municipalities across different geographic regions and security zones of the West Bank, and towns with different underlying economic conditions.

Contacts were made by cold-calling, emailing, and snowball sampling through known contacts. Two Palestinian research assistants were employed on a part-time basis to assist with recruitment of interviewees. Interviews were carried out by the author in English or Arabic with the assistance of a research assistant who could provide oral Arabic-English interpretation as needed. These interviews are described in more detail next and summarized in table A.3. The districts where the interviews were conducted are listed in the following table, however, I omit the name of the municipality to preserve the anonymity of my interlocutors.

TABLE A.3
List of interviews conducted

Number	Date	Individual	District (*muhafaza*)
2011.1	Jul 17, 2011	General director and deputy minister, Ministry of Labor	Ramallah/Al-Bireh
2011.2	Aug 7, 2011	Senior leadership, Palestine Monetary Authority	Ramallah/Al-Bireh
2014.1	Nov 9, 2014	Municipal finance manager	Jenin
2014.2	Nov 9, 2014	Municipal finance manager	Jenin
2014.3	Nov 9, 2014	General director	Jenin
2014.4	Nov 9, 2014	Current mayor	Jenin
2014.5	Nov 13, 2014	Former minister of finance	Ramallah/Al-Bireh
2014.6	Nov 16, 2014	Municipal finance manager	Tulkarm
2014.7	Nov 16, 2014	Current mayor	Tulkarm
2014.8	Nov 16, 2014	Municipal finance manager	Tulkarm
2014.9	Nov 16, 2014	Current mayor	Tulkarm
2014.10	Nov 19, 2014	Executive director of NGO	Nablus
2014.11	Nov 19, 2014	Former mayor and Ministry of Local Government staff	Nablus
2014.12	Dec 1, 2014	Senior manager in Israeli Tax Administration	West Jerusalem
2014.13	Dec 3, 2014	Former mayor	Nablus
2014.14	Dec 6, 2014	University lecturer/political activist	Bethlehem
2014.15	Dec 6, 2014	Executive director of NGO/political activist	Bethlehem
2014.16	Dec 7, 2014	Former Palestinian Legislative Council member	Ramallah/Al-Bireh
2014.17	Dec 21, 2014	Former deputy minister of finance	Ramallah/Al-Bireh
2014.18	Dec 21, 2014	PLO Executive Committee member	Ramallah/Al-Bireh
2016.1	Dec 13, 2016	Senior member of Palestinian delegation, Oslo II	Ramallah/Al-Bireh
2016.2	Dec 15, 2016	Senior member of Israeli delegation, Oslo I	By phone
2018.1	Jun 25, 2018	Current mayor	Ramallah/Al-Bireh
2018.2	Jun 25, 2018	Budget director	Ramallah/Al-Bireh
2018.3	Jun 26, 2018	Current mayor	Salfit
2018.4	Jun 26, 2018	Current mayor and general director	Salfit
2018.5	Jun 26, 2018	Current mayor	Nablus
2018.6	Jun 27, 2018	Current mayor	Bethlehem
2018.7	Jun 27, 2018	Current mayor	Bethlehem
2019.1	Jul 31, 2019	General director	Jenin
2019.2	Jul 31, 2019	Former mayor	Jenin

2019.3	Jul 31, 2019	Current mayor and two former mayors	Tubas
2019.4	Aug 1, 2019	Current mayor	Nablus
2019.5	Aug 1, 2019	Current mayor, general director, council member, and former mayor	Nablus
2019.6	Aug 3, 2019	Current mayor	Ramallah/Al-Bireh
2019.7	Aug 3, 2019	Current mayor and general director	Ramallah/Al-Bireh
2019.8	Aug 3, 2019	Former mayor	Ramallah/Al-Bireh
2019.9	Aug 4, 2019	Current mayor	Nablus
2019.10	Aug 4, 2019	Former mayor	Nablus
2019.11	Aug 4, 2019	Former mayor	Nablus
2019.12	Aug 5, 2019	Current project engineer and financial director	Hebron
2019.13	Aug 5, 2019	Former mayor	Hebron
2019.14	Aug 6, 2019	Current mayor	Ramallah/Al-Bireh
2019.15	Aug 6, 2019	Former mayor	Ramallah/Al-Bireh
2019.16	Aug 6, 2019	Former mayor	Ramallah/Al-Bireh

I recognize that my positionality as an American researcher likely affected the way that interview subjects engaged with me and perhaps the information they provided during the interviews. I took steps to mitigate risk to research assistants and all local informants, such as obtaining full, unambiguous, and continual consent; communicating the focus of the research transparently; and maintaining the confidentiality of field notes, audio recordings, and all other identifiable information, in compliance with IRB-approved procedures.

August 2011: I conducted three interviews approved by the Institutional Review Board at the University of Michigan on July 11, 2011 (ID# HUM00050809).

October–December 2014: These interviews were approved by the Institutional Review Board at the University of Michigan on August 20, 2014 (ID# HUM00091104). Between October and December 2014, I conducted eighteen in-person semi-structured interviews with national-level and local-level Palestinian politicians across the West Bank.

December 2016: I traveled to Israel and Palestine for a conference. I conducted one in-person interview and one phone interview with senior-level members of the Palestinian and Israeli negotiating teams from the Oslo era, respectively. Neither interview was audio recorded. Oral consent to use anonymized content from the conversations in future research was obtained from both respondents.

June 2018: I conducted seven interviews with eight municipal mayors and staff across four districts in the West Bank. These interviews were approved on June 13, 2018, by the Institutional Review Board at Harvard University (IRB18-0908).

July-August 2019: I completed sixteen interviews with twenty-two municipal-level politicians and municipal staff across five districts in the West Bank. This research was determined exempt from review by the Institutional Review Board at the City College of New York on July 1, 2019 (#2019–0621).

NOTES

INTRODUCTION

1. Territorially, "historic Palestine," or "Palestine," is used in this work to refer to the region as it was defined during the British Mandate. Today, that territory comprises the existing state of Israel within its 1949 armistice lines, plus the occupied territories of the West Bank, East Jerusalem, and the Gaza Strip.

2. See Mark A. Tessler, *A History of the Israeli-Palestinian Conflict*, 2nd ed. (Bloomington: Indiana University Press, 2009), 547–49; Sivan Hirsch-Hoefler and Lihi Ben Shitrit, "So, How Many Settlements Are There? Counting, Tracking, and Normalizing Jewish Settlements in the Israeli Central Bureau of Statistics (CBS) Yearbook, 1967 to the Present," *Israel/Palestine: Exploring a One State Reality* (POMEPS Studies 41, Project on Middle East Political Science, Elliott School of International Affairs, Washington, DC, 2020), 43–48. Israeli settler estimates exclude East Jerusalem. Estimates of the number of Palestinians in the West Bank come from Israeli authorities, the Palestinian Liberation Organization, and professional demographers; they range from 680,000 to 810,000. See Wael R. Ennab, "Population and Demographic Developments in the West Bank and Gaza Strip Until 1990" (United Nations Conference on Trade and Development, June 28, 1994), http://unctad.org/en/Docs/poecdcseud1.en.pdf; Allan G. Hill, "Population Growth in the Middle East Since 1945 with Special Reference to the Arab Countries of West Asia," in *Change and Development in the Middle East*, ed. John I. Clarke and Howard Bowen-Jones (London: Methuen, 1981); Hill, "The Palestinian Population of the Middle East," *Population and Development Review* 9, no. 2 (1983): 293–316; and Israel Central Bureau of Statistics, "Judea, Samaria and Gaza Area Statistics" (Jerusalem, 1980). Some of the variation depends on whether Palestinian residents of East Jerusalem are included. Along with the (non-Palestinian) territories of the Golan Heights and

the Sinai Peninsula, and the Palestinian territories of the West Bank and Gaza Strip, Israel won control of the eastern portion of the city of Jerusalem in the June 1967 war. Israel soon moved to enlarge the municipal boundaries of Jerusalem to incorporate this newly won territory, and in 1980, it would declare the city in its united form as Israel's capital despite the majority of readings of international law, and thus the international community of states, considering it occupied Palestinian territory. Unlike Palestinians in the rest of the occupied West Bank, Palestinians in Jerusalem were given the option to apply for Israeli citizenship after 1967, but they were required to pledge allegiance to the Israeli state. A small minority of Palestinians applied and were ultimately granted citizenship, while the majority of Palestinian Jerusalemites were given a permanent residency status that distinguished them from both Israeli citizens and Palestinians in the rest of the occupied territories. Ennab estimates the Palestinian population of Jerusalem in 1980 to be over 110,000.

3. Nadav G. Shelef, *Evolving Nationalism: Homeland, Identity, and Religion in Israel, 1925–2005* (Ithaca, NY: Cornell University Press, 2010), 80.

4. Rafik Halabi, *The West Bank Story: An Israeli Arab's View of Both Sides of a Tangled Conflict*, trans. Ina Friedman (New York: Harcourt Brace Jovanovich, 1981), 112.

5. Raja Shehadeh, "The Land Law of Palestine: An Analysis of the Definition of State Lands," *Journal of Palestine Studies* 11, no. 2 (1982): 82–99, https://doi.org/10.2307/2536271; Michael Galchinsky, "The Jewish Settlements in the West Bank: International Law and Israeli Jurisprudence," *Israel Studies* 9, no. 3 (2004): 115–36.

6. Emile Sahliyeh, *In Search of Leadership: West Bank Politics Since 1967* (Washington, DC: Brookings Institution Press, 1988), 63.

7. Moshe Maʿoz, *Palestinian Leadership on the West Bank: The Changing Role of the Arab Mayors Under Jordan and Israel* (London: Frank Cass, 1984), 133–36; Sahliyeh, *In Search of Leadership*, 64.

8. Sahliyeh, *In Search of Leadership*, 48.

9. Tessler, *A History of the Israeli-Palestinian Conflict*, 474, 493.

10. During the British Mandate, Palestinian political elites were active in bodies such as the Supreme Muslim Council and the Arab Higher Committee, as discussed in chapter 2, and Palestinians were also elected to local councils. However, the franchise was heavily restricted, and the British High Commissioner appointed mayors and other key positions. See, for example, Rami Zeedan, "The Palestinian Political Parties and Local Self-Governance During the British Mandate: Democracy and the Clan," in *The British Mandate in Palestine: A Centenary Volume, 1920–2020*, ed Michael J. Cohen (London: Routledge, 2020), 83–101.

11. In fact, it was Shakaʿa who posed the first question: "Why were we so late?" Slightly embarrassed, my research assistant explained that we had sat in a line of unmoving cars for over an hour at the Zaʿtara checkpoint, which Israel intermittently operated south of the city. Shakaʿa required no further explanation; this was a regular, almost mundane feature of life under military rule.

12. Interview 2014.13. More information on the interview methodology used for this research can be found in the appendix.

13. Palestinian nationalists continually resisted connecting to the grid established by the Zionist engineer Pinhas Rutenberg during the mandate. Nablus eventually established its own supply system after the 1948 war. See Fredrik Meiton, "Nation or Industry: The Non-Electrification of Nablus," *Jerusalem Quarterly* no. 80 (2019): 8.

14. In the same letter to the mayor of Tulkarm in August 1982, Shaka'a reported how Israeli authorities prevented the Nablus municipality from extending electricity lines into neighboring villages, disrupted the construction of high-voltage lines in the district, and connected the village of Sabastiya to the Israeli electricity grid "despite its village council's refusal to do so." Bassam Shaka'a, " 'Nablus Electricity Network,' a Letter from Bassam ash-Shak'a to Tulkarm Mayor, 18 February 1982 [in Arabic]," August 2, 1982, Palestine Museum Digital Archive, https://palarchive.org/index.php/Detail/objects/220408/lang/en_US.

15. According to reporting from the time, al-Nabulsi had been taking part in a protest, but eyewitness accounts claimed that she was gunned down at least half an hour after the demonstration had ended while standing on a staircase leading to a nearby apartment building. As was then reported by the *New York Times*, "at the building where Miss Nabulsi was killed there was a pool of blood on a second floor landing, and a trail of blood led to the apartment of her friend." "West Bank Girl Killed by Israeli," *New York Times*, May 17, 1976, https://www.nytimes.com/1976/05/17/archives/new-jersey-pages-west-bank-girl-killed-by-israeli-victim-was-from.html.

16. As reported by David K. Shipler, "In West Bank, Nablus Mayor Is on Pedestal," *New York Times*, December 10, 1979, sec. A., Shaka'a was "arrested and ordered deported to Jordan for remarks he made to an Israeli military officer that were allegedly sympathetic to terrorism, though it later emerged he had merely proclaimed the inevitability of terrorism as long as Israel's occupation continued."

17. David K. Shipler, "Israeli Court Bars Release of Mayor," *New York Times*, November 23, 1979, https://www.nytimes.com/1979/11/23/archives/israeli-court-bars-release-of-mayor-it-rules-that-arab-head-of.html.

18. Halabi, *The West Bank Story*, 134.

19. Shaul Mishal, *The PLO Under 'Arafat: Between Gun and Olive Branch* (New Haven, CT: Yale University Press, 1986); Yezid Sayigh, *Armed Struggle and the Search for a State* (Oxford: Oxford University Press, 1998), 479; and Tessler, *A History of the Israeli-Palestinian Conflict*, 566.

20. Meron Benvenisti, *1986 Report: Demographic, Economic, Legal, Social and Political Developments in the West Bank* (Washington, DC: American Enterprise Institute, West Bank Data Base Project, 1986), 41.

21. Adam Rasgon, "Ex-Nablus Mayor Bassam Shakaa, Who Was Injured by Jewish Terrorists, Dies at 89," *Times of Israel*, July 23, 2019, https://www.timesofisrael.com/ex-nablus-mayor-bassam-shakaa-who-was-injured-by-jewish-terrorists-dies-at-89/.

22. Audeh Rantisi and his wife, the latter of whom was British by birth, also ran an orphanage in Ramallah. Hilary and her siblings grew up with roughly fifty boys as part of their extended family at any given time, with the home expanding gradually from a few apartment units into a center with a gymnasium, full kitchen, and staff.

23. Before the 1976 municipal vote, a previous set of elections had resulted in most towns being governed by more conservative, pro-Jordanian traditional elites. After 1976, when efforts to enforce cooperation by elected municipal leaders such as Shaka'a were unsuccessful, Israel launched another effort in rural areas called the "Village Leagues," financing and arming more pliant local leaders. This, too, ultimately backfired. See, for example, Neve Gordon, *Israel's Occupation* (Berkeley: University of California Press, 2008), 111–14; and Rashid Khalidi, *The Hundred Years'*

War on Palestine: A History of Settler Colonialism and Resistance, 1917–2017 (New York: Picador, 2020), 171.

24. Palestinians also armed themselves by, for example, hurling Molotov cocktails at Israeli military installations, but iconic photos of young Palestinians throwing stones at Israeli tanks exemplified how Palestinian civilian protesters were far outmatched in firepower by the Israeli military. The young people who participated in these demonstrations came to be known as *'atfal al-hijara*, or "children of the stones." See Laetitia Bucaille, *Growing Up Palestinian: Israeli Occupation and the Intifada Generation* (Princeton, NJ: Princeton University Press, 2004); John Collins, *Occupied by Memory* (New York: NYU Press, 2004); Gordon, *Israel's Occupation*, 147–68; Wendy Pearlman, *Violence, Nonviolence, and the Palestinian National Movement* (Cambridge: Cambridge University Press, 2011); and Sayigh, *Armed Struggle and the Search for a State*, 607–37.

25. B'Tselem, "Fatalities in the first Intifada," accessed November 11, 2023, https://www.btselem.org/statistics/first_intifada_tables. Jerusalem: B'Tselem.These estimates include those killed within the occupied territories of the West Bank, East Jerusalem, and Gaza Strip and those killed within Israel, according to its 1949 armistice boundaries, between December 1987 and December 1994.

26. The concept of indirect rule is explored in more depth in chapter 1 and throughout the book. I draw on definitions from the British colonial administrator credited with originally coining the term, Lord Frederick Lugard, as well as contemporary theory and subsequent interventions from social scientists. See Frederick John Dealtry Lugard, *The Dual Mandate in British Tropical Africa* (Edinburgh: William Blackwood and Sons, 1922); Mahmood Mamdani, *Citizen and Subject: Contemporary Africa and The Legacy of Late Colonialism* (Princeton, NJ: Princeton University Press, 1996); Mamdani, "Historicizing Power and Responses to Power: Indirect Rule and Its Reform," *Social Research* 66, no. 3 (1999): 859–86; Matthew Lange, *Lineages of Despotism and Development: British Colonialism and State Power* (Chicago: University of Chicago Press, 2009); Adnan Naseemullah and Paul Staniland, "Indirect Rule and Varieties of Governance," *Governance* 29, no. 1 (2016): 13–30; Paul Staniland, *Ordering Violence: Explaining Armed Group-State Relations from Conflict to Cooperation* (Ithaca, NY: Cornell University Press, 2021); and John Gerring et al., "An Institutional Theory of Direct and Indirect Rule," *World Politics* 63, no. 3 (July 2011): 377–433. The term "native" has unfortunate paternalistic and racist connotations, which I seek to avoid. Thus, I more frequently use the terms "indigenous" or "preexisting" to describe the population (a) whose residence in the territory predates the coercive presence of the dominant power, (b) who are still present when the dominant power assumes control, and (c) whose ethnic, racial, and/or cultural identities distinguish them from subsequent immigrant and settler populations. By this definition, the Palestinian population is indigenous to the West Bank. I do not use the term to make claims regarding who or what group "originally" inhabited the territory.

27. The wording on introducing a national currency comes from the Paris Protocol. See Government of Israel and Palestinian Liberation Organization, "Gaza-Jericho Agreement, Annex IV: Protocol on Economic Relations Between the Government of the State of Israel and the P.L.O., Representing the Palestinian People" (Political Settlements Research Programme, University of Edinburgh, 1994), https://www.peaceagreements.org.

28. Later, a 2014 World Bank report claimed, "Less than 1 percent of Area C, which is already built up, is designated by the Israeli authorities for Palestinian use; the remainder is heavily restricted or off-limits to Palestinians, with 68 percent reserved for Israeli settlements, 21 percent for closed military zones, and 9 percent for nature reserves." See Orhan Niksic, Nur Nasser Eddin, and Massimiliano Cali, *Area C and the Future of the Palestinian Economy* (World Bank Studies, World Bank, Washington, DC, July 2014), 13, https://elibrary.worldbank.org/doi/abs/10.1596/978 -1-4648-0193-8.

29. Edward Said, "The Morning After," *London Review of Books*, October 21, 1993, https://www.lrb.co.uk/the-paper/v15/n20/edward-said/the-morning-after.

30. Anders Strindberg, "The Damascus-Based Alliance of Palestinian Forces: A Primer," *Journal of Palestine Studies* 29, no. 3 (2000): 60–76.

31. This definition of a "regime" is broader than the typical spectrum of categorization that is used in the positivist comparative politics literature, which is frequently centered on the extent or degree of democracy (or autocracy) in political institutions. See, for example, Mike Alvarez and Jose Antonio Cheibub, "Classifying Political Regimes," *Studies in Comparative International Development* 31, no. 2 (1996): 3.

32. Brendan O'Leary, Ian Lustick, and Thomas Callaghy, eds., *Right-Sizing the State: The Politics of Moving Borders* (Oxford: Oxford University Press, 2001).

33. The terms "ethnic," "religious," and "national" are not frequently contested as labels to distinguish Jewish Israeli from Palestinian Arab identity. However, "race" is. See the later discussion on the application of the label of "apartheid" to Israel/Palestine, where I also discuss use of the concept of race to distinguish between Jewish Israelis and Arab Palestinians.

34. On the collapse of security collaboration, see, for example, Hillel Cohen, "Society-Military Relations in a State-in-the-Making: Palestinian Security Agencies and the 'Treason Discourse' in the Second Intifada," *Armed Forces & Society* 38, no. 3 (2012): 463–85.

35. Here, I use the word "noneconomic" to imply that coercion is not being used with the primary purpose of extracting economic resources or factors of production (i.e., land, labor, capital assets, or income).

36. Amaney A. Jamal, *Barriers to Democracy: The Other Side of Social Capital in Palestine and the Arab World* (Princeton, NJ: Princeton University Press, 2009).

37. Pearlman, *Violence, Nonviolence, and the Palestinian National Movement*.

38. Yael Zeira, *The Revolution Within: State Institutions and Unarmed Resistance in Palestine* (Cambridge: Cambridge University Press, 2019); Zeira, "From the Schools to the Streets: Education and Anti-Regime Resistance in the West Bank," *Comparative Political Studies* 52, no. 8 (2019): 1131–68.

39. Emily Kalah Gade, "Social Isolation and Repertoires of Resistance," *American Political Science Review* 114, no. 2 (2020): 309–25.

40. Michelle D. Weitzel, "Access Denied: Temporal Mobility Regimes in Hebron," *Borderlands* 21, no. 1 (2022): 171–200.

41. Stephanie Dornschneider, "Exit, Voice, Loyalty . . . or Deliberate Obstruction? Non-Collective Everyday Resistance Under Oppression," *Perspectives on Politics* 21, no. 1 (2023): 126–41, https://doi.org/10.1017/S1537592720004818.

42. Dana El Kurd, *Polarized and Demobilized: Legacies of Authoritarianism in Palestine* (London: Hurst & Company, 2019).

43. Laurie A. Brand, *Palestinians in the Arab World: Institution Building and the Search for State* (New York: Columbia University Press, 1988).
44. Sarah E. Parkinson, "Money Talks: Discourse, Networks, and Structure in Militant Organizations," *Perspectives on Politics* 14, no. 4 (2016): 976–94; Parkinson, "Practical Ideology in Militant Organizations," *World Politics* 73, no. 1 (2021): 52–81; and Parkinson, *Beyond the Lines: Social Networks and Palestinian Militant Organizations in Wartime Lebanon* (Ithaca, NY: Cornell University Press, 2022).
45. Nadya Hajj, "Institutional Formation in Transitional Settings," *Comparative Politics* 46 (2014): 399–418; Nadya Hajj, *Protection Amid Chaos: The Creation of Property Rights in Palestinian Refugee Camps* (New York: Columbia University Press, 2016).
46. Nadya Hajj, *Networked Refugees: Palestinian Reciprocity and Remittances in the Digital Age*, Critical Refugee Studies (Berkeley: University of California Press, 2021).
47. Nora Stel, "Mediated Stateness as a Continuum: Exploring the Changing Governance Relations Between the PLO and the Lebanese State," *Civil Wars* 19, no. 3 (2017): 348–76.
48. See Diana B. Greenwald, "Delegating Domination: Indirect Rule in the West Bank," in *The One State Reality: What Is Israel/Palestine?*, ed. Michael Barnett et al. (Ithaca, NY: Cornell University Press, 2023), 111–13.
49. Mamdani, *Citizen and Subject*.
50. While not all would use this exact terminology, an incomplete list on such perspectives includes the following: Seth Anziska, *Preventing Palestine: A Political History from Camp David to Oslo* (Princeton, NJ: Princeton University Press, 2018); Naseer H. Aruri, "Early Empowerment: The Burden Not the Responsibility," *Journal of Palestine Studies* 24, no. 2 (1995): 33–39; Ariella Azoulay and Adi Ophir, *The One-State Condition: Occupation and Democracy in Israel/Palestine* (Stanford, CA: Stanford University Press, 2013); Andy Clarno, *Neoliberal Apartheid: Palestine/Israel and South Africa After 1994* (Chicago: University of Chicago Press, 2017); El Kurd, *Polarized and Demobilized*; Gordon, *Israel's Occupation*; Rashid Khalidi, *The Iron Cage: The Story of the Palestinian Struggle for Statehood* (Boston: Beacon, 2007); Khaled Elgindy, *Blind Spot: America and the Palestinians, from Balfour to Trump* (Washington, DC: Brookings Institution Press, 2019); Said, "The Morning After"; and Noura Erakat, *Justice for Some: Law and the Question of Palestine* (Stanford, CA: Stanford University Press, 2019).
51. Alaa Tartir, "The Palestinian Authority Security Forces: Whose Security?," (New York: Policy Brief, Al-Shabaka, May 16, 2017).
52. Gordon, *Israel's Occupation*, 176.
53. On local Palestinian government in the West Bank under Jordanian rule (1948–67) and in the early years of the Israeli occupation, see, for example, Ma'oz *Palestinian Leadership on the West Bank*; Sahliyeh, *In Search of Leadership*; and Joel S. Migdal, *Palestinian Society and Politics* (Princeton, NJ: Princeton University Press, 1980). For a highly illuminating, textured analysis of local politics in the West Bank as it relates to waste, in particular, see: Sophia Stamatopoulou-Robbins, *Waste Siege: The Life of Infrastructure in Palestine* (Stanford, CA: Stanford University Press, 2020). Most works from Palestinian scholars in the occupied territories tend to approach local politics from the perspective of public administration or public policy. See, for example, Shahir Muhammad 'Ahmad 'Ubayd, Sa'id Muhammad 'Ahmad Rubay'a, and Jamal Qasim Muhammad Habash, "*Taqyīm 'Afrad al-Mujtama' al-Maḥallī*

li-'Adā' 'A'dā' al-Majālis al-Baladiyya fī Muḥāfazat Jinīn fil-Dawra al-'Intikhābiyya Allati Jarat 'Am 2005" Al-Aqsa University Magazine 17, no. 2 (2013): 249–83; 'Ubayd, Rubay'a, and Habash, *"'Ittijāhāt Muwaẓẓafī al-Baladiyyāt Naḥu 'A'dā' al-Majālis al-Baladiyya al-Muntakhaba fī Muḥāfazat Jinīn" Al-Quds Open University Magazine* 32, no. 2 (2014): 11–45; 'Usama Shahwan, "Modernizing the Revenue Patterns of West Bank Towns," *An-Najah Journal for Research* 2, no. 6 (1992): 33–55; and Bassam Bishnaq, *Al-Tanzīm al-'Idāri lil-Muhafazāt fī Filastīn* (Ramallah: Al-Hay'ah al-Filastīniyya al-Mustaqilla li-Huqūq al-Muwāṭin, 2003). To my knowledge, the most comprehensive study of the history of municipal government available was published in 1994: Mahmud Talab al-Nammura, *Al-Filastīniyyun wa Mu'assasāt al-Hukm al-Maḥallī Bayn al-Hukm al-Dhatī wal-'Iḥtilāl wa Haqq Taqrīr al-Masīr min al-'Ahd al-'Uthmanī 'Ilā al-'Intifāḍa (1794–1994)* (self-published, 1994). A helpful source that provides an overview of top-down administration of local government in Palestine, and which includes survey data on community leaders' perceptions of local government, is Wasim I. Al-Habil, "Occupations, a Diaspora, and the Design of Local Governments for a Palestinian State" (doctoral thesis, Cleveland State University, Cleveland, OH, 2008). Maha Samman, *Trans-Colonial Urban Space in Palestine* (London: Routledge, 2013) applies theories of colonialism and space to understand urban development in the occupied territories after 1967. Scores of historical, sociological, and anthropological works have touched on local politics in Palestine, a number of which are cited in chapter 2; for example, see Beshara Doumani *Rediscovering Palestine: Merchants and Peasants in Jabal Nablus, 1700–1900* (Berkeley: University of California Press, 1995) on the Nablus region under late Ottoman rule; Lisa Taraki and Rita Giacaman, "Modernity Aborted and Reborn: Ways of Being Urban in Palestine," in *Living Palestine: Family Survival, Resistance, and Mobility Under Occupation* (Syracuse, NY: Syracuse University Press, 2006) on modernity and urban formations in Nablus, Ramallah, and Hebron; and specific works on the cities of Jerusalem, for example, Michael Dumper, *The Politics of Jerusalem Since 1967* (New York: Columbia University Press 1997) and Acre, Thomas Philipp, *Acre: The Rise and Fall of a Palestinian City* (New York: Columbia University Press, 2002). Menachem Klein, *Lives in Common: Arabs and Jews in Jerusalem, Jaffa and Hebron* (New York: Oxford University Press, 2014) explores Israel/Palestine through the lived experiences of Israelis and Palestinians in three cities: Jerusalem, Jaffa, and Hebron.

54. Diana B. Greenwald, "For Palestinians, the Local Is the National," *Jadaliyya*, May 1, 2023, https://www.jadaliyya.com/Details/44986

55. Lachlan McNamee, *Settling for Less: Why States Colonize and Why They Stop* (Princeton, NJ: Princeton University Press, 2023), 4.

56. Mamdani, *Citizen and Subject*, 20.

57. Lorenzo Veracini, *Settler Colonialism: A Theoretical Overview* (London: Palgrave Macmillan, 2010), 8.

58. Patrick Wolfe, *Settler Colonialism and the Transformation of Anthropology* (London: Cassell, 1999).

59. Patrick Wolfe, "Settler Colonialism and the Elimination of the Native," *Journal of Genocide Research* 8, no. 4 (2006): 387–409.

60. Erakat, *Justice for Some: Law and the Question of Palestine*.

61. Hilla Dayan, "Regimes of Separation: Israel/Palestine and the Shadow of Apartheid," in *The Power of Inclusive Exclusion: Anatomy of Israeli Rule in the Occupied Palestinian Territories*, ed. Adi Ophir, Michal Givoni, and Sari Hanafi (Brooklyn, NY: Zone, 2009), 281–322.

62. International Criminal Court, *Rome Statute of the International Criminal Court* (The Hague: International Criminal Court, 2021), https://www.icc-cpi.int/sites/default/files/Publications/Rome-Statute.pdf.

63. Al-Haq—Law in the Service of Man et al., "Joint Parallel Report to the United Nations Committee on the Elimination of Racial Discrimination on Israel's Seventeenth to Nineteenth Periodic Reports," November 12, 2019, https://www.alhaq.org/advocacy/16183.html; Michael Sfard, "The Occupation of the West Bank and the Crime of Apartheid: Legal Opinion" (Yesh Din, 2020), https://www.yesh-din.org/en/the-occupation-of-the-west-bank-and-the-crime-of-apartheid-legal-opinion/; B'Tselem, "A Regime of Jewish Supremacy from the Jordan River to the Mediterranean Sea: This Is Apartheid" (Position Paper, B'Tselem, 2021), https://www.btselem.org/publications/fulltext/202101_this_is_apartheid; Human Rights Watch, "A Threshold Crossed: Israeli Authorities and the Crimes of Apartheid and Persecution" (Human Rights Watch, April 27, 2021), https://www.hrw.org/report/2021/04/27/threshold-crossed/israeli-authorities-and-crimes-apartheid-and-persecution; and Amnesty International, "Israel's Apartheid Against Palestinians: Cruel System of Domination and Crime Against Humanity" (Amnesty International, February 1, 2022), https://www.amnesty.org/en/documents/mde15/5141/2022/en/.

64. Noura Erakat, Darryl Li, and John Reynolds, "Race, Palestine, and International Law," *AJIL Unbound* 117 (2023): 77–81, https://doi.org/10.1017/aju.2023.9.

65. Gordon, *Israel's Occupation*, 169.

66. El Kurd, *Polarized and Demobilized*; Alexei S. Abrahams, "Not Dark Yet: The Israel-PA Principal-Agent Relationship, 1993–2017," in *Proxy Wars: Suppressing Violence Through Local Agents*," ed. Eli Berman and David A. Lake (Ithaca, NY: Cornell University Press, 2019), 185–208; Clarno, *Neoliberal Apartheid: Palestine/Israel and South Africa After 1994*.

67. Youssef Mnaili, "Settling Palestine: Logics of Israeli (In)Direct Governance of the Occupied West Bank Since 1967" (doctoral thesis, European University Institute, Florence, Italy, 2022).

68. Somdeep Sen, *Decolonizing Palestine: Hamas Between the Anticolonial and the Postcolonial* (Ithaca, NY: Cornell University Press, 2020).

69. This suggests that it may be overly simplistic to refer to Fatah, the ruling party in the PA and dominant faction within the PLO, as Israel's "intermediary." First, according to such a critique, doing so fails to acknowledge the movement's history as one of the foundational groups of the Palestinian national liberation movement. Second, it minimizes intraparty conflict within Fatah that divides those who rule the PA from, perhaps, more rejectionist and militant factions. Because my analysis focuses on local government, it does not allow me to explore the full breadth of the party— I touch on only those elements that are serving, or have served, in some part of the PA apparatus. However, even the conversations reflected in this book—in particular in chapter 5—demonstrate that mayors and local council members affiliated with Fatah were not always outspoken loyalists of the Israeli-PA regime.

70. Sean Yom, "From Methodology to Practice: Inductive Iteration in Comparative Research," *Comparative Political Studies* 48, no. 5 (2015): 616–44.
71. Tasha Fairfield and Andrew Charman, "A Dialogue with the Data: The Bayesian Foundations of Iterative Research in Qualitative Social Science," *Perspectives on Politics* 17, no. 1 (2019): 154–67. In an earlier conference paper, the coauthors wrote, "We contend that Bayesian probability theory provides the uniquely consistent extension of deductive logic to more realistic situations where available information is imperfect or incomplete, uncertainty reigns, and hypotheses can rarely be definitively proven or disproven." See Fairfield and Charman, "Bayesian Probability: The Logic of (Political Science) Opportunities, Caveats, and Guidelines" (paper presented at the American Political Science Association Annual Meeting, San Francisco, 2015), 1.
72. More on my interview methodology can be found in the appendix and chapter 5.

1. A THEORY OF LOCAL POLITICS UNDER INDIRECT RULE

Mahmood Mamdani, *Neither Settler Nor Native: The Making and Unmaking of Permanent Minorities* (Cambridge, MA: Belknap Press of Harvard University Press, 2020), 153.
1. I use "dominant state" and "incumbent state" interchangeably. Such states are incumbent because they are entities whose external sovereignty is already widely recognized by other states and organizations in the international system. I adopt a slightly modified version of Max Weber's famous definition of the state as an organization that aspires to a monopoly on the legitimate use of violence within a specified territory. See Max Weber, *The Vocation Lectures*, ed. David Owen and Tracy B. Strong (Indianapolis: Hackett, 2004). Implicit in my definition of the state is that it is widely recognized as such an organization by the international community. Thus, in the examples mentioned earlier, the United Kingdom, South Africa, and Israel are states, whereas the movements that opposed them might be referred to as movements or organizations. What do these movements or organizations oppose? Sometimes, it may be the state itself—for example, for those seeking independence—and other times it may be the regime. "Regime" here refers to the rules that shape how political power is distributed within the state. For example, apartheid was (and, according to its generic definition in international law, still is) a regime of highly institutionalized racial discrimination. Israel's regime in the West Bank since 1967 has been described variously as one of apartheid, settler colonialism, or military rule. Finally, I use the terms "preexisting," "established," "local," and "indigenous" interchangeably to describe the population (a) whose residence in the territory predates the coercive presence of the dominant state, (b) who are still present when the dominant state asserts control, and (c) whose ethnic identities and/or cultural practices make them distinguishable from subsequent immigrant and settler populations. By this definition, the Palestinian population is indigenous to the West Bank. This definition does not require a specific claim about who, or what group, "originally" inhabited the territory.
2. See, for example, Karen Barkey, "The Ottoman Empire (1299–1923): The Bureaucratization of Patrimonial Authority," in *Empires and Bureaucracy in World History: From*

Late Antiquity to the Twentieth Century, ed. Peter Crooks and Timothy Parsons (Cambridge: Cambridge University Press, 2016), 102–26; Daron Acemoglu et al., "Indirect Rule and State Weakness in Africa: Sierra Leone in Comparative Perspective," in *African Successes, Volume IV: Sustainable Growth*, ed. Sebastian Edwards, Simon Johnson, and David N. Weil (Chicago: University of Chicago Press, 2016), 343–70.

3. Charles Tilly, *Coercion, Capital, and European States, AD 990–1992* (Malden, MA: Blackwell, 1992), 96–126.

4. Michael H. Fisher, *Indirect Rule in India: Residents and the Residency System, 1764–1858* (Delhi: Oxford University Press, 1991), quoted in Matthew Lange, *Lineages of Despostism and Development: British Colonialism and State Power* (Chicago: University of Chicago Press, 2009), 28.

5. See, for example, Acemoglu et al., "Indirect Rule and State Weakness in Africa"; Mamdani, *Citizen and Subject: Contemporary Africa and The Legacy of Late Colonialism* (Princeton, NJ: Princeton University Press, 1996); Mamdani, "Historicizing Power and Responses to Power: Indirect Rule and Its Reform," *Social Research* 66, no. 3 (1999): 859–86; Lange, *Lineages of Despotism and Development*; Shivaji Mukherjee, *Colonial Institutions and Civil War: Indirect Rule and Maoist Insurgency in India* (Cambridge: Cambridge University Press, 2021); Mukherjee, "Colonial Origins of Maoist Insurgency in India: Historical Institutions and Civil War," *Journal of Conflict Resolution* 62, no. 10 (2018): 2232–74; Adnan Naseemullah, *Patchwork States: The Historical Roots of Subnational Conflict and Competition in South Asia.* (Cambridge: Cambridge University Press, 2022); Lakshmi Iyer, "Direct Versus Indirect Colonial Rule in India: Long-Term Consequences," *Review of Economics and Statistics* 92, no. 4 (2010): 693–713; Olga Gasparyan, "Indirect Rule and Public Goods Provision: Evidence from Colonial India" (working paper, November 20, 2019), https://papers.ssrn.com/sol3/papers.cfm?abstract_id=3689339; J. C. Myers, *Indirect Rule in South Africa: Tradition, Modernity, and the Costuming of Political Power* (Rochester, NY: University of Rochester Press, 2008); and Natalie Wenzell Letsa and Martha Wilfahrt, "The Mechanisms of Direct and Indirect Rule: Colonialism and Economic Development in Africa," *Quarterly Journal of Political Science* 15, no. 4 (2020): 539–77.

6. This insight has been articulated by numerous scholars and observers of such regimes. For a discussion of how some of the literatures on British colonial India and South Africa's apartheid regime have treated this issue, see chapter 6. It is also implicit in much of the historical scholarship on Palestine reviewed in chapter 2.

7. Adnan Naseemullah and Paul Staniland, "Indirect Rule and Varieties of Governance," *Governance* 29, no. 1 (2016): 13.

8. Mamdani, *Citizen and Subject*.

9. Robert H. Bates, *Prosperity and Violence: The Political Economy of Development*, 2nd ed. (New York: Norton, 2010); Michael Mann, *The Sources of Social Power: Volume 2, The Rise of Classes and Nation-States, 1760–1914* (Cambridge: Cambridge University Press, 2012); Mancur Olson, "Dictatorship, Democracy, and Development," *American Political Science Review* 87, no. 3 (1993): 567–76; Tilly, *Coercion, Capital, and European States, AD 990–1992*.

10. Olson, "Dictatorship, Democracy, and Development."

11. Mann, *The Sources of Social Power: Volume 2*.

12. Tilly, *Coercion, Capital, and European States, AD 990–1992*, 96–126.

13. Margaret Levi, *Of Rule and Revenue* (Berkeley: University of California Press, 1988).

14. Robert H. Bates and Da-Hsiang Donald Lien, "A Note on Taxation, Development, and Representative Government," *Politics & Society* 14, no. 1 (1985): 53–70; Mark Dincecco, *Political Transformations and Public Finances* (Cambridge: Cambridge University Press, 2011); and Douglass C. North and Barry R. Weingast, "Constitutions and Commitment: The Evolution of Institutions Governing Public Choice in Seventeenth-Century England," *Journal of Economic History* 49, no. 4 (December 1989): 803–32.

15. State extraction was further delinked from the logic of war-making in research showing that elite motives and intraelite dynamics shaped the incentives for state builders to tax (or not tax) their populations. See, for example, Pablo Beramendi, Mark Dincecco, and Melissa Rogers, "Intra-Elite Competition and Long-Run Fiscal Development," *Journal of Politics* 81, no. 1 (2019); Francisco Garfias, "Elite Competition and State Capacity Development: Theory and Evidence from Post-Revolutionary Mexico," *American Political Science Review* 112, no. 2 (2018): 339–57; Isabela Mares and Didac Queralt, "The Non-Democratic Origins of Income Taxation," *Comparative Political Studies* 48, no. 14 (2015): 1974–2009; and Ryan Saylor and Nicholas C. Wheeler, "Paying for War and Building States: The Coalitional Politics of Debt Servicing," *World Politics* 69, no. 2 (2017): 366–408. Notably, these theories do not consider taxpayers' perceptions of the elites who are taxing them as influential in the state's development of fiscal capacity. Such factors occupy a more central position in the literature on tax compliance, which has largely aimed to explain variation across individuals. See, for example, James Alm, Gary H. McClelland, and William D. Schulze, "Why Do People Pay Taxes?", *Journal of Public Economics* 48 (1992): 21–38; James Alm, Betty R. Jackson, and Michael McKee, "Fiscal Exchange, Collective Decision Institutions, and Tax Compliance," *Journal of Economic Behavior and Organization* 22 (1993): 285–303; Néstor Castañeda, David Doyle, and Cassilde Schwartz, "Opting Out of the Social Contract: Tax Morale and Evasion," *Comparative Political Studies* 53, no. 7 (2020): 1175–1219; Nadja Dwenger, Henrik Kleven, Imran Rasul, and Johannes Rincke, "Extrinsic and Intrinsic Motivations for Tax Compliance: Evidence from a Field Experiment in Germany," *American Economic Journal: Economic Policy* 8, no. 3 (2016): 203–32; Lars P. Feld and Bruno S. Frey, "Trust Breeds Trust: How Taxpayers Are Treated," *Economics of Governance* 3 (2002): 87–99; and Marcia Grimes, "Organizing Consent: The Role of Procedural Fairness in Political Trust and Compliance," *European Journal of Political Research* 45 (2006): 285–315.

16. For a very small sample of this expansive literature, see Hazem Beblawi, "The Rentier State in the Arab World," *Arab Studies Quarterly* 9, no. 4 (1987): 383–98; Michael L. Ross, "What Have We Learned about the Resource Curse?," *Annual Review of Political Science* 18, no. 1 (May 11, 2015): 239–59, https://doi.org/10.1146/annurev-polisci-052213-040359; Ross, "The Political Economy of the Resource Curse," *World Politics* 51, no. 2 (January 1999): 297–322; Laura Paler, "Keeping the Public Purse: An Experiment in Windfalls, Taxes, and the Incentives to Restrain Government," *American Political Science Review* 107, no. 4 (2013): 706–25, https://doi.org/10.1017/S0003055413000415; and Stephen Haber and Victor Menaldo, "Do Natural Resources Fuel Authoritarianism? A Reappraisal of the Resource Curse," *American Political Science Review* 105, no. 1 (2011): 1–26, https://doi.org/10.1017/S0003055410000584.

17. Jeffrey Herbst, *States and Power in Africa: Comparative Lessons in Authority and Control* (Princeton, NJ: Princeton University Press, 2000).

18. Hillel David Soifer, *State Building in Latin America* (New York: Cambridge University Press, 2015).

19. Dan Slater, *Ordering Power: Contentious Politics and Authoritarian Leviathans in Southeast Asia* (Cambridge: Cambridge University Press, 2010).

20. Catherine Boone, *Political Topographies of the African State: Territorial Authority and Institutional Choice* (Cambridge: Cambridge University Press, 2003); Joel S. Migdal, *Strong Societies and Weak States: State-Society Relations and State Capabilities in the Third World* (Princeton, NJ: Princeton University Press, 1988).

21. Naseemullah, *Patchwork States.*

22. Dan Slater and Diana Kim, "Standoffish States: Nonliterate Leviathans in Southeast Asia," *TRaNS: Trans-Regional and -National Studies of Southeast Asia* 3, no. 1 (2015): 25–44.

23. See, for example, Marika Sosnowski, *Redefining Ceasefires: Wartime Order and State-building in Syria* (Cambridge: Cambridge University Press, 2023); Shamiran Mako and Alistair D. Edgar, "Evaluating the Pitfalls of External Statebuilding in Post-2003 Iraq (2003–2021)," *Journal of Intervention and Statebuilding* 15, no. 4 (August 8, 2021): 425–40, https://doi.org/10.1080/17502977.2021.1958292.

24. Jeremy Weinstein, *Inside Rebellion: The Politics of Insurgent Violence* (Cambridge: Cambridge University Press, 2007); Zachariah Mampilly, *Rebel Rulers: Insurgent Governance and Civilian Life During War* (Ithaca, NY: Cornell University Press, 2011); Ana Arjona, *Rebelocracy: Social Order in the Colombian Civil War* (Cambridge: Cambridge University Press, 2016); Claire Metelits, *Inside Insurgency: Violence, Civilians, and Revolutionary Group Behavior* (New York: NYU Press, 2010); Mara Redlich Revkin, "What Explains Taxation by Resource-Rich Rebels? Evidence from the Islamic State in Syria," *Journal of Politics* 82, no. 2 (2020): 757–64; and Zachariah Mampilly and Megan A. Stewart, "A Typology of Rebel Political Institutional Arrangements," *Journal of Conflict Resolution* 1, no. 65 (2021): 15–45.

25. Mampilly, *Rebel Rulers.*

26. Weinstein, *Inside Rebellion.*

27. Arjona, *Rebelocracy.*

28. Megan A. Stewart and Yu-Ming Liou, "Do Good Borders Make Good Rebels? Territorial Control and Civilian Casualties," *Journal of Politics* 79, no. 1 (2017): 284–301.

29. Megan A. Stewart, *Governing for Revolution: Social Transformation in Civil War* (Cambridge: Cambridge University Press, 2021).

30. This can be viewed as a particular form of what Loyle et al. call "multi-layered governance." See Cyanne E. Loyle et al., "New Directions in Rebel Governance Research," *Perspectives on Politics* 21, no. 1 (2023): 264–76.

31. Mamdani, *Citizen and Subject*, 18.

32. See, for example, Michael Hechter, *Containing Nationalism* (New York: Oxford University Press, 2001); and John Gerring et al., "An Institutional Theory of Direct and Indirect Rule," *World Politics* 63, no. 3 (July 2011): 377–433.

33. See, for example, Shireen Ally and Arianna Lissoni, eds., *New Histories of South Africa's Apartheid-Era Bantustans* (London: Routledge, 2017); Waltraud Ernst and Biswamoy Pati, eds., *India's Princely States: People, Princes and Colonialism* (London: Routledge, 2007).

34. Paul Staniland, *Ordering Violence: Explaining Armed Group-State Relations from Conflict to Cooperation* (Ithaca, NY: Cornell University Press, 2021).

35. Staniland, *Ordering Violence*, 4–6.

36. Ken Menkhaus, "Governance Without Government in Somalia: Spoilers, State Building, and the Politics of Coping," *International Security* 31, no. 3 (January 1, 2007): 74–106, https://doi.org/10.1162/isec.2007.31.3.74; Nora Stel, "Mediated Stateness as a Continuum: Exploring the Changing Governance Relations Between the PLO and the Lebanese State," *Civil Wars* 19, no. 3 (2017): 348–76.

37. Levi, *Of Rule and Revenue*.

38. Evanson N. Wamagatta, "British Administration and the Chiefs' Tyranny in Early Colonial Kenya: A Case Study of the First Generation of Chiefs from Kiambu District, 1895–1920," *Journal of Asian and African Studies* 44, no. 4 (2009): 371–88; and Uzochukwu J. Njoku, "Colonial Political Re-Engineering and the Genesis of Modern Corruption in African Public Service: The Issue of the Warrant Chiefs of South Eastern Nigeria as a Case in Point," *Nordic Journal of African Studies* 14, no. 1 (n.d.): 99–116.

39. CAVR, "Chega! The Report of the Commission for Reception, Truth and Reconciliation in Timor-Leste" (Jakarta, Indonesia: Timor-Leste Commission for Reception, Truth and Reconciliation, November 2013).

40. CAVR, "Chega!", 418.

41. See, for example, Adrian Florea, "De Facto States: Survival and Disappearance (1945–2011)," *International Studies Quarterly* 61 (2017): 337–51.

42. According to the perspectives of indigenous opponents of the regime, or even the intermediaries themselves, these coercive agents may be conceptualized differently. If the intermediary defects, they may even take actions against the dominant power in the name of the "external" security of the indigenous community. Using the label "internal" favors, in some ways, the interpretation of the dominant state.

43. Importantly, some research suggests that the reputational effects of possessing and deploying fiscal capacity can be positive because, for example, extraction is revocable, and forbearance from enforcing taxation can be used by politicians to win political support. See Alisha C. Holland, "The Distributive Politics of Enforcement," *American Journal of Political Science* 59, no. 2 (April 2015): 357–71; and Holland, "Forbearance," *American Political Science Review* 110, no. 2 (May 2016): 232–46. Furthermore, distributive capacity can come with political costs, if, for example, distribution is primarily of the *redistributive* form, or if resources are scarce enough that some communities perceive discrimination in distribution. I do not discount the possibility that distribution can generate reputational costs, especially with the expansive definition of distributive capacity that I have provided. However, in settings where the intermediary is engaging in redistribution, my theory still argues that some extractive capacity will be delegated to the intermediary to achieve redistribution. In settings where distribution (not redistribution) is politicized due to impressions (real or perceived) of favoritism, I nonetheless argue that the potential reputational costs are lower than with extraction (even if such extraction is also politicized or unevenly applied). These themes will be revisited in subsequent chapters. For example, in chapter 6, I note how distribution by the Bantustan chiefs in apartheid South Africa sometimes elicited protest and resistance. See Timothy

Gibbs, *Mandela's Kinsmen: Nationalist Elites & Apartheid's First Bantustan* (Suffolk, UK: James Currey, 2014).

44. Kenneth W. Abbott et al., "Competence-Control Theory: The Challenge of Governing Through Intermediaries," in *The Governor's Dilemma: Indirect Governance Beyond Principals and Agents*, ed. Kenneth W. Abbott, Bernhard Zangl, Duncan Snidal, and Philipp Genschel (Oxford: Oxford University Press, 2020).

45. Paul K. MacDonald, "The Governor's Dilemma in Colonial Empires," in *The Governor's Dilemma: Indirect Governance Beyond Principals and Agents*, ed. Kenneth W. Abbott, Bernhard Zangl, Duncan Snidal, and Philipp Genschel (Oxford: Oxford University Press, 2020), 49.

46. For example, Youssef Mnaili describes this kind of give-and-take between the Israeli government and the Jewish settler movement in the West Bank; "Settling Palestine: Logics of Israeli (In)Direct Governance of the Occupied West Bank Since 1967," (doctoral thesis, European University Institute, Florence, Italy, 2022).

47. Naseemullah, *Patchwork States*; Naseemullah and Staniland, "Indirect Rule and Varieties of Governance."

48. Naseemullah, *Patchwork States*, 14.

49. Mamdani, *Citizen and Subject*.

50. Brendan O'Leary, Ian Lustick, and Thomas Callaghy, eds. *Right-Sizing the State: The Politics of Moving Borders* (Oxford: Oxford University Press, 2001).

51. Alisha C. Holland, *Forbearance as Redistribution: The Politics of Informal Welfare in Latin America* (Cambridge: Cambridge University Press, 2017) 233, emphasis in original.

52. Holland, *Forbearance as Redistribution*, 234.

53. Holland, *Forbearance as Redistribution*, 14–15.

54. On the politics of distribution, see the following helpful reviews: Miriam Golden and Brian Min, "Distributive Politics Around the World," *Annual Review of Political Science* 16 (2013): 73–99; and Allen Hicken, "Clientelism," *Annual Review of Political Science* 14, no. 1 (June 15, 2011): 289–310, https://doi.org/10.1146/annurev.polisci.031908.220508.

55. On the political incentives for democratically elected leaders to target electricity provision, in particular, see B. Min, *Power and the Vote: Elections and Electricity in the Developing World* (Cambridge: Cambridge University Press, 2015). Important exceptions to the focus on democracies include, for example, Lisa Blaydes, *Elections and Distributive Politics in Mubarak's Egypt* (Cambridge: Cambridge University Press, 2010); Michael Albertus, *Autocracy and Redistribution: The Politics of Land Reform* (Cambridge: Cambridge University Press, 2015); and Christiana Parreira, "Power Politics: Armed Non-State Actors and the Capture of Public Electricity in Post-Invasion Baghdad," *Journal of Peace Research* 58, no. 4 (2021): 749–62.

56. Max Weber, *The Theory of Social and Economic Organization*, ed. Talcott Parsons (New York: Free Press, 1964).

57. Fabienne Peter, "Political Legitimacy," in *Stanford Encyclopedia of Philosophy* (Stanford, CA: Stanford University, revised April 27, 2017), https://stanford.library.sydney.edu.au/archives/sum2021/entries/legitimacy/.

58. Michael Hechter, *Alien Rule* (Cambridge: Cambridge University Press, 2013).

59. Sean Gailmard, "Accountability and Principal-Agent Theory," in *The Oxford Handbook of Public Accountability*, ed. Mark Bovens, Robert Goodin, and Thomas Schillemans (New York: Oxford University Press, 2014), 90–105.

60. International Monetary Fund, "Macroeconomic and Fiscal Framework for the West Bank and Gaza—First Review of Progress" (Staff Report for the Meeting of the Ad-Hoc Liaison Committee, International Monetary Fund, London, May 2, 2008), 7.

2. REGIMES AND LOCAL GOVERNANCE
IN THE WEST BANK BEFORE 1967

1. Unless otherwise noted, "Palestine" refers to the territory defined by the geographic borders of the British Mandate. However, conceptions of Palestine varied over time and, in the Ottoman period, included not just the district of Jerusalem and its surroundings; the label was also sometimes used to include parts of what is now Jordan and southern Lebanon. "Palestinian," when used in this chapter, references residents of Palestine of Arab descent. While at the time, all residents, including Jewish residents, e.g., would have been appropriately referred to as "Palestinian," I keep the terminology limited to the Arab population to be consistent with how Palestinian peoplehood is defined today.

2. See, for example, Engin Akarli, *The Long Peace: Ottoman Lebanon, 1861–1920* (Berkeley: University of California Press, 1993); and Ussama Makdisi, "After 1860: Debating Religion, Reform, and Nationalism in the Ottoman Empire," *International Journal of Middle East Studies* 34, no. 4 (2002): 601–17, https://doi.org/10.1017/S0020743802004014.

3. Abigail Jacobson, *From Empire to Empire: Jerusalem Between Ottoman and British Rule*, Space, Place and Society (Syracuse, NY: Syracuse University Press, 2011), 4; Falestin Naili, "The De-Municipalization of Urban Governance: Post-Ottoman Political Space in Jerusalem," *Jerusalem Quarterly* 76 (2018), 8.

4. 'Adel Manna', "Eighteenth- and Nineteenth-Century Rebellions in Palestine," *Journal of Palestine Studies* 24, no. 1 (1994): 51–66.

5. Manna`, "Eighteenth- and Nineteenth-Century Rebellions in Palestine," 52.

6. Manna', "Eighteenth- and Nineteenth-Century Rebellions in Palestine," 53. Importantly, Manna' describes how grievances associated with taxation were a common thread in eighteenth- and nineteenth-century rebellions against Ottoman rule. A revolt in the Galilee was led by Zahir al-'Umar al-Zaydani, a tax collector who sought to add more territory under his rule, expanding to include most of the Galilee and moving his "seat of government" to Acre. When he, in collaboration with the ruler of Egypt, 'Ali Bey al-Kabir, tried to occupy and control Damascus, the Ottomans quashed his movement. However, as Manna' describes, his rebellion was evidence of the "the increasing influence of local forces in the Arab *vilayets* [provinces] as the Ottoman state weakened and was no longer able to impose direct authority on those regions" (57).

7. Manna`, "Eighteenth- and Nineteenth-Century Rebellions in Palestine," 53.

8. Weldon C. Matthews, "Book Review: *The Rise and Fall of a Palestinian Dynasty: The Husaynis, 1700–1948* by Ilan Pappé," *Journal of World History* 23, no. 2 (2012): 435–38; Ilan Pappé, *The Rise and Fall of a Palestinian Dynasty: The Husaynis, 1700–1948* (Berkeley: University of California Press, 2010).

9. Manna`, "Eighteenth- and Nineteenth-Century Rebellions in Palestine," 54.

10. Manna', "Eighteenth- and Nineteenth-Century Rebellions in Palestine," 58–59.

11. Manna', "Eighteenth- and Nineteenth-Century Rebellions in Palestine," 59–60, emphasis added.

12. Naili, "The De-Municipalization of Urban Governance," 8–9.
13. Naili, "The De-Municipalization of Urban Governance," 9.
14. Beshara Doumani, *Rediscovering Palestine: Merchants and Peasants in Jabal Nablus, 1700–1900* (Berkeley: University of California Press, 1995), 10.
15. Manna', "Eighteenth- and Nineteenth-Century Rebellions in Palestine," 61.
16. Lisa Taraki and Rita Giacaman, "Modernity Aborted and Reborn: Ways of Being Urban in Palestine," in *Living Palestine: Family Survival, Resistance, and Mobility Under Occupation*, ed. Lisa Taraki (Syracuse, NY: Syracuse University Press, 2006), 6.
17. Taraki and Giacaman, "Modernity Aborted and Reborn," 7, citing Alexander Schölch, *Palestine in Transformation, 1856–1882: Studies in Social, Economic and Political Development*, trans. William C. Young and Michael C. Gerrity (Washington, DC: Institute of Palestine Studies, 1993), 119.
18. Taraki and Giacaman, "Modernity Aborted and Reborn," 11; Yehuda Karmon, "Changes in the Urban Geography of Hebron During the Nineteenth Century," in *Studies on Palestine During the Ottoman Period*, ed. Moshe Ma'oz (Jerusalem: Gefen, 1975), 79.
19. Suad Amiry, *Throne Village Architecture: Palestinian Rural Mansions in the Eighteenth and Nineteenth Centuries* (Ramallah: Riwaq Centre for Cultural Preservation, 2003), 216, paraphrased by Taraki and Giacaman, "Modernity Aborted and Reborn," 11–12.
20. Manna', "Eighteenth- and Nineteenth-Century Rebellions in Palestine," 52.
21. Manna', "Eighteenth- and Nineteenth-Century Rebellions in Palestine," 60.
22. Sherene Seikaly, *Men of Capital: Scarcity and Economy in Mandate Palestine* (Stanford, CA: Stanford University Press, 2016), 14.
23. Rami Zeedan, "The Palestinian Political Parties and Local Self-Governance During the British Mandate: Democracy and the Clan," in *The British Mandate in Palestine: A Centenary Volume, 1920–2020*, ed. Michael Joseph Cohen (London: Routledge, 2020), 87.
24. Shira Robinson, *Citizen Strangers: Palestinians and the Birth of Israel's Liberal Settler State* (Stanford, CA: Stanford University Press, 2013), 16; Rashid Khalidi, *The Iron Cage: The Story of the Palestinian Struggle for Statehood* (New York: Picador, 2020).
25. Seikaly, *Men of Capital*, 113.
26. Seikaly, *Men of Capital*, 90.
27. Seikaly, *Men of Capital*, 135, 136.
28. Seikaly, Men of Capital, 137.
29. Seikaly, *Men of Capital*, 131.
30. Naili, "The De-Municipalization of Urban Governance," 10.
31. Naili, "The De-Municipalization of Urban Governance," 11.
32. Naili, "The De-Municipalization of Urban Governance," 12.
33. Hillel Cohen, *Army of Shadows: Palestinian Collaboration with Zionism, 1917-1948* (Berkeley: University of California Press, 2008), 1.
34. Hillel Cohen, *Army of Shadows: Palestinian Collaboration with Zionism, 1917–1948* (Berkeley: University of California Press, 2008), 2.
35. Cohen, *Army of Shadows*, 78.
36. Cohen, *Army of Shadows*, 83.
37. Cohen, *Army of Shadows*, 83.
38. Cohen, *Army of Shadows*, 68.
39. Zeedan, "The Palestinian Political Parties and Local Self-Governance During the British Mandate," 91.
40. Zeedan, "The Palestinian Political Parties and Local Self-Governance During the British Mandate," 91.

41. Spiro Munayyer, "The Fall of Lydda," *Journal of Palestine Studies* 27, no. 4 (July 1, 1998): 80–98, https://doi.org/10.2307/2538132.

42. Munayyer, "The Fall of Lydda."

43. Mark A. Tessler, *A History of the Israeli-Palestinian Conflict* (Bloomington: Indiana University Press, 2009), 281.

44. Robinson, *Citizen Strangers*, 39.

45. Robinson, *Citizen Strangers*.

46. Robinson, *Citizen Strangers*.

47. See, for example, Tawfiq Zayyad, "The Fate of the Arabs in Israel," *Journal of Palestine Studies* 6, no. 1 (1976): 92–103, https://doi.org/10.2307/2535721.

48. Tessler estimates that 420,000 Palestinian refugees from the 1947–1949 violence ended up in the West Bank. Alternative estimates put the population at the end of 1948 between 415,000 and 426,000—which, presumably, would have already included many refugees—and the 1950 population at around 764,900, according to Ennab. Mark A. Tessler, *A History of the Israeli-Palestinian Conflict*, 2nd ed. (Bloomington: Indiana University Press, 2009), 280; Wael R. Ennab, "Population and Demographic Developments in the West Bank and Gaza Strip Until 1990" (study prepared for United Nations Conference on Trade and Development, June 28, 1994), http://unctad.org/en/Docs/poecdcseud1.en.pdf.

49. Janine A. Clark, *Local Politics in Jordan and Morocco: Strategies of Centralization and Decentralization* (New York: Columbia University Press, 2018), 50–51.

50. Laurie Brand, *Jordan's Inter-Arab Relations: The Political Economy of Alliance-Making* (New York: Columbia University Press, 1995).

51. Clark, *Local Politics in Jordan and Morocco*, 51.

52. Clark, *Local Politics in Jordan and Morocco*, 39.

53. Yoav Alon, "The Tribal System in the Face of the State-Formation Process: Mandatory Transjordan, 1921–46," *International Journal of Middle East Studies* 37 (2005): 228; quoted in Clark, *Local Politics in Jordan and Morocco*, 46.

54. Moshe Ma'oz, *Palestinian Leadership on the West Bank: The Changing Role of the Arab Mayors Under Jordan and Israel* (London: Frank Cass, 1984), 28–29.

55. Ma'oz, *Palestinian Leadership on the West Bank*, 26–39.

56. Glenn E. Robinson, *Building a Palestinian State: The Incomplete Revolution* (Bloomington: Indiana University Press, 1997), 10. See also Shaul Mishal, "Palestinian Society and Politics," in *Palestinian Society and Politics*, ed. Joel S. Migdal (Princeton, NJ: Princeton University Press, 1980).

57. Menachem Klein, *Lives in Common: Arabs and Jews in Jerusalem, Jaffa and Hebron* (New York: Oxford University Press, 2014), 142–43.

58. Clark, *Local Politics in Jordan and Morocco*, 52.

59. Emile Sahliyeh, *In Search of Leadership: West Bank Politics Since 1967* (Washington, DC: Brookings Institution Press, 1988), 44; Ma'oz, *Palestinian Leadership on the West Bank*, 77.

3. THE ORIGINS AND DEVELOPMENT
OF ISRAEL'S INDIRECT RULE REGIME

1. I make this argument in briefer form in Diana B. Greenwald, "Military Rule in the West Bank," in *Israel/Palestine: Exploring A One State Reality* (POMEPS Studies 41, Project on Middle East Political Science, Elliott School of International Affairs,

Washington, DC, 2020), https://pomeps.org/pomeps-studies-41-israel-palestine
-exploring-a-one-state-reality.

2. Joel Perlmann, *The 1967 Census of the West Bank and Gaza Strip: A Digitized Version* (Annandale-on-Hudson, NY: Levy Economic Institute of Bard College, November 2011–February 2012), http://www.levyinstitute.org/palestinian-census/.

3. Tessler, *A History of the Israeli-Palestinian Conflict*, 399.

4. Tessler, *A History of the Israeli-Palestinian Conflict*, 401.

5. Tessler, *A History of the Israeli-Palestinian Conflict*, 404–5.

6. Israeli sovereignty in East Jerusalem is not internationally recognized, and Palestinians still claim the city as the capital of their eventual state.

7. Ariella Azoulay and Adi Ophir, *The One-State Condition: Occupation and Democracy in Israel/Palestine* (Stanford, CA: Stanford University Press, 2013).

8. Ariella Azoulay and Adi Ophir, *The One-State Condition: Occupation and Democracy in Israel/Palestine* (Stanford, CA: Stanford University Press, 2013), 3.

9. Azoulay and Ophir, *The One-State* Condition, 3, quoting David Ronen, *The GSS Year* [in Hebrew] (Tel Aviv: Ministry of Defense, 1989), 18.

10. Shelef quotes Meir from the Mapai Secretariat meeting of September 24, 1967; see Nadav G. Shelef, *Evolving Nationalism: Homeland, Identity, and Religion in Israel, 1925–2005* (Ithaca, NY: Cornell University Press, 2010), 46.

11. Gershom Gorenberg, *The Accidental Empire: Israel and the Birth of the Settlements, 1967–1977* (New York: Times Books, 2006).

12. Gorenberg, *The Accidental Empire*.

13. Gorenberg, *The Accidental Empire*.

14. Diana Buttu, "Review: *The Accidental Empire: Israel and the Birth of the Settlements, 1967–1977* by Gershom Gorenberg," *Journal of Palestine Studies* 36, no. 2 (2007): 97–98, https://doi.org/10.1525/jps.2007.36.2.97.

15. Golda Meir, " 'Excerpts from Interview with Mrs. Meir,' *International Herald Tribune*, 31 January 1972, p. 4," *Bulletin of Peace Proposals* 3, no. 3 (1972): 257.

16. Gorenberg, *The Accidental Empire*.

17. Moshe Maʿoz, *Palestinian Leadership on the West Bank: The Changing Role of the Arab Mayors Under Jordan and Israel* (London: Frank Cass, 1984), 62.

18. Maʿoz, *Palestinian Leadership on the West Bank*, 63, emphasis added.

19. Usamah Shahwan, *Public Administration in Palestine Past and Present* (Lanham, MD: University Press of America, 2003).

20. Maʿoz, *Palestinian Leadership on the West Bank*, 69–71.

21. Rashid Khalidi, *The Iron Cage: The Story of the Palestinian Struggle for Statehood* (Boston: Beacon, 2007), 141.

22. Maʿoz, *Palestinian Leadership on the West Bank*, 73, emphasis added.

23. Ian S. Lustick, *Unsettled States, Disputed Lands: Britain and Ireland, France and Algeria, Israel and the West Bank and Gaza* (Ithaca, NY: Cornell University Press, 1993), 10–11.

24. Foundation for Middle East Peace, "Comprehensive Settlement Population 1972–2011," January 13, 2012, http://fmep.org/resource/comprehensive-settlement-population
-1972-2010/.

25. Tessler, *A History of the Israeli-Palestinian Conflict*, 548.

26. Tessler, *A History of the Israeli-Palestinian Conflict*; Lustick, *Unsettled States, Disputed Lands*.

27. Gad Barzilai and Ilan Peleg, "Israel and Future Borders: Assessment of a Dynamic Process," *Journal of Peace Research* 31, no. 1 (1994): 59–73.
28. Avi Shlaim, "Prelude to the Accord: Likud, Labor, and the Palestinians," *Journal of Palestine Studies* 23, no. 2 (1994): 7.
29. Tessler, *A History of the Israeli-Palestinian Conflict*, 528.
30. Tessler, *A History of the Israeli-Palestinian Conflict*, 529. See also: Anziska, *Preventing Palestine*.
31. "Camp David Accords; September 17, 1978" (Avalon Project, Yale Law School Lillian Goldman Law Library), accessed September 24, 2023, https://avalon.law.yale .edu/20th_century/campdav.asp.
32. Lustick, *Unsettled States, Disputed Lands*, 360.
33. Quoted in Shlaim, "Prelude to the Accord," 10.
34. Lustick, *Unsettled States, Disputed Lands*, 41.
35. Lustick, *Unsettled States, Disputed Lands*, 361.
36. Trudy Rubin, "West Bank Tactics May Erode Israeli Democracy," *Christian Science Monitor*, August 1983.
37. Shelef, *Evolving Nationalism*.
38. Shelef, *Evolving Nationalism*, 161.
39. Tessler, *A History of the Israeli-Palestinian Conflict*, 552.
40. World Bank, *Developing the Occupied Territories: An Investment in Peace* (report, International Bank for Reconstruction and Development and the World Bank, Washington, DC, September 1993).
41. Migdal, *Palestinian Society and Politics*, 47.
42. Wendy Pearlman, *Violence, Nonviolence, and the Palestinian National Movement* (Cambridge: Cambridge University Press, 2011); Tessler, *A History of the Israeli-Palestinian Conflict*.
43. Interview 2014.14. See chapter 5 for more details on field-based interviews conducted for this project.
44. Menachem Shalev, "The Looming Conflict," *Jerusalem Post*, July 28, 1989.
45. Shlaim, "Prelude to the Accord."
46. Barzilai and Peleg, "Israel and Future Borders."
47. Tessler, *A History of the Israeli-Palestinian Conflict*, 748–49.
48. Ehud Ya'ari, "It Just Won't Work," *Jerusalem Report*, December 3, 1992.
49. Peter Bakogeorge, "Deported Palestinians Return to Israel from Exile," *Southam News*, December 16, 1993, sec. A.
50. Sarah Helm, "Maps Dispute Draws New Battle of Jericho," *The Independent*, November 24, 1993.
51. Israel Ministry of Foreign Affairs, "The Israeli-Palestinian Interim Agreement," 1995, https://www.gov.il/en/Departments/General/the-israeli-palestinian-interim -agreement.
52. Note that this distribution of territory reflects Oslo II, as well as subsequent redeployments conducted as part of the Wye River Memorandum in 1998 and the Sharm El-Sheikh Memorandum in 1999.
53. Salem Ajluni, "The Palestinian Economy and the Second Intifada," *Journal of Palestine Studies* 32, no. 3 (2003): 66.
54. Ajluni, "The Palestinian Economy and the Second Intifada," 67–69.

4. PALESTINIAN LOCAL GOVERNMENT UNDER ISRAELI INDIRECT RULE: QUANTITATIVE FINDINGS

1. Lt. Gen. Keith Dayton, "The Soref Symposium Michael Stein Address on U.S. Middle East Policy" (Washington Institute for Near East Policy, Washington, D.C., May 7, 2009), emphasis added. The grammatical construction is, perhaps intentionally, ambiguous. Must the Palestinian security forces be held accountable only to the PA executive—after 2005, that was President Mahmoud Abbas—or to the Palestinian people themselves?

2. Jamal reviews the 2006 legislative election and argues that Hamas's victory resulted from its long-term organizational strategy and its focus on grass-roots, local mobilization of voters—both of which, the author claims, distinguished it from Fatah and the leftist opposition. See Manal A. Jamal, "Beyond Fateh Corruption and Mass Discontent: Hamas, the Palestinian Left and the 2006 Legislative Elections," *British Journal of Middle Eastern Studies* 40, no. 3 (2013): 273–94.

3. Brynjar Lia, *A Police Force Without a State: A History of the Palestinian Security Forces in the West Bank and Gaza* (Reading, UK: Ithaca, 2006).

4. This was demonstrated during the second intifada, when Israel ordered the shuttering of Palestinian police stations in Area B while leaving Area A stations open. In a 2005 meeting between Israeli and Palestinian counterparts, Isma'il Jabr, the head of the Palestinian delegation, referenced the closure of these stations, noting: "We want our jurisdiction in Area B. . . . We want the police stations to be re-opened." Al Jazeera Palestine Papers, "Meeting Minutes: Redeployment Coordination Committee" (February 2005). Importantly, despite a breakdown in Oslo institutions during the second intifada, the boundaries of Areas A, B, and C were restored after the uprising. Palestinian police stations in Area B that had been shuttered were reopened.

5. Palestinian Center for Policy and Survey Research, "Who Needs Security?" (Report No. 2, Palestinian Center for Policy and Survey Research, Ramallah, February 2017). These findings draw on four polls conducted between June and December 2016, two of which were representative samples of the West Bank Palestinian population ($n = 830$ for each) and two of which were restricted to non-Area A areas ($n = 2,107$ and $n = 1,490$).

6. Palestinian Center for Policy and Survey Research, "Who Needs Security?" This finding is from the two polls restricted to non-Area A respondents in August and December 2016.

7. Palestinian vehicles are permitted only on certain roads in the West Bank, as Israel has created segregated infrastructure, including a network of roads built to exclusively serve Jewish Israeli settlers in the West Bank. The distance traveled along roads is also a crude measure of the effort that Palestinian police would need to exert to respond to an incident; longer routes are more likely to pass through Area C, which the PA needs Israeli permission to traverse.

8. Ministry of the Interior, "Police Stations in the Governorates," 2022, accessed September 26, 2023, https://www.palpolice.ps/police-map. Thanks to Zane Jarrar for assistance in obtaining and processing the police station data, Alexei Abrahams for assistance in obtaining the road network data, and UNOCHA for consenting to share this data with researchers such as myself.

9. For more on the origins of municipal land borders, see the statistical appendix in this volume. Generating *shareabuilt* was a two-part process: first, assigning built-up areas to municipalities based on municipal land borders, and second, calculating the share of those built-up areas that fall within Area A.

10. Area C comprises the 60 percent of the West Bank where there is no permitted Palestinian security presence. This land consists of the Jewish settlements, areas designated for the settlements to expand, Israeli outposts and military bases, and some clusters of smaller Palestinian and Bedouin communities. Area C is thus an area of zero Palestinian policing capacity. Because my analysis is restricted to towns and cities with more than 1,000 residents—and thus I do not examine smaller villages or encampments—there are no municipalities in my data set with a majority of their built-up area located in Area C. However, many municipalities have substantial shares of their land in Area C where all forms of Palestinian development are heavily restricted and often forbidden by Israeli authorities. Of the 107 municipalities included in the data set, 46—or 43 percent of all municipalities, with a total of 346,000 residents in 2007—are fully located in Areas B and C. This means that none of their developed, built-up areas and none of their land is located in Area A. Scores of Palestinian villages that do not meet the size threshold to be part of my municipal dataset face the same situation.

11. The roads are coded for whether or not Palestinians are prohibited from driving on them. For municipality origins, we computed the centroid of the largest built-up area in each municipality. For police station destinations, we computed route lengths using only roads that Palestinian vehicles are permitted to drive on. I thank Atsuko Sakurai for her assistance in creating the municipality origins and computing road distances using the QNEAT plug-in for QGIS.

12. Map 4.1 shows some built-up Palestinian areas that fall within the Israeli-defined municipal boundaries of the city of Jerusalem, where Israel and the city government, not the PA, currently maintain authority. Thus, these areas do not fall within Area A, B, or C of the West Bank, and most, but not all, fall on the Israeli side of the separation wall. While the PA Ministry of Local Government does contain data on building cover in these areas, the PA has no ability to operate in these areas, and thus the municipalities containing these built-up areas are not included in our data set.

13. See, for example, Dana El Kurd, *Polarized and Demobilized: Legacies of Authoritarianism in Palestine* (London: Hurst & Co., 2019); Jamil Hilal, "Problematizing Democracy in Palestine," *Comparative Studies of South Asia, Africa and the Middle East* 23 (2003): 163–72; Amaney A. Jamal, *Barriers to Democracy: The Other Side of Social Capital in Palestine and the Arab World* (Princeton, NJ: Princeton University Press, 2009); and Yezid Sayigh, *Policing the People, Building the State: Authoritarian Transformation in the West Bank and Gaza* (Washington, DC: Carnegie Endowment for International Peace, February 2011).

14. Hassan Balawi, "Palestinian Municipal Elections: A Gradual Change," in *IEMed Mediterranean Yearbook 2006* (Barcelona: European Institute of the Mediterranean, 2006), https://www.iemed.org/publication/palestinian-municipal-elections-a -gradual-change/; Palestinian National Authority, "*Qānūn Raqam (1) li-Sanat 1997 bi-Sha'n al-Hayāt al-Maḥalliyya al-Filastīniyya*" (Ramallah: Palestinian National Authority, 1997), http://muqtafi.birzeit.edu.

15. Mohsen Mohammad Saleh, "The Islamic Resistance Movement (Hamas): An Over-view of Its Experience & History, 1987–2005," in *Islamic Resistance Movement—Hamas: Studies of Thought & Experience* (Beirut: Al-Zaytouna Centre for Studies & Consultations, 2017), 27–61.

16. Saleh, "The Islamic Resistance Movement (Hamas)," 60. While I do not have access to Saleh's municipality-level data, the author generously shared many of the pri-mary and secondary sources he used to code municipalities. This enabled me to cross-check my own coding against these sources. My coding of election results dif-fers among several towns from one of these sources, a report from the Middle East Studies Centre, "*Ittijāhāt al-Nākhibīn al-Filastīniyyīn fi Intikhābāt al-Baladiyyāt wa Riʾāsat al-Sulṭa*" (Strategic Report, Center for Middle East Studies, Amman, 2006).

17. The seven West Bank municipalities are Beit Awwa, Dura, Hebron, and Yatta in Hebron district; Abwein and Atara in Ramallah district; and Tulkarm in Tulkarm district. Many speculated that the Fatah leadership canceled the polls in these towns to avoid further losses (see, e.g., Saleh, "The Islamic Resistance Movement (Hamas)," 59).

18. There is no formal process by which a selected mayor must form a coalition to gov-ern. In fact, a number of mayors and former mayors interviewed in chapter 5 spoke about the importance of setting aside partisan divisions between council members once it came time to govern. However, some mayors relied more directly on partners from other parties or other electoral lists, whereas others governed with a more nar-row group of supporting council members.

19. Online forums sympathetic to the opposition—such as the Palestinian Network for Dialogue (*Shabakat Filastīn lil-Ḥiwār*) and the Palestinian Information Center (*al-Markaz al-Filastīnī al-ʾIʿlamī*)—offered details that could be cross-checked with local sources.

20. In theory, a continuous measure of the vote or seat share of each party would be pref-erable to this simple categorical measure. The change of electoral system between the second and third rounds of the elections means that the strategic calculus facing voters changed, along with the way in which votes were translated into seats. This means that vote or seat share measures may capture these changes in the institu-tional process, and the effects of those changes on voter behavior, rather than the overall relative performance of the parties. As a first priority, research assistants were directed to fill gaps in the partisan identifications (if any) of those candidates and lists that won seats, and they used local media and additional sources to cross-check the published results. Due to finite research budgets and resources, we were not able to return to the data set and completely code the partisan affiliations of losing candidates and lists, which we would have needed to compute vote shares.

21. The 107 units include towns with a population over 1,000 and that were classified as municipalities (rather than villages) by the Palestinian Authority during the period of analysis. See the statistical appendix for more details on how this list compares with the 116 used by Rafeef Abdelrazek, *West Bank and Gaza—Local Government Performance Assessment: An Assessment of Service Delivery Outcomes and Perfor-mance Drivers in the West Bank and Gaza* (Washington, DC: World Bank, June 14, 2017). There is not always a precise population threshold above which a popula-tion center becomes a municipality, but villages are generally restricted to populated areas numbering less than 2,000 to 3,000 residents whose leadership council is not

chosen through free elections but by representatives of the villages' largest clans. However, elections have been introduced in some villages in recent years.

22. European Institute of Public Administration et al., "Southern Neighborhood Area Countries—Palestine" (Brussels: Division of Powers, European Committee of the Regions, 2016), https://portal.cor.europa.eu/divisionpowers/Pages/Palestine-Introduction.aspx; Palestinian National Authority, *Qānūn Raqam (1) li-Sanat 1997 bi-Sha'n al-Hay'āt al-Maḥalliyya al-Filastīniyya.*

23. The Palestinian Central Bureau of Statistics (PCBS) population projections begin in 2007 when the census was conducted; thus, I impute 2006 by assuming the same locality-specific population growth rate from 2006 to 2007 that was observed between 2007 and 2008.

24. The latter category—service fees—does not include water or electricity provision, which are captured in a distinct variable described later.

25. In a report published during the period covered by the panel data, the notes that only 58 municipalities (out of 132 in both the West Bank and Gaza) were providing electricity themselves. Nonetheless, fees from electricity and water comprised an estimated 50 percent of aggregate municipal budgets in 2008. World Bank, *West Bank and Gaza Municipal Finance and Service Provision (vol. 2): Annexes* (English) (report, World Bank Sustainable Development Department, Middle East and North Africa Region, Washington, DC, January 2010), 75.

26. There are similar institutions for the northern governorates (Northern Electricity Distribution Company, or NEDCO, and Tubas Electricity Distribution Company, TEDCO), and for the south (Southern Electricity Company, or SELCO, and the Hebron Electric Power Company, HEPCO).

27. These dynamics are explored more in chapter 5, where it seems that some municipalities were more adamant about retaining municipal control over electricity revenues and expressed more skepticism toward the regional utilities. Insights from chapter 5 suggest that this skepticism could be found among both Fatah and opposition politicians.

28. World Bank, "Securing Water for Development in West Bank and Gaza" (Water Global Practice Sector Note, World Bank, Washington, DC, 2018); World Bank, *Securing Energy for Development in the West Bank and Gaza* (report, World Bank, Washington, DC, 2017).

29. With the institution's characteristic focus on public financial and macroeconomic stability, the World Bank describes how even as late as 2018, municipalities were diverting revenues from water provision to other budgetary needs: "the absence of ring-fencing of water tariff accounts means that water revenues may be diverted [by municipalities] to general revenues. . . . Although few LGUs [local government units, i.e., municipalities] derive an accounting surplus from their water operations, many simply retain a share of the water revenues to finance other operations and do not pay for their bulk water. . . . Unless the financing of LGUs is put on a more solid footing, LGUs will have limited incentive to separate their water operations as autonomous cost accounting centers, and even if they do, they may find other ways to divert water revenues to their own account." World Bank, "Securing Water for Development in West Bank and Gaza."

30. This variable also sometimes includes transfers from the Municipal Development and Lending Fund (MDLF), established in 2005. The MDLF is a nominally autonomous governmental institution, but its board of directors is dominated by government ministers—including the minister of local government, who serves as its

chair—and local representatives whose membership on the board is approved by the central government.

31. Organisation for Economic Co-Operation and Development/United Cities and Local Government, "Middle East and West Asia: Palestinian Authority" (Country Profiles of World Observatory on Subnational Government Finance and Investment, OECD, Paris, 2019), https://www.sng-wofi.org/country-profiles/.

32. This particular measure demonstrates a strong positive skew with the median (16.32 NIS/capita) well below the mean (54.46 NIS/capita), due in part to the outlier of Ramallah.

33. In January 2010, 3.72 NIS equaled US$1.00, according to the International Monetary Fund's International Financial Statistics Database. Constant 2010 dollars are used in all subsequent currency conversions unless otherwise noted.

34. See Table A.1. Ramallah's outlier status on $\overline{opc_i}$ pulls the mean upward; dropping Ramallah gives a mean of 37.19 NIS/capita and a maximum of 436.74.

35. Spending dedicated to each area is further broken down into operational and non-operational expenses; the former includes sector-specific spending and the latter includes salaries and overhead related to the provision of that good or service. The only exceptions are the market and slaughterhouse expenditures, which are simply aggregated into one category.

36. Ramallah is again an outlier in the "other" category due to high spending on loan repayments and other atypical investments that are applicable to Ramallah as the *de facto* capital city. Dropping Ramallah from this category reduces the mean of $\overline{otherpc_i}$ to 10.69 and the maximum value to 304.03.

37. I do not include capital development projects in the analysis for a couple of reasons. First, the revenues for these projects come in the form of grants from donors, while municipalities sometimes supplement it with their own revenues from surpluses or savings from previous years. In reviewing these portions of the municipal budget files, one notes that municipalities almost always reported balancing their capital development budgets so that spending matches revenues, the majority of which are from foreign donors. Undoubtedly, municipalities are required to fulfill reporting requirements for each of their donors. While this is speculative, I anticipate that municipalities may have incentives to demonstrate that donor grants have been fully spent and, perhaps additionally, that they are matching donor grants with their own funding. Thus, I have some concerns about data reliability. Perhaps more importantly, donor development funding tends to be project driven, very rarely resulting in fiscal support for existing municipal staff and institutions. I do not expect that occasional donor projects routed through municipalities will depress incentives for municipalities to generate their own regular sources of revenue or to carry out their typical spending. (As noted earlier, transfers from the central PA government did not appear to generate such effects.) Nonetheless, when interpreting the findings, we should be aware that idiosyncratic donor-funded projects may have altered specific municipality-year budget observations in unobserved ways.

38. There are eleven governorates in the West Bank: Bethlehem, Hebron, Jenin, Jericho, Jerusalem, Nablus, Qalqilya, Ramallah/Al-Bireh, Salfit, Tubas, and Tulkarm.

39. Alexei S. Abrahams, "Hard Traveling: Unemployment and Road Infrastructure in the Shadow of Political Conflict," *Political Science Research and Methods* 10 (2022):

545–66; Palestinian Central Bureau of Statistics, "Census Final Results—Population Report West Bank 2007," 2007, https://www.pcbs.gov.ps.

40. The numerator for *est* is taken from tables in the governorate yearbooks titled "Number of Establishments in Operation and Employed Persons in the Private Sector, Non Governmental Organization Sector and Government Companies." The numerator for *houseunits* is taken from tables titled "Number of Occupied Housing Units." Although the tables characterize that the data are for 2008, footnotes in the yearbooks confirm that the 2007 census is the original source for these observations.

41. World Bank, "West Bank and Gaza Municipal Finance and Service Provision." In cross-referencing these data with some personnel information available from Ministry of Local Government budget files, they appear to be from late 2007.

42. For both municipality origins and district capital destinations, we computed the centroid of the largest built-up area within each municipality. For district capital destinations, we computed route lengths using only roads on which Palestinian vehicles are permitted to drive. Settlement, outpost, and military base destinations were obtained from the Palestinian Ministry of Local Government. Unfortunately, these data are from 2014. We do not have a detailed record of how many of the outposts were created between the 2004–5 elections and 2014. I thank Atsuko Sakurai for her assistance in creating the municipality origins and district capital destinations and for computing all road distances using the QNEAT plug-in for QGIS and SQL queries to obtain shortest distances.

43. Tareq Baconi, *Hamas Contained: The Rise and Pacification of Palestinian Resistance* (Stanford, CA: Stanford University Press, 2018), 77.

44. Palestinian Center for Policy and Survey Research, "Poll Number 11: While Three Quarters of the Palestinians Welcome Sharon's Plan of Withdrawal from Gaza . . .," (Palestinian Center for Policy and Survey Research, Ramallah, March 14–17, 2004), http://www.pcpsr.org/sites/default/files/p11epdf.pdf; "Poll Number 12: In the Context of the Sharon Disengagement Plan . . ." (Palestinian Center for Policy and Survey Research, Ramallah, June 24–27, 2004), http://www.pcpsr.org/sites/default/files/p12epdf.pdf; "Poll Number 13: After Four Years of Intifada . . ." (Palestinian Center for Policy and Survey Research, Ramallah, September 23–26, 2004), http://www.pcpsr.org/sites/default/files/p13epdf.pdf; and "Poll Number 14: First Serious Signs of Optimism Since the Start of Intifada" (Palestinian Center for Policy and Survey Research, Ramallah, December 1–5, 2004), http://www.pcpsr.org/sites/default/files/p14epdf.pdf.

45. As noted previously, PCBS locality-specific population estimates are available for census years 1997, 2007, and each year after that. In estimations not shown, I find that the log of the population in 1997 ($p < 0.05$), the population in 2006 ($p < 0.05$), and the log of the population in 2006 ($p < 0.01$) are all positively associated with Hamas victory. I use the latter in the regressions shown here. Although this captures municipal population size in the year following the local elections, I do not anticipate that changes in population between 2005 and 2006 would pose a threat to inference here. The coefficient on *log_pop06* drops to a lower level of statistical significance ($p < 0.1$) in column 11 when governorate-fixed effects are included. None of the individual governorate coefficients is statistically significant in this estimation (Ramallah is the excluded category). If we begin with 10 separate null hypotheses that the coefficient for each of the control variables is significantly different from zero at $\alpha = 0.05$, then

the p-value for each significant coefficient would need to be less than 0.005 to survive a Holm-Bonferroni correction. The coefficient on log_pop06 predicting Hamas
victory survives this test in columns 3 and 7 of table 4.1. Thus, we cannot rule out
that the other coefficients are significant at $\alpha = 0.05$ due to chance.

46. Note that I do not include the number of municipal employees per 1,000 residents
($munemp$) in these specifications. That is a variable for which reverse causality is a
concern if, for example, newly elected municipal councils hired or fired staff soon
after taking office. Because there are fairly strong correlations between some of the
economic measures, I combine these variables into an index for some of the analysis.
However, for now, I analyze these variables separately to identify noteworthy bivariate correlations.

47. The online appendix is available at: https://dianabgreenwald.com/mayors-in-the
-middle/.

48. Husam ʻIzz al-Din, "Natāʼij al-Intikhābāt al-Maḥalliyya Tuʼakkid Iktisāḥ Ḥamās lil-
Mudun al-Kubrā wa Taqqadum Fataḥ fi al-Manāṭiq al-Rīfiyya," Al-Ayyam, December 17, 2005; Saleh, "The Islamic Resistance Movement (Hamas)."

49. Pairwise correlation coefficients for the three measures range from 0.32 to 0.64. I
find that variation in a town's employment rate ($emprate$), its number of housing
units ($houseunits$), and its number of business establishments (est) can be summarized by a common latent factor. Factor analysis was performed using the factor
command in Stata using the principal factor method and orthogonal varimax rotation. One factor was retained with an eigenvalue greater than zero, and the factor
loadings were $emprate = 0.392$, $est = 0.735$, and $houseunits = 0.717$. Thus, I construct
an index in which each variable is demeaned and rescaled to range from 0 to 5. The
$econ\_index$ for each municipality is the sum of each demeaned and rescaled variable divided by the number of variables that are nonmissing for that observation.
(So, for example, if est is missing for a particular observation, $econ\_index$ is the sum
of the demeaned, rescaled versions of $emprate$ and $houseunits$ divided by 2.) Thus,
$econ\_index$ also ranges from 0 to 5.

50. Avidit Acharya, Matthew Blackwell, and Maya Sen, "Explaining Causal Findings
Without Bias: Detecting and Assessing Direct Effects," American Political Science
Review 110, no. 3 (2016): 512–29. Unlike Acharya et al., however, I am not concerned
with modeling the local party in power as a mediator, nor is the main goal to recover
the controlled direct effect of the economic variables with the mediator fixed at
certain values. Instead, I seek to isolate the possible effect of the party variable on
revenues, removing economic sources of variation from the party variable so that I
am not capturing underlying reasons Fatah, Hamas, or independents came to power
in the first place but, rather, the possible effects of their rule once in office.

51. If we begin with fourteen separate null hypotheses that the coefficient for $fatahsum$
or $resid\_if$ will be significantly different from zero at $\alpha = 0.05$ for each of the seven
dependent variables, then the p-value for each significant coefficient would need to
be less than 0.004 to survive a Holm-Bonferroni correction. The coefficients on
$fatahsum$ and $resid\_fs$ in columns 7 and 8, respectively, where fines per capita is the
dependent variable, do not survive this correction. Thus, we cannot rule out that
these results are generated due to chance.

52. For example, both municipal self-generated revenues and total expenditures
dropped in 2007 due to the temporary freezing of international aid to the Palestinian

Authority; year fixed effects would absorb these common shocks to municipal budgets.

53. Recent literature has problematized two-way fixed-effects models due to their strong assumptions (Kosuke Imai and In Song Kim, "On the Use of Two-Way Fixed Effects Regression Models for Causal Inference with Panel Data," *Political Analysis* 29 [2021]: 405–15) and their interpretability (Jonathan Kropko and Robert Kubinec, "Interpretation and Identification of Within-Unit and Cross-Sectional Variation in Panel Data Models," *PLoS ONE* 15, no. 4 [2020]: e0231349). Further, because a number of my independent variables do not vary over time (or do not vary much, as is the case with the party variable for many towns), municipal fixed effects would sweep away both unobserved features of municipalities that shape revenue collection and, possibly, part of the relationship between party and revenues that we are trying to observe here.

54. To decide which variables to include, I added each of the time-invariant controls to the baseline lagged dependent variable model one at a time, retaining control variables with significant coefficients (not shown). The shortest distance to the nearest governorate capital or nearest Israeli settlement, the presence of a refugee camp, and the shortest distance to the nearest police station are not significant, so they are not retained.

55. Instead of municipal fixed effects, these are targeted variables that capture features of a local economy that are broadly accepted as shaping the tax base.

56. The most conservative approach to correcting for the multiple comparison problem here would begin with thirty separate null hypotheses—one for each of columns 2–11 of table 4.3, holding that the coefficient on *hamas* (or *resid_h*, the substitute residual term) will not be significantly different from zero, with ten identical nulls for a Fatah dummy (or substitute residual) and ten more for an Independent dummy (or substitute residual). As such, the *p*-value for each significant coefficient would need to be less than 0.002 to survive a Holm-Bonferroni correction. The coefficients shown on *hamas* and *resid_h* in table 4.3 do not pass this threshold.

57. When Nablus is dropped from the sample, the coefficient on *hamas* or the residual substitute variable (*resid_h*) remains significant at the 5 percent level in column 2 and at the 10 percent level in columns 3, 4, 5, and 7. When Al-Bireh is dropped from the sample, the coefficient on *hamas* or *resid_h* remains significant at the 5 percent level in column 2 and at the 10 percent level in columns 3, 4, 5, 6, 7, and 10. When Ramallah is dropped from the sample, the coefficient on *hamas* or *resid_h* remains significant at the 5 percent level in columns 2, 4, 5, 7, 9, and 10 and at the 10 percent level in columns 3, 6, 8, and 11.

58. International Crisis Group, *Enter Hamas: The Challenges of Political Integration* (Middle East Report No. 39, International Crisis Group, Brussels, January 18, 2006), 12. https://www.refworld.org/docid/43cf8a1a4.html.

59. International Crisis Group, *Enter Hamas*, 12.

60. Revenue from utilities bears no discernible relationship to the policing zones. This is consistent with the logic described earlier, whereby municipal control over electricity provision in particular is contingent on the district where the municipality is located. While those in Bethlehem, Ramallah, and Jericho districts had little choice in turning over this service to a public-private utility, municipality-specific factors may have shaped whether or not towns in other districts retained control of their own electricity provision. There is no reason to suspect these factors are related to PA policing capacity in the town.

61. The Holm-Bonferroni method would require the p-values for each of the estimates of $\hat{\beta}_2$, $\hat{\beta}_4$, and $\hat{\beta}_5$ to be less than 0.05/9, or 0.006, since the model is estimated with Fatah, Hamas, and independent dummies, respectively, substituted for $party_{it}$. The estimated coefficients shown in table 4.4 do not meet this threshold, and thus we cannot rule out that the resulting significance on the estimated marginal effects to be discussed are due to chance.

62. An increase of one standard deviation in the share of an opposition-controlled municipality's land located in Area C is associated with a decrease of 5.64 NIS (US$1.52) per capita, or 80,138 NIS (approximately US$21,543) for a town with the average 2010 population size.

63. Following Brambor et al., the standard error of interest is

$$\widehat{\frac{\sigma \delta Y}{\delta X}} = \sqrt{var\left(\widehat{\beta_3}\right) + var\left(\widehat{\beta_5}\right) + 2cov\left(\widehat{\beta_3}\widehat{\beta_5}\right)}.$$ All marginal effects and standard errors

are calculated using the margins command in Stata. Thomas Brambor, William Roberts Clark, and Matt Golder, "Understanding Interaction Models: Improving Empirical Analyses," *Political Analysis* 14 (2006): 63–82.

64. This is simply an additive sum of all revenues per capita shown in table 4.2. Since sector-specific spending can be highly variable from year to year, we might expect current year revenues to be a more robust predictor of spending than the previous year's spending.

65. For a review of the distinction between these concepts, see Allen Hicken, "Clientelism," *Annual Review of Political Science* 14, no. 1 (June 15, 2011): 289–310, https://doi.org/10.1146/annurev.polisci.031908.220508.

66. Access to utility revenues does not appear to correlate with the local party in power. I separate the sample into municipalities that generated any utility revenue over the seven-year period (83) versus those that generated none (17) and find that this is uncorrelated with either the party that won the plurality of seats in the elections or the party in power in 2006. While that does not account for historical political factors that might have influenced municipal control over utilities in the past, it is reassuring that the partisan identification of municipal councils that took office after the 2004–5 elections was unrelated to their access to this revenue source. Finally, it is important to note that the estimated coefficients on *fatah* and *resid_f* terms in table 4.5 do not meet the revised significance level implied by the Holm-Bonferroni method, since I estimate the models shown for each of the other ten disaggregated spending types, plus epc_{it}, as noted earlier. Thus, we cannot fully rule out the possibility that the significant relationship between Fatah rule and year-to-year changes in utility spending is due to chance.

67. All data below the 1st percentile (bottom 1 percent of cases) are set to the 1st percentile's value and all data above the 99th percentile are set to the 99th percentile's value.

68. When budget balance per capita, rather than the total value of the budget balance, is used as the dependent variable, the coefficient on *fatahsum* is significant only at a weaker, 10 percent threshold, and it drops from statistical significance when the outliers of Nablus and Ramallah are excluded. See the online appendix.

69. The only partial exception is that in municipality years under Fatah control, less was spent on cultural and social activities (*cusopc*) than was the case with their opposition counterparts, although for some specifications, the relationship is significant only at the $p < 0.1$ threshold. (These estimations are also shown in the online appendix.)

70. See, for example, Sara Roy, *Hamas and Civil Society in Gaza: Engaging the Islamist Sector* (Princeton, NJ: Princeton University Press, 2013); Benoît Challand, "A Nahḍa of Charitable Organizations? Health Service Provision and the Politics of Aid in Palestine," *International Journal of Middle East Studies* 40 (2008): 227–47; and Amit Loewenthal, Sami H. Miaari, and Anke Hoeffler, "Aid and Radicalization: The Case of Hamas in the West Bank and Gaza," *Journal of Development Studies* 59, no. 8 (April 10, 2023): 1187–1212, https://doi.org/10.1080/00220388.2023.2197546.

5. PALESTINIAN LOCAL GOVERNMENT UNDER ISRAELI INDIRECT RULE: QUALITATIVE FINDINGS

1. See the appendix at the end of this volume for more details on interview methodology and the de-identified list of interview subjects.
2. Peter Cohn, "Election Night, Beit Ummar," 2013, accessed October 1, 2023, https://vimeo.com/62637511.
3. Alisha Holland, "Forbearance," *American Political Science Review* 110, no. 2 (May 2016): 232–46; Holland, *Forbearance as Redistribution: The Politics of Informal Welfare in Latin America* (Cambridge: Cambridge University Press, 2017); and Holland, "The Distributive Politics of Enforcement," *American Journal of Political Science* 59, no. 2 (April 2015): 357–71.
4. Holland, "Forbearance."
5. WAFA, "*Quwwāt al-Iḥtilāl Tastawlī ʿalā ʾAḥad Manāzil Baldat Tuqūʿ wa Tuḥawwiluhu ʾilā Nuqṭa Murāqiba ʿAskariyya,*" *Palestinian News & Information Agency*, June 14, 2006, https://www.wafa.ps/ar_page.aspx?id=QuviHma61780190736aQuviHm.
6. *Shabakat Filastīn lil-Ḥiwār* blog post. Full citation details are omitted to maintain the anonymity of the interview subject.
7. WAFA news article. Full citation details are omitted to maintain the anonymity of the interview subject.
8. According to Article 55 of the Fourth Geneva Convention, the occupying power "has the duty of ensuring the food and medical supplies of the population," and Article 56 tasks the occupying power with "ensuring and maintaining, with the co-operation of national and local authorities, the medical and hospital establishments and services, public health and hygiene in the occupied territory." Electricity and water provision are clearly necessary basic goods required to meet these conditions. See Secretariat of the United Nations, "Convention (IV) Relative to the Protection of Civilian Persons in Time of War" (August 12, 1949), https://ihl-databases.icrc.org/en/ihl-treaties/gciv-1949?activeTab=1949GCs-APs-and-commentaries.
9. I omit the respondent's sector of work to maintain anonymity.
10. Holland, "Forbearance"; Holland, *Forbearance as Redistribution.*

6. HISTORIES AND FUTURES OF INDIRECT RULE: SITUATING THE PALESTINIAN CASE IN COMPARATIVE CONTEXT

1. Each poll is carried out on a stratified random sample of approximately twelve hundred respondents across the West Bank and Gaza Strip. Each survey is designed to be nationally representative of the Palestinian population across the occupied

territories. For more on methodology and individual poll results, see Palestinian Center for Policy and Survey Research, "Index PSR Polls," 2023 polls, accessed October 2, 2023, https://www.pcpsr.org/en/node/154.

2. Coalition for Accountability and Integrity—AMAN, "Annual Corruption Report 2008" (Jerusalem: AMAN, 2009).

3. Tariq Dana, "Crony Capitalism in the Palestinian Authority: A Deal Among Friends," *Third World Quarterly* 41, no. 2 (2020): 247–63.

4. Miriam A. Golden and Paasha Mahdavi, "The Institutional Components of Political Corruption," in *Routledge Handbook of Comparative Political Institutions*, ed. Jennifer Gandhi and Rubén Ruiz-Rufino (London: Routledge, 2015), 404–20.

5. Leila Farsakh, "Palestinian Economic Development: Paradigm Shifts Since the First Intifada," *Journal of Palestine Studies* 45, no. 2 (2016): 67.

6. Dan Sobovitz, *The Occupation Corrupts? Quantitative Analysis of Corruption in the Palestinian Authority* (Working Paper No. 50, Hertie School of Governance, Columbia University, New York, June 2010), https://edoc.vifapol.de/opus/volltexte/2013/4264/pdf/50.pdf.

7. Nora Stel, "Mediated Stateness as a Continuum: Exploring the Changing Governance Relations Bbetween the PLO and the Lebanese State," *Civil Wars* 19, no. 3 (2017): 348–76.

8. Sarah E. Parkinson, "Money Talks: Discourse, Networks, and Structure in Militant Organizations," *Perspectives on Politics* 14, no. 4 (2016), 978.

9. Nadya Hajj, *Protection Amid Chaos: The Creation of Property Rights in Palestinian Refugee Camps* (New York: Columbia University Press, 2016), 83–111.

10. Hajj, *Protection Amid Chaos.*

11. Hajj, *Protection Amid Chaos*, 109.

12. Parkinson, "Money Talks," 986.

13. Mahmood Mamdani, *Citizen and Subject: Contemporary Africa and the Legacy of Late Colonialism* (Princeton, NJ: Princeton University Press, 1996).

14. Mahmood Mamdani, *Neither Settler Nor Native: The Making and Unmaking of Permanent Minorities* (Cambridge, MA: Belknap Press of Harvard University Press, 2020), 13–14.

15. Mamdani, *Neither Settler Nor Native*, 23.

16. "The Census of British India of 1871–72," *Journal of the Statistical Society of London* 39, no. 2 (1876): 411–16.

17. In fact, the British had begun experimenting with indirect rule in the Indian subcontinent prior to 1858. See Michael K. Fisher, "Indirect Rule in the British Empire: The Foundations of the Residency System in India (1764–1858)," *Modern Asian Studies* 18, no. 3 (1984): 402–4. In the early stages, Fisher notes, the British East India Company deployed "Residents" and "Political Agents," who "served more as [a] diplomatic body than as the means for indirect control over the other regional states of India," (402). However, after 1798, the company made significant military advances, choosing to annex some territories while exercising "a position of indirect control over some of the larger states including Awadh, Hyderabad, and Mysore" (402). Sadly, as Fisher noted at the time, the Indians who were enmeshed in this early version of indirect rule disappear from the narrative: "Many Indians did . . . serve as members of the staffs of Residencies and Political Agencies. The presence, experience, and advice of these clerks, translators, and attendants no doubt influenced the decisions

and actions of their British superiors, although to a degree that can never accurately be measured. In this study of the Residency system, these Indian subordinates must therefore remain the nameless parts of a complex organization" (403–4). See, for example, Callie Wilkinson, "Weak Ties in a Tangled Web? Relationships Between the Political Residents of the English East India Company and Their Munshis, 1798–1818," *Modern Asian Studies* 53, no. 5 (2019): 1574–1612, https://doi.org/10.1017 /S0026749X17000932.

18. Olga Gasparyan, "Indirect Rule and Public Goods Provision: Evidence from Colonial India" (working paper, November 20, 2019), https://papers.ssrn.com/sol3/papers .cfm?abstract_id=3689339; Lakshmi Iyer, "Direct Versus Indirect Colonial Rule in India: Long-Term Consequences," *Review of Economics and Statistics* 92, no. 4 (2010): 693–713; and Ajay Verghese, *The Colonial Origins of Ethnic Violence in India* (Stanford, CA: Stanford University Press, 2016).

19. Abhijit Banerjee and Lakshmi Iyer, "History, Institutions, and Economic Performance: The Legacy of Colonial Land Tenure Systems in India," *American Economic Review* 95, no. 4 (2005): 1190–1213; Alexander Lee, "Land, State Capacity, and Colonialism: Evidence from India," *Comparative Political Studies* 52, no. 3 (2019): 412–44; and Shivaji Mukherjee, "Colonial Origins of Maoist Insurgency in India: Historical Institutions and Civil War," *Journal of Conflict Resolution* 62, no. 10 (2018): 2232–74. While Lee distinguishes the effects of *zamindari* (landlord-dominated) versus non-*zamindari* (cultivator-dominated) areas on state capacity and subsequent economic outcomes, Mukherjee distinguishes the princely-state-based definition of indirect rule from the land-tenure-based definition but finds that both, through different mechanisms, increase the probability of later Naxalite insurgency.

20. Adnan Naseemullah, *Patchwork States: The Historical Roots of Subnational Conflict and Competition in South Asia* (Cambridge: Cambridge University Press, 2022).

21. Banerjee and Iyer, "History, Institutions, and Economic Performance," 1193.

22. Barbara Ramusack, *The Indian Princes and Their States*, New Cambridge History of India III, 6 (Cambridge: Cambridge University Press, 2004), 171.

23. Lee, "Land, State Capacity, and Colonialism," 425.

24. Lee, "Land, State Capacity, and Colonialism," 425.

25. Lee, "Land, State Capacity, and Colonialism"; Shivaji Mukherjee, *Colonial Institutions and Civil War: Indirect Rule and Maoist Insurgency in India* (Cambridge: Cambridge University Press, 2021). Mukherjee's strongest empirical findings on long-run policing capacity distinguish the princely states from the directly annexed areas; thus, they employ the second definition of indirect rule discussed later.

26. Walter Hauser, "The Indian National Congress and Land Policy in the Twentieth Century," *Indian Economic & Social History Review* 1, no. 1 (July 1, 1963): 58–59, https://doi.org/10.1177/001946466400100104.

27. Hauser, "The Indian National Congress and Land Policy in the Twentieth Century," 65.

28. Naseemullah, *Patchwork States*, 15–16.

29. Karen Leonard, "Reassessing Indirect Rule in Hyderabad: Rule, Ruler, or Sons-in-Law of the State?," *Modern Asian Studies* 37, no. 2 (2003): 364, https://doi.org/10.1017 /S0026749X0300204X.

30. Hira Singh, "Colonial and Postcolonial Historiography and the Princely States: Relations of Power and Rituals of Legitimation," in *India's Princely States: People, Princes and Colonialism*, ed. Waltraud Ernst and Biswamoy Pati (London: Routledge, 2007), 16.

31. Singh, "Colonial and Postcolonial Historiography and the Princely States: Relations of Power and Rituals of Legitimation," 16.
32. Throughout this volume, I have adopted the preferred term "intermediary." It still may be problematic that this term implies that the actor is who the dominant state hopes they will be, but actors may refuse the label, or their own actions and behavior might undermine its relevance. However, I still find "intermediary" to be more agnostic than "agent" or the even more coarse term, "collaborator," and that it can encompass a range of possible actions other than collaboration with the dominant power. Nonetheless, I do make the assumption that intermediaries can be distinguished from other actors by the role they play within the regime.
33. Ramusack, *The Indian Princes and Their States*, 170.
34. However, not all of what came to be considered the princely states after 1858 were formed through treaties, and, of course, many important British declarations of policy were made unilaterally. Ramusack, *The Indian Princes and Their States*, 48–52.
35. Ramusack describes how the princes drew on the concept of *rajadharma*, or the kingly duties, which "included offering protection to prospective subjects; adjudicating disputes among social groups including kinspeople, clans and castes; patronizing religious leaders and institutions; and distributing gifts . . . to other cultural activities and social groups claiming kingly support." Because this concept is rooted in Hinduism, one would expect that it did not result in additional legitimacy among non-Hindu subjects. Ramusack, *The Indian Princes and Their States*, 4–5.
36. Ramusack, *The Indian Princes and Their States*, 48–49, emphasis added.
37. William Stevenson Meyer et al., "The Native States," *Imperial Gazetteer of India* IV, no. Administrative (1907): 85.
38. Ramusack, *The Princes and Their States*, 172.
39. Ramusack, *The Indian Princes and Their States*, 173 (emphasis added).
40. Shakti Kak, "The Agrarian System of the Princely State of Jammu and Kashmir," in *India's Princely States: People, Princes and Colonialism*, ed. Waltraud Ernst and Biswamoy Pati (London: Routledge, 2007), 68.
41. Fisher, "Indirect Rule and the British Empire," 402–3 (emphasis added).
42. Fisher, "Indirect Rule in the British Empire," 406.
43. Ramusack, *The Indian Princes and Their States*, 216.
44. Ramusack, *The Indian Princes and Their States*, 216.
45. Kishore Chandra Mishra, "Prajamandal Movements in the Feudatory States of Western Orissa," *Proceedings of the Indian History Congress* 69 (2008): 543–53.
46. Pravin J. Patel, "Trade Union Movement in a Princely State: Tradition, Industrialisation and Social Change," *Contributions to Indian Sociology* 45, no. 1 (February 1, 2011): 31–34, https://doi.org/10.1177/006996671004500102.
47. Patel, "Trade Union Movement in a Princely State," 39.
48. Patel, "Trade Union Movement in a Princely State," 31; Manu Bhagavan, *Sovereign Spheres: Princes, Education and Empire in Colonial India* (Delhi: Oxford University Press, 2003), 132; Ramusack, *The Indian Princes and Their States*, 216.
49. John McLeod, *Sovereignty, Power, Control: Politics in the States of Western India, 1916–1947*, Brill's Indological Library, vol. 15 (Leiden: Brill, 1999), 45.
50. Patel, "Trade Union Movement in a Princely State," 40–41; Bhagavan, *Sovereign Spheres*, 162.
51. Patel, "Trade Union Movement in a Princely State," 40.

52. Ramusack, *The Indian Princes and Their States*, 222.
53. Mridu Rai, *Hindu Rulers, Muslim Subjects: Islam, Rights, and the History of Kashmir*, Kindle ed. (Delhi: Permanent Black, 2004), 15.
54. Rai, *Hindu Rulers, Muslim Subjects*, 18–19.
55. Rai, *Hindu Rulers, Muslim Subjects*, 271–96.
56. Rai, *Hindu Rulers, Muslim Subjects*, 298.
57. Ramusack, *The Indian Princes and Their States*, 240.
58. Ramusack, *The Indian Princes and Their States*, 240.
59. George Kunnath, "Janathana Sarkar (People's Government): Rebel Governance and Agency of the Poor in India's Maoist Guerrilla Zones," *Identities* 29, no. 1 (January 2, 2022): 45–62, https://doi.org/10.1080/1070289X.2021.1928981.
60. On the role of Maoist ideology in rebel governance, see also Megan A. Stewart, *Governing for Revolution: Social Transformation in Civil War* (Cambridge: Cambridge University Press, 2021).
61. See, for example, Alan Lester, *Imperial Networks: Creating Identities in Nineteenth-Century South Africa and Britain* (London: Routledge, 2001); Saul Dubow, *Racial Segregation and the Origins of Apartheid in South Africa, 1919–36*, St Antony's Series (London: Palgrave Macmillan, 1989); Andy Clarno, *Neoliberal Apartheid: Palestine/Israel and South Africa After 1994* (Chicago: University of Chicago Press, 2017); Hermann Giliomee, "The Making of the Apartheid Plan, 1929–1948," *Journal of Southern African Studies* 29, no. 2 (June 1, 2003): 373–92, https://doi.org/10.1080/03057070306211.
62. Mamdani, *Citizen and Subject*.
63. Mamdani, *Citizen and Subject*, 102; Laurie Platzky, Cherryl Walker, and Surplus People Project (South Africa), *The Surplus People: Forced Removals in South Africa* (Johannesburg: Ravan, 1985); Dhiru V. Soni and Brij Maharaj, "Emerging Urban Forms in Rural South Africa," *Antipode* 23, no. 1 (January 1, 1991): 47–67, https://doi.org/10.1111/j.1467-8330.1991.tb00402.x.
64. The distinction between directly and indirectly ruled areas under apartheid were not as simple as urban versus rural, since, as Mamdani notes, governance of the migrant worker hostels and, for example, Black townships in Natal mimicked the structure of indirect rule in some ways. Mamdani, *Citizen and Subject*, 261–62, 274–75.
65. Bertil Egerö, *South Africa's Bantustans: From Dumping Grounds to Battlefronts* (discussion paper, Scandinavian Institute of African Studies, Uppsala: Nordiska Afrikainstitutet, 1991), 16.
66. Egerö, *South Africa's Bantustans*, 16.
67. Carolyn E. Holmes, *The Black and White Rainbow: Reconciliation, Opposition, and Nation-Building in Democratic South Africa* (Ann Arbor: University of Michigan Press, 2020), 36; Hermann Giliomee and Lawrence Schlemmer, "The Changing Political Functions of the Homelands," in *Up Against the Fences: Poverty, Passes and Privilege in South Africa* (New York: St. Martin's, 1985), 39–56.
68. Andrew Manson and Bernard Mbenga, "Bophuthatswana and the North-West Province: From Pan-Tswanaism to Mineral-Based Ethnic Assertiveness," in *New Histories of South Africa's Apartheid-Era Bantustans*, ed. Shireen Ally and Arianna Lissoni (London: Routledge, 2017), 135–55.
69. Timothy Gibbs, *Mandela's Kinsmen: Nationalist Elites & Apartheid's First Bantustan* (Suffolk, UK: James Currey, 2014), 132–54.

70. Shireen Ally and Arianna Lissoni, *New Histories of South Africa's Apartheid-Era Bantustans* (London: Routledge, 2017).

71. Laura Evans, "South Africa's Bantustans and the Dynamics of 'Decolonisation': Reflections on Writing Histories of the Homelands," in *New Histories of South Africa's Apartheid-Era Bantustans*, ed. Shireen Ally and Arianna Lissoni (London: Routledge, 2017), 182.

72. Gibbs, *Mandela's Kinsmen*, 25, 52–53.

73. Gibbs, *Mandela's Kinsmen*, 55.

74. Gibbs, *Mandela's Kinsmen*, 58.

75. Eliphas Mukonoweshuro, "Between Verwoerd and the ANC: Profiles of Contemporary Repression, Deprivation, and Poverty in South Africa's 'Bantustans,'" *Social Justice* 18, no. 1/2 (1991): 172.

76. Gibbs, *Mandela's Kinsmen*, 66–69.

77. Gibbs, *Mandela's Kinsmen*, 112–17.

78. Nicholas Rush Smith, *Contradictions of Democracy: Vigilantism and Rights in Post-Apartheid South Africa* (New York: Oxford University Press, 2019), 38–56.

79. Vha-Musanda Vho-Shandukani Mudzunga, "Autobiography of an Underground Political Activist," in *New Histories of South Africa's Apartheid-Era Bantustans*, ed. Shireen Ally and Arianna Lissoni (London: Routledge, 2017), 196.

80. Vha-Musanda Vho-Shandukani Mudzunga, "Autobiography of an Underground Political Activist," in *New Histories of South Africa's Apartheid-Era Bantustans*, ed. Shireen Ally and Arianna Lissoni (London: Routledge, 2017), 196–97.

81. Helen Wieffering, "The Deepening Costs of 4 Gaza Wars in 13 Years, in 4 Charts," *Associated Press*, August 25, 2021, https://apnews.com/article/middle-east-united-nations-israel-palestinian-gaza-hamas-186d89b5fa8ae171c166f6162d6ea3da.

82. Gisha, "Gaza Up Close," June 28, 2023, https://features.gisha.org/gaza-up-close/.

83. Somdeep Sen, *Decolonizing Palestine: Hamas Between the Anticolonial and the Postcolonial* (Ithaca, NY: Cornell University Press, 2020), 106.

84. United Nations Office for the Coordination of Humanitarian Affairs. "Hostilities in the Gaza Strip and Israel: Flash Update #104," January 28, 2024, https://www.ochaopt.org/. Accessed: January 29, 2024.

85. Tyler Bartlam, Kathryn Fox, Ari Shapiro, Greg Myre, "Unpacking Netanyahu's intentions for the future of Gaza," National Public Radio: *All Things Considered*, November 17, 2023, https://www.npr.org/2023/11/17/1213890350/unpacking-netanyahus-intentions-for-the-future-of-gaza.

86. Egerö, *South Africa's Bantustans*.

87. Diana Greenwald, "Delegating Domination: Indirect Rule in the West Bank," in *The One State Reality: What Is Israel/Palestine?*, ed. Michael Barnett, Nathan Brown, Marc Lynch, and Shibley Telhami (Ithaca, NY: Cornell University Press, 2023).

88. Robert H. Bates and Da-Hsiang Donald Lien, "A Note on Taxation, Development, and Representative Government," *Politics & Society* 14, no. 1 (1985): 53–70.

89. Dana El Kurd, *Polarized and Demobilized: Legacies of Authoritarianism in Palestine* (London: Hurst & Co., 2019).

90. On the Muslim Brotherhood in Egypt, see, for example, Steven T. Brooke, *Winning Hearts and Votes: Social Services and the Islamist Political Advantage* (Ithaca, NY: Cornell University Press, 2019); and Tarek Masoud, *Counting Islam: Religion, Class, and Elections in Egypt* (Cambridge: Cambridge University Press, 2014). On Hamas and

social service provision in Gaza, see, for example, Sara Roy, *Hamas and Civil Society in Gaza: Engaging the Islamist Sector* (Princeton, NJ: Princeton University Press, 2013).

91. Karin Laub and Mohammed Daraghmeh, "Fatah Fails to Win Strong Nod in West Bank Vote," *Associated Press*, October 20, 2012, https://www.usatoday.com/story /news/world/2012/10/20/palestinians-elections-west-bank/1645993/; BBC Worldwide Monitoring, "Hamas, Fatah Officials Trade Accusations Over Boycott of Gaza Municipal Polls," *BBC Monitoring Middle East—Political*, October 23, 2012.

92. Greenwald, "For Palestinians, the Local Is the National," Jadaliyya, May 1, 2023. https:// www.jadaliyya.com/Details/44986/For-Palestinians,-the-Local-is-the-National.

93. Egerö, *South Africa's Bantustans*, 6.

94. Gibbs, *Mandela's Kinsmen*, 5.

95. One example is that of Fathi Hazim. Hazim is a retired colonel in the Palestinian Authority security services. In April 2022, Hazim's son allegedly carried out an armed attack against Israeli civilians in Tel Aviv, killing two. Israel chased down and killed the younger Hazim that night, while Fathi later made a defiant speech to hundreds of young men outside his home in Jenin refugee camp, commending his son's actions and armed resistance against Israel. Despite his former position, he has since become a caustic critic of Israeli-PA collaboration, expressing support for Palestinian armed resistance, and remains wanted for arrest by Israeli authorities at the time of writing. In January 2023, Hazim suffered "swelling, tumors and blood poisoning," with some alleging he was poisoned by Israel. Ahmed Abu Artema, "West Bank Restiveness a Sign of Changing Times," *Electronic Intifada*, May 27, 2022, https://electronicintifada. net/content/west-bank-restiveness-sign-changing-times/35546; Elior Levy, "Israel Still on the Hunt for Father of Tel Aviv Gunman," *Yedioth Ahronoth*, April 12, 2022, https://www.ynetnews.com/article/skgrhkeeq; and Tzvi Joffre, "Palestinians Accuse Israel of 'Poisoning' Father of Dizengoff Terrorist," *Jerusalem Post*, January 9, 2023.

96. Antonio Gramsci, *Prison Notebooks*, vol. 2, ed. and trans. Joseph A. Buttigieg (New York: Columbia University Press, 2011), 32–33.

METHODOLOGICAL APPENDIX

1. The cartographic borders of Areas A, B, and C were drawn behind closed doors. Qualitative sources suggest that the Israeli military establishment in particular had disproportionate influence over the geographic divisions that were finalized in the Oslo II agreement. The composition of the negotiating teams that concluded Oslo II were different from the teams that agreed on Oslo I. In a phone interview with the author, a senior member of the Israeli delegation for Oslo I was quick to note that they were not involved in the subsequent negotiations that led to Oslo II (Interview 2016.2; see table A.3). According to the same individual, the Israeli military was "overly involved in the [Oslo II] negotiations to compensate" for their minimized role in Oslo I. A senior member of the Palestinian delegation to the Oslo II nego-tiations described that his team had "no maps, no satellite images," and no exist-ing institutions that could provide such data (Interview 2016.1). This respondent recalled relying on the maps that the Israeli delegation brought with them.

2. One district was subjected to a much more deterministic selection process: Jerusa-lem. There are ten municipalities and more than a dozen smaller villages in the West

Bank that immediately surround the city of Jerusalem but fall outside Israel's uni-laterally defined municipal boundaries for the city; thus, they are governed by the Oslo Accords rather than Israeli local and national institutions. Since Israel began construction of the separation barrier in the early 2000s, these towns have also been physically walled off from the city of Jerusalem. These towns—formally part of the PA's Jerusalem district, not Israel's—had nearly all of their developed areas desig-nated as Area B. For these towns, the divisions created by the Oslo Accords ensured that the Palestinian police would have relatively little authority. This applies to 10 municipalities in my dataset: Abu Dis, al-'Eizariyya, al-Ram, 'Anata, al-Sawahira al-Sharqiyya, Biddu, Beit 'Anan, Beit Surik, Bir Nabala, and Qatanna.

3. Rafeef Abdelrazek, *West Bank and Gaza—Local Government Performance Assess-ment: An Assessment of Service Delivery Outcomes and Performance Drivers in the West Bank and Gaza* (Washington, DC: World Bank, June 14, 2017).

4. Israel Central Bureau of Statistics, "Judea, Samaria and Gaza Area Statistics" (Jeru-salem, 1980).

5. Joel Perlmann, *The 1967 Census of the West Bank and Gaza Strip: A Digitized Version* (Annandale-on-Hudson, NY: Levy Economic Institute of Bard College, November 2011–February 2012), http://www.levyinstitute.org/palestinian-census/.

6. Palestinian Central Bureau of Statistics, *Population, Housing and Establishment Cen-sus-1997*, Statistical Reports Series (Ramallah: Palestinian National Authority, 1999).

7. First, I use the 1967 census estimates of population by municipality and assume a constant growth rate of 0.91 percent (based on Wael Ennab's estimates of the growth rate in the West Bank from 1962 to 1967) between 1967 and 1982 to arrive at the ini-tial 1982 figures. Ennab, "Population and Demographic Developments in the West Bank and Gaza Strip Until 1990"(study prepared for United Nations Conference on Trade and Development, June 28, 1994), http://unctad.org/en/Docs/poecdcseud1 .en.pdf. From 1982 on, I assume a constant 4.5 percent rate through 1994. This is the estimated annual population growth rate provided in the World Bank *World Development Indicators* for the West Bank and Gaza for 1991 to 1997. The second set of estimates I use interpolates municipal populations back in time using the 1997 PCBS figures and assuming a constant 4.5 percent annual population growth rate going back to 1982.

BIBLIOGRAPHY

Abbott, Kenneth W., Philipp Genschel, Duncan Snidal, and Bernhard Zangl. "Competence-Control Theory: The Challenge of Governing Through Intermediaries." In *The Governor's Dilemma: Indirect Governance Beyond Principals and Agents*, ed. Kenneth W. Abbott, Bernhard Zangl, Duncan Snidal, and Philipp Genschel. Oxford: Oxford University Press, 2020.

Abdelrazek, Rafeef. *West Bank and Gaza—Local Government Performance Assessment: An Assessment of Service Delivery Outcomes and Performance Drivers in the West Bank and Gaza*. Washington, DC: World Bank, June 14, 2017.

Abrahams, Alexei S. "Hard Traveling: Unemployment and Road Infrastructure in the Shadow of Political Conflict." *Political Science Research and Methods* 10 (2022): 545–66.

——. "Not Dark Yet: The Israel-PA Principal-Agent Relationship, 1993–2017." In *Proxy Wars: Suppressing Violence Through Local Agents*, ed. Eli Berman and David A. Lake, 185–208. Ithaca, NY: Cornell University Press, 2019.

Abu Artema, Ahmed. "West Bank Restiveness a Sign of Changing Times." *Electronic Intifada*, May 27, 2022. https://electronicintifada.net/content/west-bank-restiveness -sign-changing-times/35546.

Acemoglu, Daron, Isaías N. Chaves, Philip Osafo-Kwaako, and James A. Robinson. "Indirect Rule and State Weakness in Africa: Sierra Leone in Comparative Perspective." In *African Successes, Volume IV: Sustainable Growth*, ed. Sebastian Edwards, Simon Johnson, and David N. Weil, 343–70. Chicago: University of Chicago Press, 2016.

Acharya, Avidit, Matthew Blackwell, and Maya Sen. "Explaining Causal Findings Without Bias: Detecting and Assessing Direct Effects." *American Political Science Review* 110, no. 3 (2016): 512–29.

Ajluni, Salem. "The Palestinian Economy and the Second Intifada." *Journal of Palestine Studies* 32, no. 3 (2003): 64–73.

Akarli, Engin. *The Long Peace: Ottoman Lebanon, 1861–1920.* Berkeley: University of California Press, 1993.

Al Jazeera Palestine Papers. "Meeting Minutes: Redeployment Coordination Committee." February 2005.

Albertus, Michael. *Autocracy and Redistribution: The Politics of Land Reform.* Cambridge: Cambridge University Press, 2015.

Al-Habil, Wasim I. "Occupations, a Diaspora, and the Design of Local Governments for a Palestinian State." Doctoral thesis, Cleveland State University, 2008.

Al-Haq—Law in the Service of Man, BADIL Resource Center for Palestinian Residency and Refugee Rights, Palestinian Center for Human Rights, Al Mezan Center for Human Rights, Addameer Prisoner Support and Human Rights Association, Civic Coalition for Palestinian Rights in Jerusalem, Cairo Institute for Human Rights Studies, and Habitat International Coalition—Housing and Land Rights Network. "Joint Parallel Report to the United Nations Committee on the Elimination of Racial Discrimination on Israel's Seventeenth to Nineteenth Periodic Reports," November 12, 2019. https://www.alhaq.org/advocacy/16183.html.

Ally, Shireen, and Arianna Lissoni, eds. *New Histories of South Africa's Apartheid-Era Bantustans.* London: Routledge, 2017.

Alm, James, Betty R. Jackson, and Michael McKee. "Fiscal Exchange, Collective Decision Institutions, and Tax Compliance." *Journal of Economic Behavior and Organization* 22 (1993): 285–303.

Alm, James, Gary H. McClelland, and William D. Schulze. "Why Do People Pay Taxes?", *Journal of Public Economics* 48 (1992): 21–38.

Alon, Yoav. "The Tribal System in the Face of the State-Formation Process: Mandatory Transjordan, 1921–46." *International Journal of Middle East Studies* 37 (2005): 213–40.

Alvarez, Mike, and Jose Antonio Cheibub. "Classifying Political Regimes." *Studies in Comparative International Development* 31, no. 2 (1996): 3–36.

Amiry, Suad. *Throne Village Architecture: Palestinian Rural Mansions in the Eighteenth and Nineteenth Centuries.* Ramallah: Riwaq Centre for Cultural Preservation, 2003.

Amnesty International. "Israel's Apartheid Against Palestinians: Cruel System of Domination and Crime Against Humanity." Amnesty International, February 1, 2022. https://www.amnesty.org/en/documents/mde15/5141/2022/en/.

Anziska, Seth. *Preventing Palestine: A Political History from Camp David to Oslo.* Princeton, NJ: Princeton University Press, 2018.

Arjona, Ana. *Rebelocracy: Social Order in the Colombian Civil War.* Cambridge: Cambridge University Press, 2016.

Aruri, Naseer H. "Early Empowerment: The Burden Not the Responsibility." *Journal of Palestine Studies* 24, no. 2 (1995): 33–39.

Azoulay, Ariella, and Adi Ophir. *The One-State Condition: Occupation and Democracy in Israel/Palestine.* Stanford, CA: Stanford University Press, 2013.

Baconi, Tareq. *Hamas Contained: The Rise and Pacification of Palestinian Resistance.* Stanford, CA: Stanford University Press, 2018.

Bakogeorge, Peter. "Deported Palestinians Return to Israel from Exile." *Southam News,* December 16, 1993, sec. A.

Balawi, Hassan. "Palestinian Municipal Elections: A Gradual Change." In *IEMed Mediterranean Yearbook 2006*. Barcelona: European Institute of the Mediterranean, 2006. https://www.iemed.org/publication/palestinian-municipal-elections-a-gradual-change/.

Banerjee, Abhijit, and Lakshmi Iyer. "History, Institutions, and Economic Performance: The Legacy of Colonial Land Tenure Systems in India." *American Economic Review* 95, no. 4 (2005): 1190–1213.

Barkey, Karen. "The Ottoman Empire (1299–1923): The Bureaucratization of Patrimonial Authority." In *Empires and Bureaucracy in World History: From Late Antiquity to the Twentieth Century*, ed. Peter Crooks and Timothy Parsons, 102–26. Cambridge: Cambridge University Press, 2016.

Barzilai, Gad, and Ilan Peleg. "Israel and Future Borders: Assessment of a Dynamic Process." *Journal of Peace Research* 31, no. 1 (1994): 59–73.

Bates, Robert H. *Prosperity and Violence: The Political Economy of Development*. 2nd ed. New York: Norton, 2010.

Bates, Robert H., and Da-Hsiang Donald Lien. "A Note on Taxation, Development, and Representative Government." *Politics & Society* 14, no. 1 (1985): 53–70.

BBC Worldwide Monitoring. "Hamas, Fatah Officials Trade Accusations Over Boycott of Gaza Municipal Polls." *BBC Monitoring Middle East—Political*, October 23, 2012.

Beblawi, Hazem. "The Rentier State in the Arab World." *Arab Studies Quarterly* 9, no. 4 (1987): 383–98.

Benvenisti, Meron. *1986 Report: Demographic, Economic, Legal, Social and Political Developments in the West Bank*. Washington, DC: American Enterprise Institute, West Bank Data Base Project, 1986.

Beramendi, Pablo, Mark Dincecco, and Melissa Rogers. "Intra-Elite Competition and Long-Run Fiscal Development." *Journal of Politics* 81, no. 1 (2019).

Bhagavan, Manu. *Sovereign Spheres: Princes, Education and Empire in Colonial India*. Delhi: Oxford University Press, 2003.

Bishnaq, Bassam. *Al-Tanzīm al-'Idāri lil-Muhafazāt fī Filastīn*. Ramallah: Al-Hay'ah al-Filastīniyya al-Mustaqilla li-Huqūq al-Muwāṭin, 2003.

Blaydes, Lisa. *Elections and Distributive Politics in Mubarak's Egypt*. Cambridge: Cambridge University Press, 2010.

Boone, Catherine. *Political Topographies of the African State: Territorial Authority and Institutional Choice*. Cambridge: Cambridge University Press, 2003.

Brambor, Thomas, William Roberts Clark, and Matt Golder. "Understanding Interaction Models: Improving Empirical Analyses." *Political Analysis* 14 (2006): 63–82.

Brand, Laurie A. *Jordan's Inter-Arab Relations: The Political Economy of Alliance-Making*. New York: Columbia University Press, 1995.

——. *Palestinians in the Arab World: Institution Building and the Search for State*. New York: Columbia University Press, 1988.

Brooke, Steven T. *Winning Hearts and Votes: Social Services and the Islamist Political Advantage*. Ithaca, NY: Cornell University Press, 2019.

B'Tselem. "A Regime of Jewish Supremacy from the Jordan River to the Mediterranean Sea: This Is Apartheid." Position Paper. Jerusalem: B'Tselem, 2021. https://www.btselem.org/publications/fulltext/202101_this_is_apartheid.

——. "Fatalities in the first Intifada." Accessed November 11, 2023. Jerusalem: B'Tselem. https://www.btselem.org/statistics/first_intifada_tables.

Bucaille, Laetitia. *Growing Up Palestinian: Israeli Occupation and the Intifada Generation.* Princeton, NJ: Princeton University Press, 2004.

Buttu, Diana. "Review: *The Accidental Empire: Israel and the Birth of the Settlements, 1967–1977* by Gershom Gorenberg." *Journal of Palestine Studies* 36, no. 2 (2007): 97–98. https://doi.org/10.1525/jps.2007.36.2.97.

"Camp David Accords; September 17, 1978." Avalon Project, Yale Law School Lillian Goldman Law Library. Accessed September 24, 2023. https://avalon.law.yale.edu/20th_century/campdav.asp.

Castañeda, Néstor, David Doyle, and Cassilde Schwartz. "Opting Out of the Social Contract: Tax Morale and Evasion." *Comparative Political Studies* 53, no. 7 (2020): 1175–1219.

CAVR. "Chega! The Report of the Commission for Reception, Truth and Reconciliation in Timor-Leste." Jakarta, Indonesia: Timor-Leste Commission for Reception, Truth and Reconciliation, November 2013.

Challand, Benoît. "A Naḥḍa of Charitable Organizations? Health Service Provision and the Politics of Aid in Palestine." *International Journal of Middle East Studies* 40 (2008): 227–47.

Clark, Janine A. *Local Politics in Jordan and Morocco: Strategies of Centralization and Decentralization.* New York: Columbia University Press, 2018.

Clarno, Andy. *Neoliberal Apartheid: Palestine/Israel and South Africa after 1994.* Chicago: University of Chicago Press, 2017.

Coalition for Accountability and Integrity—AMAN. "Annual Corruption Report 2008." Jerusalem: AMAN, 2009.

Cohen, Hillel. *Army of Shadows: Palestinian Collaboration with Zionism, 1917–1948.* Berkeley: University of California Press, 2008.

——. "Society-Military Relations in a State-in-the-Making: Palestinian Security Agencies and the 'Treason Discourse' in the Second Intifada." *Armed Forces & Society* 38, no. 3 (2012): 463–85.

Cohn, Peter. "Election Night, Beit Ummar." 2013. Accessed October 1, 2023. https://vimeo.com/62637511.

Collins, John. *Occupied by Memory.* New York: NYU Press, 2004.

Cuinet, Vital. *Syrie, Liban et Palestine. Géographie Administrative, Statistique, Descriptive et Raisonnée* [with maps.]. Paris, 1896. https://access.bl.uk/item/viewer/ark:/81055/vdc_000000008292#?cv=527&c=0&m=0&s=0&xywh=-3416%2C-1839%2C9887%2C6100.

Dana, Tariq. "Crony Capitalism in the Palestinian Authority: A Deal Among Friends." *Third World Quarterly* 41, no. 2 (2020): 247–63.

Dayan, Hilla. "Regimes of Separation: Israel/Palestine and the Shadow of Apartheid." In *The Power of Inclusive Exclusion: Anatomy of Israeli Rule in the Occupied Palestinian Territories*, ed. Adi Ophir, Michal Givoni, and Sari Hanafi, 281–322. Brooklyn, NY: Zone, 2009.

Dayton, Lt. Gen. Keith. "The Soref Symposium Michael Stein Address on U.S. Middle East Policy." Presented at the the Washington Institute for Near East Policy, Washington, DC, May 7, 2009.

Dincecco, Mark. *Political Transformations and Public Finances.* Cambridge: Cambridge University Press, 2011.

Dornschneider, Stephanie. "Exit, Voice, Loyalty . . . or Deliberate Obstruction? Non-Collective Everyday Resistance Under Oppression." *Perspectives on Politics* 21, no. 1 (2023): 126–41. https://doi.org/10.1017/S1537592720004818.

Doumani, Beshara. *Rediscovering Palestine: Merchants and Peasants in Jabal Nablus, 1700–1900*. Berkeley: University of California Press, 1995.

DrRandomFactor. "South Africa & South West Africa Bantustans Map." Wikimedia Commons, April 29, 2017. https://commons.wikimedia.org/wiki/File:South_Africa _%26_South_West_Africa_Bantustans_Map.svg.

Dubow, Saul. *Racial Segregation and the Origins of Apartheid in South Africa, 1919–36*. St Antony's Series. London: Palgrave Macmillan, 1989.

Dumper, Michael. *The Politics of Jerusalem Since 1967*. New York: Columbia University Press, 1997.

Dwenger, Nadja, Henrik Kleven, Imran Rasul, and Johannes Rincke. "Extrinsic and Intrinsic Motivations for Tax Compliance: Evidence from a Field Experiment in Germany." *American Economic Journal: Economic Policy* 8, no. 3 (2016): 203–32.

Edinburgh Geographical Institute. "Political Divisions of the Indian Empire [map]." *Imperial Gazetteer Atlas of India* 26 (1909): 20.

Egerö, Bertil. *South Africa's Bantustans: From Dumping Grounds to Battlefronts*. Discussion paper. Scandinavian Institute of African Studies. Uppsala: Nordiska Afrikainstitutet, 1991.

El Kurd, Dana. *Polarized and Demobilized: Legacies of Authoritarianism in Palestine*. London: Hurst & Co., 2019.

Elgindy, Khaled. *Blind Spot: America and the Palestinians, from Balfour to Trump*. Washington, DC: Brookings Institution Press, 2019.

Ennab, Wael R. "Population and Demographic Developments in the West Bank and Gaza Strip Until 1990." Study prepared for United Nations Conference on Trade and Development, June 28, 1994. http://unctad.org/en/Docs/poecdcseud1.en.pdf.

Erakat, Noura. *Justice for Some: Law and the Question of Palestine*. Stanford, CA: Stanford University Press, 2019.

Erakat, Noura, Darryl Li, and John Reynolds. "Race, Palestine, and International Law." *AJIL Unbound* 117 (2023): 77–81. https://doi.org/10.1017/aju.2023.9.

Ernst, Waltraud, and Biswamoy Pati, eds. *India's Princely States: People, Princes and Colonialism*. London: Routledge, 2007.

European Institute of Public Administration, European Center for the Regions, Centre for European Policy Studies, and Centre for Strategy & Evaluation Services. "Southern Neighborhood Area Countries—Palestine." Division of Powers European Committee of the Regions, 2016. https://portal.cor.europa.eu/divisionpowers/Pages/Palestine -Introduction.aspx.

Evans, Laura. "South Africa's Bantustans and the Dynamics of 'Decolonisation': Reflections on Writing Histories of the Homelands." In *New Histories of South Africa's Apartheid-Era Bantustans*, ed. Shireen Ally and Arianna Lissoni, 173–93. London: Routledge, 2017.

Fairfield, Tasha, and Andrew Charman. "Bayesian Probability: The Logic of (Political Science) Opportunities, Caveats, and Guidelines." Paper presented at the American Political Science Association Annual Meeting, San Francisco, CA, 2015.

——. "A Dialogue with the Data: The Bayesian Foundations of Iterative Research in Qualitative Social Science." *Perspectives on Politics* 17, no. 1 (2019): 154–67.

Farsakh, Leila. "Palestinian Economic Development: Paradigm Shifts Since the First Intifada." *Journal of Palestine Studies* 45, no. 2 (2016): 55–71.

Feld, Lars P., and Bruno S. Frey. "Trust Breeds Trust: How Taxpayers Are Treated." *Economics of Governance* 3 (2002): 87–99.

Fisher, Michael H. *Indirect Rule in India: Residents and the Residency System, 1764–1858.* Delhi: Oxford University Press, 1991.
——. "Indirect Rule in the British Empire: The Foundations of the Residency System in India (1764–1858)." *Modern Asian Studies* 18, no. 3 (1984): 393–428.
Florea, Adrian. "De Facto States: Survival and Disappearance (1945–2011)." *International Studies Quarterly* 61 (2017): 337–51.
Foundation for Middle East Peace. "Comprehensive Settlement Population 1972–2011." January 13, 2012. http://fmep.org/resource/comprehensive-settlement-population -1972-2010/.
Gade, Emily Kalah. "Social Isolation and Repertoires of Resistance." *American Political Science Review* 114, no. 2 (2020): 309–25.
Gailmard, Sean. "Accountability and Principal-Agent Theory." In *The Oxford Handbook of Public Accountability*, ed. Mark Bovens, Robert Goodin, and Thomas Schillemans, 90–105. New York: Oxford University Press, 2014.
Galchinsky, Michael. "The Jewish Settlements in the West Bank: International Law and Israeli Jurisprudence." *Israel Studies* 9, no. 3 (2004): 115–36.
Garfias, Francisco. "Elite Competition and State Capacity Development: Theory and Evidence from Post-Revolutionary Mexico." *American Political Science Review* 112, no. 2 (2018): 339–57.
Gasparyan, Olga. "Indirect Rule and Public Goods Provision: Evidence from Colonial India." Working paper. November 20, 2019. https://papers.ssrn.com/sol3/papers .cfm?abstract_id=3689339.
Gerring, John, Daniel Ziblatt, Johan Van Gorp, and Julian Arevalo. "An Institutional Theory of Direct and Indirect Rule." *World Politics* 63, no. 3 (July 2011): 377–433.
Gibbs, Timothy. *Mandela's Kinsmen: Nationalist Elites & Apartheid's First Bantustan.* Suffolk, UK: James Currey, 2014.
Giliomee, Hermann. "The Making of the Apartheid Plan, 1929-1948." *Journal of Southern African Studies* 29, no. 2 (June 1, 2003): 373–92. https://doi.org/10.1080/03057070306211.
Giliomee, Hermann, and Lawrence Schlemmer. "The Changing Political Functions of the Homelands." In *Up Against the Fences: Poverty, Passes and Privilege in South Africa*, 39–56. New York: St. Martin's, 1985.
Gisha. "Gaza Up Close." June 28, 2023. https://features.gisha.org/gaza-up-close/.
Golden, Miriam A., and Paasha Mahdavi. "The Institutional Components of Political Corruption." In *Routledge Handbook of Comparative Political Institutions*, ed. Jennifer Gandhi and Rubén Ruiz-Rufino, 404–20. London: Routledge, 2015.
Golden, Miriam, and Brian Min. "Distributive Politics Around the World." *Annual Review of Political Science* 16 (2013): 73–99.
Gordon, Neve. *Israel's Occupation.* Berkeley: University of California Press, 2008.
Gorenberg, Gershom. *The Accidental Empire: Israel and the Birth of the Settlements, 1967–1977.* New York: Times Books, 2006.
Government of Israel and Palestinian Liberation Organization. "Gaza-Jericho Agreement, Annex IV: Protocol on Economic Relations Between the Government of the State of Israel and the P.L.O., Representing the Palestinian People." Political Settlements Research Programme, University of Edinburgh, 1994. https://www.peace agreements.org.
Gramsci, Antonio. *Prison Notebooks*, vol. 2. Ed. and trans. Joseph A. Buttigieg. New York: Columbia University Press, 2011.

Greenwald, Diana B. "Delegating Domination: Indirect Rule in the West Bank." In *The One State Reality: What Is Israel/Palestine?*, ed. Michael Barnett, Nathan Brown, Marc Lynch, and Shibley Telhami. Ithaca, NY: Cornell University Press, 2023.
——. "For Palestinians, the Local Is the National." Jadaliyya, May 1, 2023. https://www.jadaliyya.com/Details/44986/For-Palestinians,-the-Local-is-the-National.
——. "Military Rule in the West Bank." POMEPS Studies 41. Project on Middle East Political Science, Elliott School of International Affairs, Washington, DC, 2020. https://pomeps.org/pomeps-studies-41-israel-palestine-exploring-a-one-state-reality.
Grimes, Marcia. "Organizing Consent: The Role of Procedural Fairness in Political Trust and Compliance." *European Journal of Political Research* 45 (2006): 285–315.
Haber, Stephen, and Victor Menaldo. "Do Natural Resources Fuel Authoritarianism? A Reappraisal of the Resource Curse." *American Political Science Review* 105, no. 1 (2011): 1–26. https://doi.org/10.1017/S0003055410000584.
Hajj, Nadya. "Institutional Formation in Transitional Settings." *Comparative Politics* 46 (2014): 399–418.
——. *Networked Refugees: Palestinian Reciprocity and Remittances in the Digital Age.* Critical Refugee Studies. Berkeley: University of California Press, 2021.
——. *Protection Amid Chaos: The Creation of Property Rights in Palestinian Refugee Camps.* New York: Columbia University Press, 2016.
Halabi, Rafik. *The West Bank Story: An Israeli Arab's View of Both Sides of a Tangled Conflict.* Trans. Ina Friedman. New York: Harcourt Brace Jovanovich, 1981.
Hauser, Walter. "The Indian National Congress and Land Policy in the Twentieth Century." *Indian Economic & Social History Review* 1, no. 1 (July 1, 1963): 57–65. https://doi.org/10.1177/001946466400100104.
Hechter, Michael. *Alien Rule.* Cambridge: Cambridge University Press, 2013.
——. *Containing Nationalism.* New York: Oxford University Press, 2001.
Helm, Sarah. "Maps Dispute Draws New Battle of Jericho." *The Independent*, November 24, 1993.
Herbst, Jeffrey. *States and Power in Africa: Comparative Lessons in Authority and Control.* Princeton, NJ: Princeton University Press, 2000.
Hicken, Allen. "Clientelism." *Annual Review of Political Science* 14, no. 1 (June 15, 2011): 289–310. https://doi.org/10.1146/annurev.polisci.031908.220508.
Hilal, Jamil. "Problematizing Democracy in Palestine." *Comparative Studies of South Asia, Africa and the Middle East* 23 (2003): 163–72.
Hill, Allan G. "The Palestinian Population of the Middle East." *Population and Development Review* 9, no. 2 (1983): 293–316.
——. "Population Growth in the Middle East Since 1945 with Special Reference to the Arab Countries of West Asia." In *Change and Development in the Middle East*, ed. John I. Clarke and Howard Bowen-Jones. London: Methuen, 1981.
Hirsch-Hoefler, Sivan, and Lihi Ben Shitrit. "So, How Many Settlements Are There? Counting, Tracking, and Normalizing Jewish Settlements in the Israeli Central Bureau of Statistics (CBS) Yearbook, 1967 to the Present." *Israel/Palestine: Exploring a One State Reality*, POMEPS Studies 41. Project on Middle East Political Science, Elliott School of International Affairs, Washington, DC, 2020, 43–48.
Holland, Alisha C. "The Distributive Politics of Enforcement." *American Journal of Political Science* 59, no. 2 (April 2015): 357–71.
——. "Forbearance." *American Political Science Review* 110, no. 2 (May 2016): 232–46.

——. *Forbearance as Redistribution: The Politics of Informal Welfare in Latin America.* Cambridge: Cambridge University Press, 2017.

Holmes, Carolyn E. *The Black and White Rainbow: Reconciliation, Opposition, and Nation-Building in Democratic South Africa.* Ann Arbor: University of Michigan Press, 2020.

Human Rights Watch. "A Threshold Crossed: Israeli Authorities and the Crimes of Apartheid and Persecution." Human Rights Watch, April 27, 2021. https://www.hrw .org/report/2021/04/27/threshold-crossed-israeli-authorities-and-crimes-apartheid-and -persecution.

Imai, Kosuke, and In Song Kim. "On the Use of Two-Way Fixed Effects Regression Models for Causal Inference with Panel Data." *Political Analysis* 29 (2021): 405–15.

International Criminal Court. *Rome Statute of the International Criminal Court.* The Hague, 2021. https://www.icc-cpi.int/resource-library/core-legal-texts.

International Crisis Group. *Enter Hamas: The Challenges of Political Integration.* Middle East Report No. 39. Brussels: International Crisis Group, January 18, 2006., https:// www.refworld.org/docid/43cf8a1a4.html.

International Monetary Fund. "Macroeconomic and Fiscal Framework for the West Bank and Gaza—First Review of Progress." Staff Report for the Meeting of the Ad-Hoc Liaison Committee. London: International Monetary Fund, May 2, 2008.

Israel Central Bureau of Statistics. "Judea, Samaria and Gaza Area Statistics." Jerusalem, 1980.

Israel Ministry of Foreign Affairs. "The Israeli-Palestinian Interim Agreement," 1995. https:// www.gov.il/en/Departments/General/the-israeli-palestinian-interim-agreement.

Iyer, Lakshmi. "Direct Versus Indirect Colonial Rule in India: Long-Term Consequences." *Review of Economics and Statistics* 92, no. 4 (2010): 693–713.

'Izz al-Din, Husam. "*Naṭā'ij al-Intikhābāt al-Maḥalliyya Tu'akkid Iktisāḥ Ḥamās lil-Mudun al-Kubrā wa Taqqadum Fataḥ fi al-Manāṭiq al-Rīfiyya.*" *Al-Ayyam*, December 17, 2005.

Jacobson, Abigail. *From Empire to Empire: Jerusalem Between Ottoman and British Rule.* Space, Place and Society. Syracuse, NY: Syracuse University Press, 2011.

Jamal, Amaney A. *Barriers to Democracy: The Other Side of Social Capital in Palestine and the Arab World.* Princeton, NJ: Princeton University Press, 2009.

Jamal, Manal A. "Beyond Fateh Corruption and Mass Discontent: Hamas, the Palestinian Left and the 2006 Legislative Elections." *British Journal of Middle Eastern Studies* 40, no. 3 (2013): 273–94.

Joffre, Tzvi. "Palestinians Accuse Israel of 'Poisoning' Father of Dizengoff Terrorist." *Jerusalem Post*, January 9, 2023.

Kak, Shakti. "The Agrarian System of the Princely State of Jammu and Kashmir." In *India's Princely States: People, Princes and Colonialism*, ed. Waltraud Ernst and Biswamoy Pati, 68–84. London: Routledge, 2007.

Karmon, Yehuda. "Changes in the Urban Geography of Hebron During the Nineteenth Century." In *Studies on Palestine During the Ottoman Period*, ed. Moshe Ma'oz, 70–86. Jerusalem: Gefen, 1975.

Khalidi, Rashid. *The Hundred Years' War on Palestine: A History of Settler Colonialism and Resistance, 1917–2017.* New York: Picador, 2020.

——. *The Iron Cage: The Story of the Palestinian Struggle for Statehood.* Boston: Beacon, 2007.

Klein, Menachem. *Lives in Common: Arabs and Jews in Jerusalem, Jaffa and Hebron.* New York: Oxford University Press, 2014.

Kropko, Jonathan, and Robert Kubinec. "Interpretation and Identification of Within-Unit and Cross-Sectional Variation in Panel Data Models." *PloS ONE* 15, no. 4 (2020): e0231349.

Kunnath, George. "Janathana Sarkar (People's Government): Rebel Governance and Agency of the Poor in India's Maoist Guerrilla Zones." *Identities* 29, no. 1 (January 2, 2022): 45–62. https://doi.org/10.1080/1070289X.2021.1928981.

Lange, Matthew. *Lineages of Despotism and Development: British Colonialism and State Power*. Chicago: University of Chicago Press, 2009.

Laub, Karin, and Mohammed Daraghmeh. "Fatah Fails to Win Strong Nod in West Bank Vote." *Associated Press*, October 20, 2012. https://advance-lexis-com.ccny-proxy1.libr .ccny.cuny.edu/api/document?collection=news&id=urn:contentItem:56VV-B4V1 -DXYN-64K8-00000-00&context=1516831.

Lee, Alexander. "Land, State Capacity, and Colonialism: Evidence from India." *Comparative Political Studies* 52, no. 3 (2019): 412–44.

Leonard, Karen. "Reassessing Indirect Rule in Hyderabad: Rule, Ruler, or Sons-in-Law of the State?", *Modern Asian Studies* 37, no. 2 (2003): 363–79. https://doi.org/10.1017 /S0026749X0300204X.

Lester, Alan. *Imperial Networks: Creating Identities in Nineteenth-Century South Africa and Britain*. London: Routledge, 2001.

Letsa, Natalie Wenzell, and Martha Wilfahrt. "The Mechanisms of Direct and Indirect Rule: Colonialism and Economic Development in Africa." *Quarterly Journal of Political Science* 15, no. 4 (2020): 539–77.

Levi, Margaret. *Of Rule and Revenue*. Berkeley: University of California Press, 1988.

Levy, Elior. "Israel Still on the Hunt for Father of Tel Aviv Gunman." *Yedioth Ahronoth*, April 13, 2022. https://www.ynetnews.com/article/skgrhkeeq.

Lia, Brynjar. *A Police Force Without a State: A History of the Palestinian Security Forces in the West Bank and Gaza*. Reading, UK: Ithaca Press, 2006.

Loewenthal, Amit, Sami H. Miaari, and Anke Hoeffler. "Aid and Radicalization: The Case of Hamas in the West Bank and Gaza." *Journal of Development Studies* 59, no. 8 (April 10, 2023): 1187–1212. https://doi.org/10.1080/00220388.2023.2197546.

Loyle, Cyanne E., Kathleen Gallagher Cunningham, Reyko Huang, and Danielle F. Jung. "New Directions in Rebel Governance Research." *Perspectives on Politics* 21, no. 1 (2023): 264–76.

Lugard, Frederick John Dealtry. *The Dual Mandate in British Tropical Africa*. Edinburgh: William Blackwood and Sons, 1922.

Lustick, Ian S. *Unsettled States, Disputed Lands: Britain and Ireland, France and Algeria, Israel and the West Bank and Gaza*. Ithaca, NY: Cornell University Press, 1993.

MacDonald, Paul K. "The Governor's Dilemma in Colonial Empires." In *The Governor's Dilemma: Indirect Governance Beyond Principals and Agents*, ed. Kenneth W. Abbott, Bernhard Zangl, Duncan Snidal, and Philipp Genschel. Oxford: Oxford University Press, 2020.

Makdisi, Ussama. "After 1860: Debating Religion, Reform, and Nationalism in the Ottoman Empire." *International Journal of Middle East Studies* 34, no. 4 (2002): 601–17. https://doi.org/10.1017/S0020743802004014.

Mako, Shamiran, and Alistair D. Edgar. "Evaluating the Pitfalls of External Statebuilding in Post-2003 Iraq (2003–2021)." *Journal of Intervention and Statebuilding* 15, no. 4 (August 8, 2021): 425–40. https://doi.org/10.1080/17502977.2021.1958292.

Mamdani, Mahmood. *Citizen and Subject: Contemporary Africa and the Legacy of Late Colonialism.* Princeton, NJ: Princeton University Press, 1996.

——. "Historicizing Power and Responses to Power: Indirect Rule and Its Reform." *Social Research* 66, no. 3 (1999): 859–86.

——. *Neither Settler Nor Native: The Making and Unmaking of Permanent Minorities.* Cambridge, MA: Belknap Press of Harvard University Press, 2020.

Mampilly, Zachariah. *Rebel Rulers: Insurgent Governance and Civilian Life During War.* Ithaca, NY: Cornell University Press, 2011.

Mampilly, Zachariah, and Megan A. Stewart. "A Typology of Rebel Political Institutional Arrangements." *Journal of Conflict Resolution* 1, no. 65 (2021): 15–45.

Mann, Michael. *The Sources of Social Power: Volume 2, The Rise of Classes and Nation-States, 1760-1914.* Cambridge: Cambridge University Press, 2012.

Manna', 'Adel. "Eighteenth- and Nineteenth-Century Rebellions in Palestine." *Journal of Palestine Studies* 24, no. 1 (1994): 51–66.

Manson, Andrew, and Bernard Mbenga. "Bophuthatswana and the North-West Province: From Pan-Tswanaism to Mineral-Based Ethnic Assertiveness." In *New Histories of South Africa's Apartheid-Era Bantustans*, ed. Shireen Ally and Arianna Lissoni, 135–55. London: Routledge, 2017.

Ma'oz, Moshe. *Palestinian Leadership on the West Bank: The Changing Role of the Arab Mayors under Jordan and Israel.* Frank Cass, 1984.

Mares, Isabela, and Didac Queralt. "The Non-Democratic Origins of Income Taxation." *Comparative Political Studies* 48, no. 14 (2015): 1974–2009.

Masoud, Tarek. *Counting Islam: Religion, Class, and Elections in Egypt.* Cambridge: Cambridge University Press, 2014.

Matthews, Weldon C. "Book Review: *The Rise and Fall of a Palestinian Dynasty: The Husaynis, 1700–1948* by Ilan Pappé." *Journal of World History* 23, no. 2 (2012): 435–38.

McLeod, John. *Sovereignty, Power, Control: Politics in the States of Western India, 1916–1947.* Brill's Indological Library, vol. 15. (Leiden: Brill, 1999.

McNamee, Lachlan. *Settling for Less: Why States Colonize and Why They Stop.* Princeton, NJ: Princeton University Press, 2023.

Meir, Golda. " 'Excerpts from Interview with Mrs. Meir,' *International Herald Tribune*, 31 January 1972, p. 4." *Bulletin of Peace Proposals* 3, no. 3 (1972): 257.

Meiton, Fredrik. "Nation or Industry: The Non-Electrification of Nablus." *Jerusalem Quarterly*, no. 80 (2019): 8.

Menkhaus, Ken. "Governance Without Government in Somalia: Spoilers, State Building, and the Politics of Coping." *International Security* 31, no. 3 (January 1, 2007): 74–106. https://doi.org/10.1162/isec.2007.31.3.74.

Metelits, Claire. *Inside Insurgency: Violence, Civilians, and Revolutionary Group Behavior.* New York: NYU Press, 2010.

Meyer, William Stevenson, Richard Burn, James Sutherland Cotton, and Herbert Hope Risley. "The Native States." *Imperial Gazetteer of India* IV, no. Administrative (1907): 85.

Middle East Studies Centre. "*Itijahat an-Nakhibin al-Falastinin fi Intikhabat al-Baladiyyat wa R'iasa al-Sulta.*" Strategic Report. Amman: Center for Middle East Studies, 2006.

Migdal, Joel S. *Palestinian Society and Politics.* Princeton, NJ: Princeton University Press, 1980.

——. *Strong Societies and Weak States: State-Society Relations and State Capabilities in the Third World*. Princeton, NJ: Princeton University Press, 1988.

Miller, Ylana. *Government and Society in Rural Palestine, 1920–1948*. Austin: University of Texas Press, 1985.

Min, B. *Power and the Vote: Elections and Electricity in the Developing World*. Cambridge: Cambridge University Press, 2015.

Ministry of the Interior. "Police Stations in the Governorates," 2022. Accessed September 26, 2023, https://www.palpolice.ps/police-map.

Mishal, Shaul. "Palestinian Society and Politics." In *Palestinian Society and Politics*, Joel S. Migdal. Princeton, NJ: Princeton University Press, 1980.

——. *The PLO Under 'Arafat: Between Gun and Olive Branch*. New Haven, CT: Yale University Press, 1986.

Mishra, Kishore Chandra. "Prajamandal Movements in the Feudatory States of Western Orissa." *Proceedings of the Indian History Congress* 69 (2008): 543–53.

Mnaili, Youssef. "Settling Palestine: Logics of Israeli (In)Direct Governance of the Occupied West Bank Since 1967." Doctoral thesis, European University Institute, Florence, Italy, 2022.

Mudzunga, Vha-Musanda Vho-Shandukani. "Autobiography of an Underground Political Activist." In *New Histories of South Africa's Apartheid-Era Bantustans*, ed. Shireen Ally and Arianna Lissoni, 194–99. London: Routledge, 2017.

Mukherjee, Shivaji. *Colonial Institutions and Civil War: Indirect Rule and Maoist Insurgency in India*. Cambridge: Cambridge University Press, 2021.

——. "Colonial Origins of Maoist Insurgency in India: Historical Institutions and Civil War." *Journal of Conflict Resolution* 62, no. 10 (2018): 2232–74.

Mukonoweshuro, Eliphas. "Between Verwoerd and the ANC: Profiles of Contemporary Repression, Deprivation, and Poverty in South Africa's 'Bantustans.'" *Social Justice* 18, no. 1/2 (1991): 170–85.

Munayyer, Spiro. "The Fall of Lydda." *Journal of Palestine Studies* 27, no. 4 (July 1, 1998): 80–98. https://doi.org/10.2307/2538132.

Myers, J. C. *Indirect Rule in South Africa: Tradition, Modernity, and the Costuming of Political Power*. Rochester, NY: University of Rochester Press, 2008.

Naïli, Falestin. "The De-Municipalization of Urban Governance: Post-Ottoman Political Space in Jerusalem." *Jerusalem Quarterly* 76 (2018): 8–13.

al-Nammura, Mahmud Talab. *Al-Filastīniyyun wa Mu'assasāt al-Hukm al-Maḥallī Bayn al-Hukm al-Dhatī wal-'Iḥtilāl wa Haqq Taqrīr al-Masīr min al-'Ahd al-'Uthmanī 'Ilā al-'Intifāḍa (1794–1994)*. Published by author, 1994.

Naseemullah, Adnan. *Patchwork States: The Historical Roots of Subnational Conflict and Competition in South Asia*. Cambridge: Cambridge University Press, 2022.

Naseemullah, Adnan, and Paul Staniland. "Indirect Rule and Varieties of Governance." *Governance* 29, no. 1 (2016): 13–30.

Niksic, Orhan, Nur Nasser Eddin, and Massimiliano Cali. *Area C and the Future of the Palestinian Economy*. World Bank Studies. Washington, DC: World Bank, July 2014. https://elibrary.worldbank.org/doi/abs/10.1596/978-1-4648-0193-8.

Njoku, Uzochukwu J. "Colonial Political Re-Engineering and the Genesis of Modern Corruption in African Public Service: The Issue of the Warrant Chiefs of South Eastern Nigeria as a Case in Point." *Nordic Journal of African Studies* 14, no. 1 (n.d.): 99–116.

North, Douglass C., and Barry R. Weingast. "Constitutions and Commitment: The Evolution of Institutions Governing Public Choice in Seventeenth-Century England." *Journal of Economic History* 49, no. 4 (December 1989): 803–32.

'Ubayd, Shahir, Muhammad 'Ahmad, Sa'id Muhammad 'Ahmad Rubay'a, Jamal Qasim Muhammad Habash. "*'Ittijāhāt Muwaẓẓafī al-Baladiyyāt Naḥu 'A'ḍā' al-Majālis al-Baladiyya al-Muntakhaba fī Muḥāfazat Jinīn.*" *Al-Quds Open University Magazine* 32, no. 2 (2014): 11–45.

——. "*Taqyīm 'Afrad al-Mujtama' al-Maḥallī li-'Adā' 'A'ḍā' al-Majālis al-Baladiyya fī Muḥāfazat Jinīn fil-Dawra al-'Intikhābiyya Allati Jarat 'Am 2005.*" *Al-Aqsa University Magazine* 17, no. 2 (2013): 249–83.

Organisation for Economic Co-Operation and Development/United Cities and Local Government. "Middle East and West Asia: Palestinian Authority." Country Profiles of World Observatory on Subnational Government Finance and Investment. Paris: OECD, 2019). https://www.sng-wofi.org/country-profiles/.

O'Leary, Brendan, Ian Lustick, and Thomas Callaghy, eds. *Right-Sizing the State: The Politics of Moving Borders.* Oxford: Oxford University Press, 2001.

Olson, Mancur. "Dictatorship, Democracy, and Development." *American Political Science Review* 87, no. 3 (1993): 567–76.

Paler, Laura. "Keeping the Public Purse: An Experiment in Windfalls, Taxes, and the Incentives to Restrain Government." *American Political Science Review* 107, no. 4 (2013): 706–25. https://doi.org/10.1017/S0003055413000415.

Palestinian Center for Policy and Survey Research. "Index PSR Polls." 2023 polls. Accessed October 2, 2023. https://www.pcpsr.org/en/node/154.

——. "Poll Number 11: While Three Quarters of the Palestinians Welcome Sharon's Plan of Withdrawal from Gaza . . ." Ramallah: Palestine Center for Policy and Survey Research, March 14–17, 2004. http://www.pcpsr.org/sites/default/files/p11epdf.pdf.

——. "Poll Number 12: In the Context of the Sharon Disengagement Plan . . ." Ramallah: Palestine Center for Policy and Survey Research, June 24–27, 2004. http://www.pcpsr.org/sites/default/files/p12epdf.pdf.

——. "Poll Number 13: After Four Years of Intifada . . ." Ramallah: Palestine Center for Policy and Survey Research, September 23–26, 2004. http://www.pcpsr.org/sites/default/files/p13epdf.pdf.

——. "Poll Number 14: First Serious Signs of Optimism Since the Start of Intifada." Ramallah: Palestine Center for Policy and Survey Research, December 1–5, 2004. http://www.pcpsr.org/sites/default/files/p14epdf.pdf.

——. "Who Needs Security?" Ramallah: Palestinian Center for Policy and Survey Research, February 2017.

Palestinian Central Bureau of Statistics. "Census Final Results—Population Report West Bank 2007," 2007. https://www.pcbs.gov.ps.

——. *Population, Housing and Establishment Census-1997.* Statistical Reports Series. Ramallah: Palestinian National Authority, 1999.

Palestinian National Authority. *Qanun raqam (1) l-sana 1997 b-sha'an al-hi'aat al-ma7aliyya al-falastiniyya* (1997). http://muqtafi.birzeit.edu.

Pappé, Ilan. *The Rise and Fall of a Palestinian Dynasty: The Husaynis, 1700–1948.* Berkeley: University of California Press, 2010.

Parkinson, Sarah E. *Beyond the Lines: Social Networks and Palestinian Militant Organizations in Wartime Lebanon.* Ithaca, NY: Cornell University Press, 2022.

——. "Money Talks: Discourse, Networks, and Structure in Militant Organizations." *Perspectives on Politics* 14, no. 4 (2016): 976–94.

——. "Practical Ideology in Militant Organizations." *World Politics* 73, no. 1 (2021): 52–81.

Parreira, Christiana. "Power Politics: Armed Non-State Actors and the Capture of Public Electricity in Post-Invasion Baghdad." *Journal of Peace Research* 58, no. 4 (2021): 749–62.

Patel, Pravin J. "Trade Union Movement in a Princely State: Tradition, Industrialisation and Social Change." *Contributions to Indian Sociology* 45, no. 1 (February 1, 2011): 27–54. https://doi.org/10.1177/006996671004500102.

Pearlman, Wendy. *Violence, Nonviolence, and the Palestinian National Movement.* Cambridge: Cambridge University Press, 2011.

Perlmann, Joel. *The 1967 Census of the West Bank and Gaza Strip: A Digitized Version.* Annandale-on-Hudson, NY: Levy Economic Institute of Bard College, November 2011–February 2012. http://www.levyinstitute.org/palestinian-census/.

Peter, Fabienne. "Political Legitimacy." In *Stanford Encyclopedia of Philosophy.* Stanford, CA: Stanford University, rev. April 27, 2017. https://stanford.library.sydney.edu.au/archives/sum2021/entries/legitimacy/.

Philipp, Thomas. *Acre: The Rise and Fall of a Palestinian City.* New York: Columbia University Press, 2002.

Platzky, Laurie, Cherryl Walker, and Surplus People Project (South Africa). *The Surplus People: Forced Removals in South Africa.* Johannesburg: Ravan, 1985.

Rai, Mridu. *Hindu Rulers, Muslim Subjects: Islam, Rights, and the History of Kashmir.* Kindle ed. Delhi: Permanent Black, 2004.

Ramusack, Barbara. *The Indian Princes and Their States.* New Cambridge History of India III, 6. Cambridge: Cambridge University Press, 2004.

Rasgon, Adam. "Ex-Nablus Mayor Bassam Shakaa, Who Was Injured by Jewish Terrorists, Dies at 89." *Times of Israel,* July 23, 2019. https://www.timesofisrael.com/ex-nablus-mayor-bassam-shakaa-who-was-injured-by-jewish-terrorists-dies-at-89/.

Revkin, Mara Redlich. "What Explains Taxation by Resource-Rich Rebels? Evidence from the Islamic State in Syria." *Journal of Politics* 82, no. 2 (2020): 757–64.

Robinson, Glenn E. *Building a Palestinian State: An Incomplete Revolution.* Bloomington: Indiana University Press, 1997.

Robinson, Shira. *Citizen Strangers: Palestinians and the Birth of Israel's Liberal Settler State.* Stanford, CA: Stanford University Press, 2013.

Ronen, David. *The GSS Year.* [In Hebrew]. Tel Aviv: Ministry of Defense, 1989.

Ross, Michael L. "The Political Economy of the Resource Curse." *World Politics* 51, no. 2 (January 1999): 297–322.

——. "What Have We Learned About the Resource Curse?", *Annual Review of Political Science* 18, no. 1 (May 11, 2015): 239–59. https://doi.org/10.1146/annurev-polisci-052213-040359.

Roy, Sara. *Hamas and Civil Society in Gaza: Engaging the Islamist Sector.* Princeton, NJ: Princeton University Press, 2013.

Rubin, Trudy. "West Bank Tactics May Erode Israeli Democracy." *Christian Science Monitor,* August 1983.

Sahliyeh, Emile. *In Search of Leadership: West Bank Politics since 1967.* Washington, DC: Brookings Institution Press, 1988.

Said, Edward. "The Morning After." *London Review of Books*, October 21, 1993. https://www.lrb.co.uk/the-paper/v15/n20/edward-said/the-morning-after.

Saleh, Mohsen Mohammad. "The Islamic Resistance Movement (Hamas): An Overview of Its Experience & History, 1987–2005." In *Islamic Resistance Movement—Hamas: Studies of Thought & Experience*, 27–61. Beirut: Al-Zaytouna Centre for Studies & Consultations, 2017.

Samman, Maha. *Trans-Colonial Urban Space in Palestine*. London: Routledge, 2013.

Sayigh, Yezid. *Armed Struggle and the Search for a State*. Oxford: Oxford University Press, 1998.

——. *Policing the People, Building the State: Authoritarian Transformation in the West Bank and Gaza*. Washington, DC: Carnegie Endowment for International Peace, February 2011.

Saylor, Ryan, and Nicholas C. Wheeler. "Paying for War and Building States: The Coalitional Politics of Debt Servicing." *World Politics* 69, no. 2 (2017): 366–408.

Schölch, Alexander. *Palestine in Transformation, 1856–1882: Studies in Social, Economic and Political Development*. Trans. William C. Young and Michael C. Gerrity. Washington, DC: Institute of Palestine Studies, 1993.

Secretariat of the United Nations. "Convention (IV) Relative to the Protection of Civilian Persons in Time of War" (August 12, 1949). https://ihl-databases.icrc.org/en/ihl-treaties/gciv-1949?activeTab=1949GCs-APs-and-commentaries.

Seikaly, Sherene. *Men of Capital: Scarcity and Economy in Mandate Palestine*. Stanford, CA: Stanford University Press, 2016.

Sen, Somdeep. *Decolonizing Palestine: Hamas Between the Anticolonial and the Postcolonial*. Ithaca, NY: Cornell University Press, 2020.

Sfard, Michael. "The Occupation of the West Bank and the Crime of Apartheid: Legal Opinion." Yesh Din, 2020. https://www.yesh-din.org/en/the-occupation-of-the-west-bank-and-the-crime-of-apartheid-legal-opinion/.

Shahwan, Usamah. "Modernizing the Revenue Patterns of West Bank Towns." *An-Najah Journal for Research* 2, no. 6 (1992): 33–55.

——. *Public Administration in Palestine Past and Present*. Lanham, MD: University Press of America, 2003.

Shaka'a, Bassam. " 'Nablus Electricity Network', a Letter from Bassam ash-Shak'a to Tulkarm Mayor, 18 February 1982 [in Arabic]," August 2, 1982. Palestine Museum Digital Archive. https://palarchive.org/index.php/Detail/objects/220408/lang/en_US.

Shalev, Menachem. "The Looming Conflict." *Jerusalem Post*, July 28, 1989.

Shehadeh, Raja. "The Land Law of Palestine: An Analysis of the Definition of State Lands." *Journal of Palestine Studies* 11, no. 2 (1982): 82–99. https://doi.org/10.2307/2536271.

Shelef, Nadav G. *Evolving Nationalism: Homeland, Identity, and Religion in Israel, 1925–2005*. Ithaca, NY: Cornell University Press, 2010.

Shipler, David K. "In West Bank, Nablus Mayor Is on Pedestal." *New York Times*, December 10, 1979, sec. A. https://www.nytimes.com/1979/12/10/archives/in-west-bank-nablus-mayor-is-on-pedestal-close-ties-to-the-plo-fled.html.

——. "Israeli Court Bars Release of Mayor." *New York Times*, November 23, 1979. https://www.nytimes.com/1979/11/23/archives/israeli-court-bars-release-of-mayor-it-rules-that-arab-head-of.html.

Shlaim, Avi. "Prelude to the Accord: Likud, Labor, and the Palestinians." *Journal of Palestine Studies* 23, no. 2 (1994): 5–19.

Singh, Hira. "Colonial and Postcolonial Historiography and the Princely States: Relations of Power and Rituals of Legitimation." In *India's Princely States: People, Princes and Colonialism*, ed. Waltraud Ernst and Biswamoy Pati, 15–29. London: Routledge, 2007.

Slater, Dan. *Ordering Power: Contentious Politics and Authoritarian Leviathans in Southeast Asia*. Cambridge: Cambridge University Press, 2010.

Slater, Dan, and Diana Kim. "Standoffish States: Nonliterate Leviathans in Southeast Asia." *TraNS: Trans-Regional and -National Studies of Southeast Asia* 3, no. 1 (2015): 25–44.

Smith, Nicholas Rush. *Contradictions of Democracy: Vigilantism and Rights in Post-Apartheid South Africa*. New York: Oxford University Press, 2019.

Sobovitz, Dan. *The Occupation Corrupts? Quantitative Analysis of Corruption in the Palestinian Authority* (Working Paper No. 50, Hertie School of Governance, Columbia University, New York, June 2010), https://edoc.vifapol.de/opus/volltexte/2013/4264/pdf/50.pdf.

Soifer, Hillel David. *State Building in Latin America*. New York: Cambridge University Press, 2015.

Soni, Dhiru V., and Brij Maharaj. "Emerging Urban Forms in Rural South Africa." *Antipode* 23, no. 1 (January 1, 1991): 47–67. https://doi.org/10.1111/j.1467-8330.1991.tb00402.x.

Sosnowski, Marika. *Redefining Ceasefires: Wartime Order and Statebuilding in Syria*. Cambridge: Cambridge University Press, 2023.

Staniland, Paul. *Ordering Violence: Explaining Armed Group-State Relations from Conflict to Cooperation*. Ithaca, NY: Cornell University Press, 2021.

Stel, Nora. "Mediated Stateness as a Continuum: Exploring the Changing Governance Relations Between the PLO and the Lebanese State." *Civil Wars* 19, no. 3 (2017): 348–76.

Stewart, Megan A. *Governing for Revolution: Social Transformation in Civil War*. Cambridge: Cambridge University Press, 2021.

Stewart, Megan A., and Yu-Ming Liou. "Do Good Borders Make Good Rebels? Territorial Control and Civilian Casualties." *Journal of Politics* 79, no. 1 (2017): 284–301.

Strindberg, Anders. "The Damascus-Based Alliance of Palestinian Forces: A Primer." *Journal of Palestine Studies* 29, no. 3 (2000): 60–76.

Taraki, Lisa, and Rita Giacaman. "Modernity Aborted and Reborn: Ways of Being Urban in Palestine." In *Living Palestine: Family Survival, Resistance, and Mobility Under Occupation*, ed. Lisa Taraki, 1–50. Syracuse, NY: Syracuse University Press, 2006.

Tartir, Alaa. "The Palestinian Authority Security Forces: Whose Security?" Policy Brief. Al-Shabaka, May 16, 2017.

Tessler, Mark A. *A History of the Israeli-Palestinian Conflict*. 2nd ed. Bloomington: Indiana University Press, 2009.

"The Census of British India of 1871–72." *Journal of the Statistical Society of London* 39, no. 2 (1876): 411–16.

Tilly, Charles. *Coercion, Capital, and European States, AD 990–1992*. Malden, MA: Blackwell, 1992.

United Nations Office for the Coordination of Humanitarian Affairs, "Hostilities in the Gaza Strip and Israel: Flash Update #104," January 28, 2024, https://www.ochaopt.org. Accessed: January 29, 2024.

Veracini, Lorenzo. *Settler Colonialism: A Theoretical Overview*. London: Palgrave Macmillan, 2010.

Verghese, Ajay. *The Colonial Origins of Ethnic Violence in India*. Stanford, CA: Stanford University Press, 2016.

———. "*Quwwāt al-Iḥtilāl Tastawlī ʿalā ʾAḥad Manāzil Baldat Tuqūʿ wa Tuḥawwiluhu ʾilā Nuqta Murāqiba ʿAskariyya.*" *Palestinian News & Information Agency*, June 14, 2006. https://www.wafa.ps/ar_page.aspx?id=QuviHma61780190736aQuviHm.

Wamagatta, Evanson N. "British Administration and the Chiefs' Tyranny in Early Colonial Kenya: A Case Study of the First Generation of Chiefs from Kiambu District, 1895—1920." *Journal of Asian and African Studies* 44, no. 4 (2009): 371–88.

Weber, Max. *The Theory of Social and Economic Organization.* Ed. Talcott Parsons. New York: Free Press, 1964.

———. *The Vocation Lectures.* [1919]. Ed. David Owen and Tracy B. Strong. Indianapolis: Hackett Publishing, 2004.

Weinstein, Jeremy. *Inside Rebellion: The Politics of Insurgent Violence.* Cambridge: Cambridge University Press, 2007.

Weitzel, Michelle D. "Access Denied: Temporal Mobility Regimes in Hebron." *Borderlands* 21, no. 1 (2022): 171–200.

"West Bank Girl Killed by Israeli." *New York Times*, May 17, 1976. https://www.nytimes.com/1976/05/17/archives/new-jersey-pages-west-bank-girl-killed-by-israeli-victim-was-from.html.

Wieffering, Helen. "The Deepening Costs of 4 Gaza Wars in 13 Years, in 4 Charts." *Associated Press*, August 25, 2021. https://apnews.com/article/middle-east-united-nations-israel-palestinian-gaza-hamas-186d89b5fa8ae171c166f6162d6ea3da.

Wilkinson, Callie. "Weak Ties in a Tangled Web? Relationships Between the Political Residents of the English East India Company and Their Munshis, 1798–1818." *Modern Asian Studies* 53, no. 5 (2019): 1574–1612. https://doi.org/10.1017/S0026749X17000932.

Wolfe, Patrick. "Settler Colonialism and the Elimination of the Native." *Journal of Genocide Research* 8, no. 4 (2006): 387–409.

———. *Settler Colonialism and the Transformation of Anthropology.* London: Cassell, 1999.

World Bank. *Developing the Occupied Territories: An Investment in Peace.* Washington, DC: International Bank for Reconstruction and Development and the World Bank, 1993.

———. *Securing Energy for Development in the West Bank and Gaza.* Report. Washington, DC: World Bank, 2017.

———. "Securing Water for Development in West Bank and Gaza." Water Global Practice Sector Note. Washington, DC: World Bank, 2018.

———. *West Bank and Gaza Municipal Finance and Service Provision(vol. 2): Annexes* (English). Report. Washington, DC: World Bank Sustainable Development Department, Middle East and North Africa Region, January 2010.

Yaʾari, Ehud. "It Just Won't Work." *Jerusalem Report*, December 3, 1992.

Yom, Sean. "From Methodology to Practice: Inductive Iteration in Comparative Research." *Comparative Political Studies* 48, no. 5 (2015): 616–44.

Zayyad, Tawfiq. "The Fate of the Arabs in Israel." *Journal of Palestine Studies* 6, no. 1 (1976): 92–103. https://doi.org/10.2307/2535721.

Zeedan, Rami. "The Palestinian Political Parties and Local Self-Governance During the British Mandate: Democracy and the Clan." In *The British Mandate in Palestine: A Centenary Volume, 1920–2020*, ed. Michael J. Cohen, 83–101. London: Routledge, 2020.

Zeira, Yael. "From the Schools to the Streets: Education and Anti-Regime Resistance in the West Bank." *Comparative Political Studies* 52, no. 8 (2019): 1131–68.

———. *The Revolution Within: State Institutions and Unarmed Resistance in Palestine.* Cambridge: Cambridge University Press, 2019.

INDEX

Abbas, Mahmoud, 10, 106, 115
Abdullah, Mohammad, 206
Absentee Property Law, 77
administrative detention, 176, 177–179
African National Congress (ANC), 16,
    211–212
AISPC. *See* All India States People's
    Conference
'Ali, Muhammad, 70
All India States People's Conference
    (AISPC), 203
Allon, Yigal, 89
AMAN. *See* Coalition for Integrity and
    Accountability
'Amin al-Husayni, Muhammad, 71
Amnesty International, 18
ANC. *See* African National Congress
annexation, 3, 98, 195; via Israeli
    settlements, 84, 100; in Jerusalem, 87;
    by Jordan, 61, 78; of West Bank, 83,
    185, 221
anti-corruption platform, of Hamas,
    122–123
apartheid, 15, 194; discrimination relation
    to, 241n1; extraction relation to, 209;
    indirect rule relation to, 191, 265n64;

international community response to,
    18–19; resistance to, 212–213; in South
    Africa, 16, 21, 28, 29–30, 207–208; in
    West Bank, 221
Aqsa mosque, al-, 65
Arab Higher Committee, 234n10
Arafat, Yasser, 6–7, 105; at Camp David
    Summit, 101–102; Oslo Accords and,
    99; PLO led by, 90–91
Area A, 101, 102, *111*, *113*, 223–224;
    Area C compared to, 170; coercion
    in, 229; municipalities in, 140;
    policing in, 163, 164, 166, 169, 223;
    revenue mobilization in, 145; during
    second intifada, 110, 252n4; security
    in, 110, 111
Area B, *113*, 223–224, 267n2; coercion in,
    229; Fatah-affiliated mayors in, 147–
    148; municipalities in, 140; policing
    in, 147–148, 163, 164–166, 168–169;
    during second intifada, 252n4
Area C, 112, *113*, 128, 224; Israeli
    settlements in, 101, 237n28; Israel
    relation to, 171, 172; municipalities in,
    140; PA relation to, 252n7; policing in,
    166, 170, 252n10; during second